AAT

NVQ FOUNDATION

COURSE **COMPANION**   Units 1-4

Income and Receipts

Payments

Ledger Balances and the
Initial Trial Balance

Information for Management

BPP)))

LEARNING MEDIA

Sixth edition May 2007
First edition 2001

ISBN 9780 7517 2892 7 (previous ISBN 07517 2605 2)

British Library Cataloguing-in-Publication Data
A catalogue record for this book is available from the British Library

Published by

BPP Learning Media Ltd
BPP House
Aldine Place
London
W12 8AA

www.bpp.com/learningmedia

Printed in Great Britain by Page Bros
Mile Cross Lane
Norwich
NR6 6SA

CONTENTS

INTRODUCTION

BPP Learning Media's Companions range of AAT materials is ideal for students who like to get to grips with the essentials and study on the move.

The range comprises:

- **Course Companions**, covering all the knowledge and understanding and performance criteria specified by the Standards of Competence and needed by students, with numerous illustrations, practical examples and activities for students to use to consolidate their learning.

- **Revision Companions**, ideal for classroom courses, which contain an additional range of graded activities for each chapter of the Course Companion, plus specially written practice assessments and answers for the Units, the AAT's own specimen assessment and a selection of Unit 3 exams up to December 2006. Full answers to all activities and assessments, prepared by BPP Learning Media, are included.

- **Tutor Companions**, providing a further bank of questions, answers and practice assessments for classroom use, available separately only to lecturers whose colleges adopt the Companions for the relevant Units.

This Course Companion for NVQ Foundation Units 1 to 4 has been written specifically to ensure comprehensive yet concise coverage of the Standards of Competence and performance criteria. It is fully up to date as at April 2007.

Each chapter contains:

- clear, step by step explanation of the topic

- logical progression and linking from one chapter to the next, using a case study approach throughout

- numerous illustrations and practical examples

- interactive activities within the text of the chapter itself, with answers at the back of the book

- a bank of questions of varying complexity, again with answers supplied at the back of the book

The emphasis in all activities and questions is on the practical application of the skills acquired.

If you have any comments about this book, please e-mail pippariley@bpp.com or write to Pippa Riley, Publishing Projects Director, BPP Learning Media Ltd, BPP House, Aldine Place, London W12 8AA.

STANDARDS OF COMPETENCE

The Structure of the Standards for the AAT Units

Each Unit commences with a statement of the knowledge and understanding which underpin competence in the Unit's elements.

The Unit of Competence is then divided into elements of competence describing activities which the student should be able to perform.

Each element includes:

a)   a set of **performance criteria**. This defines what constitutes competent performance.

b)   a **range statement**. This defines the situations, contexts, methods etc in which competence should be displayed.

Unit 1 Recording Income and Receipts

Unit Commentary

This Unit relates to the role of invoicing and receiving payments. The first element involves you in manually preparing and coding invoices and credit notes for goods and services supplied, and entering the details in both a manual and computerised accounting system. The element also requires you to prepare statements of account manually, and as computerised output. It is expected that you will communicate with customers politely and effectively, in response to their queries or when chasing payments.

The second element is concerned with checking and recording receipts in a manual and computerised system. The element requires you to deal with receipts in a variety of different forms and, therefore, to complete paying-in documents where necessary. You are required to deal with unusual features relating to wrongly completed cheques, out-of-date cheques, debit or credit card limits exceeded and disagreement with supporting documentation. Where these features are outside of your own area of responsibility the element expects you to refer them to an appropriate person.

Elements contained within this unit are:

Element: 1.1   Process documents relating to goods and services supplied

Element: 1.2   Process receipts

Knowledge and Understanding

To perform this unit effectively you will need to know and understand:

The Business Environment		Chapter
1	Income and receipt transactions, including assoicated documentation (Element 1.1)	1, 2
2	Basic contract law regarding income and receipts, Sale of Goods Act (Elements 1.1 & 1.2)	19
3	Document retention policies for income and receipts (Elements 1.1 & 1.2)	19
4	General principles of VAT regarding income and receipts (Element 1.1)	2
5	Types of discounts available to customers (Element 1.1)	2
6	Cheques from customers, including crossings and endorsements (Element 1.2)	5
7	The use of banking documentation (Element 1.2)	7
8	Automated payments from customers (Element 1.2)	5
9	Credit limits (Elements 1.1 & 1.2)	2
10	Basic data protection law regarding customers (Element 1.2)	19

Element 1.1 Process documents relating to goods and services supplied

Performance Criteria

In order to perform this element successfully you need to:

		Chapter
A	Accurately prepare **invoices** and **credit notes** in accordance with organisational requirements and check against **source documents**	2
B	Ensure invoices and credit notes are correctly **authorised** before being sent to customers	2
C	Ensure invoices and credit notes are correctly **coded**	2
D	Enter invoices and credit notes into **books of prime entry** according to organisational procedures	4
E	Enter invoices and credit notes in the appropriate **ledgers**	4
F	Produce **statements** of account for despatch to debtors	8
G	**Communicate** politely and effectively with customers regarding accounts, using the relevant information from the aged debtors analysis	8

Range Statement

Performance in this element relates to the following contexts:

Invoices and credit notes:

- Pricing
- Price extensions
- Discounts
- VAT

Source documents:

- Quotations
- Purchase orders
- Delivery notes
- Sales orders

Coded:

- Manual systems
- Computerised systems

Statements:

- Manual
- Computerised

Ledgers:

- Manual main ledger
- Manual subsidiary ledger
- Computerised ledgers

Books of prime entry:

- Manual sales daybook
- Manual sales returns daybook
- Relevant computerised records

Communicate:

- Respond to queries
- Chase payments

Element 1.2 Process receipts

Performance Criteria

In order to perform this element successfully you need to:

		Chapter
A	Check **receipts** against relevant supporting information	5
B	Enter receipts in appropriate **accounting records**	6
C	Prepare paying-in documents and reconcile to relevant records	7
D	Identify **unusual features** and either resolve or refer to the appropriate person	5

Range Statement

Performance in this element relates to the following contexts:

Receipts:

- Cash
- Cheques
- An automated payment

Accounting records:

- Manual cash book
- Manual main ledger and subsidiary ledger
- Computerised records

Unusual features:

- Wrongly completed cheques
- Out-of-date cheques
- Credit and debit card limits exceeded
- Disagreement with supporting documentation

Unit 2 Making and Recording Payments

Unit Commentary

This Unit relates to the organisation's expenditure. It includes dealing with documentation from suppliers and ordering and delivery documentation, preparing payments, recording expenditure in the appropriate records, and making payments relating to invoices, wages and salaries, and petty cash.

The first element is concerned with ensuring calculations and records of expenditure are correct and deducting available discounts. You are required to code and enter documents in a manual and computerised accounting system. You are also required to handle both verbal and written communications with suppliers in a polite and effective manner. However, you are not expected to deal with goods supplied under leasing or hire purchase contracts at this level.

The second element relates to preparing authorised payments, relating to creditors, payroll and petty cash. This involves you in selecting appropriate payment methods and ensuring that all payments are recorded and entered into the accounting records, both manual and computerised. This element also requires you to take responsibility for ensuring the security of relevant payment methods and to refer queries to the appropriate person.

Elements contained within this unit are:

Element: 2.1   Process documents relating to goods and services received

Element: 2.2   Process payments

Knowledge and Understanding

To perform this unit effectively you will need to know and understand:

The Business Environment	Chapter
1 Payment transactions, including associated documentation (Element 2.1)	9
2 Basic contract law regarding payments; Sale of Goods Act (Elements 2.1 & 2.2)	19
3 Document retention policies for payments (Elements 2.1 & 2.2)	19
4 General principles of VAT regarding payments (Element 2.1)	9
5 Types of discounts available from suppliers (Element 2.1)	9
6 Payment cheques, including crossings and endorsements (Element 2.2)	5
7 Automated payments to suppliers (Elements 2.1 & 2.2)	5, 11
8 Different ordering systems: Internet, verbal and written (Element 2.1)	9
9 Documentation for payments (Element 2.2)	11
10 Basic data protection law regarding suppliers (Element 2.2)	19

Element 2.1 Process documents relating to goods and services received

Performance Criteria

In order to perform this element successfully you need to:

		Chapter
A	Check suppliers' invoices and credit notes against relevant **documents** for validity	9
B	Check **calculations** on suppliers' invoices and credit notes for accuracy	9
C	Identify and deduct available **discounts**	9
D	Correctly **code** invoices and credit notes	9
E	Correctly enter invoices and credit notes into **books of prime entry** according to organisational procedures	10
F	Enter invoices and credit notes in the appropriate **ledgers**	10
G	Identify **discrepancies** and either resolve or refer to the appropriate person if outside own authority	9
H	**Communicate** appropriately with suppliers regarding accounts	12

Range Statement

Performance in this element relates to the following contexts:

Documents:

- Orders
- Suppliers' invoices
- Delivery notes
- Credit notes

Calculations:

- Pricing
- Price extensions and VAT
- Bulk, trade and settlement discounts

Code:

- Manual systems
- Computerised systems

Discounts:

- Settlement

Books of prime entry:

- Manual purchases day book
- Manual purchases returns day book
- Relevant computerised records

Ledgers:

- Manual main ledger
- Manual subsidiary ledger
- Computerised ledgers

Discrepancies:

- Incorrect calculations
- Non-delivery of goods charged
- Duplicated invoices
- Incorrect discounts

Communicate:

- Orally
- In writing

Element 2.2 Process payments

Performance Criteria

In order to perform this element successfully you need to:

		Chapter
A	Calculate **payments** from relevant **documentation**	11, 13, 14
B	Schedule payments and obtain authorisation	11, 14
C	Use the appropriate **payment method** and timescale, in accordance with organisational procedures	11, 14
D	Enter payments into **accounting records**	12, 13, 14
E	Identify **queries** and resolve or refer to the appropriate person	11
F	Ensure security and confidentiality is maintained according to organisational requirements	11, 14

Range Statement

Performance in this element relates to the following contexts:

Payments:

- Payroll
- Creditors
- Petty cash

Documentation:

- Petty cash claims
- Suppliers' statements
- Payslips
- Cheque requisitions

Payment method:

- Cash
- Cheques
- An automated payment

Accounting records:

- Manual cash book
- Manual petty cash book
- Manual main ledger
- Manual subsidiary ledger
- Computerised records

Queries relating to:

- Unauthorised claims for payment
- Insufficient supporting evidence
- Claims exceeding authorised limit

Unit 3 Preparing Ledger Balances and an Initial Trial Balance

Unit Commentary

This Unit relates to the internal checks involved in an organisation's accounting processes. The first element is primarily concerned with comparing individual items on the bank statement with entries in the cashbook and identifying any discrepancies. This involves recording details from the relevant primary documentation in the cashbook, manual and computerised, and calculating the totals and balances of receipts and payments. You are also required to identify any discrepancies, such as differences identified by the matching process.

The second element requires you to total the relevant accounts and to reconcile the control accounts, within a computerised and a manual accounting system. You are also required to resolve or refer any discrepancies and to ensure security and confidentiality. The third element involves drafting an initial trial balance manually and producing a trial balance from a computerised accounting system. You will be expected to identify and rectify discrepancies, which may occur in a manual accounting system, and create a suspense account where necessary.

Elements contained within this unit are:

Element: 3.1   Balance bank transactions

Element: 3.2   Prepare ledger balances and control accounts

Element: 3.3   Draft an initial trial balance

Knowledge and Understanding

To perform this unit effectively you will need to know and understand:

The Business Environment	Chapter
1 Types of business transactions and the documents involved (Elements 3.1 & 3.2)	1, 2, 9
2 General principles of VAT applicable to the transactions (Element 3.1)	3, 9
3 General bank services and operation of bank clearing system (Element 3.1)	7
4 Function and form of banking documentation (Element 3.1)	7, 15

Element 3.1 Balance bank transactions

Performance Criteria

In order to perform this element successfully you need to:

		Chapter
A	Record details from the relevant **primary documentation** in the **cashbook** and **ledgers**	15
B	Correctly calculate totals and balances of receipts and payments	15
C	Compare individual items on the bank statement and in the **cashbook** for accuracy	15
D	Identify **discrepancies** and prepare a **bank reconciliation statement**	15

Range Statement

Performance in this element relates to the following contexts:

Primary documentation:

- Credit transfer
- Standing order and direct debit schedules
- Bank statement

Cash book and ledgers:

- Manual
- Computerised

Discrepancies:

- Differences identified by the matching process

Bank reconciliation statement:

- Manual
- Computerised

Element 3.2 Prepare ledger balances and control accounts

Performance Criteria

In order to perform this element successfully you need to:

		Chapter
A	Make and **record** authorised **adjustments**	16
B	Total relevant accounts in the main ledger	16
C	Reconcile **control accounts** with the totals of the balance in the subsidiary ledger	16
D	Reconcile petty cash **control account** with cash in hand and subsidiary records	16
E	Identify **discrepancies** arising from the reconciliation of **control accounts** and either resolve or refer to the appropriate person	16
F	Ensure documentation is stored securely and in line with the organisation's confidentiality requirements	16

Range Statement

Performance in this element relates to the following contexts:

Record:

- Manual journal
- Computerised journal

Adjustments:

- To correct errors
- To write off bad debts

Control accounts:

- Sales ledger
- Purchase ledger
- Non-trade debtors
- Manual
- Computerised

Discrepancies:

- Manual sales ledger and manual purchases ledger control account not agreeing with subsidiary ledger
- Cash in-hand not agreeing with subsidiary record and control account

Element 3.3 Draft an initial trial balance

Performance Criteria

In order to perform this element successfully you need to:

		Chapter
A	Prepare the draft **initial trial balance** in line with the organisation's policies and procedures	17
B	Identify **discrepancies** in the balancing process	18
C	Identify reasons for imbalance and **rectify** them	18
D	Balance the trial balance	18

Range Statement

Performance in this element relates to the following contexts:

Trial balance:

- Manual
- Computerised

Discrepancies in a manual accounting system:

- Incorrect double entries
- Missing entries and wrong calculations

Rectify imbalances in a manual accounting system by:

- Adjusting errors
- Creating a suspense account

Unit 4 Supplying Information for Management Control

Unit Commentary

This Unit is about recognising and providing basic management information. This involves information relating to both costs and income and includes the comparison of actual costs and income against the previous period's data, the corresponding period's data and forecast data.

The first element involves recognising cost centres. It should be noted that in some organisations profit centres or investment centres will be used in place of cost centres, and these will differ depending on the organisation. The element also involves recognising elements of costs, coding income and expenditure and identifying and reporting obvious errors, such as the wrong code or excessive volumes. You are required to extract information relating to the three elements of costs: materials, labour and expenses. The element, however, does not specifically relate to manufacturing as materials will include items such as consumables in service industries, and the majority of costs will probably be labour costs in those circumstances.

The second element is concerned with extracting information from a particular source, for example the previous period's data, and comparing that information with actual costs and income, in line with the organisational requirements. You are required to report discrepancies between the two in the appropriate format, ensuring confidentiality requirements are adhered to.

Elements contained within this unit are:

Element: 4.1   Code and extract information

Element: 4.2   Provide comparisons on costs and income

Knowledge and Understanding

To perform this unit effectively you will need to know and understand:

The Business Environment	**Chapter**
1 Types of cost centres, including profit centres and investment centres (Element 4.1)	20
2 Costs, including wages, salaries, services and consumables (Element 4.1)	21

Element 4.1 Code and extract information

Performance Criteria

In order to perform this element successfully you need to:

		Chapter
A	Recognise appropriate **cost centres** and elements of costs	21
B	Extract **income** and **expenditure** details from the relevant sources	21
C	**Code** income and expenditure correctly	22
D	Refer any problems in obtaining the necessary information to the appropriate person	22
E	Identify and report errors to the appropriate person	22

Range Statement

Performance in this element relates to the following contexts:

Elements of costs:

- Materials
- Labour
- Expenses

Sources:

- Purchase orders
- Purchase invoices
- Sales orders
- Sales invoices
- Policy manual
- Payroll

Information:

- Cost
- Income
- Expenditure

Errors:

- Wrong codes
- Excessive volumes

Element 4.2 Provide comparisons on costs and income

Performance Criteria

In order to perform this element successfully you need to:

		Chapter
A	Clarify **information** requirements with the appropriate person	23
B	Compare **information** extracted from a particular **source** with actual results	23
C	Identify discrepancies	23
D	Provide comparisons to the appropriate person in the required **format**	23
E	Follow organisational **requirements for confidentiality** strictly	23

Range Statement

Performance in this element relates to the following contexts:

Information:

- Costs
- Income

Sources:

- Previous period's data
- Corresponding period's data
- Forecast data
- Ledgers

Format:

- Letter
- Memo
- E-mail
- Note
- Word-processed report

Confidentiality requirements:

- Sharing of information
- Storage of documents

chapter 1:
INTRODUCTION TO BUSINESS

chapter coverage 📖

This opening chapter of the Course Companion serves as a brief introduction to the world of business. The topics that are to be covered are:

✍ introduction to the different types of business organisation

✍ the general types of transactions that businesses have and ways of classifying them

✍ the different types of industry or business environment that you might have to deal with

✍ different types of accounting systems

✍ a brief introduction to the overall purpose of accounting and the final product of the accounting procedure, the financial statements

---

KNOWLEDGE AND UNDERSTANDING AND PERFORMANCE CRITERIA COVERAGE

Units 1, 2 and 3

knowledge and understanding – the business environment

1.1, 2.1, 3.1 income and receipt transactions and payment transactions, including associated documentation

knowledge and understanding – accounting methods

1.14, 2.15, 3.8 operation of manual accounting systems
1.15, 2.16, 3.9 operation of computerised accounting systems, including output

Units 1, 2, 3 and 4

knowledge and understanding – the organisation

TYPES OF BUSINESS

A business can be set up in a variety of different ways depending upon its nature, its size and its organisation.

Sole trader

The simplest type of business is that of a SOLE TRADER. A sole trader is someone who trades under their own name. Many, many businesses are sole traders, from electricians through to accountants. Being a sole trader does not mean that the owner is the only person working in the business. Some sole traders are the only person in the business but many will also employ a number of other staff. Even so, in most cases the owner will be in charge of most of the business functions such as buying and selling the goods or services and doing the bookkeeping and producing accounts. In some instances however the sole trader will employ an external bookkeeper, who may also be a sole trader, in order to regularly update the accounting records.

The owner of the business is the one who contributes the capital to the business, although it might also have loans, either commercial or from friends. The owner is also the only party to benefit from the profits of the business and this will normally be done by the owner taking money or goods out of the business and these are known as DRAWINGS.

Partnership

A PARTNERSHIP is a group of individuals who are trading together with the intention of making a profit. Partnerships are often created as a sole trader's business expands and more capital and expertise is needed within the business. Typical partnerships are those of accountants, solicitors and dentists and usually comprise between 2 and 20 partners. As partnerships will tend to be larger than sole traders there will tend to be more employees and a greater likelihood of a bookkeeper being employed to maintain the accounting records.

Each of the partners will contribute capital to the business and will normally take part in the business activities. The profits of the business will be shared between the partners and this is normally done by setting up a partnership agreement whereby the financial rights of each partner are set out. Just as with sole traders the partners will tend to withdraw part of the profits that are due to them in the form of drawings from the business, although in some cases partners may also be paid a salary by the business.

Limited company

Most larger businesses will be formed as LIMITED COMPANIES. A limited company is where the owners of the business are the shareholders but the business is often managed by a completely different set of people, the directors. In legal terms a limited company is a completely separate entity from the owners, the shareholders. Many companies are run as private limited companies (Ltd) and often the shareholders and the directors are the same people. The largest companies however are public limited companies (PLC) and in these companies the shareholders and the directors are completely different. The directors run the company on behalf of the shareholders, the owners, and are accountable to the shareholders for their management of the business and stewardship of the assets.

The shareholders provide the capital for the business by buying shares in the company and they share in the profits of the company by being paid dividends. The accounting records that are required for a limited company are regulated by law and most companies will tend to have a large and comprehensive accounting function.

Limited liability

The main difference between the trading of a sole trader and a partnership on the one hand and a company on the other is the concept of limited liability. If the business of a sole trader or a partnership is declared bankrupt then the owner or owners are personally liable for any outstanding debts of the business. However the shareholders of a company have limited liability which means that once they have fully paid for their shares then they cannot be called upon for any more money if the company is declared bankrupt. All that they will lose is the amount that they have paid for their shares.

TYPES OF TRANSACTIONS

Whether a business is run as a sole trader, partnership or company it will still carry out all of the same types of business transactions although on different scales.

Typical transactions that all businesses will undertake include the following:

- selling goods or services;
- buying goods to resell;
- paying expenses;
- paying wages;
- buying long term assets for use in the business;

- paying money into the bank;

- withdrawing cash from the bank;

- paying the owners (either as drawings or dividends);

- paying taxes such as VAT.

It is vital that each and every one of these transactions is correctly recorded in the accounting records of the business and much of this is what will be covered later in this Course Companion.

As well as recording the everyday transactions, the accounting records will also provide valuable information to the owners or directors of the business. The records should be able to indicate how much money is owed by the business and to whom, how much is owing to the business and from whom, what long term assets the business has and how much stock is being held. Again if the business is to run efficiently the accounting records must be capable of providing accurate information on all of these areas.

When we consider the types of transactions of a business there are two important distinctions that must be made. These are CASH and CREDIT TRANSACTIONS and CAPITAL and REVENUE TRANSACTIONS.

Cash transactions are where payment is made or received immediately. A cash transaction is not limited to payments and receipts made in notes and coins, cash transactions are also made by cheque, credit card or debit card. The important factor is the timing of the payment.

Credit transactions by contrast are transactions whereby the goods or services are given or received now but it is agreed that payment is to be made or received at a future date. This will normally involve the issue or receipt of an invoice and the creation of a DEBTOR or a CREDITOR.

Activity 1

A sale is made for £100 and it is agreed that this will be paid for in cash in two weeks' time. Is this a cash transaction or a credit transaction?

Capital transactions are the purchase and sale of items that are to be used in the business for a considerable period of time rather than being purchased for resale. This might include the purchase of buildings, machinery, office furniture or motor vehicles. These long term assets of the business, known as FIXED ASSETS, can be purchased either for cash or more usually on credit. Capital transactions should not be confused with the initial capital that the owners of a business pay into the business.

Revenue transactions are the everyday income and expenses of the business. These will include the sales, the purchase of goods for resale, the general running expenses of the business and the payment of wages. Again these transactions can either be for cash or on credit.

Activity 2

A new car is purchased for use in the business and is paid for at the time of the purchase by cheque. Is this a capital or revenue transaction?

TYPES OF INDUSTRY

We have been talking in general terms about the types of transactions that a business will tend to undertake. You should be aware however that there are many different types of business working in different types of industry and each will have very different types of transactions. For the purposes of the Foundation Units there are three types of industry or business environment that you are likely to have to deal with.

MANUFACTURING ORGANISATIONS are businesses which actually make the goods that they are to sell on to other businesses. Therefore such organisations will tend to be buying the raw materials that are necessary in order to make the goods and then paying the wages of the employees that make these goods.

RETAIL ORGANISATIONS will buy in already made goods in order to sell on to the final customer. Such organisations will be buying finished goods rather than raw materials and will be paying the wages of the shop assistants who are selling the goods to customers. Many retail organisations will tend to have high property costs as they will need to purchase or rent the buildings in which to house the shops.

SERVICE ORGANISATIONS are businesses that do not manufacture or sell a physical product but instead provide a service such as accountants or a transport company. Such organisations will tend not to buy many physical goods but will have high wages and salaries costs and expenses.

TYPES OF ACCOUNTING SYSTEM

As you will be starting to realise business life is complicated and all businesses of whatever size or form will need an accounting system that is capable of accurately recording all of the transactions of the business and producing a picture of what the business owns and owes periodically. Without such an accounting system the owners would not know how the business was doing nor be able to keep track of payments that needed to be made and receipts that should be being received.

Most businesses, unless very small, will have an accounting system that is based upon double entry bookkeeping methods. These will be considered in more detail in a later chapter. In general terms however the accounting system must be capable of recording each of the transactions made and categorising them as the correct type of transactionx such as sales, purchases, telephone bills etc. The accounting system may be manual or it may be computerised or it may be a mixture of the two.

Manual accounting systems

Manual accounting systems are where the accounting records are maintained by hand and are written up by the bookkeeper or the accounts department staff. Although totally manual accounting systems are becoming increasingly rare with the introduction of computerised accounting packages and personal computers, most of the material in assessments will be based upon a manual system as this will be the best method of testing competence in the performance criteria. It is also essential that even in a computerised accounting environment, accounting technicians understand what the computer system is performing.

Computerised accounting systems

In practice, even a very small, part-time, one-person business will benefit from the use of a computer for accounting purposes, even if it is just a collection of spreadsheets.

Moreover, some banks now insist that their business customers have a computerised system, as part of the conditions of allowing them to have a business bank account in the first place.

A fully computerised accounting system, with separate but linked ledgers and so on, can be purchased for less than £100, and it quickly pays for itself because you can be sure that this is far less than an accounting firm would charge for putting the records in good order! It usually takes longer to set up a computerised system than it does a manual one, but this only needs to be done once.

Once the system is set up the advantages are considerable.

- The risk of error is considerably reduced (not eliminated, but much reduced).

- Laborious, repetitive tasks can be automated and done at the click of a button.

- Computerised systems are much quicker at analysing accounting data and putting it into the proper format.

What's the difference?

From the point of view of the user of a computerised system, the accounting functions that the computer carries out will appear to be the much same as those that are carried out by hand in a manual system.

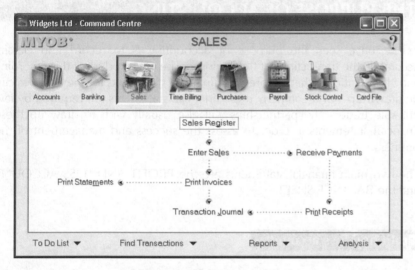

Behind the scenes the records are actually kept in a very different way, but you are unlikely to need to know about that - at least not for your AAT studies at any level.

If you work for a small firm of accountants there will no doubt still be a few clients who have not yet made the leap into computing, and new businesses may wait a while before deciding on which system to use, so those are two more good reasons why it is still very important to know about manual systems.

If you work in an established company's accounting department it is most unlikely that you will ever deal with anything other than a computerised system.

Evidence and BPP support

The AAT's Standard of Competence require students to provide evidence of competence in the IT aspects of accounting at Foundation level. This may be in the form of evidence from the workplace or it may be provided by completing a simulation.

- We will illustrate the use of computerised systems at appropriate points throughout this book.

- Our examples are taken from a number of the most popular packages for small businesses, such as Sage and QuickBooks, to give you a flavour of the similarities and differences between packages.

- Unit 21 covers working with computers in more depth. There is a full chapter on computerised accounting systems, and a simulation, in the BPP Combined Companion for Units 21, 22 and 23.

THE PURPOSE OF ACCOUNTING

As we have seen the purpose of accounting is to record and classify accurately the transactions of the business. The end product of this recording and classification is that, at intervals, financial statements for the business can be drawn up. For a company these financial statements are required by law but sole traders and partnerships will also usually wish to draw up these financial statements in order to assess the success and management of the business.

The two main financial statements are the PROFIT AND LOSS ACCOUNT and the BALANCE SHEET.

Profit and loss account

INCOME less EXPENSES = PROFIT OR LOSS

The profit and loss account shows how the business has performed during the last accounting period, typically six months or a year. It summarises all of the income of the business from sales etc and deducts all of the expenses. The expenses will include the cost of goods that have been purchased for resale, the cost of making any goods for resale, the costs of employing any staff and all of the other everyday costs of running the business.

If the income is greater than the expenses a profit has been made, but if expenses exceed income then a loss has occurred.

Balance sheet

The balance sheet is a list of the monetary value of all of the ASSETS and LIABILITIES of the business on the last day of the accounting period. Assets are amounts that the business owns and liabilities are amounts that the business owes.

FIXED ASSETS plus CURRENT ASSETS minus LIABILITIES = CAPITAL

We have already seen that the fixed assets of a business are those assets that are held for long term use in the business. The CURRENT ASSETS are the shorter term assets of the business. These will include the STOCK of the business which is the stock of any goods that are due to be sold but have not yet been sold. There will also be debtors of the business which are amounts that are owed to the business usually from customers to whom credit sales have been made. It will also include any cash or bank balances that the business may have.

The liabilities of the business will include creditors which are the amounts that the business owes to other parties. These could be trade creditors to whom money is owed for goods that have been purchased on credit, money owed for wages, loans that are outstanding or amounts owed to the tax authorities.

The total of the assets minus the liabilities should be equal to the CAPITAL of the business. The capital is made up of the initial amount that the owner or owners paid into the business plus any accumulated profits of the business minus any drawings or dividends that the owners have taken. This is the amount that is effectively owed back to the owner.

For the purposes of these Units you do not need to prepare a profit and loss account or a balance sheet but it is useful to be aware at this stage of the final product of all of the accounting that you will be doing in these units.

CHAPTER OVERVIEW

- there are three main types of business - a sole trader, a partnership or a limited company

- many transactions will be undertaken by a business and these can be categorised as cash and credit transactions and capital and revenue transactions

- different types of organisations will have predominantly different types of transactions - the types of industry that you may have to deal with are manufacturing, retail and service organisations

- accounting systems can either be manual or computerised or a combination of the two

- regardless of the type of system, the final product of the accounting system is to produce the financial statements - these are made up chiefly of the profit and loss account and the balance sheet

KEY WORDS

Sole trader a business that is run by an individual trading under his own name

Drawings amounts taken out of the business by the owner

Partnership a business run by a number of individuals trading together

Limited company a business that is owned by the shareholders and run by the directors - the owners have limited liability

Cash transactions transactions whereby payment is immediate

Credit transactions transactions whereby payment is to be made at some future date

Capital transactions purchases of assets for long term use in the business

Revenue transactions all other day to day income and expenses

Debtor someone who owes money to the business

Creditor someone to whom the business owes money

Manufacturing organisation a business that makes the goods that it is to sell

Retail organisation a business that buys in ready made goods in order to sell to customers

Service organisation a business that provides a service rather than a physical product

Fixed assets assets held for long term use in the business

Profit and loss account statement showing income less expenses equalling a profit or a loss

Balance sheet statement showing the assets and liabilities of the business on a particular date

Assets amounts that the business owns

Liabilities amounts that the business owes

Current assets short term assets of the business

Stock goods purchased for eventual resale but as yet unsold

Capital the amount owed back to the owner of the business

HOW MUCH HAVE YOU LEARNED?

1   What is meant by limited liability for shareholders in a limited company?

2   For each of the following transactions determine whether it should be classified as a cash or credit transaction.

   a)   Purchase of a motor van with an agreed payment date in one month's time

   b)   Sale of goods which are paid for by credit card

   c)   Purchase of computer discs by cheque

   d)   Purchase of computer discs which are accompanied by an invoice

   e)   Sale of goods which are paid for by cheque

3   For each of the following transactions determine whether it should be classified as a capital or revenue transaction.

   a)   Purchase of a computer for resale to a customer by a computer retailer

   b)   Purchase of a computer by a computer retailer for use in the sales office

   c)   Payment of wages by an accounting firm

   d)   Purchase of a building by a property developer to serve as a Head Office

4   What are the main items that will appear in a profit and loss account?

5   Assets are split into two main categories in the balance sheet, what are they?

6   What does the capital figure represent in the balance sheet?

chapter 2:
BUSINESS DOCUMENTS – SALES

chapter coverage 📖

This chapter considers all of the documents involved in making sales, in particular credit sales, and the checks that must be made on those documents. The topics that are to be covered are:

✍ the general types of transactions that businesses have and ways of classifying them

✍ the documents involved in cash sales

✍ the documents involved in credit sales

✍ value added tax (VAT) and its operation and collection

✍ VAT calculations on sales invoices

✍ trade and cash or settlement discounts and the VAT complications of a cash discount

✍ customer statements

✍ the checks that must be made when preparing a sales invoice and/or credit note in a manual system

✍ the procedure for preparing credit notes

✍ the checks required in a computerised accounting system

✍ the procedures for authorisation and coding of sales invoices and credit notes

Unit 1

knowledge and understanding – the business environment

1   income and receipt transactions, including associated documentation
4   general principles of VAT regarding income and receipts
5   types of discounts available to customers
9   credit limits

knowledge and understanding – accounting methods

13   methods of coding data

knowledge and understanding – the organisation

24   organisational procedures for authorisation and coding of sales invoices

Performance criteria – element 1.1

A   accurately prepare invoices and credit notes in accordance with organisational requirements and check against source documents

B   ensure invoices and credit notes are correctly authorised before being sent to customers

C   ensure invoices and credit notes are correctly coded

CASH SALES

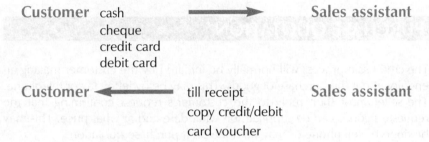

As we discussed in the previous chapter, business transactions can be either cash transactions or credit transactions. Therefore the sales that a business makes may be for cash or may be on credit.

It is most likely that sales will be for cash in a retail based organisation which has a shop or a number of shops. The customers will purchase goods and will pay for them by cash, cheque, credit card or debit card. The sales assistant will in return hand over the goods and a receipt.

Customer cash ──────────────▶ **Sales assistant**
cheque
credit card
debit card

Customer ◀────────── till receipt **Sales assistant**
copy credit/debit
card voucher

In a later chapter of the Course Companion we will consider the validity of cheque and credit/debit card receipts in more detail.

However in general terms the sales assistant must check the following when making the sale:

- the correct amount is entered into the till;

- the correct change is given if payment is made in cash;

- if payment is by cheque that the cheque is for the correct amount;

- the credit or debit card voucher is made out for the correct amount.

The till should then automatically produce a receipt for the customer showing the correct amount.

CREDIT SALES

For a credit sale there is much more documentation involved than for a cash sale and the time scale of the transaction is much longer, possibly taking a number of months from start to finish. The diagram below gives an overview of the main documents potentially involved in a credit sale and all of these documents will be discussed in more detail later in the chapter.

student notes ✍

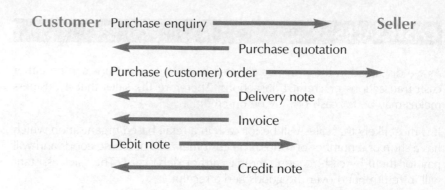

Customer		Seller
	Purchase enquiry ⟶	
	⟵ Purchase quotation	
	Purchase (customer) order ⟶	
	⟵ Delivery note	
	⟵ Invoice	
	Debit note ⟶	
	⟵ Credit note	

PURCHASE QUOTATION

The credit sale process will normally be initiated by the customer making an enquiry about the purchase of goods. This may be by letter, fax or telephone. The seller must then reply to the customer's request confirming that the requested goods can be supplied, on what date and at what price. This may be done by telephone or may be done on a purchase quotation.

HOW IT WORKS

Southfield Electrical is a supplier of a wide range of electrical appliances to high street electrical stores such as Whitehill Superstores. Earlier today, Southfield Electrical sales department received a telephone call from the purchasing manager of Whitehill Superstores enquiring whether they can supply six Zanpoint dishwashers as soon as possible. Southfield are able to supply these goods and the sales department sends out the following quotation.

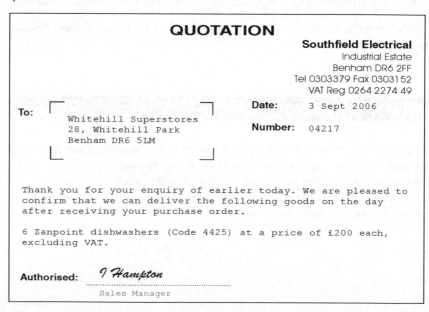

QUOTATION

Southfield Electrical
Industrial Estate
Benham DR6 2FF
Tel 0303379 Fax 0303152
VAT Reg 0264 2274 49

To:
Whitehill Superstores
28, Whitehill Park
Benham DR6 5LM

Date: 3 Sept 2006

Number: 04217

Thank you for your enquiry of earlier today. We are pleased to confirm that we can deliver the following goods on the day after receiving your purchase order.

6 Zanpoint dishwashers (Code 4425) at a price of £200 each, excluding VAT.

Authorised: *I Hampton*
Sales Manager

PURCHASE ORDER

Once the purchasing manager at Whitehill has received this quotation then if the price and terms are acceptable his department will produce the purchase order shown next. Purchase orders are sometimes also referred to as CUSTOMER ORDERS. The meaning is exactly the same.

PURCHASE ORDER

WHITEHILL SUPERSTORES
28 Whitehill Park
Benham DR6 5LM
Tel 0303446 Fax 0303447

To: Southfield Electrical
Industrial Estate
Benham
DR6 2FF

Number: 32011

Date: 5 Sept 2006

Delivery address: Whitehill Superstores
28, Whitehill Park
Benham DR6 5LM

Product code	Quantity	Description	Unit list price £
4425	6	Zanpoint Dishwasher	200 (excluding VAT)

Authorised by: *P. Winterbottom*   **Date:** *5 Sept 2006*

Let's consider the details of this purchase order:

- the purchase order has its own unique, sequential number which will be quoted on subsequent documentation such as the delivery note and invoice;

- the address to which the goods are to be delivered is given, as this may be different from the address of the purchasing department if there is, for example, a separate warehouse;

- the product is described in words but is also given its product code – coding is useful in all areas of the accounting process and this is a first example of a code being used to identify goods and transactions. If a code is used as well as words it helps to reduce the chances of an error being made in the sale;

- the price has been confirmed in order to avoid any misunderstanding at a later date;

- the purchase order must be signed and authorised by an appropriate person within Whitehill Superstores.

Activity 1

Who issues a purchase order, the buyer or the seller of goods?

CREDIT LIMITS

When a purchase order is received from a customer one of the first checks that should be made is to determine whether your business wants to sell these goods to this customer on credit. There is always a risk involved in selling goods on credit. The goods are being delivered to the customer with only the promise of payment in the future.

Most businesses will therefore guard against the risk of not being paid by a customer and one method of dealing with this risk is to set a CREDIT LIMIT for each customer. This is then the maximum amount that that particular customer should ever be allowed to owe the business at any one time.

Therefore when Southfield receives the purchase order the credit manager or the person responsible for credit customers should initially check how much Whitehill already owes, what Whitehill's credit limit is and whether this new purchase will take Whitehill's debt over the credit limit.

In this case Whitehill's account is checked and Whitehill currently owe Southfield £316.40. As they have been given a credit limit of £5,000 there is no problem and the sale can progress.

Even if a purchase order would take a customer over their credit limit it is not necessarily automatic that the sale will not be authorised. The person in the organisation who is responsible for credit limits may review the customer's account and if they are a good customer with a good record of payment then the credit limit might be increased in order to accommodate the sale.

DELIVERY NOTE

Once the purchase order has been received by the sales department of Southfield Electrical it will be checked against the purchase quotation number 04217 to ensure that this was the quantity and price that had been quoted to Whitehill. It should also be checked that the purchase order has been properly authorised by Whitehill – as Whitehill are likely to be a regular customer then it is likely that the Southfield sales department will know who normally authorises such purchase orders.

Once these checks have been carried out then the delivery of the goods must be organised. The sales department will draw up the DELIVERY NOTE shown next to accompany the dishwashers.

```
┌─────────────────────────────────────────────────────────┐
│                    DELIVERY NOTE                          │
│                                                           │
│                               Southfield Electrical       │
│                                  Industrial Estate        │
│                                  Benham DR6 2FF           │
│                             Tel 0303379 Fax 0303152       │
│                                                           │
│  Delivery address:                                        │
│                                                           │
│  ┌  Whitehill Superstores  ┐                              │
│     28, Whitehill Park         Number: 34619              │
│     Benham DR6 5LM             Date: 6 Sept 2006          │
│                                Order number: 32011        │
│  └                         ┘                              │
└─────────────────────────────────────────────────────────┘
```

Product code	Quantity	Description
4425	6	Zanpoint Dishwasher

Received by: [Signature] .... **Print name:** ....

Date: ....

We will now look in detail at the delivery note:

- the address of the delivery is included so that the carrier knows where to take the goods;

- the delivery note has its own unique, sequential number which can be used on other documentation and in any dispute;

- the purchase order number relating to this delivery is also included in order to be able to match the delivery note to the purchase order easily;

- a precise description of the goods is given both by including the description in words and including the product code. Again this is important as the goods despatched must be exactly what the customer has ordered;

- as the delivery note leaves Southfield it is unsigned. The signature that is required is that of the person receiving the dishwashers at Whitehill. The stores department at Whitehill must check that the goods that have been delivered were the ones ordered and stated on the delivery note. If there is any discrepancy then this must be recorded on the delivery note;

- the delivery note will normally have two carbon copies. Once the delivery note has been signed to confirm that the correct goods have been delivered, then the carrier will keep one copy as proof of delivery and the further copy will be returned to Southfield again as proof of delivery and acceptance by Whitehill;

- there is no need to include any price information on the delivery note as this is not relevant at this stage.

Activity 2

Why is the delivery note important?

INVOICE

The next stage in the process is for Southfield Electrical to produce a sales INVOICE. This is a request for payment for the dishwashers from Whitehill Superstores and details precisely how much is due and when. The invoice that the sales department prepares is shown next.

INVOICE

Southfield Electrical
Industrial Estate
Benham DR6 2FF
Tel 0303379 Fax 0303152
VAT Reg 0264 2274 49

To: Whitehill Superstores
28, Whitehill Park
Benham DR6 5LM

Invoice number: 56314

Date/tax point: 7 Sept 2006

Order number: 32011

Account number: SL 44

Quantity	Description	Stock code	Unit amount £	Total £
6	Zanpoint Dishwasher	4425	200	1,200.00

Net total		1,200.00
VAT @ 17S%		210.00
Invoice total		1,410.00

Terms
Net 30 days
E & OE

Let's now look at the details of the invoice:

- it must show the seller's name, address and VAT registration number (VAT will be considered in more detail later in the chapter);

- it has its own unique, sequential number. Usually at least two copies of the invoice will be produced, one being sent to Whitehill and one remaining in the accounts department of Southfield until payment is received;

- the date of the invoice (also known as the tax point) must be included as this is important information for Whitehill. It shows when the invoice is due for payment – in this case 30 days after the invoice date (see later);

- the purchase order number is included in order for the invoice to be matched with the purchase order and most probably filed together by Southfield;

- the account number is another example of coding in accounting. Eventually Southfield will have to enter this invoice into the accounting records and this account number shows exactly which account relates to Whitehill;

- the details of the goods are again included both in words and product code;

- the price of the dishwashers, excluding VAT, as quoted to Whitehill is then shown per unit. To find the total price the quantity is multiplied by the unit price. To this price must be added the VAT which is currently charged at 17.5%. The resulting total is the amount that Whitehill must pay;

- the term "net 30 days" shows that payment is due 30 days after the invoice date. "E & OE" is a standard term on documents meaning "errors and omissions excepted" which means that if an error has been made in drawing up the invoice Southfield can amend it and are due the corrected amount.

DEBIT NOTE

Let us now suppose that when the stores manager at Whitehill Superstores inspected the dishwashers he found that one had been damaged. This was noted on the delivery note and the one dishwasher was returned to Southfield Electrical. Obviously Whitehill does not want to have to pay for this machine, and therefore the accounts department raises a DEBIT NOTE. This debit note is effectively requesting a credit note from Southfield which will reflect that only five good machines have been supplied and not six.

DEBIT NOTE

WHITEHILL SUPERSTORES
28 Whitehill Park
Benham DR6 5LM
Tel 0303446 Fax 0303447

To:	Southfield Electrical Industrial Estate Benham DR6 2FF	

Debit note number:	0466
Date/tax point:	8 Sept 2006
Order number	32011
Delivery note number:	34619

Quantity	Description	Stock code	Unit amount	Total
			£	£
1	Zanpoint Dishwasher	4425	200	200.00

Net total	200.00
VAT	35.00
Gross total	235.00

Reason: *Goods damaged. Dent in front door panel*

Authorised by: *N Jones*
Stores manager

Date: *7 Sept 2006*

Let's now look at the detail of the debit note:

- as with all of these documents it has its own unique, sequential number;

- the order number and delivery note number allow this to be easily traced to the correct delivery of goods;

- the debit note is effectively requesting a credit note from Southfield so it must show all relevant details of the goods delivered, in particular the quantity of the damaged goods and the unit price quoted;

- the debit note is requesting a reduction of the total amount due for this dishwasher which includes the VAT and therefore the gross total must be shown;

- the reason for the debit note should also be given, in this case it is damaged goods, but it might also be delivery of a smaller quantity than that which was ordered;

- finally the debit note must be authorised and dated otherwise it will not be accepted by Southfield.

CREDIT NOTE

When the damaged dishwasher is returned to Southfield then notification should be sent to the accounts department of a potential problem. When the accounts department receives the debit note from Whitehill the details will then be checked with Southfield's stores department to ensure that the dishwasher was in fact returned and was damaged. When all checks have been satisfactorily made, then Southfield will issue a CREDIT NOTE to Whitehill which reverses the part of the sales invoice that relates to the damaged dishwasher.

CREDIT NOTE

SOUTHFIELD ELECTRICAL
INDUSTRIAL ESTATE
Benham DR6 2FF
Tel 0303379 Fax 0303152
VAT Reg 0264 2274 49

Invoice to:

Whitehill Superstores
28, Whitehill Park
Benham DR6 5LM

Credit note number: 08641
Date/tax point: 12 Sept 2006
Order number 32011
Account number: SL 44

Quantity	Description	Stock code	Unit amount £	Total £
1	Zanpoint Dishwasher	4425	200.00	200.00

Net total		200.00
VAT		35.00
Gross total		235.00

Reason for credit note:

Damaged goods

If we look at the credit note it can be seen that it is almost identical to an invoice. The only differences are:

- it is described as a credit note;
- it has a unique, sequential credit note number;
- a reason for the credit is noted at the bottom of the credit note.

Activity 3

What is the difference between a debit note and a credit note?

VAT

Having outlined the document flow for a sale on credit it is now necessary to consider the area of VALUE ADDED TAX (or VAT) in some more detail.

VAT is due to HM Revenue and Customs (HMRC) on many goods that are sold. It is a tax that is paid by the final consumer of the goods but is collected along the way by each seller in the goods chain. It was previously dealt with by HM Customs & Excise, which has now been merged with the Inland Revenue to form one taxation authority.

VAT registration

If the sales of a business exceed a certain amount for a year, currently £64,000, then a business must register for VAT. This means that they have a VAT registration number which must be included on invoices and other business documents.

What it also means is that it must charge VAT on all of its taxable supplies or sales at the standard rate, normally 17.5%. This is known as OUTPUT VAT.

There is however a benefit, in that the VAT that the business pays when buying from suppliers or paying expenses can be recovered back from HMRC and is known as INPUT VAT.

Usually every three months the business must complete a VAT return showing the output and input VAT. The excess of output VAT over input VAT must be paid with the VAT return. However if the input VAT exceeds the output VAT then a refund is due from HMRC.

HOW IT WORKS

Let's follow a simple manufacturing process through the VAT payment process.

Business	Transaction		HMRC
Supplier of wood	Sells wood to table manufacturer for £160 + VAT of £28		
	Sale value	£160	
	Output VAT	£28	£28
Table manufacturer	Purchases wood from supplier for £160 + VAT of £28 Sells table to retailer for £280 + VAT of £49		
	Sale value	£280	
	Purchases value	£160	
	Output VAT – Input VAT (49 – 28)	£21	£21
Retailer	Purchases table from manufacturer for £280 + VAT of £49		
	Sells table to customer for £360 + VAT of £63		
	Sale value	£360	
	Purchases value	£280	
	Output VAT – Input VAT (63 – 49)	£14	£14
Customer	Purchases table for £360 + VAT of £63		
	Pays retailer (360 + 63)	£423	£0
Total VAT paid to HMRC			£63

Note that it is the final consumer who bears the cost of the VAT, because the table cost him £423 not £360. The consumer does not himself have to pay this to HMRC as this has already been done throughout the chain of manufacture and sale.

Activity 4

What are output VAT and input VAT?

RATES OF VAT

The rate used in the previous example was the standard rate of 17.5% which will be the rate that will normally be required in these Units.

However you should be aware that there are also items that are zero-rated for VAT purposes such as food and children's clothing. This means that the seller of these items charges VAT at zero percent (ie no VAT) but can reclaim input VAT on his expenses and purchases.

Other items are exempt from VAT, such as postal services. The difference with exempt supplies is that not only is no output VAT charged on the sales but no input VAT on expenses and purchases can be reclaimed.

VAT CALCULATIONS

You will be dealing with VAT when preparing sales invoices and will need to perform accurate calculations of the VAT on these sales. Whenever you are calculating VAT amounts the rule is that you always round the VAT down to the nearest penny.

The two main calculations that you might be required to make are as follows.

Calculating the VAT on a net amount

The net amount for an invoice totals £235.46. What is the VAT on this amount?

The VAT is calculated as 17.5% of £235.46. This means that the fraction $\frac{17.5}{100}$ needs to be applied to £235.46.

$$\text{VAT to be charged} = £235.46 \times \frac{17.5}{100} = 41.2055$$

This should be rounded down to £41.20.

Activity 5

If the net amount of an invoice is £337.58 then how much VAT is charged?

Calculating the VAT and net amount from a VAT inclusive figure

The total of the price of goods plus the VAT is £375.80. How much VAT is included in this price and what is the net price of the goods?

This time the £375.80 includes 17.5% VAT and therefore to find the VAT part of that, the fraction $\dfrac{17.5}{117.5}$ must be applied to the VAT inclusive amount.

$$VAT = £375.80 \times \frac{17.5}{117.5} = 55.9702$$

This must be rounded down to £55.97. Therefore the net price of the goods is £375.80 – £55.97 = £319.83.

Activity 6

If the total price of goods is £442.68 inclusive of VAT then how much VAT has been charged and what is the net price of the goods?

DISCOUNTS

When selling goods to customers a business may not always charge all customers the full list price of the goods – the business may offer a discount. There are two types of discount that we must consider.

Trade discounts

A TRADE DISCOUNT is a percentage reduction from the list price of goods that a business may offer to some customers. The reasons for offering this reduced price might be due to the fact that this is a regular and valued customer, or it could be offered as an incentive to a new customer to buy.

The amount of the trade discount will be shown on the face of the invoice as a deduction from the list price.

HOW IT WORKS

Continuing with Southfield Electrical and Whitehill Superstores, suppose now that the initial price quotation from Southfield was the list price of £200 per dishwasher but Whitehill were to be allowed a trade discount of 10%.

The invoice would now appear as follows.

INVOICE

Southfield Electrical
Industrial Estate
Benham DR6 2FF
Tel 0303379 Fax 0303152
VAT Reg 0264 2274 49

To: Whitehill Superstores
28, Whitehill Park
Benham DR6 5LM

Invoice number: 56314

Date/tax point: 7 Sept 2006

Order number: 32011

Account number: SL 44

Quantity	Description	Stock code	Unit amount £	Total £
6	Zanpoint Dishwasher	4425	200	1,200.00
Less:	10% discount			120.00

Net total		1,080.00
VAT @ 17½%		189.00
Invoice total		1,269.00

Terms
Net 30 days
E & OE

This is how the calculations were made:

Step 1 Calculate the total price before the discount by multiplying the quantity by the list price
6 x £200 = £1,200.00

Step 2 Calculate the trade discount as 10% of this total list price
£1,200.00 x 10% (10/100) = £120.00

Step 3   Deduct the trade discount from the total list price to reach the invoice net total

£1,200.00 – £120.00 = £1,080.00

Step 4   Calculate the VAT at 17.5% of the invoice net total

£1,080.00 x 17.5% (17.5/100) = £189.00

Step 5   Calculate the invoice total by adding the VAT to the net total

£1,080.00 + £189.00 = £1,269.00

Activity 7

Goods with a list price of £2,450.00 are to be sent to a customer. The customer is allowed a trade discount of 15% and VAT is to be charged at 17.5%. What is the invoice total?

Cash or settlement discount

A CASH DISCOUNT or SETTLEMENT DISCOUNT is a percentage discount of the total invoice value that is offered to a customer to encourage that customer to pay up or settle the invoice earlier. For example if it is normal policy to request that payment is made by customers 30 days after the invoice date, a cash discount of 4% might be offered for payment within 10 days of the invoice date.

A cash discount differs from a trade discount in that although the seller offers the discount to the customer it is up to the customer to decide whether or not to accept the offer of the discount. Therefore the discount does not appear on the face of the invoice but it will be noted at the bottom of the invoice in the "Terms" section.

There is one complication here with VAT. If a cash discount is offered then the VAT is calculated on the assumption that the cash discount is taken up by the customer and therefore the VAT calculation is made based upon the net invoice total **after deducting** the cash discount.

HOW IT WORKS

Continuing with Southfield and Whitehill suppose now that Southfield not only offers the 10% trade discount but also a 4% cash discount for settlement within 10 days of the invoice date.

This is what the invoice would look like:

INVOICE

Southfield Electrical
Industrial Estate
Benham DR6 2FF
Tel 0303379 Fax 0303152
VAT Reg 0264 2274 49

To: Whitehill Superstores
28, Whitehill Park
Benham DR6 5LM

Invoice number: 56314

Date/tax point: 7 Sept 2006

Order number: 32011

Account number: SL 44

Quantity	Description	Stock code	Unit amount £	Total £
6	Zanpoint Dishwasher	4425	200	1,200.00
Less:	10% discount			120.00

Net total		1,080.00
VAT		181.44
Invoice total		1,261.44

Terms
4% discount for settlement within 10 days of invoice date, otherwise net 30 days
E & OE

Now let's look at the calculations involved here. The figures are exactly the same as on the previous invoice until the VAT section is reached. So we will now look at how to calculate the VAT.

Step 1 Calculate the amount of the cash discount offered by finding 4% of the net invoice total
£1,080.00 x 4% (4/100) = £43.20

Step 2 In a working, deduct the cash discount from the net invoice total
£1,080.00 – £43.20 = £1,036.80

Step 3 Calculate the VAT at 17.5% on the invoice total minus the cash discount
£1,036.80 x 17.5% (17.5/100) = £181.44 (remember to round down to the nearest penny)

Step 4   Add this VAT amount into the net invoice total to arrive at the total invoice amount

£1,080.00 + £181.44 = £1,261.44

Step 5   State the terms of the cash discount at the bottom of the invoice.

Activity 8

Goods with a value of £368.40 are to be sold to a customer and the customer is offered a 3% settlement discount for payment received within 14 days of the invoice date. What is the invoice total?

OTHER TERMS

We have already come across some of the terms that might appear on an invoice but there are a few further common ones that you should be aware of:

- ex-works means that the price of the goods does not include delivery so there will be a delivery charge as well

- carriage paid means that the price of the goods does include the cost of delivery

- COD means cash on delivery and therefore payment must be made by the customer at the time that the goods are delivered.

STATEMENTS

There is one final document that is part of the document cycle for credit sales and that is the CUSTOMER STATEMENT. It is common practice to send out to customers on a regular basis, usually monthly, a statement showing all the invoices and credit notes that have been sent to the customer that month together with any amounts outstanding from previous months, along with any payments received from the customer in the month.

A typical statement might look like this:

STATEMENT

Southfield Electrical
Industrial Estate
Benham DR6 2FF
Tel 0303379 Fax 0303152
VAT Reg 0264 2274 49

To: Whitehill Superstores
28, Whitehill Park
Benham
DR6 5LM

Account number: SL 44

Date: 30 Sept 2006

Date	Details	Debit	Credit	Balance
01.09.06	Balance b/f			316.40
07.09.06	Invoice 56314	1,410.00		1,726.40
12.09.06	Credit 08641		235.00	1,491.40
20.09.06	Payment received - Thank you		316.40	1,175.00

Amount now due   1,175.00

Let's now consider the entries on this statement:

- it is addressed to Whitehill Superstores and again, in order to ease finding the relevant information, the customer's account code is included;

- the balance b/f (brought forward) indicates that Whitehill owed Southfield £316.40 at the start of the month – note that this has been received from Whitehill on 20 September;

- the invoice on the 7 September is shown together with the credit note sent out on 12 September – at this stage do not worry about the terms debit and credit or which column each entry goes into: this will become clear later in the Course Companion;

- after each entry the balance is shown which represents the amount currently owing by Whitehill;

- by the end of September the amount due is the net of the invoice and the credit note, £1,410.00 – £235.00 = £1,175.00.

CHECKING INVOICES

There are a lot of important details and calculations involved in preparing an invoice and it is extremely important that these details and calculations are done properly and thoroughly checked.

We will now work through the whole process of preparing a sales invoice in a manual accounting system in order to illustrate all of the checks that must be made.

HOW IT WORKS

You work for Southfield Electrical and are responsible for preparing sales invoices. Today is 8 October 2006 and you have on your desk the following purchase order from Whitehill Superstores for which an invoice must be prepared.

PURCHASE ORDER

WHITEHILL SUPERSTORES
28 Whitehill Park
Benham DR6 5LM
Tel 0303446 Fax 0303447

To: Southfield Electrical
Industrial Estate
Benham
DR6 2FF

Number: 32174

Date: 2 Oct 2006

Delivery address: Whitehill Superstores
28, Whitehill Park
Benham DR6 5LM

Product code	Quantity	Description	Unit list price £
6160	4	Hosch Washing Machine	300.00
3172	10	Temax Mixer	40.00

Authorised by: *P. Winterbottom*   **Date:** *2 Oct 2006*

student notes ✎

Step 1   You must first check that the goods were in fact sent to Whitehill and therefore you find the delivery note that relates to purchase order 32174. This is given below.

DELIVERY NOTE

Southfield Electrical
Industrial Estate
Benham DR6 2FF
Tel 0303379 Fax 0303152

Delivery address:

Whitehill Superstores
28, Whitehill Park
Benham DR6 5LM

Number: 34772
Date: 5 Oct 2006
Order number: 32174

Product code	Quantity	Description
6160	4	Hosch Washing Machine
3172	9	Temax Mixer

Received by: [Signature]   *J. Jones*   **Print name:** *J. JONES*

Date: *5 Oct 2006*

Step 2   You should note that only 9 mixers were delivered and accepted (the delivery note is signed) and therefore only 9 mixers must be invoiced not the 10 that were ordered. You might also make a note to follow up why only 9 and not 10 were delivered, or to inform the appropriate person in your organisation.

Step 3   The prices quoted on the purchase order are the unit list prices. You must now check that these list prices are correct. An extract from Southfield's price list is given below.

PRICE LIST EXTRACT

CODE	DESCRIPTION	UNIT PRICE £
HOSCH		
6040	Tumble dryer	250.00
6050	Tumble dryer	280.00
6060	Tumble dryer	300.00
6140	Washing machine	220.00
6150	Washing machine	260.00
6160	Washing machine	300.00
6170	Washing machine	340.00
TEMAX		
3160	Food processor	100.00
3162	Food processor	120.00
3164	Food processor	140.00
3170	Mixer	35.00
3172	Mixer	40.00
3174	Mixer	46.00

As you can see the prices included on the purchase order do indeed agree with the list prices and therefore can be used on the invoice.

Step 4   You must now find the customer file for Whitehill Superstores which will show details of addresses, account codes, credit limits and discounts allowed.

The customer file for Whitehill Superstores shows the following:

- account code number – SL44;

- 10% trade discount is allowed;

- 4% cash discount for settlement within 10 days, otherwise net 30 days;

- delivery charges are included in the list price.

Step 5   You now have all of the information required to start preparing the sales invoice. The final invoice is now shown and we will then work through the remaining steps in completing it.

INVOICE

Southfield Electrical
Industrial Estate
Benham DR6 2FF
Tel 0303379 Fax 0303152
VAT Reg 0264 2274 49

To: Whitehill Superstores
28, Whitehill Park
Benham DR6 5LM

Invoice number: 56483

Date/tax point: 8 Oct 2006

Order number: 32174

Account number: SL 44

Quantity	Description	Stock code	Unit amount £	Total £
4	Hosch Washing Machine	6160	300.00	1,200.00
9	Temax Mixer	3172	40.00	360.00
				1,560.00
Less:	10% discount			156.00

Net total	1,404.00
VAT @ 17½%	235.87
Invoice total	1,639.87

Terms
4% discount for settlement within 10 days of invoice date, otherwise 30 days net
E & OE
Carriage Paid

Step 6 Enter the customer's name and address and account number from the customer file. The invoice number is the next number in sequence after the previous invoice. Enter today's date.

Step 7 Enter the quantities, codes and descriptions from the delivery note – remember that only 9 mixers were delivered.

Step 8 Enter the unit prices from the price list. Calculate the total list price by multiplying the quantity by the list price
4 x £300 = £1,200.00
9 x £40 = £360.00

Step 9 Calculate the total list price by adding together the totals for each product
£1,200.00 + £360.00 = £1,560.00

Step 10 Calculate the trade discount as 10% of the total list price
£1,560.00 x 10% (10/100) = £156.00
Deduct the trade discount to arrive at the net invoice total
£1,560.00 – £156.00 = £1,404.00

Step 11 To calculate the VAT, first of all determine the amount of cash discount
£1,404.00 x 4% (4/100) = £56.16
In a working deduct this from the net invoice total
£1,404.00 – £56.16 = £1,347.84
Calculate the VAT at 17.5% based on the amount after the discount has been deducted
£1,347.84 x 17.5% (17.5/100) = £235.87

Alternatively, the VAT can be calculated as follows:

	£
Net invoice total	1,404.00
VAT 1,404.00 x 0.96 x 0.175 =	235.87

Step 12 Add the VAT calculated to the net invoice total to arrive at the gross invoice total
£1,404.00 + £235.87 = £1,639.87

Step 13 Enter the relevant terms at the bottom of the invoice, in this case the cash discount terms, E & OE (standard term) and carriage paid as delivery charges are included.

student notes

student notes✎

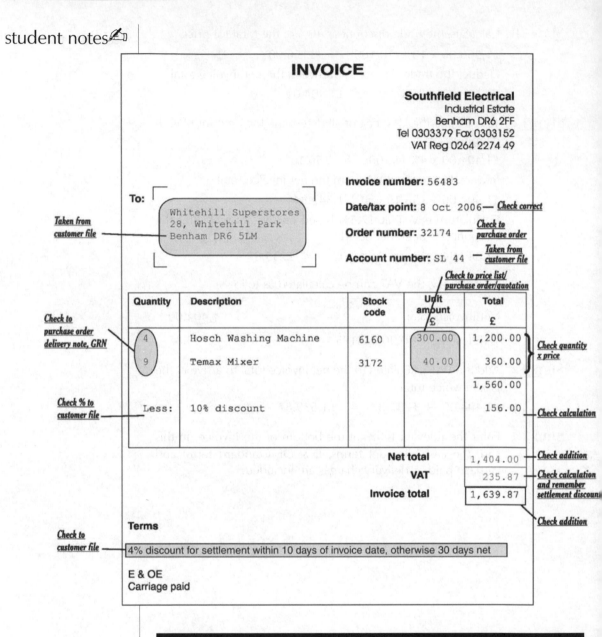

INVOICE

Southfield Electrical
Industrial Estate
Benham DR6 2FF
Tel 0303379 Fax 0303152
VAT Reg 0264 2274 49

Invoice number: 56483

Date/tax point: 8 Oct 2006 — *Check correct*

To:
Whitehill Superstores
28, Whitehill Park
Benham DR6 5LM

Taken from customer file

Order number: 32174 — *Check to purchase order*

Account number: SL 44 — *Taken from customer file*

Check to price list/ purchase order/quotation

Quantity	Description	Stock code	Unit amount £	Total £
4	Hosch Washing Machine	6160	300.00	1,200.00
9	Temax Mixer	3172	40.00	360.00
				1,560.00
Less:	10% discount			156.00

Check to purchase order delivery note, GRN

Check % to customer file

Check quantity x price

Check calculation

Net total		1,404.00
VAT		235.87
Invoice total		1,639.87

Check addition

Check calculation and remember settlement discount

Check addition

Terms

Check to customer file

4% discount for settlement within 10 days of invoice date, otherwise 30 days net

E & OE
Carriage paid

CHECKING CREDIT NOTES

When preparing or checking a credit note the same type of procedures need to be followed as those for an invoice. The following approach should be followed:

- check that the goods were actually returned;

- ensure that the credit note is being issued to the correct customer;

- check that the goods returned are the ones on the credit note by checking the product or stock code;

- check the price of the returned goods on the price list;

- check the calculations on the credit note eg quantity x unit price = total price;

- check that any trade discounts have been allowed for on the price of the goods returned;

- check that the VAT has been correctly calculated.

Activity 9

Why is it important to check credit notes thoroughly before sending them out to customers?

COMPUTERISED ACCOUNTING SYSTEM

The checks carried out in the previous section of the chapter were based upon a manual accounting system. In a computerised accounting system some of these checks are not necessary as the computer will accurately carry out the calculations on an invoice or credit note.

However, what is particularly important in a computerised system is that the data input is correct. This will largely be in the form of codes and therefore it is important that the correct codes are being used.

When producing a sales invoice in a computerised accounting system the following codes are likely to be used:

- customer code – this will bring up the customer name. address and credit details including discounts offered;

- purchase order number and delivery note number – these must be checked as in a manual system to ensure that the correct quantities are being invoiced;

- product codes – when the correct product code is input then the up to date list price will be applied to the quantity.

Therefore in a computerised accounting system the emphasis is on checking that the data input is correct.

Issuing invoices in a computerised system

Remember that in theory the purpose of a computer system is the same as that of a manual system, and it is intended to achieve the same ends. In computer terminology a file is a collection of data with common features. A price list or a customer list could be held as a computer file.

A computerised invoicing program makes use of two data files:

- the customer file (name, address, credit limit, discount policy);
- the product file (description and selling prices of each product).

The program will work something like this:

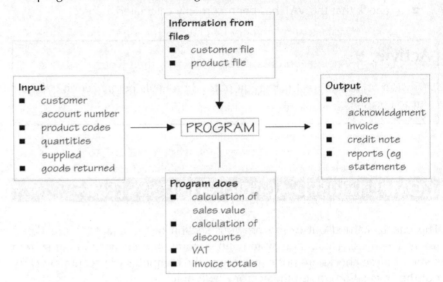

This may look complicated, but the computer is doing all the work. All the user needs to do in practice is select the relevant customer and product codes from drop menus and enter the quantities. All the rest of the information will be looked up or calculated by the system. Then you just click on Save.

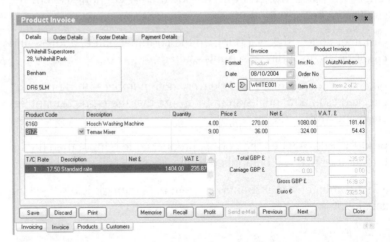

Note that there is also a Memorise button in the system illustrated. That means that if this were a regular monthly order the invoice could be created even more quickly next month, just by copying the previous example. The computer would even know that it should change the date.

Activity 10

Can you see any differences between the computer invoice entry screen and the manual invoice illustrated on previous pages?

The reports produced can include customer statements, and also:

- summaries of goods sold (eg 17 dishwashers so the company knows when to reorder);

- sales by product line (to see which are popular or profitable);

- sales by customer (to see which are the biggest customers);

- sales by geographical area (can help to identify for example where more resource may be needed, or where a marketing exercise is necessary);

- total VAT on sales (and total gross or net sales);

- total discounts allowed (is it too much?);

- check the calculations on the credit note eg quantity x unit price = total price;

- check that any trade discounts have been allowed for on the price of the goods returned;

- check that the VAT has been correctly calculated.

AUTHORISATION AND CODING OF INVOICES

A sales invoice is a very important document for a business. It is the source of the business's income and therefore the invoice must be accurate. As such, once the invoice has been prepared it will be checked and once the checking process has taken place will be marked as checked. This might be with a simple signature or with a standardised rubber stamp showing exactly what checks have been carried out, eg calculations, price lists, account codes etc.

The precise checks and method of indicating that those checks have been carried out will differ from organisation to organisation. However the final outcome will be that the invoice will be authorised by the appropriate person in the organisation and then sent out to the customer. There should be checks in place to ensure that an invoice that has not been authorised cannot be sent out to a customer. This also applies to credit notes.

As part of the checking and authorising process, sales invoices and credit notes must also be coded for their eventual inclusion in the accounting records. The invoice or credit note should always include the account code for the customer; if you remember with Whitehill Superstores this was SL44. The coding might also indicate what type of sale was made. In some organisations the sales are categorised according to the type of product or the geographical region of the sale. If this is the policy of the organisation then each invoice must be correctly coded to show the type of product or where the sale was made.

CHAPTER OVERVIEW

- when cash sales are made the only documentation that is usually required is for the customer to be given a copy of the till roll receipt, and if payment is made by credit or debit card a copy of the voucher

- when credit sales are made however, there are potentially many documents involved

- the process is started by an initial purchase enquiry from the prospective customer

- the seller then answers the enquiry with a telephone or written price quotation

- the customer then confirms the purchase with a purchase order

- at this stage the customer's credit limit should be checked to ensure it is not exceeded

- the goods are despatched to the customer together with a delivery note that must be signed by the customer upon receipt of the goods and a copy returned to the seller

- the seller then sends out an invoice requesting payment from the customer

- upon return of any goods from the customer or receipt of a debit note the seller will send out a credit note effectively cancelling all or part of the invoice

- most businesses will be registered for VAT and must therefore add VAT at 17.5%, the standard rate, to the price of the goods charged to the customer

- if the customer is not satisfied with the goods or they are damaged in any way and have to be returned then the customer may send a debit note with the goods being returned

- the seller may offer the customer a trade discount and/or a cash or settlement discount. A trade discount is a reduction of list price and is shown on the face of the invoice. A cash discount is offered to the customer who may or may not take up the offer. This is shown at the bottom of the invoice as part of the terms

- a statement is sent out to customers on a regular basis, normally monthly, showing invoices and credit notes issued during the month, payments received (if any) and the final amount outstanding from the customer at the end of the month

KEY WORDS

Purchase order sent from the customer to the seller confirming the required purchase

Customer order another term for a purchase order

Credit limit the maximum amount that each customer should owe at any point in time

Delivery note document sent to the customer with the goods being despatched which must be signed by the customer confirming receipt of the goods

Invoice sent out by the seller to the customer to request payment for the goods

Debit note sent from the customer to the seller when goods are returned to request a credit note

Credit note sent from the seller to the customer when goods are returned in order to cancel or reverse all or part of the invoice

VAT a tax levied by HM Revenue and Customs which must be added to the selling price of goods at all stages in the manufacturing process, paid over to HMRC at each stage of the process and borne by the final consumer

Output VAT VAT on sales

Input VAT VAT on purchases and expenses

CHAPTER OVERVIEW cont.

- many checks are necessary when preparing an invoice to ensure that it is for the correct goods, to the correct customer and for the correct amount

- similar checks are also required for credit notes, in particular details of the goods that have been returned

- there are also a number of different types of checks that are required in a computerised accounting system on sales invoices and credit notes

- finally each organisation will have its own procedures that should be followed for authorisation and coding of sales invoices and credit notes

KEY WORDS

Trade discount a percentage discount off the list price of goods offered to some long standing customers

Cash/settlement discount a percentage discount off the total invoice value offered to some customers in order to provide an incentive to pay the invoice amount early

Customer statement a statement sent out to credit customers on a regular basis showing the amount outstanding and due from the customer at the end of the period

1 Which type of document would be used for the following purposes?

    a) To inform the customer of the amount due for a sale;
    b) To inform the seller of the quantities required;
    c) To inform the seller that some of the delivery was not of the standard or type required;
    d) To inform the customer of the quantity delivered;
    e) To inform the customer that the invoiced amount was overstated.

2 Explain briefly what is included on a delivery note and what its purposes are.

3 What are the main items that should appear on a sales invoice?

4   a) A sale is made for £288.59 plus VAT. How much VAT should be charged?

    b) A sale is made for £288.59 including VAT. How much VAT has been charged and what is the net amount of the sale?

5 For each of the following VAT inclusive amounts, calculate the VAT and the net amount.

    a) £3,152,90
    b) £446.28
    c) £168.35

6   a) A customer is purchasing 23 items each with a list price of £56.00. A trade discount of 15% is given to this customer.

    Calculate the total cost before the discount, the discount, the net of discount price, the VAT and the total cost.

    b) Suppose that a cash discount of 3% is also offered. Calculate the same figures on this basis.

7   Given below are a purchase order and related delivery note and sales invoice. Check them carefully and note any problems that you discover stating how you would deal with them.

PURCHASE ORDER

WHITEHILL SUPERSTORES
28 Whitehill Park
Benham DR6 5LM
Tel 0303446 Fax 0303447

To: Southfield Electrical
Industrial Estate
Benham
DR6 2FF

Number: 32202

Date: 16 Oct 2006

Delivery address: Whitehill Superstores
28, Whitehill Park
Benham DR6 5LM

Product code	Quantity	Description	Unit list price £
7460	11	Magifen Vacuum	210.00
3264	7	Temax Food Processor	65.00
9406	15	Kensharp Toaster	15.00

Authorised by: *P. Winterbottom* ....   **Date:** *16 Oct 2006* ....

DELIVERY NOTE

Southfield Electrical
Industrial Estate
Benham DR6 2FF
Tel 0303379 Fax 0303152

Delivery address:

Whitehill Superstores
28, Whitehill Park
Benham DR6 5LM

Number: 34816
Date: 18 Oct 2006
Order number: 32202

Product code	Quantity	Description
3264	7	Temax Food Processor
9406	12	Kensharp Toaster
7460	11	Magifen Vacuum

Received by: [Signature] *J. Jones*   **Print name:** *J. JONES*

Date: *18 Oct 2006*

INVOICE

Southfield Electrical
Industrial Estate
Benham DR6 2FF
Tel 0303379 Fax 0303152
VAT Reg 0264 2274 49

To: Whitehill Superstores
28, Whitehill Park
Benham DR6 5LM

Invoice number: 56501

Date/tax point: 22 Oct 2006

Order number: 32202

Account number: SL 44

Quantity	Description	Stock code	Unit amount £	Total £
7	Temax Food Processor	3264	65.00	455.00
15	Kensharp Toaster	9406	15.00	225.00
11	Magifen Vacuum	7460	220.00	2,420.00
				3,100.00
Less:	10% discount			310.00

Net total	2,790.00
VAT	468.72
Invoice total	3,258.72

Terms
4% discount for settlement within 10 days of invoice date, otherwise net 30 days
E & OE
Carriage Paid

8 Given below is a sales invoice. Check it carefully and state what is wrong with it and calculate the correct figures.

INVOICE

Southfield Electrical
Industrial Estate
Benham DR6 2FF
Tel 0303379 Fax 0303152
VAT Reg 0264 2274 49

To: G. Bender & Sons
14, High St.
Wentford
DR10 6LT

Invoice number: 56503

Date/tax point:

Order number: 32216

Account number:

Quantity	Description	Stock code	Unit amount £	Total £
21	Zanpoint Tumble Dryer	4610	180.00	3,870.00
10	Temax Mixer	3172	40.00	400.00
				4,270.00
Less:	15% discount			683.20

Net total	3,586.80
VAT	627.69
Invoice total	4,214.49

Terms
5% cash discount for payment within 10 days, otherwise 30 days net
E & OE

9 Given below is a credit note and the related debit note from the customer. Check them carefully and state what is wrong with the credit note and calculate the correct figures.

CREDIT NOTE

SOUTHFIELD ELECTRICAL
INDUSTRIAL ESTATE
Benham DR6 2FF
Tel 0303379 Fax 0303152
VAT Reg 0264 2274 49

To:		Credit note number:	08669
B. B. Berry Ltd		Date/tax point:	22 Oct 2006
Industrial Estate		Order number	40102
Benham		Account number:	5416
DR6 5FW			

Quantity	Description	Stock code	Unit amount	Total
			£	£
3	Zanpoint fridge	4770	220.00	660.00
2	Temax whisk	3212	6.99	19.38
			Net total	679.38
			VAT	118.90
			Gross total	560.48

Reason for credit note:

Goods not ordered

....

DEBIT NOTE

B. B. BERRY LTD
Industrial Estate
Benham DR6 5FW
Tel 0303412 Fax 0303413
VAT Reg 0671 2168 34

To:

Southfield Electrical
Industrial Estate
Benham
DR6 2FF

Debit note number: 0611
Date/tax point: 16 Oct 2006
Order number 40102

Quantity	Description	Stock code	Unit amount	Total
			£	£
3	Zanpoint Fridge	4770	220.00	660.00
2	Temax Whisk	3212	6.99	13.98
				673.98
Less:	20% discount			134.80

Net total	539.18
VAT	94.35
Gross total	633.53

Reason for return: *Not ordered*

chapter 3:
DOUBLE ENTRY BOOKKEEPING

chapter coverage 📖

Now that we have considered the preparation and authorisation of invoices and credit notes, the next stage is to enter these documents into the accounting records. Therefore in this chapter the basics of double entry bookkeeping are introduced so that these can be applied to credit sales, and to other types of transaction later in the Course Companion.

The topics that are to be covered are:

✍ the dual effect of each transaction for a business

✍ recording transactions in ledger accounts

✍ balancing ledger accounts

✍ different types of accounting system

✍ preparing a simple trial balance

✍ the different ledgers in an accounting system

KNOWLEDGE AND UNDERSTANDING AND PERFORMANCE CRITERIA COVERAGE

Units 1, 2 and 3

knowledge and understanding – accounting methods

1.11, 2.11, 3.5 double entry bookkeeping, including balancing accounts

Unit 3

knowledge and understanding – accounting methods

15 inter-relationship of accounts - double entry system
18 function and form of the trial balance

DOUBLE ENTRY BOOKKEEPING

Traditionally, accounting is based upon a system of double entry bookkeeping. The fundamental principle of this is that each and every transaction has two effects on a business.

A further important concept in accounting is that the owner is a completely separate entity from the business itself. Therefore if the owner pays money into the business or takes money out then this must be recorded by the business.

HOW IT WORKS

We will look at the initial transactions of a small business to illustrate this.

- Ben Charles sets up in business on 1 May 2006 by paying £10,000 into a business bank account from his redundancy money.

Effect 1

Cash into the business of £10,000

Effect 2

The business owes Ben £10,000

- Ben buys some goods for resale for £1,000 in cash

Effect 1

Purchases of £1,000 have been made

Effect 2

Cash of £1,000 is used up

- Ben buys some goods for resale for £2,000 on credit

Effect 1

Purchases of £2,000 have been made

Effect 2

A creditor for £2,000 exists

- Ben pays rent for premises of £600

Effect 1

A rent expense of £600 has been incurred

Effect 2

Cash of £600 is used up

- Sales of £1,500 for cash are made by selling the goods that were bought for cash

Effect 1

Cash has increased by £1,500

Effect 2

Sales of £1,500 have been made

- Sales of £1,800 are made on credit for half of the goods bought on credit

Effect 1
A debtor for £1,800 exists

Effect 2
Sales of £1,800 have been made

- Ben purchases a computer to help with the accounting process at a cost of £1,000 and pays for this by cheque

Effect 1
The business now has a fixed asset worth £1,000

Effect 2
Cash has decreased by £1,000

- Ben buys computer discs and other stationery for £200 by cheque

Effect 1
A revenue expense of £200 is incurred

Effect 2
Cash is decreased by £200

- Ben takes out £500 from the business for his own living expenses

Effect 1
Drawings of £500 have taken place

Effect 2
Cash is decreased by £500

- Ben pays his creditor £1,500

Effect 1
The creditor is reduced by £1,500

Effect 2
Cash is reduced by £1,500

- Ben's credit customer pays £1,400 by cheque

Effect 1
Cash is increased by £1,400

Effect 2
The debtor's amount is reduced by £1,400

Activity 1

What are the two effects of the following transactions?

a) Purchase of goods on credit
b) Sale of goods on credit
c) Receipt of money for sale of goods on credit
d) Payment of a creditor

LEDGER ACCOUNTS

All of these transactions, and indeed both sides of each transaction, need to be recorded in the accounting records of the organisation.

The traditional and manual method of recording these transactions is in a LEDGER ACCOUNT.

Ledger simply means book, and each type of transaction would occupy a whole page of the book or ledger, looking something like this:

Date	Ref	Narrative	£	Date	Ref	Narrative	£

You will note that there are two sides to this ledger account. As we have already seen, each transaction has two effects and consequently the two sides of the ledger account become vital. These ledger accounts are often known as T accounts due to their visual impact!

Each ledger account will have a title which explains which transaction it is recording eg, sales, purchases, capital etc.

Each side of the ledger account has both a name and a purpose. This is where it becomes technical! The left hand side is the DEBIT side and the right hand side is the CREDIT side.

For every transaction that a business makes there must be a debit entry in one account and an equal and opposite credit entry in another account. The trick is knowing which accounts to put the debit and credit entries into.

GENERAL RULES FOR DOUBLE ENTRY

There are some general rules for double entry bookkeeping which can help you to determine where debit and credit entries should be made:

- if cash is paid out of the business, then the cash account is always credited – therefore some other account must be debited;

- if cash comes into the business, then the cash account is always debited – therefore some other account must be credited;

- assets are always recorded on the debit side of their account;

- liabilities are always recorded on the credit side of their account;

- expenses are always debit entries in their account;

- income is always a credit entry in its account.

Asset account

	£		£
Debit entry	X		

Liability account

	£		£
		Credit entry	X

Expense account

	£		£
Debit entry	X		

Income account

	£		£
		Credit entry	X

HOW IT WORKS

So we will now return to Ben Charles's business and enter each of his initial transactions into ledger accounts. For this example we will simplify the ledger accounts slightly, not worrying about the date or any reference, just concentrating on the debit and the credit entry.

Ben sets up in business on 1 May 2006 by paying £10,000 into a business bank account

Money has come into the business therefore the cash or bank account must be debited. The money paid in is from the owner of the business and is therefore capital of the business so the credit entry is to the capital account.

Bank account

	£		£
Capital	10,000		

Capital account

	£		£
		Bank	10,000

Note how the description of each item denotes where the other side of the entry is.

Ben buys some goods for resale for £1,000 in cash

Money is going out of the business so the bank account must be credited.

The payment was for goods for resale which are known as PURCHASES so this is the account that must be debited.

Bank account				
	£			£
Capital	10,000	Purchases		1,000

Purchases account			
	£		£
Bank	1,000		

Ben buys some goods for resale for £2,000 on credit

Again these goods are purchases so the purchases account must be debited.

The transaction is not for cash this time so there is no entry into the bank account, instead the credit entry is to a creditors account – remember that liabilities (ie a creditor) are always a credit entry.

Purchases account			
	£		£
Bank	1,000		
Creditors	2,000		

Creditors account			
	£		£
		Purchases	2,000

Ben pays rent for premises of £600 in cash

Money out of the business; therefore credit the bank account.

The rent is an expense of the business so the rent account must be debited – expenses are always debit entries in their accounts.

Bank account				
	£			£
Capital	10,000	Purchases		1,000
		Rent		600

student notes ✐

Rent account

	£		£
Bank	600		

Sales of £1,500 for cash are made by selling the goods that were bought for cash

Cash is coming into the business from these SALES therefore debit the bank account.

The credit is to the sales account – remember that income is always a credit entry.

Bank account

	£		£
Capital	10,000	Purchases	1,000
Sales	1,500	Rent	600

Sales account

	£		£
		Bank	1,500

Sales of £1,800 are made on credit for half of the goods bought on credit

Again we have a sale so the sales account must be credited.

This time however there is no cash coming in so it is not the bank account that is debited, instead a debtor account is where the debit entry is made – remember that assets (ie a debtor) are always a debit entry.

Sales account

	£		£
		Bank	1,500
		Debtors	1,800

Debtors account

	£		£
Sales	1,800		

Ben purchases a computer to help with the accounting process at a cost of £1,000 and pays for this by cheque

Money out of the business, so a credit to the bank account.

student notes

A fixed asset has been purchased so a debit is required in a fixed asset account – remember that assets always have debit entries in their account.

Bank account

	£		£
Capital	10,000	Purchases	1,000
Sales	1,500	Rent	600
		Fixed asset	1,000

Fixed asset account

	£		£
Bank	1,000		

Ben buys computer discs and other stationery for £200 by cheque

Money out of the business, so a credit to the bank account.

The stationery and discs are an expense to the business so a stationery account will be opened and debited.

Bank account

	£		£
Capital	10,000	Purchases	1,000
Sales	1,500	Rent	600
		Fixed asset	1,000
		Stationery	200

Stationery account

	£		£
Bank	200		

Ben takes out £500 from the business for his own living expenses

Money out of the business, so credit the bank account.

This is the owner taking money out of the business which is known as DRAWINGS, so a drawings account is debited.

Bank account

	£		£
Capital	10,000	Purchases	1,000
Sales	1,500	Rent	600
		Fixed asset	1,000
		Stationery	200
		Drawings	500

Drawings account

	£		£
Bank	500		

Ben pays his creditor £1,500

Money out of the business, so credit the bank account.

The money is being paid to his creditor therefore it is reducing his liability to that creditor. The creditors account is debited to reflect this.

Bank account

	£		£
Capital	10,000	Purchases	1,000
Sales	1,500	Rent	600
		Fixed asset	1,000
		Stationery	200
		Drawings	500
		Creditors	1,500

Creditors account

	£		£
Bank	1,500	Purchases	2,000

Ben's credit customer pays £1,400 by cheque

This is money being received into the business so the bank account is debited.

The credit entry is to the debtors account, as this receipt is reducing the amount that the debtor owes the business.

Bank account

	£		£
Capital	10,000	Purchases	1,000
Sales	1,500	Rent	600
Debtors	1,400	Fixed asset	1,000
		Stationery	200
		Drawings	500
		Creditors	1,500

Debtors account

	£		£
Sales	1,800	Bank	1,400

Activity 2

For each of the following transactions state which account should be debited and which account credited:

a)   Purchase of goods on credit
b)   Sale of goods on credit
c)   Receipt of money for sale of goods on credit
d)   Payment of a creditor

BALANCING THE LEDGER ACCOUNTS

Once all of the accounting entries have been put into the ledger accounts for a period then it is likely that the owner or managers of a business will want to know certain things such as what is the balance on the bank account, how many sales have there been in the period, how much do we owe our creditors at the end of the period etc?

These questions can be answered by balancing the ledger accounts.

HOW IT WORKS

We will illustrate the balancing process by using Ben Charles's ledger accounts for his initial period of trading. Lets start with the bank account.

Bank account

	£		£
Capital	10,000	Purchases	1,000
Sales	1,500	Rent	600
Debtors	1,400	Fixed asset	1,000
		Stationery	200
		Drawings	500
		Creditors	1,500

Step 1   Total both the debit and the credit columns making a note of the totals for each.

Debit column total £12,900
Credit column total £4,800

Step 2   Put the largest of the two totals as the column total for both the debit and credit columns leaving at least one empty line at the bottom of each column.

Bank account

	£		£
Capital	10,000	Purchases	1,000
Sales	1,500	Rent	600
Debtors	1,400	Fixed asset	1,000
		Stationery	200
		Drawings	500
		Creditors	1,500
	12,900		12,900

Step 3 At the bottom of the column with the smaller actual total put in the figure that makes the column total to the larger figure. This is called the balance carried down (Bal c/d).

Bank account

	£		£
Capital	10,000	Purchases	1,000
Sales	1,500	Rent	600
Debtors	1,400	Fixed asset	1,000
		Stationery	200
		Drawings	500
		Creditors	1,500
		Balance c/d	8,100
	12,900		12,900

Step 4 Show this balancing figure on the opposite side of the account below the total and describe it as the balance brought down (Bal b/d).

Bank account

	£		£
Capital	10,000	Purchases	1,000
Sales	1,500	Rent	600
Debtors	1,400	Fixed asset	1,000
		Stationery	200
		Drawings	500
		Creditors	1,500
		Balance c/d	8,100
	12,900		12,900
Balance b/d	8,100		

This is showing us that we have an asset (a debit balance) of £8,100 of cash in the bank account.

Now we will balance all of the other accounts for Ben Charles in the same way.

Capital account

	£		£
		Bank	10,000

When an account has only one entry, like the capital account, there is no need for the balancing exercise as this single entry is the balance ie, a credit balance of £10,000.

Purchases account

	£		£
Bank	1,000		
Creditors	2,000	Balance c/d	3,000
	3,000		3,000
Balance b/d	3,000		

This shows that purchases totalled £3,000 for the period.

Creditors account

	£		£
Bank	1,500	Purchases	2,000
Balance c/d	500		
	2,000		2,000
		Balance b/d	500

This shows that Ben still owes his creditor £500 at the end of the period.

Rent account

	£		£
Bank	600		

The balance on the rent account is simply this debit of £600.

Sales account

	£		£
		Bank	1,500
Balance c/d	3,300	Debtors	1,800
	3,300		3,300
		Balance b/d	3,300

This shows that sales totalled £3,300 for the period.

Debtors account

	£		£
Sales	1,800	Bank	1,400
		Balance c/d	400
	1,800		1,800
Balance b/d	400		

This shows that Ben's debtor still owes £400 at the end of the period.

Fixed asset account

	£		£
Bank	1,000		

This is simply the balance on the fixed asset account showing that the business has a fixed asset that cost £1,000.

Stationery account

	£		£
Bank	200		

The stationery expense for the period was £200.

Drawings account

	£		£
Bank	500		

The owner's drawings for the period totalled £500.

Activity 3

Balance the following ledger account and state what the balance represents.

Debtors account

	£		£
Sales	2,600	Bank	1,800
Sales	1,400	Bank	1,200
Sales	3,700	Bank	2,000
Sales	1,300		

63

THE TRIAL BALANCE

Once all of the accounts have been balanced then a very useful exercise is often carried out. This is the preparation of a TRIAL BALANCE.

The trial balance is simply a list of all of the debit and credit balances on each of the ledger accounts. The purpose of the trial balance is that it forms a check on the accuracy of the entries in the ledger accounts. If the debits in the trial balance do not equal the credits then this indicates that there has been an error in the double entry. The trial balance will be considered in more detail later in this Course Companion.

HOW IT WORKS

Now we will complete Ben Charles's accounts for the period by preparing a trial balance.

Step 1 List the balance brought down on each account as a debit or credit as appropriate.

	Debits £	Credits £
Bank	8,100	
Capital		10,000
Purchases	3,000	
Creditors		500
Rent	600	
Sales		3,300
Debtors	400	
Fixed assets	1,000	
Stationery	200	
Drawings	500	

Step 2 Total the debit column and the credit column and check that they are equal.

	Debits £	Credits £
Bank	8,100	
Capital		10,000
Purchases	3,000	
Creditors		500
Rent	600	
Sales		3,300
Debtors	400	
Fixed assets	1,000	
Stationery	200	
Drawings	500	
	13,800	13,800

TYPES OF LEDGER

The ledger accounts that we have been considering so far are all kept together in one LEDGER or book. This is known as the MAIN LEDGER or sometimes nominal ledger or general ledger.

There are also two other types of ledger, known as the SUBSIDIARY LEDGERS. These are the SUBSIDIARY (SALES) LEDGER and the SUBSIDIARY (PURCHASES) LEDGER.

The subsidiary (sales) ledger is a collection of ledger accounts for each individual debtor of the business.

The subsidiary (purchases) ledger is a collection of ledger accounts for each individual creditor of the business.

HOW IT WORKS

A business has three credit customers, A, B and C. The following transactions occur with them during a period.

Sales to credit customers:

	£
A	400
B	600
C	500

The double entry in the main ledger for a sale on credit is to credit sales and debit the sales ledger control account, which so far we have called debtors. In practice it is called the SALES LEDGER CONTROL ACCOUNT, because it reflects the total of all the accounts in the subsidiary (sales) ledger.

Therefore the double entry in the main ledger will be as follows.

Main ledger

Sales account

£		£
	Sales ledger control	400
	Sales ledger control	600
	Sales ledger control	500

Sales ledger control account

	£		£
Sales	400		
Sales	600		
Sales	500		

However this sales ledger control account gives no detail of the individual debtors and how much is due from each of them. To rectify this, an account is held for each debtor in the subsidiary (sales) ledger. This is usually in the form of a ledger account with the same debit and credit entries that would be used in the main ledger. However the big difference is that in the subsidiary (sales) ledger there is no double entry taking place. The accounts in the subsidiary (sales) ledger are not part of the double entry system of the main ledger but completely separate "memorandum" accounts. They just give information.

The entries in the subsidiary (sales) ledger for these three debtors would be as follows.

Subsidiary (sales) ledger

A's account

	£		£
Sales	400		

B's account

	£		£
Sales	600		

C's account

	£		£
Sales	500		

Now suppose that £300 is received from A and £250 from C. We will look at the entries for these receipts in the main ledger and in the subsidiary (sales) ledger.

In the main ledger, money in means a debit to the bank account and therefore a credit to the sales ledger control account. In the subsidiary (sales) ledger the individual accounts will also be credited with the money received.

Main ledger

Bank account

	£		£
Sales ledger control	300		
Sales ledger control	250		

Sales ledger control account

	£		£
Sales	400	Bank	300
Sales	600	Bank	250
Sales	500		

Subsidiary (sales) ledger

A's account

	£		£
Sales	400	Bank	300

B's account

	£		£
Sales	600		

C's account

	£		£
Sales	500	Bank	250

Activity 4

A credit customer James Daniels buys goods from your business on credit for £1,000 and later pays £800 by cheque. Record these transactions in his debtors account in the subsidiary (sales) ledger.

HOW IT WORKS

The same principles apply when dealing with creditors in the subsidiary (purchases) ledger. The double entry for purchases on credit and money paid to creditors takes place in the main ledger in the PURCHASES LEDGER CONTROL ACCOUNT, and then each individual creditor account in the subsidiary (purchases) ledger is also updated.

Suppose that our business has three credit suppliers, D, E and F.

The following transactions take place with these suppliers:

Purchases on credit	D	£200
	E	£350
	F	£100
Payments made	D	£100
	E	£250

These transactions must now be recorded in the main ledger and the subsidiary (purchases) ledger.

Main ledger

Purchases account

	£		£
Purchases ledger control	200		
Purchases ledger control	350		
Purchases ledger control	100		

Purchases ledger control account

	£		£
Bank	100	Purchases	200
Bank	250	Purchases	350
		Purchases	100

Bank account

	£		£
		Purchases ledger control	100
		Purchases ledger control	250

Subsidiary (purchases) ledger

D's account

	£		£
Payment	100	Purchases	200

E's account

	£		£
Payment	250	Purchases	350

F's account

	£		£
		Purchases	100

CHAPTER OVERVIEW

- the principles behind double entry bookkeeping are that every transaction has two effects on a business and that the owner is a separate entity from the business itself

- the two effects of each transaction are recorded in ledger accounts with a debit in one account and a credit entry in another account

- if money is paid out of the business then the bank account is credited. Money coming into the business is debited to the bank account

- assets and expenses are recorded on the debit side of their accounts

- liabilities and income are recorded on the credit side of their accounts

- money paid into the business by the owner is recorded in a capital account and money or goods taken out of the business by the owner are recorded in a drawings account

- ledger accounts are balanced by totalling both sides of the account, inserting the larger total at the bottom of both the debit and credit sides and putting in the figure that makes the smaller side of the account add back to this total. This is called the balance carried down and this balance is brought down on the other side of the account below the total

- a trial balance is prepared by listing all of the debit balances and credit balances brought down and checking the total of these balances to ensure that they agree

- all of the double entry takes place in ledger accounts in the main ledger. There are however two subsidiary ledgers – the subsidiary (sales) ledger and the subsidiary (purchases) ledger

- the subsidiary (sales) ledger has an account for each individual debtor showing all of the sales made to that debtor and money received from the debtor

- the subsidiary (purchases) ledger has an account for each individual creditor showing all purchases from that creditor and all payments made to the creditor

KEY WORDS

Double entry bookkeeping a system of accounting where the two effects of each transaction are recorded

Ledger accounts the accounts in which each transaction is recorded – there will be a ledger account for each type of transaction such as sales and purchases and for every type of asset and liability

Debit the debit side of a ledger account is the left hand side

Credit the credit side of a ledger account is the right hand side

Purchases for accounting purposes purchases are the goods that are bought with the intention of re-selling them

Sales for accounting purposes sales are the sale of goods or services which the business trades in

Drawings the money or goods that the owner takes out of the business

Trial balance a list of all of the debit and credit balances brought down on the ledger accounts

Ledger this is where all accounts of a similar type are kept

Main ledger this is where the double entry takes place for all of the transactions of the business

Subsidiary ledgers these are where supporting or memorandum ledger accounts are kept

Subsidiary (sales) ledger a collection of individual accounts for each credit customer

Subsidiary (purchases) ledger a collection of individual accounts for each credit supplier

Sales ledger control account the ledger account in the main ledger which records all transactions with debtors

Purchases ledger control account the ledger account in the main ledger which records all transactions with creditors

HOW MUCH HAVE YOU LEARNED?

1 What are the two effects for accounting purposes of the following transactions?

a) Money paid into the business by the owner
b) Purchases on credit
c) Purchase of machinery by cheque, for use in the business
d) Sales on credit
e) Money taken out of the business by the owner

2 Fred Jones set up in business on 1 June 2006 by putting £25,000 into a business bank account. Given below are his transactions for the month of June:

a) purchased a delivery van with a cheque for £8,000
b) purchased goods for resale with a cheque for £6,000
c) paid 3 months rent by cheque totalling £2,400
d) sold goods on credit for £2,700
e) purchased office stationery for cash of £100
f) purchased goods on credit for £4,500
g) sold goods on credit for £5,200
h) sold goods for cash for £1,200
i) paid telephone bill by cheque totalling £140
j) sold goods on credit for £3,000
k) paid creditors £2,500
l) withdrew £1,200 from the bank account for personal use
m) received £3,600 from debtors

Write up these transactions in Fred's ledger accounts.

3 Balance off each of the accounts in Fred's ledger showing clearly the balance carried down and brought down and prepare a trial balance.

4 Explain what is meant by the main ledger and the subsidiary ledgers. Give examples of the subsidiary ledgers.

chapter 4:
ACCOUNTING FOR CREDIT SALES

chapter coverage 📖

In this chapter we will be looking at entering details of credit sales and sales returns into the accounting records. The topics that are covered are:

✍ books of prime entry and the sales day book

✍ posting the sales day book

✍ the sales returns day book

✍ entering credit notes in the sales day book

✍ an analysed sales day book

KNOWLEDGE AND UNDERSTANDING AND PERFORMANCE CRITERIA COVERAGE

Unit 1

knowledge and understanding – accounting methods

11 double entry bookkeeping, including balancing accounts
18 relationship between accounting system and the ledger

Performance criteria – element 1.1

D enter invoices and credit notes into books of prime entry according to organisational procedures

E enter invoices and credit notes in the appropriate ledgers

BOOKS OF PRIME ENTRY

In the previous chapter we looked at the double entry bookkeeping for the transactions of a business. In those examples we entered each individual transaction directly into the ledger accounts, and using double entry principles this meant that each transaction was in fact entered twice.

In practice in a manual system this would be impractical and therefore a step is built into the process before the ledger account entries are made.

The first stage of the accounting process is to enter details of transaction documents into the BOOKS OF PRIME ENTRY. These books of prime entry are often known as day books, as in theory at least, they would be written up every day.

TRANSACTION DOCUMENTS → BOOKS OF PRIME ENTRY → LEDGER ACCOUNTS

We are concerned at this stage with sales invoices and credit notes. All of the sales invoices for a period are initially recorded in their book of prime entry which is known as the SALES DAY BOOK.

A typical sales day book would look like this.

Date	Customer	Invoice number	Ref	Gross £	VAT £	Net £
2006						
1 May	Grigsons Ltd	10356	SL 21	193.87	28.87	165.00
1 May	Hail & Co	10357	SL 05	103.40	15.40	88.00
1 May	Harris & Sons	10358	SL 17	117.50	17.50	100.00
2 May	Jaytry Ltd	10359	SL 22	303.15	45.15	258.00
3 May	Millings Ltd	10360	SL 31	470.00	70.00	400.00
3 May	Frate Haulage	10361	SL 09	184.47	27.47	157.00

The writing up of the sales day book for a period would have the following steps:

Step 1   Find the sales invoices that have been authorised for issue since the sales day book was last written up, or copies of the sales invoices that have been sent out to customers since the day book was last written up. You will be able to check that there are no invoices missing as the invoice numbers should be in sequence. All of the information that you need to enter into the sales day book should be on the face of the sales invoice.

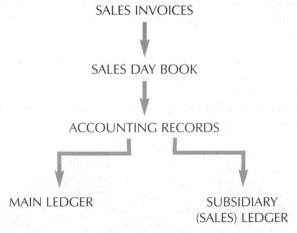

Step 2 Enter the date of the invoice, the name of the customer and the invoice number in the appropriate columns.

Step 3 The reference column is also sometimes headed up "folio". This is the column where you should enter the account code number for the customer. This should be on the face of the invoice and is the customer's code in the subsidiary sales ledger and therefore is often given the prefix "SL". This reference code is important as it will help with the eventual entry of these figures into the ledger accounts.

Step 4 Enter the invoice totals. The gross column is the eventual invoice total including VAT. The VAT is the amount shown on the face of the invoice. The net amount is the invoice total minus the VAT and this will normally be a subtotal on the face of the invoice.

Activity 1

An invoice shows the following totals:

	£
Goods total	1,235.57
VAT	216.22
Invoice total	1,451.79

Which columns in the sales day book would each total appear in?

POSTING THE SALES DAY BOOK

Once the details of the sales invoices for a period have been entered into the sales day book, the next stage is to transfer the details to the accounting records.

SALES INVOICES

↓

SALES DAY BOOK

↓

ACCOUNTING RECORDS

MAIN LEDGER   SUBSIDIARY (SALES) LEDGER

In order to do this the sales day book must first be totalled. This totalling process is also sometimes known as CASTING. The day book used before has now been totalled.

Date	Customer	Invoice number	Ref	Gross £	VAT £	Net £
2006						
1 May	Grigsons Ltd	10356	SL 21	193.87	28.87	165.00
1 May	Hail & Co	10357	SL 05	103.40	15.40	88.00
1 May	Harris & Sons	10358	SL 17	117.50	17.50	100.00
2 May	Jaytry Ltd	10359	SL 22	303.15	45.15	258.00
3 May	Millings Ltd	10360	SL 31	470.00	70.00	400.00
3 May	Frate Haulage	10361	SL 09	184.47	27.47	157.00
				1,372.39	204.39	1,168.00

Whenever casting a day book it is very easy to make errors in your additions. Therefore it is always advisable to CROSS CAST the day book as well. This means adding the net total to the VAT to ensure that it adds back to the gross total – if it does not then an error has been made in the casting (1,168.00 + 204.39 = £1,372.39).

Now for entering the totals into the main ledger. Remember the main ledger is where the double entry takes place so let us consider the double entry required here.

The sales day book represents the sales on credit that have been made by the business so we shall now consider what each total represents.

Net total: The net total is the total of credit sales – the business makes no profit out of charging VAT as it is paid over to HM Revenue and Customs, therefore the VAT is excluded from the sales total. This net total must be a credit entry in the sales account.

Gross total: The gross total is the amount that the customer must pay to your business – the goods total plus the VAT. Therefore this is the amount of your debtor and the gross total is a debit entry in the sales ledger control account.

VAT total: The VAT total is the amount of VAT that is owed to HMRC and as such is a credit entry in the VAT account.

So these totals must now be posted or entered into the ledger accounts in the main ledger.

Main ledger

Sales ledger control account

	£		£
Sales Day Book	1,372.39		

Sales account

	£		£
		Sales Day Book	1,168.00

VAT account

	£		£
		Sales Day Book	204.39

Note that there are three different entries for these transactions but as always in double entry the total of the debit entries must equal the total of the credit entries:

Debit		£1,372.39
Credits	£1,168.00 + £204.39 =	£1,372.39

You should also note that the reference is no longer to the other account that is to be debited or credited but instead is the source document for the entry, the sales day book. This is often shortened to SDB.

Activity 2

Name the accounts that the following totals from the sales day book will be posted to and whether they are a debit or a credit entry:

a)   Total, ie gross figure
b)   VAT
c)   Net figure

The ledger account postings do not stop here however as each individual invoice total must also be entered into the individual debtor accounts in the subsidiary (sales) ledger.

Step 1   Find the individual customer's account in the subsidiary (sales) ledger using the account code in the reference column.

Step 2   Enter the gross total of the invoice, the amount the customer actually owes, on the debit side of his account.

Subsidiary (sales) ledger

Grigsons Ltd		SL21
	£	£
SDB – 10356	193.87	

Hail & Co		SL 05
	£	£
SDB – 10357	103.40	

Harris & Sons		SL 17
	£	£
SDB – 10358	117.50	

Jaytry Ltd		SL 22
	£	£
SDB – 10359	303.15	

Millings Ltd		SL 31
	£	£
SDB – 10360	470.00	

Frate Haulage		SL 09
	£	£
SDB – 10361	184.47	

The reference for each entry is again the sales day book (SDB) but the invoice number is also entered as this may be useful when dealing with customer enquiries or preparing statements for customers.

SALES RETURNS AND CREDIT NOTES

We have already considered the preparation of credit notes for valid and authorised sales returns. Now we will look at the accounting for credit notes.

As with sales invoices they are initially entered in their own book of prime entry known as the SALES RETURNS DAY BOOK. This will look very similar to the sales day book with the same details required to be entered.

Date	Customer	Credit note number	Ref	Gross £	VAT £	Net £
2006 4 May 5 May	Grigsons Ltd Harris & Sons	CN668 CN669	SL 21 SL 17	70.50 94.00	10.50 14.00	60.00 80.00

The only difference here is that the credit note number is entered rather than an invoice number. Again all of the details required can be found on the face of the credit note or copy credit note that is used to write up the day book.

As with the sales day book the sales returns day book must now be totalled and posted to the ledgers.

Date	Customer	Credit note number	Ref	Gross £	VAT £	Net £
2006 4 May 5 May	Grigsons Ltd Harris & Sons	CN668 CN669	SL 21 SL 17	70.50 94.00	10.50 14.00	60.00 80.00
				164.50	24.50	140.00

Again remember to check that the column totals do add back to the gross total (140.00 + 24.50 = 164.50).

Now the sales returns day book details must be entered into the accounting records.

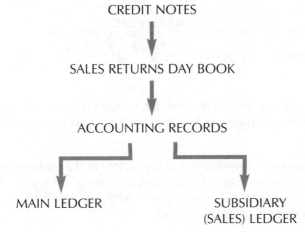

CREDIT NOTES

↓

SALES RETURNS DAY BOOK

↓

ACCOUNTING RECORDS

MAIN LEDGER   SUBSIDIARY
(SALES) LEDGER

POSTING THE SALES RETURNS DAY BOOK

In the main ledger the three column totals must be entered into the ledger accounts. The double entry is the reverse of that for a sale on credit but let's consider the logic behind each entry:

Gross total As the customer has returned these goods they will no longer have to pay for them. Therefore debtors are decreased which means that this total is a **credit** entry in the sales ledger control account.

Net total The net total is the total of sales returns for the period which is effectively the reverse of a sale. Therefore a **debit** entry is required in the sales returns account.

VAT As no sale has been made of these returned goods the VAT is no longer due to HMRC. Therefore a **debit** entry is made in the VAT account.

Main ledger

Sales ledger control account

	£		£
SDB	1,372.39	Sales Returns Day Book	164.50

Sales returns account

	£		£
Sales Returns Day Book	140.00		

VAT account

	£		£
Sales Returns Day Book	24.50	SDB	204.39

Again note that the total of the two debit entries is equal to the credit entry. The reference is to the Sales Returns Day Book and is often abbreviated to SRDB.

Now we must enter each individual credit note in the customer's account in the subsidiary (sales) ledger. The amount to be used is the gross amount and the debtor's account must be credited with this figure to show that the customer no longer owes this amount.

Grigsons Ltd — SL 21

	£		£
SDB – 10356	193.87	SRDB – CN 668	70.50

Harris & Sons		SL 17
£		£
SDB – 10358	117.50	SRDB – CN 669	94.00

The reference given is to the source document, the Sales Returns Day Book (SRDB) and the credit note number is also shown as this may be useful for further processing and enquiries.

Activity 3

Name the accounts in the main ledger and subsidiary (sales) ledger that would be debited and credited for the issue of a credit note.

CREDIT NOTES AND THE SALES DAY BOOK

In the previous paragraphs we saw that credit notes for sales returns were entered in a Sales Returns Day Book. However in some organisations a separate Sales Returns Day Book is not considered necessary. Instead the credit notes are entered into the Sales Day Book together with the sales invoices for the period. They are distinguished from the sales invoices by each of the figures, gross, net and VAT, being shown with brackets around them.

If this system is in operation then great care should be taken when casting and posting the sales day book. When the casting is done you must remember to deduct the figures in brackets. When posting to the main ledger the totals will already be net of any credit notes and therefore no separate entries are needed for the credit notes. In particular there is no separate sales returns account, as the sales returns have been netted off against the sales and the net total credited to the sales account. When posting to the individual debtors accounts in the subsidiary (sales) ledger, remember to enter the credit notes, shown in brackets, on the credit side of the debtor's account.

ANALYSED SALES DAY BOOK

Some organisations operate a slightly different type of sales day book which shows the analysis of sales into different categories.

For example an organisation that makes sales of its products around the country may wish to analyse its sales by geographical area. Its analysed sales day book might look something like this:

student notes✍

Date	Customer	Invoice number	Ref	Gross £	VAT £	North £	South £	East £	West £
1 June	AB Ltd	936	SL 23	117.50	17.50		100.00		
1 June	CD & Co	937	SL03	235.00	35.00			200.00	
2 June	EF Ltd	938	SL45	63.45	9.45	54.00			
3 June	GH Ltd	939	SL18	141.00	21.00				120.00
4 June	IJ Bros	940	SL25	70.50	10.50		60.00		
				627.45	93.45	54.00	160.00	200.00	120.00

This type of sales day book breaks down the actual sales, the net amounts from the invoices, into their separate areas. The posting of this sales day book in the main ledger would require a separate sales account for each area as follows:

Sales ledger control account

	£		£
SDB	627.45		

VAT account

	£		£
		SDB	93.45

Sales account – north

	£		£
		SDB	54.00

Sales account – south

	£		£
		SDB	160.00

Sales account – east

	£		£
		SDB	200.00

Sales account – west

	£		£
		SDB	120.00

You can again check that all of the credit entries do add up to the total of the debit entry (93.45 + 54.00 + 160.00 + 200.00 + 120.00 = 627.45).

An organisation may also wish to analyse its sales by type of product. For example a computer manufacturer may wish to analyse sales between computers, printers and scanners. In this case there would be a column for each and a sales account for each. If an analysed sales day book is used and a separate sales returns day book is kept then this must also be analysed in the same manner.

Activity 4

An extract from an invoice for a computer manufacturer that analyses its sales into those for computers, printers and scanners is given below:

		£
1	GH3 Computer	800.00
1	Z3 Colour printer	300.00
1	S4 Scanner	200.00
		1,300.00
VAT		227.50
Invoice total		1,527.50

Show how this invoice would be entered into the analysed sales day book.

SPREADSHEET ANALYSIS

Here is the analysed sales day book from earlier in the chapter set out as a spreadsheet.

	A	B	C	D	E	F	G	H	I	J
1	Date	Customer	Invoice number	Ref	Gross	Vat	North	South	East	West
2					£	£	£	£	£	£
3	1 June	AB Ltd	936	SL 23	117.50	17.50		100.00		
4	1 June	CD & Co	937	SL03	235.00	35.00			200.00	
5	2 June	EF Ltd	938	SL45	63.45	9.45	54.00			
6	3 June	GH Ltd	939	SL18	141.00	21.00				120.00
7	4 June	IJ Bros	940	SL25	70.50	10.50		60.00		
8					627.45	93.45	54.00	160.00	200.00	120.00

Spreadsheets are very useful, especially for very repetitive or numerical tasks. However, remember that if it has been set up wrongly or data has been entered wrongly without any form of checking, the spreadsheet itself may contain errors. Just because the computer produced it, it doesn't mean that it's correct!

Spreadsheets are covered in more detail later in this Course Companion when we are dealing with Unit 4.

COMPUTERISED SALES PACKAGES

Some very small businesses may produce all their sales documents with a word processor, and then enter the details into a spreadsheet as a simple, day book style list.

This may well be adequate for a business that has very few transactions, very few customers and only a few stock items or services.

It is not a 'package' in the proper sense of a word, though: it is exactly the same as a manual system, except that the spreadsheet list can be added up by computer and can more easily be sorted (by date, by customer, by product etc) to give different views of the data.

Invoicing packages

An advance upon this very simple word-processor/spreadsheet approach is an 'invoicing package'. These are usually very cheap or even freely downloadable from the Internet.

The illustration below is based on the order entry template which is available as part of the Microsoft Access database package. For some businesses this might be all that is needed for sales document generation and recording.

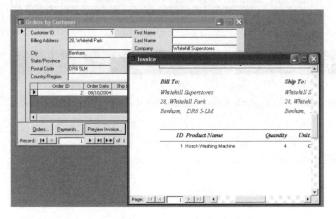

The advantage of a system such as this is that all the customer details and product details are stored permanently in the database, so they only have to be entered in full once, and then just edited if they ever change.

A variety of reports may be available that could then be used both as input for manually-kept accounting ledgers or other computerised systems, and as generally useful information for managing the business.

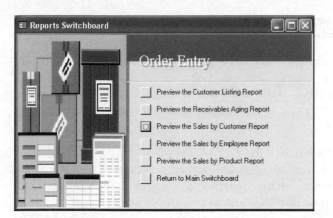

Integrated systems

The word 'integrated' simply means that the different parts of the accounting system are linked together.

A typical computerised accounting package integrates ALL the ledgers, so it *does not use day books* in the traditional, manual sense (although sales day book style listings can still be obtained, if required, in the form of a report).

In an integrated system just creating an invoice and then posting it has the effect of updating ALL the ledgers at the same time, in one go. There is no risk of double-entry errors or incorrect addition. If there is also an integrated stock system that will be updated correctly, too, without any extra effort.

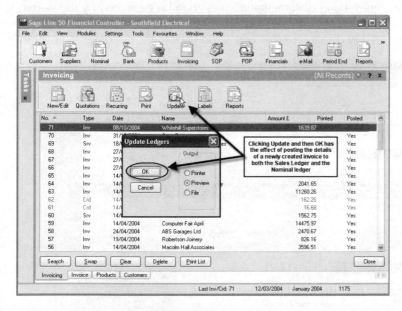

As mentioned earlier, a fully integrated package may cost as little as £100 and this is the solution we would recommend for any but the tiniest of businesses because it will very quickly begin to save the user time and therefore money.

student notes ✏

Modular accounting systems

Larger businesses will have separate departments devoted to separate accounting tasks. For instance you may find yourself working in a customer service department that posts all the sales transactions but has no involvement in matters such as credit control, and no need to get involved with the main ledger.

Larger systems, of which one of the best known is SAP, are made up of many separate 'modules', which are separate packages dedicated to a particular accounting task - sales invoicing, purchasing, treasury (cash management), stock management, payroll, fixed, and so on.

If you work in a sales department in a large business like this you will probably find that you can only enter data into the customer/invoicing part of the accounting system, although you can access data from other modules such as stock (to see if there is enough stock available to meet a customer's order).

In other words, behind the scenes modular systems usually work in the same way as integrated systems, but the users of a particular module only need to see the part of the system that is relevant to their job.

E-commerce

Yet another possibility for computerised sales is that the documentation and records will be created by the customers themselves, for instance if they order a product over the Internet and pay with a debit or credit card. All the necessary accounting entries and documentation may then be generated by the system, simply as a result of various computers talking to each other and automatically e-mailing delivery details, invoices and so on back to the customer.

Activity 5

Look at the Amazon webpage illustration above. If the user clicks on 'Buy now with 1-Click' do you think that means that entries will be posted directly into Amazon's accounting system? Explain your answer.

CHAPTER OVERVIEW

- in order to reduce the number of entries necessary in the ledger accounts, documents of the same type are initially recorded in the books of prime entry

- sales invoices are all recorded initially in the sales day book. The sales day book is written up using authorised sales invoices before they are sent out to customers, or copy invoices if the originals have already been despatched

- once the details are entered into the sales day book it must be totalled and the totals entered into the ledger accounts in the main ledger

- each individual sales invoice must also be entered into the individual debtor's account in the subsidiary (sales) ledger

- credit notes are initially recorded in the sales returns day book. The details are taken either from the original credit note or a copy

- the sales returns day book must also be regularly totalled and posted to the main ledger and the subsidiary (sales) ledger

- in some organisations credit notes are shown in the sales day book with brackets around the figures instead of maintaining a separate sales returns day book

- some organisations find it useful to analyse their sales by product or geographical location and therefore would use an analysed sales day book

---

KEY WORDS

Books of prime entry the books in which the details of the organisation's transactions are initially recorded prior to entry into the ledger accounts

Sales day book primary record for recording sales invoices, ie credit sales

Casting an accounting term for adding up a column of figures

Cross cast adding up the totals of a number of columns to check that they add back to the total

Sales returns day book the primary record for recording credit notes, ie sales returns

Analysed sales day book a sales day book where the net figures are analysed into the different types of sales

---

HOW MUCH HAVE YOU LEARNED?

1 Briefly explain how credit sales and sales returns (with VAT) are accounted for in the main ledger.

2 Given below are a number of sales invoices for Southfield Electrical.

   a) Write up the sales day book using these invoices
   b) Total the columns of the sales day book
   c) Post the sales day book to the main ledger and to the subsidiary (sales) ledger.

INVOICE

Southfield Electrical
Industrial Estate
Benham DR6 2FF
Tel 0303379 Fax 0303152
VAT Reg 0264 2274 49

To: Dagwell Enterprises
Dagwell House
Hopchurch Rd
Winnish
DR2 6LT

Invoice number: 56401

Date/tax point: 21 Sept 2006

Order number: 6123

Account number: SL 15

Quantity	Description	Stock code	Unit amount £	Total £
3	Milo Dishwasher	8641	310.00	930.00
Less:	15% discount			139.50

Net total		790.50
VAT		138.33
Invoice total		928.83

Terms
Net 30 days
E & OE

INVOICE

Southfield Electrical
Industrial Estate
Benham DR6 2FF
Tel 0303379 Fax 0303152
VAT Reg 0264 2274 49

To:
G. Thomas & Co
48, High Street
Cabland
DR3 8QT

Invoice number: 56402

Date/tax point: 21 Sept 2006

Order number: 6124

Account number: SL 30

Quantity	Description	Stock code	Unit amount £	Total £
16	Zanpoint Tumble Dryer	3462	220.00	3,520.00
11	Temax Kettle	6180	15.00	165.00
				3,685.00
Less:	20% discount			737.00

Net total		2,948.00
VAT		495.26
Invoice total		3,443.26

Terms
4% discount for settlement within 10 days of invoice date, otherwise net 30 days
E & OE

INVOICE

Southfield Electrical
Industrial Estate
Benham DR6 2FF
Tel 0303379 Fax 0303152
VAT Reg 0264 2274 49

To:

Polygon Stores
Grobler Street
Parrish
DR7 4TT

Invoice number: 56403

Date/tax point: 22 Sept 2006

Order number: 6127

Account number: SL 03

Quantity	Description	Stock code	Unit amount £	Total £
4	Milo Dishwasher	8641	310.00	1,240.00
2	Milo Washing Machine	8649	290.00	580.00
				1,820.00
Less:	10% discount			182.00

Net total		1,638.00
VAT		286.65
Invoice total		1,924.65

Terms
Net 30 days
E & OE

INVOICE

Southfield Electrical
Industrial Estate
Benham DR6 2FF
Tel 0303379 Fax 0303152
VAT Reg 0264 2274 49

To: Weller Enterprises
Booker House
Industrial Estate
Benham
DR6 2FM

Invoice number: 56404

Date/tax point: 23 Sept 2006

Order number: 6128

Account number: SL 18

Quantity	Description	Stock code	Unit amount £	Total £
2	Habark cooker	1264	480.00	960.00

Net total	960.00
VAT	161.28
Invoice total	1,121.28

Terms
4% discount for settlement within 10 days of invoice date, otherwise net 30 days
E & OE

3   Given below are two credit notes.

a)   Use the credit notes to write up the sales returns day book

b)   Total the sales returns day book

c)   Post the sales returns day book to the main ledger and the subsidiary ledger, the sales ledger

CREDIT NOTE

SOUTHFIELD ELECTRICAL
INDUSTRIAL ESTATE
Benham DR6 2FF
Tel 0303379 Fax 0303152
VAT Reg 0264 2274 49

Invoice to:

Q Q Stores
23 Queens Rd
Winnish
DR2 7PJ

Credit note number: 08660
Date/tax point: 21 Sept 2006
Order number: 6021
Account number: SL 37

Quantity	Description	Stock code	Unit amount	Total
			£	£
1	Zanpoint Fridge	3676	330.00	330.00
Less:	10% discount			33.00

Net total	297.00
VAT	51.97
Gross total	348.97

Reason for credit note:

Damaged goods

CREDIT NOTE

SOUTHFIELD ELECTRICAL
INDUSTRIAL ESTATE
Benham DR6 2FF
Tel 0303379 Fax 0303152
VAT Reg 0264 2274 49

Invoice to:

    Dagwell Enterprises
    Dagwell House
    Hopchurch Rd
    Winnish
    DR2 6LT

Credit note number: 08661
Date/tax point: 23 Sept 2006
Order number: 5983
Account number: SL 15

Quantity	Description	Stock code	Unit amount	Total
			£	£
6	Temax Coffee maker	6470	40.00	240.00
Less:	15% discount			36.00
			Net total	204.00
			VAT	35.70
			Gross total	239.70

Reason for credit note:

    Goods not ordered
....

4   Your organisation records sales invoices and credit notes in the sales day book. One of your tasks today is to write up the sales day book from the invoices and credit notes given below and the post the transactions to the main ledger and the subsidiary (sales) ledger.

Invoice no. 44263	1 June	To J Jepson SL34	£118.00 + VAT
Invoice no. 44264	2 June	To S Beck and Sons SL01	£315.00 + VAT
Credit note 3813	2 June	To Scroll Ltd SL16	£18.50 + VAT
Invoice no. 44265	3 June	To Penfold Ltd SL 23	£164.70 + VAT
Invoice no. 44266	4 June	To S Beck and Sons SL01	£256.40 + VAT
Invoice no. 44267	4 June	To J Jepson SL34	£144.00 + VAT
Credit note 3814	5 June	To Penfold Ltd SL23	£16.80 + VAT

chapter 5:
RECEIVING MONEY

chapter coverage 📖

In this chapter we will start to consider the procedures that must be carried out when receiving money. The topics that are to be covered are:

✍ receiving cash, cheques and credit/debit card payments in a retail environment

✍ the requirements for a valid cheque and the checks that should be carried out when accepting a cheque

✍ the meaning of crossings on cheques

✍ the effect of an endorsement on a cheque

✍ the procedure to be carried out when a cheque is supported by a cheque guarantee card

✍ the procedure for accepting payment by credit card

✍ the procedure for accepting payment by debit card

✍ the procedure when receiving cheques through the post from credit customers

✍ the procedure when receiving automated payments from customers directly into the bank account

Units 1 and 2

<u>knowledge and understanding – the business environment</u>

1.6, 2.6 cheques from customers, including crossings and endorsements and payment cheques, including crossings and endorsements
1.8, 2.7 automated payments from customers and automated payments to suppliers

<u>knowledge and understanding – accounting methods</u>

1.19, 2.20 credit card procedures
1.20, 2.23 methods of handling and storing money, including the security aspects

Performance criteria – element 1.2

A   check receipts against relevant supporting information
D   identify unusual features and either resolve or refer to the appropriate person

RECEIVING MONEY IN A RETAIL ENVIRONMENT

In a retail environment customers are likely to pay for their purchases in a variety of different ways, for example:

- in cash;
- by cheque;
- by credit card;
- by debit card.

Whatever the method of payment, if you are receiving the money then it is important that you always check the following:

- the payment is for the correct amount and that any change given is calculated and counted correctly;

- the method of payment is valid – this applies particularly to cheques and credit and debit cards;

- any documentation required is correctly filled out, signed and dealt with correctly.

CASH

Where sales are being made for cash it is normal practice to have a cash till which will record the sale, calculate any change required, produce a receipt for the purchase and store the cash received. Therefore the main responsibility of the person operating the till is to input the correct price for the goods and to correctly count out the change that the till has calculated.

A further consideration with cash sales is however the security of the money itself. Most modern tills can only be opened, other than when a sale is made, by using a key that is held by a responsible official. The tills should however be emptied on a regular basis and the cash stored in a safe on the premises until it can be paid into the bank. The payment of monies into the bank and the practical and security arrangements necessary will be considered in a later chapter.

CHEQUES

A CHEQUE may be defined as 'a written order to the bank, signed by the bank's customer to pay a certain amount, specified in words and figures, to another specified person'.

Pre-printed cheque books are issued by most banks and building societies to both business and personal customers and cheques are an extremely common method of making payment for goods and services.

There are three parties involved in a cheque:

- the DRAWEE – the bank who has issued the cheque and will have to pay the cheque;

- the PAYEE – the person to whom the cheque is being paid;

- the DRAWER – the person who is writing and signing the cheque in order to make a payment.

A typical cheque is shown below and we will consider the details on the face of the cheque and the checks that should be carried out when receiving a cheque as payment.

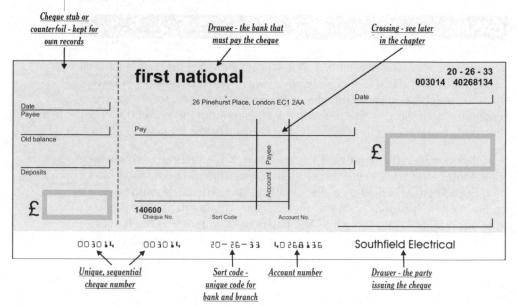

When you receive a cheque from a customer it will of course be filled out and there are a number of checks that you must make to ensure that the cheque is valid. A completed cheque is shown below and we then go through the checks that should be carried out.

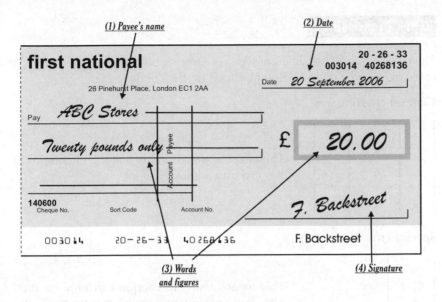

(1) Payee's name   *(2) Date*

(3) Words and figures   *(4) Signature*

1) Check that the payee's name, ie your organisation, is correct. In many retail organisations this is not relevant as customers cheques will be stamped with the organisation's name rather than the customer having to write it out.

2) Check that the date is today's date. A cheque should not be dated later than today's date as it cannot be paid into the your account until the date on the cheque. Also check that the cheque does not have an earlier date on it. A cheque has a limited life and is out of date or "stale" after six months.

3) Check that the words and figures for the amount of the cheque are the same. If they do not agree then the bank may return the cheque and not credit it to your account.

4) Finally check that the cheque has been signed.

If any of the words, dates or figures on the cheque are incorrect then the customer should be asked to amend them and to initial the amendment.

CHEQUE CROSSINGS

When an example of a cheque was considered earlier it was noted that the two parallel lines on the cheque were known as a CROSSING. A cheque with these parallel lines (with or without any words printed between the lines) is known as a crossed cheque and the effect of the crossing is that the cheque can only be paid into a bank account, it cannot be exchanged for cash at a bank by the payee.

student notes

Types of crossing

There are a number of different types of crossing on cheques that you might come across which have different effects on the cheque.

General crossing

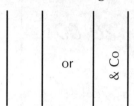

The effect of this is simply that the cheque must be paid into a bank account

Special crossing

This means that the cheque can only be paid into this specific branch of the bank, ie the Benham branch of the Northern bank

Not negotiable

This is a cheque that can be endorsed to another party (see next paragraph)

Account payee

This cheque can only be paid into the account of the payee on the cheque and cannot be endorsed (see next paragraph)

In practice most pre-printed bank cheques have an account payee crossing.

Activity 1

What is the effect of a crossing on a cheque?

ENDORSEMENTS

If a cheque is uncrossed or has a crossing other than an account payee crossing, then it is possible for that cheque to be endorsed. An ENDORSEMENT of a cheque is a method by which the payee of the cheque can transfer the cheque to another party. This is done by the payee signing the back of the cheque and usually naming the person to whom the cheque is to be endorsed.

HOW IT WORKS

Consider this cheque.

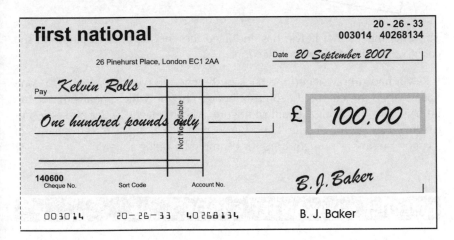

This cheque has been made out to Kelvin Rolls, the payee, and as it is a crossed cheque it must be paid into a bank account. However suppose that Kelvin owed £100 to Jane Spears. Rather than Kelvin paying this cheque into his bank account and writing a cheque of his own to Jane for £100, as this cheque has a 'not negotiable' crossing, Kelvin can endorse this cheque over to Jane.

student notes

This is done on the back of the cheque like this:

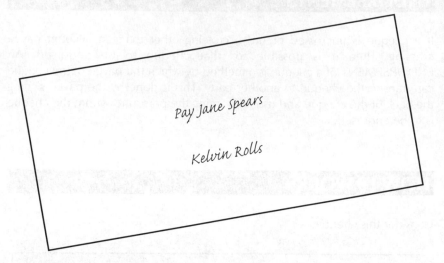

Pay Jane Spears

Kelvin Rolls

This now means that Kelvin has endorsed the cheque over to Jane and she can now pay it into her bank account.

If Kelvin had simply signed the back of the cheque without stating 'Pay Jane Spears' then the cheque becomes a bearer cheque which means that it can be paid into the bank account of anyone who manages to get possession of it. Obviously such a cheque has a big security risk if it gets into the hands of someone who has no right to it, for example by being stolen.

CHEQUE GUARANTEE CARDS

When a cheque book is issued to a customer by a bank a CHEQUE GUARANTEE CARD normally accompanies it. The cheque guarantee card is an assurance to a retailer that the cheque will be paid, up to a certain limit – normally £50 or £100, provided that certain conditions are met:

- the guarantee card has the same name and account number as the cheque;

- the cheque is signed before the expiry date on the card;

- the cheque is signed in the presence of the payee;

- the card has not been defaced or altered in any way;

- the payee writes the card number on the back of the cheque.

A typical cheque guarantee card is shown here.

Guarantee limit

Account number

Expiry date

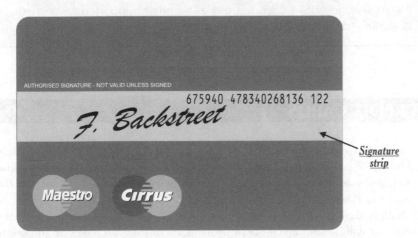

Signature strip

If a cheque is offered as the form of payment for goods then it is normal practice to ask for the cheque guarantee card as this ensures that your organisation will be paid the cheque amount by the bank.

When the customer gives you the cheque guarantee card it is important that you check the details carefully. The checks that you should carry out are:

■   make sure, to the best of your ability, that the cheque card is not stolen or forged – the best check is to run your finger along the signature strip, if it feels perfectly smooth then it has probably not been tampered with in any way;

■   check that the amount of the cheque is within the guarantee amount – the card only covers one cheque so it is not possible to write two £100 cheques for £200 of purchases and for the payment to be guaranteed;

- check that the cheque has been dated before the expiry date of the card;

- check that the account name agrees with that on the cheque itself;

- check that the account number agrees with that on the cheque – the account number is the last 8 numbers of the numbers on the face of the card;

- check that the signature on the cheque agrees with that on the guarantee card;

- check the cheque for the normal details, payee name, date, words and figures;

- write the card number on the back of the cheque.

Activity 2

If a retailer accepts a cheque from a customer supported by a cheque guarantee card how does the retailer benefit?

CREDIT CARDS

A further common method of paying for goods is by CREDIT CARD. A customer must apply to a bank or credit card company for a credit card, and upon its issue a credit limit (which cannot be exceeded) is set for the customer. The customer can pay for goods and services with the credit card at outlets that accept that particular card. At the end of each month the customer will be sent a statement showing all of the purchases on the credit card for the month, the total outstanding on the credit card, the minimum payment required and the date by which payment should reach the credit card company. The customer can then choose whether to pay off the full amount outstanding on the card or only part of it. Any unpaid outstanding amount will have interest charged to it which will appear on the next credit card statement.

From the retailers point of view he will have to pay the credit card company a small percentage (normally up to 5%) for the right to accept payment by their credit card. Most retail outlets will accept a number of different types of credit card, eg Visa, Mastercard.

A typical credit card is shown below.

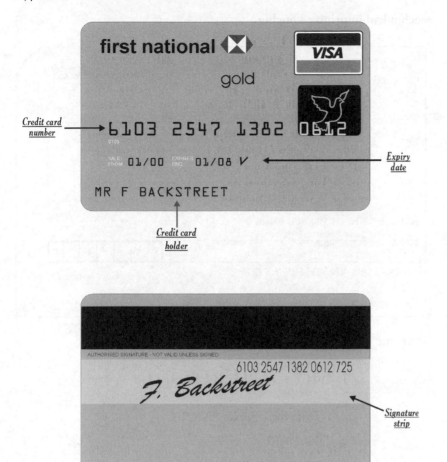

When accepting a credit card as the form of payment the retailer will either process it through a mechanical imprinter or through an electronic swipe machine attached to the till.

The mechanical imprinter is where the card is laid flat in the imprinter and the blank credit card voucher is placed on top of it. The embossed details on the card are then transferred onto the voucher by passing the top part of the imprinter over the receipt and card. This form of processing is now quite unusual and it is far more common for a card to be 'swiped' as detailed below.

On an electronic till the credit card is 'swiped' through the machine and the credit card details are read by the machine off the strip on the back of the card. These details are then transferred to the receipt produced by the till and the cardholder verifies the transaction by keying in their PIN number or by signing the slip.

student notes ✍

Examples of the two types of credit card voucher or receipt are shown below.

Mechanical imprinter voucher

4543 6101 5018 0612			NatWest STREAMLINE
01/02 01/04 V			Date 26/9/00 · Send? · Take?
MRS JUDITH L SMITH			Dept. Schools · Sales No · Initials AB
			Quan./Descrip. Schools
791 5905 24 S SIMMONDS TUNBRIDGE WELLS			Amount 42 00

RETAILER: CHECK THE SIGNATURE !

Cardholder authority: Please debit my account

Sales confirmed - Cardholder's signature | Authorisation code | Total £ \ \ \ 4 2 0 0

CARDHOLDER: PLEASE RETAIN THIS COPY

Electronic till voucher

THE PICTURE HOUSE

HIGH STREET

UCKFIELD, E SUSSEX.

VAT number	192496821
VISA/MASTERCARD	4543610150189612
Card details	0201
Date: 11/11/00	Time : 20:01:14

GOODS	£9.50
TOTAL SALE	£9.50

VAT RATE	NET	VAT	TOTAL
17.50%	8.09	1.41	9.50

Please debit my account with the total amount.

Sign : ----------------------------

Please keep this copy for your records.

005042897   2084   0322

Checks to be made – mechanical imprinter

The procedure and checks that should be carried out when using a mechanical imprinter are as follows:

- run your finger over the signature strip to check that the card has not been tampered with;

- check the expiry date of the card – it cannot be accepted if the expiry date has passed;

- check the list of stolen cards that will be provided by the credit card company to ensure that this credit card number is not on the list;

- place the card and voucher on the imprinter and pass the top of the imprinter over both to transfer the card details onto the voucher;

- enter the date, the type of goods or service being sold and the total amount of the sale on the voucher – most credit card companies will set a floor limit for transactions and if the sale is for more than this floor limit then the company must be telephoned for an authorisation code – this code must also be entered onto the voucher;

- the customer should be asked to check the amount on the voucher and to sign it – check that the signature is the same as that on the back of the card;

- the top copy of the voucher is then given to the customer and the carbons removed from between the other copies and the other three copies are retained by the retailer.

Checks to be made – electronic till voucher

The procedures to be followed are similar if an electronic swipe machine is being used although some of the checks are carried out automatically by the machine:

- the card should be swiped through the machine – the machine will then automatically check that the card has not expired or is not stolen;

- the goods details and total are entered into the cash machine – if the machine is on-line with the credit card company and if the floor limit is exceeded the machine will automatically authorise the transaction and provide the authorisation code (it will also check that the customer has not exceeded the credit card limit) – if not on-line then a telephone call will be required for an authorisation code;

- the customer enters their PIN number into the keypad connected to the till to confirm the transaction and their identity;

■   a two part voucher or receipt will be produced by the machine and the top copy of the voucher is given to the customer and the other copy retained by the retailer.

DEBIT CARDS

Many banks now provide their customers with a DEBIT CARD, eg Switch and Delta cards. These look very similar to credit cards but their purpose is very different. When a debit card is used to pay for a transaction, the amount of the sale is automatically debited from the customer's bank account by Electronic Funds Transfer at Point of Sale (EFTPOS) and credited to the retailer's bank account.

The procedure for accepting a debit card as payment is similar to that for a credit card:

■   the card should be checked to ensure that it has not been tampered with and that today's date is before the expiry date on the card;

■   the card is swiped through the machine and the customer's bank account is checked to ensure that the funds are available;

■   the customer enters their PIN number into the retailer's keypad to verify their identity;

■   the machine provides a two part receipt and the customer is given the top copy of the voucher whilst the retailer retains the other copy.

Activity 3

What is the essential difference between a credit card and a debit card?

RECEIVING PAYMENTS BY POST

Where an organisation sells its goods or services on credit by providing the customer with a sales invoice, the majority of the payments that it receives will be cheques sent through the post. Each morning when the post is opened there must be strict procedures in place for checking these cheques and ensuring their security.

When the post is opened, as each cheque and any documentation sent with it is found, the details of the cheque should be initially recorded on a REMITTANCE LIST. A remittance list is simply a list showing the details of each cheque received that day. A typical remittance list might look like this:

REMITTANCE LIST

Date	Sender	Amount £	Discount £
25 September	Polygon Stores	2,137.63	
25 September	Dagwell Enterprises	1,316.74	
25 September	QQ Stores	918.70	

At this stage the discount column will remain empty, any discount taken will be recorded later when the discount is checked.

All of the cheques received and any documentation with them should then be kept with the remittance list and passed to the person responsible for checking the receipts.

Checking receipts

Correct amount

The first check that must be carried out is that the cheque has been made out for the correct amount. In order to do this you will need to know what invoices are being paid by this cheque. In many situations a REMITTANCE ADVICE will be received with the cheque detailing precisely what the payment relates to.

The remittance advice may have been prepared by the customer or it may be a completed remittance advice sent out by your organisation either with the regular statements that are sent to customers or with the sales invoice itself.

Here is a typical remittance advice:

REMITTANCE ADVICE

To: Southfield Electrical
Industrial Estate
Benham
DR6 2FF
Tel 0303379 Fax 0303152

From: Dagwell Enterprises

Date: 22 September 2006

Reference	Amount	Paid (✔)
30112	723.80	✔
30126	811.59	✔
CN2351	218.65	✔
30164	928.83	
CN2377	239.70	

CHEQUE ENCLOSED	£1,316.74

student notes

You must check that the total of the invoices and credit notes indicated as being paid does agree to the cheque amount (£723.80 + £811.59 – £218.65 = £1,316.74).

If the customer has prepared the remittance advice by completing the invoice and credit note amounts then you should also check that correct amounts have been included. This can be done either by finding copies of the original invoices and credit notes or by examining the sales ledger account for that customer in the subsidiary ledger, the sales ledger.

Valid cheque

When payment is received in the form of a cheque then you must ensure that the cheque itself is valid using the checks discussed earlier in this chapter:

- date;
- payee;
- words and figures;
- signature.

Discounts

If the customer has taken advantage of a settlement discount then very careful checks must be made to ensure that this discount is valid and correct.

- Has this customer been offered a settlement discount? This can be checked either by examining the copy of the sales invoice or finding the masterfile for this customer which will include details of address, credit limit and any trade and settlement discounts that are routinely offered to this customer.

- Has the invoice been paid within the timescale set for the discount? For this the copy of the sales invoice should be examined to determine the invoice date and the terms of the settlement discount. For example if a sales invoice was dated 10 September and a settlement discount was offered for payment received within 10 days, if the cheque was received before or on 20 September it would be valid, but if payment arrived after this date then the claiming of the discount would not be valid.

- Has the discount been correctly calculated? Again the copy invoice will need to be checked for this as due to the VAT complication with settlement discounts, the discount has to be calculated as a percentage of the VAT exclusive amount and the VAT then added on.

HOW IT WORKS

An extract from a sales invoice shows the following:

	£
Goods total	589.37
VAT	99.01
	688.38

4% settlement discount for payment received within 10 days of invoice date, otherwise net 30 days

The discount that can be deducted is 4% of the net total £589.37

$$£589.37 \times 4/100 = £23.57$$

Therefore the cheque that is received should be for £688.38 – £23.57 = £664.81

Discounts and the remittance list

Once any settlement discount has been checked for validity and for being the correct deduction, the amount of the discount should be entered onto the remittance list.

For example the final version of the remittance list considered earlier might look like this:

REMITTANCE LIST			
Date	Sender	Amount £	Discount £
25 September	Polygon Stores	2,137.63	72.77
25 September	Dagwell Enterprises	1,316.74	44.82
25 September	QQ Stores	918.70	

In some situations a customer may send a cheque with no remittance advice or other supporting documentation. In this case it will be necessary to examine the customer's account in the sales ledger in order to determine which invoices are being paid by this cheque.

HOW IT WORKS

Southfield Electrical have received this cheque through the post with no accompanying documentation.

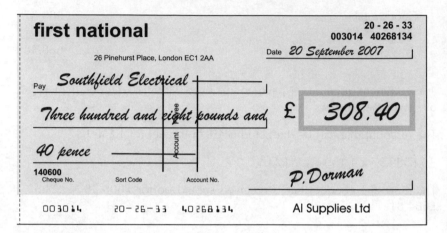

Clearly this cheque is from A1 Supplies Ltd and therefore the account for this customer should be found in the sales ledger. The customer's account shows the following:

A1 Supplies Ltd				SL41
		£		£
3 Sept	SDB – 30118	115.68	12 Sept SDB-CN2355	35.97
8 Sept	SDB – 30131	228.69		
15 Sept	SDB – 30144	147.25		
19 Sept	SDB – 30159	279.46		

By trial and error you will find that the following invoices less the credit note add up to the cheque total:

	£
30118	115.68
30131	228.69
CN 2355	(35.97)
	308.40

Procedure for cheques received in the post

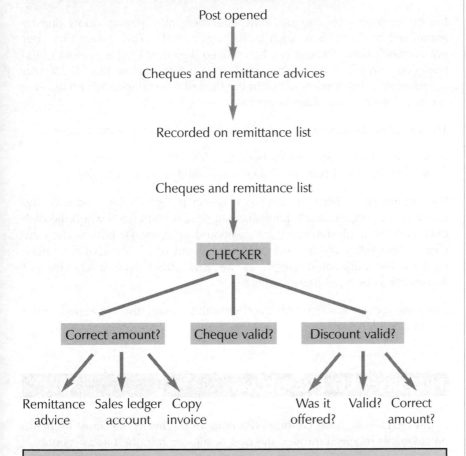

Post opened

Cheques and remittance advices

Recorded on remittance list

Cheques and remittance list

CHECKER

Correct amount?   Cheque valid?   Discount valid?

Remittance   Sales ledger   Copy   Was it   Valid?   Correct
advice   account   invoice   offered?   amount?

Activity 4

Goods with a net total of £368.45 were sold to a customer and VAT of £62.54 was added to the net value to give a gross invoice total of £430.99. The invoice was dated 20 November and a cheque for £418.06 was received today, 28 November. The invoice terms stated that a 3% settlement discount was offered for payment received within 14 days of the invoice date. Is the receipt for the correct amount?

AUTOMATED PAYMENTS

Instead of paying by cheque some customers may pay amounts due by automated bank payment such as bank giro credit. This means that your organisation's bank account will be credited directly with the amount of the payment. Normally the customer will send your organisation notification that the payment is being made, often in the form of a remittance advice showing precisely which invoices are being paid.

The same checks should be carried out as for a receipt of a cheque:

- has the correct amount been transferred?
- if a discount has been taken is this valid and correct?

If no remittance advice or other notification is sent by the customer, the credit to your organisation's bank account should be noticed when the cash book and the bank statement are compared on a regular basis. When the credit is spotted, it will be necessary to work out which invoices have been paid by this automated credit, as we saw above with a cheque not accompanied by a remittance advice.

Once the receipt has been checked then this should also be added to the remittance list.

ERRORS AND PROBLEMS

In this chapter we have considered a number of checks that must be made on payments received through the post or directly into the bank account:

- is the payment for the correct amount?
- is the cheque valid?
- has the discount been correctly calculated and should it have been taken?

Once all these checks have been carried out and there are no problems with the receipt then either the remittance list or the cheque itself should be evidenced in some way so that it is clear that this receipt has been checked and is correct. The easiest method is for each entry on the remittance list to be initialled by the checker once they are happy with the validity of the receipt, but different organisations will have different methods.

If however there is a problem with the cheque, or the amount, or the discount then this must be reported to the appropriate person within the organisation as some action will be needed. In most cases the customer will need to be informed of the problem and might possibly be asked to issue a replacement cheque. Such communications with customers will be considered in a later chapter.

CHAPTER OVERVIEW

- cash will normally only be received in a retail business – modern tills will calculate any change that is required but the correct price of the goods and money offered by the customer must be input into the till

- a cheque will have three parties to it – the drawee, the payee and the drawer

- four main checks must be made when a cheque is given as payment – the payee's name is correct, the cheque is correctly dated and not stale or post-dated, the words and figures agree, the cheque is signed

- a cheque crossing is two parallel lines on the face of the cheque and means that the cheque can only be paid into a bank account – there are general crossings, special crossings, not negotiable crossing and account payee crossing

- a cheque can be endorsed if it is uncrossed or has a not negotiable crossing – this is done by the payee signing the back of the cheque and stating who the cheque should now be paid to

- when a cheque is supported by a cheque guarantee card, further checks are required – the guarantee card has the same name and account number as the cheque, it has not expired, the cheque is signed in the presence of the payee and the signature is the same as on the back of the card. The payee writes the card number on the back of the cheque

- if a customer pays by credit card this can be processed by a mechanical imprinter or an electronic swiping machine

- a number of checks must be made when payment is made by credit card – the card has not been tampered with, the card has not expired, it has not been stolen, an authorisation code is sought if the sale is above the organisation's floor limit and the customer's PIN number verifies their identity

- debit cards can be used for payment which means that the customer's bank account is automatically debited and your organisation's account is credited – similar checks must be carried out as those for a credit card payment

---

KEY WORDS

Cheque a written order to a bank, signed by the bank's customer, to pay a certain amount to another party

Drawee the bank who has issued the cheque and who will have to pay it

Payee the person to whom the cheque is being paid

Drawer the person writing and signing the cheque

Crossing two vertical parallel lines on a cheque which mean that it can only be paid into a bank account

Endorsement a method of transferring a cheque to another party by the payee signing the back of the cheque

Cheque guarantee card a card that ensures that, if correct procedures are followed, a cheque will be paid by the bank

Credit card a method of payment whereby the customer can purchase goods now and pay the credit card company at a later date

Debit card a method of payment that automatically debits the customer's bank account and credits the retailer's bank account at the time of the sale

Remittance list a listing of all of the receipts of the business for a period, usually that day

Remittance advice a document accompanying a receipt showing which invoices less credit notes are being paid

CHAPTER OVERVIEW cont.

- organisations that make credit sales will receive most payments in the form of cheques through the post – these will be recorded initially on a remittance list

- the receipt must be thoroughly checked – is it for the correct amount? – is the cheque valid? – is any discount deducted valid and correct?

- if no remittance advice is received with the cheque then the customer's sales ledger account must be examined to determine which invoices (less credit notes) are being paid

- customers may make payments directly into the organisation's bank account by bank giro credit – similar checks should be carried out as for the receipt of a cheque

- if any errors, discrepancies or problems do arise with the receipts then they should be reported to the appropriate person within the organisation

HOW MUCH HAVE YOU LEARNED?

1   Here is a cheque.

Who is

a)   the drawer
b)   the drawee
c)   the payee?

Explain briefly what each term means

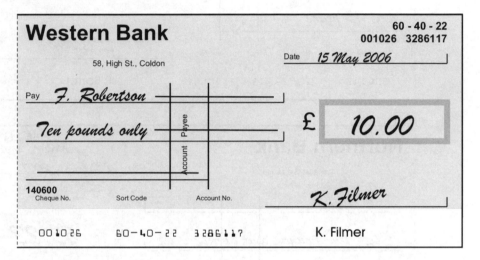

Western Bank	60 - 40 - 22
	001026 3286117
58, High St., Coldon	Date *15 May 2006*

Pay *F. Robertson*

Ten pounds only

£   *10.00*

140600
Cheque No.   Sort Code   Account No.

K. Filmer

001026   60-40-22   3286117   K. Filmer

2   Given below are three cheques which you have received today, 15 November 2007. Examine each one and comment on their validity.

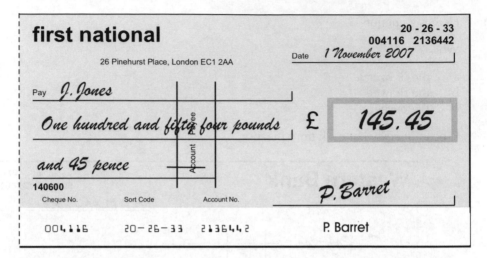

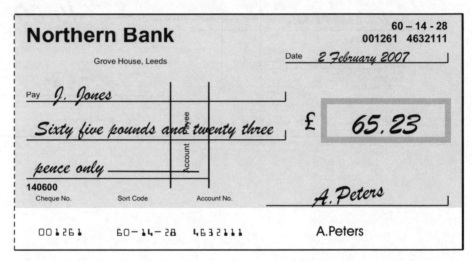

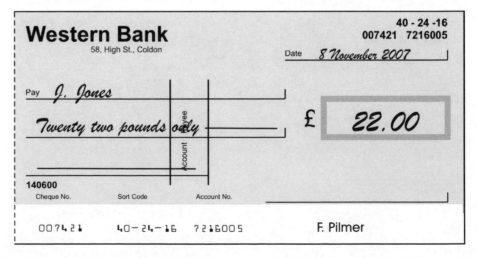

3 Given below are three crossed cheques. Explain what each crossing means.

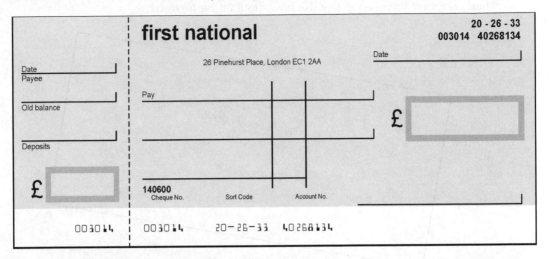

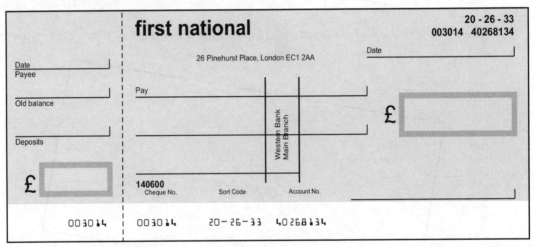

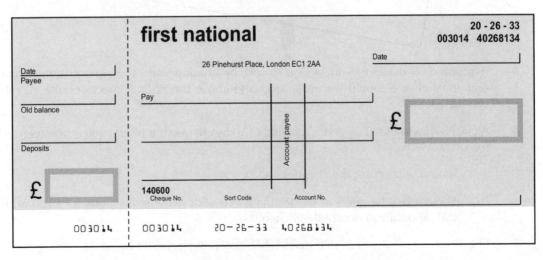

4   Dawn Evans has received a cheque made payable to her with a not negotiable crossing. If she had endorsed the cheque like this how should it be treated?

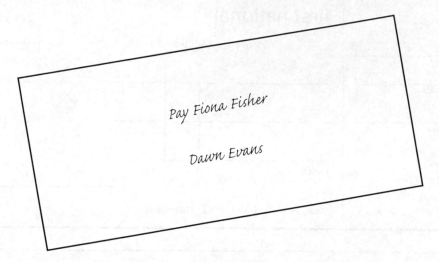

If alternatively she had endorsed the cheque in the following way what could happen to it?

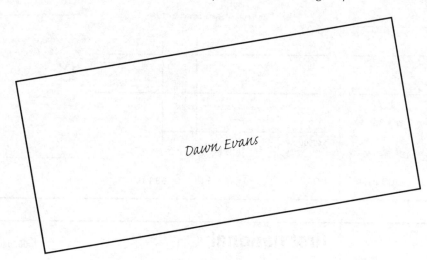

5   If payment is made to you by a customer by cheque with a cheque guarantee card what additional checks should you make over and above the normal checks on the validity of the cheque itself?

6   A customer wishes to buy goods totalling £150 by cheque but his cheque guarantee card is only for £100.

    a)   Should you accept the cheque?

    b)   Alternatively he offers to pay for the goods with two cheques, one for £100 and one for £50. Should you accept these cheques?

7   List the checks that you should make when accepting payment by credit card.

8   What is the essential difference between a credit card and a debit card?

9 What does EFTPOS stand for and what does it mean?

10 The following cheques have been received by your organisation through the post today, 15 October 2007. Record them on a remittance list.

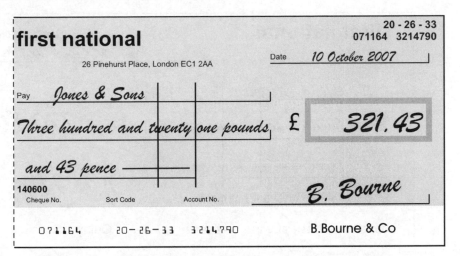

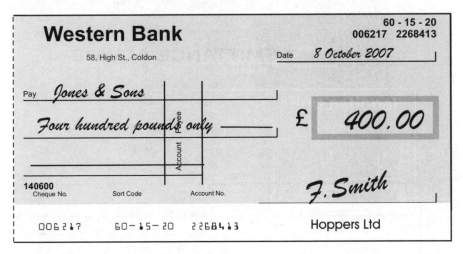

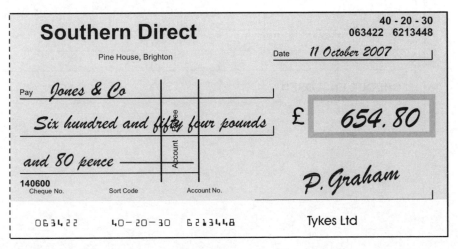

11 Here are two cheques received by Southfield Electrical in the post this morning and the accompanying remittance advices. Check that the correct amount has been sent in each case. Today's date is 22 October 2007.

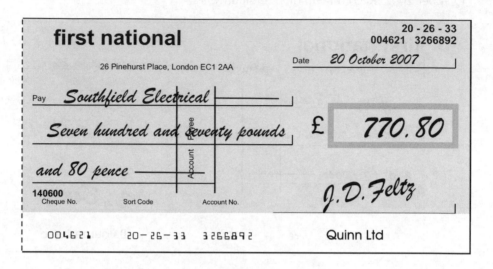

first national

20 - 26 - 33
004621 3266892

26 Pinehurst Place, London EC1 2AA

Date 20 October 2007

Pay Southfield Electrical

Seven hundred and seventy pounds £ 770.80

and 80 pence

140600
Cheque No.   Sort Code   Account No.

J. D. Feltz

004621   20-26-33   3266892   Quinn Ltd

REMITTANCE ADVICE

To: Southfield Electrical
Industrial Estate
Benham
DR6 2FF
Tel 0303379 Fax 0303152

From: Quinn Ltd

Date: 20 October 2007

Reference	Amount	Paid (✓)
30128	325.61	✓
CN2269	18.80	✓
30201	463.27	✓

CHEQUE ENCLOSED	£770.08

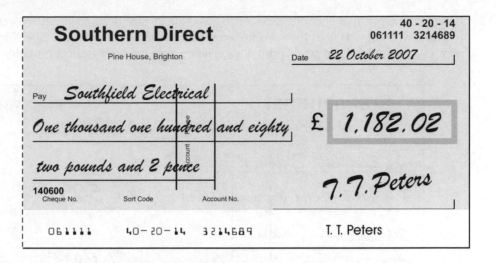

REMITTANCE ADVICE

To: Southfield Electrical
Industrial Estate
Benham
DR6 2FF
Tel 0303379 Fax 0303152

From: T.T. Peters

Date: 22 October 2007

Reference	Amount	Paid (✓)
30196	556.28	✓
30217	180.53	✓
30223	267.03	
30237	454.21	✓

CHEQUE ENCLOSED	£1,182.02

12 Given below are two cheques received by Southfield Electrical, today 20 November 2007, together with extracts from the sales invoices that are being paid in each case. Check that the correct amount has been paid and if not explain where the error has been made.

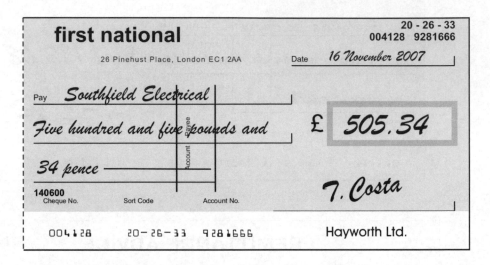

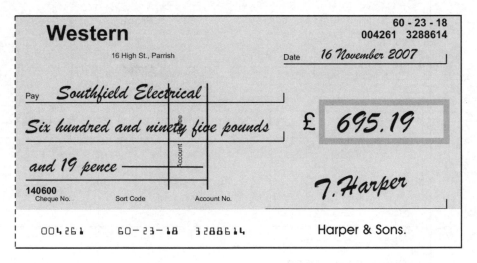

Invoice number	30227	
Date:	7 November	
To:	Hayworth Ltd	
		£
Goods value		448.00
VAT		75.26
Invoice total		523.26

4% settlement discount for payment received within 10 days of invoice date, otherwise 30 days net

Invoice number	30256	
Date:	12 November	
To:	Harper & Sons	
		£
Goods value		620.00
VAT		104.16
Invoice total		724.16

4% settlement discount for payment received within 10 days of invoice date, otherwise 30 days net

---

13 Southfield Electrical have received a cheque from a customer, Long Bros, for £226.79 with no accompanying documentation. The sales ledger account for this customer is given below. Determine which invoices are being paid by this cheque.

	Long Bros		SL 42
	£		£
SDB – 30219	88.37	SDB CN2381	15.80
SDB – 30234	157.35		
SDB – 30239	85.24		
SDB – 30250	265.49		

126

chapter 6:
RECORDING RECEIPTS

chapter coverage 📖

In this chapter we will consider the entry of the checked receipts into the accounting system. The topics that are to be covered are:

✍ the layout of an analysed cash receipts book

✍ the entries to be made into the cash receipts book

✍ totalling and checking the totals of the cash receipts book

✍ posting the cash receipts book to the main ledger

✍ posting the cash receipts book to the subsidiary (sales) ledger

✍ dealing with automated receipts

✍ the importance of coding in the accounting system

✍ the use of posting sheets

✍ computerised accounting systems

KNOWLEDGE AND UNDERSTANDING AND PERFORMANCE CRITERIA COVERAGE

Unit 1

knowledge and understanding – accounting methods

12 accounting for receipts from credit customers and customers without credit accounts
13 methods of coding data
14 operation of manual accounting systems
15 operation of computerised accounting systems, including output
16 the use of the cash book and petty cash book as part of the double entry system or as books of prime entry
17 batch control
18 relationship between the accounting system and the ledger

Performance criteria – element 1.2

B enter receipts in appropriate accounting records

PRIMARY RECORDS

As we saw in an earlier chapter all of the transactions of a business are normally recorded in books of prime entry before being posted to the main ledger and any relevant subsidiary ledgers.

For receipts of monies the book of prime entry is known as the CASH RECEIPTS BOOK. All money being paid to the organisation is recorded in the cash receipts book whether it is payments by cash, cheque, credit card, debit card or directly through the banking system.

The cash receipts book is, however, slightly different in nature from other books of prime entry. In most organisations the cash receipts book is not only the book of prime entry for receipts of money but it is also part of the double entry bookkeeping system in that it forms the debit side of the bank ledger account. Therefore all of the entries made in the cash receipts book are already debited in the main ledger and all that remains in the main ledger is to post the credit entries.

The types of receipts that an organisation will have will depend entirely upon the nature of its business. However for most businesses the following are typical:

- cash sales;
- money received from debtors for credit sales;
- money paid into the business by the owner;
- bank interest;
- miscellaneous income such as receipts from the sale of fixed assets.

Most businesses will have an ANALYSED CASH RECEIPTS BOOK which reflects the most common types of receipts.

The layout of a typical cash book is shown here:

Date	Details	Ref	Total	VAT	Cash sales	Sales ledger	Sundry	Discounts allowed
			£	£	£	£	£	£

Date – the date recorded will be the date the income was received or written up in the cash book depending upon the organisation's policy.

Details – the details should be sufficient to describe the transaction so that it can easily be analysed and checked at a later date, eg if a receipt from a debtor, the name of that debtor.

Ref – the reference will depend upon the type of receipt. If it is a receipt from a debtor then the reference will normally be the sales ledger code number for that debtor. If it is a receipt for cash sales or bank interest then the reference may be the main ledger code for sales or interest or simply a reference to the main ledger to distinguish it from sales ledger receipts.

Total – the figure in the total column is the total amount of the receipt.

VAT – when money is received from a debtor no VAT is recorded, as the VAT was recorded and posted to the VAT account when the original sales invoice was entered into the Sales Day Book. However when cash sales which include VAT are made, the VAT element must be entered in this column.

Cash sales – the net amount of the cash sale, the total cash minus the VAT, is recorded in this column. Remember that when we talk about a cash sale we mean a sale that is not on credit – the actual receipt could be in the form of cash, cheque, credit or debit card.

Sales ledger – this column is used to record receipts from credit customers. The details of VAT and net and gross amounts were recorded in the Sales Day Book when the sales invoice was sent out to the customer. When the customer pays the invoice only the total of the actual payment needs to be recorded here. The amount is the actual value of the cheque received, so after deduction of any settlement discount that was offered (see below).

Sundry – the sundry column is used for other miscellaneous receipts that do not occur on a regular basis. It is important that their "details" and reference coding are detailed enough for the receipt to be eventually posted to the correct main ledger account.

Discount allowed – the DISCOUNT ALLOWED column is known as a 'memorandum column'. What is recorded here is the amount of any settlement discount that has been deducted by the credit customer before making the payment. This column will be used when making the postings from the cash receipts book to the main ledger and the subsidiary ledger.

Activity 1

When should VAT be recorded in the Cash Receipts Book?

HOW IT WORKS

Southfield Electrical supplies local high street dealers with a wide range of electrical goods. Most of these dealers trade on credit terms with Southfield, but a few customers, small sole traders, are required to pay at the time of the sale.

The monies received this week, the week ended 28 September, are recorded on the weekly remittance list:

REMITTANCE LIST

£

Dagwell Enterprises, cheque	336.50 – £14.02 discount taken
Polygon Stores, cheque	158.20
Peter Hayward, cheque	227.95 – cash sale
G Thomas & Co, cheque	269.43 – £11.23 discount taken
Whitehill Superstores, cheque	673.58 – £28.07 discount taken
Benham Garages, cheque	1,400.00 – sale of motor car
Weller Enterprises, cheque	225.49
John Cooper, cash	75.20 – cash sale

You are also provided with the sales ledger account codes for the credit customers:

Polygon Stores	SL 03
Dagwell Enterprises	SL 15
Weller Enterprises	SL 18
Whitehill Superstores	SL 24
G Thomas & Co	SL 30

These transactions must now be written up in the Cash Receipts Book.

Date	Details	Ref	Total	VAT	Cash sales	Sales ledger	Sundry	Discounts allowed
			£	£	£	£	£	£
28/9	Dagwell Ent	SL15	336.50			336.50		14.02
28/9	Polygon Stores	SL03	158.20			158.20		
28/9	Peter Hayward	ML	227.95	33.95	194.00			
28/9	G Thomas & Co	SL30	269.43			269.43		11.23
28/9	Whitehill Superstores	SL24	673.58			673.58		28.07
28/9	Benham Garages – sale of car	ML	1,400.00				1,400.00	
28/9	Weller Ent.	SL18	225.49			225.49		
28/9	John Cooper	ML	75.20	11.20	64.00			

Reference – the sales ledger account code is used as the reference for the receipts from credit customers, as eventually these amounts will need to be posted to their individual debtor accounts in the subsidiary (sales) ledger. For the cash sales and the proceeds from sale of the motor car the reference ML refers to the main ledger indicating that the only entries for these amounts will be in the main ledger.

Total and analysis columns – each receipt is entered into the total column and then into the appropriate analysis column – if the money is from a credit customer it is analysed into the sales ledger column, if from cash sales the analysis is into the VAT and cash sales columns and the sale of the car is in the sundry column.

VAT – when monies are received from credit customers there is no entry for VAT as this has already been analysed and accounted for in the Sales Day book. However the money received for cash sales is inclusive of VAT and the VAT must be calculated and included in the VAT column:

Peter Hayward   VAT = £227.95 x 17.5/117.5 =   £33.95
John Cooper   VAT = £75.20 x 17.5/117.5 =   £11.20

There is no VAT on the sale of the car.

Sundry – the entry in the sundry column must be described in the details so that it can eventually be posted to the correct account in the main ledger.

Discounts allowed – although only the actual amount of the cheques received from credit customers is included in the Cash Receipts Book, the amount of any discount that the customer has taken must be noted in the discount allowed column as this is important for the eventual posting of the receipts.

Activity 2

If cash sales are made for £893.00 including VAT what entries should be made in the Cash Receipts Book?

TOTALLING THE CASH RECEIPTS BOOK

Once the Cash Receipts Book has been written up for a period, it must be totalled in order for the postings to the main ledger to take place.

Step 1   Each column of the Cash Receipts Book should be totalled.

Step 2   The casting should be checked by cross-casting the column totals to ensure that they add back to the 'total' column total. Take care here as the discount allowed column should not be included in the cross-casting – this column is a memorandum column only and does not form part of the total cash received.

student notes ✍

HOW IT WORKS

Southfield's Cash Receipts Book will now be totalled and the totals checked by cross-casting.

Date	Details	Ref	Total	VAT	Cash sales	Sales ledger	Sundry	Discounts allowed
			£	£	£	£	£	£
28/9	Dagwell Ent	SL15	336.50			336.50		14.02
28/9	Polygon Stores	SL03	158.20			158.20		
28/9	Peter Hayward	ML	227.95	33.95	194.00			
28/9	G Thomas & Co	SL30	269.43			269.43		11.23
28/9	Whitehill Superstores	SL24	673.58			673.58		28.07
28/9	Benham Garages – sale of car	ML	1,400.00				1,400.00	
28/9	Weller Ent.	SL18	225.49			225.49		
28/9	John Cooper	ML	75.20	11.20	64.00			
			3,366.35	45.15	258.00	1,663.20	1,400.00	53.32

Cross-cast check:

	£
VAT	45.15
Cash sales	258.00
Sales ledger	1,663.20
Sundry	1,400.00
Total	3,366.35

Remember not to include the discount allowed column in this cross-casting as this is not part of the cash actually received.

POSTING THE CASH RECEIPTS BOOK TO THE MAIN LEDGER

Now we need to consider the posting of the column totals to the main ledger in order to complete the double entry. Remember that the Cash Receipts Book is normally part of the main ledger as well as being a book of prime entry, and therefore the "total" column is effectively the debit entry for each of these cash receipts in the main ledger.

The postings that remain are the credit entries for each of the column totals:

	£
VAT account	45.15
Sales account	258.00
Sales ledger control account	1,663.20
Disposal of fixed assets account	1,400.00
Total	3,366.35

The total of these credit entries is equal to the total of the debit entries in the Cash Receipts Book.

Do not worry about the Disposal of fixed assets account as this is only for illustration. You do not have to deal with this at Foundation.

HOW IT WORKS

Each of these accounts will now be posted with the relevant total. You will notice that each of the accounts being used have a balance brought down on them. This is the OPENING BALANCE on the account and is the same as the balance carried down when the account was last balanced.

The opening balance on the VAT account shows that at the start of today Southfield owe (a credit balance therefore a liability) £6,348.20 to HM Revenue and Customs.

VAT account

£		£
	Balance b/d	6,348.20
	Cash Receipts Book	45.15

The opening balance on the sales account (a credit as it is an income account) shows that sales of £225,389.16 have been made so far this year.

Sales account

£		£
	Balance b/d	225,389.16
	Cash Receipts Book	258.00

The opening balance on the sales ledger control account (a debit as it is an asset account) shows that debtors currently owe Southfield £8,378.34.

Sales ledger control account

£		£
Balance b/d 8,378.34	Cash Receipts Book	1,663.20

The entry in the sales ledger control account is a credit entry as the money from the debtors is reducing the amount that is owed.

There is no opening balance on this account as it is rarely used.

Disposal of fixed asset account			
	£		£
		Cash Receipts Book	1,400.00

Note that each of the entries into the main ledger accounts have been referenced to the Cash Receipts Book. In future this will be abbreviated to CRB.

DISCOUNTS ALLOWED

We have not quite completed the entries to the main ledger accounts as we still have to deal with the discounts allowed.

For the discounts allowed both a debit and a credit entry are required. The credit entry is to the sales ledger control account as the discount allowed is effectively another method of reducing the amount owed by the debtor.

Suppose that a sales invoice for £100 was sent to a debtor and the debtor paid £95 by cheque, taking advantage of a settlement discount of £5. The debtors account would be debited with the invoice and credited with the cash.

Debtor account			
	£		£
Invoice	100.00	Cash	95.00

Without an entry for the discount it would appear that the debtor still owed £5. Therefore the debtor's account must be credited with the discount allowed in order to clear the debt.

Debtor account			
	£		£
Invoice	100.00	Cash	95.00
		Discount allowed	5.00

The **debit** entry for the discount is to a discount allowed account. This is a debit entry because to Southfield the discount is an expense. They have foregone some of the monies due in order to ensure that payment is made more quickly.

HOW IT WORKS

The total of the discount allowed column for Southfield, £53.32 will now be posted.

Discount allowed account

	£		£
CRB	53.32		

Sales ledger control account

	£		£
Balance b/d	8,378.34	Cash receipts book	1,663.20
		CRB – discount	53.32

Activity 3

What is the double entry for discounts allowed to credit customers?

POSTING THE CASH RECEIPTS BOOK TO THE SUBSIDIARY (SALES) LEDGER

Every receipt from credit customers must be entered not only in the main ledger as part of the totals posted but also in the subsidiary (sales) ledger.

Therefore each item in the 'Sales ledger' column must be entered into the individual debtors' accounts in the subsidiary (sales) ledger. The entry for the receipt will be a credit entry in the account in order to reduce the amount owing by the debtor.

Remember also that, just as in the main ledger, any discount allowed to that customer must also be credited to his individual account.

As in the main ledger, each of the debtor accounts are now shown with opening balances representing the amount that that debtor owed to Southfield at the start of the day.

HOW IT WORKS

Subsidiary ledger

Dagwell Enterprises			SL 15
	£		£
Balance b/d	1,360.72	CRB	336.50
		CRB – discount	14.02

Polygon Stores			SL 03
	£		£
Balance b/d	442.60	CRB	158.20

G Thomas & Co			SL 30
	£		£
Balance b/d	280.66	CRB	269.43
		CRB – discount	11.23

Whitehill Superstores			SL 24
	£		£
Balance b/d	2,457.28	CRB	673.58
		CRB – discount	28.07

Weller Enterprises			SL 18
	£		£
Balance b/d	225.49	CRB	225.49

Activity 4

The opening balance on a debtor's account, J Thomlinson, is £146.78. Show how this would appear in the sales ledger account for this customer.

AUTOMATED RECEIPTS

Some credit customers may choose not to send your organisation a cheque directly, but to arrange payment of the amount due via the banking system. For example a customer may pay money directly into your organisation's bank account using the bank giro credit system. This will be covered in more detail later in this Course Companion, when dealing with payments.

However at this stage it is important to ensure that such receipts are also included when writing up the Cash Receipts Book. As we saw in the previous chapter, when automated receipts are paid into your organisation's bank account it is normal practice for the customer to send a remittance advice detailing the payment that has been made. This receipt would then be included on the remittance list and entered into the Cash Receipts Book with the other forms of receipt.

In some rare situations your organisation may not be informed of the payment directly into its bank account and therefore the amount could not be entered into the Cash Receipts Book. However such a situation can be rectified by careful comparison of the Cash Receipts Book and the bank statement. This will be covered in detail later in this Course Companion.

REFERENCING THE LEDGER ACCOUNTS

The ledger accounts that we have been preparing have been kept simple by including only the minimum of information. However in practice each time an entry is made in the ledger accounts it would firstly be dated with the date that it was entered into the ledger. The second point is that instead of simply referencing the entry to the CRB for example, it would be normal practice to show what page of the Cash Receipts Book, eg CRB31.

CASH RECEIPTS BOOK AND THE MAIN LEDGER

We have noted earlier in this chapter that the Cash Receipts Book is normally not only a book of prime entry but also part of the main ledger. For this reason only the analysis columns in the Cash Receipts Book need to be credited to the relevant ledger accounts in the main ledger, as the total column is effectively the debit entry to the bank account in the main ledger.

However in some businesses the Cash Receipts Book is purely a book of prime entry and not part of the main ledger. In these cases the total column total must be debited to the Bank ledger account in the main ledger as well as the analysis column totals being credited to the relevant accounts.

CODING

So far in this Course Companion we have come across a variety of types of coding:

- purchase orders, delivery notes, sales invoices and credit notes are all given a unique, sequential number;

- the products ordered and sent out are identified by their stock code;

- the number of each invoice/credit note is included in the sales day book and sales returns day book;

- entries for debtors in the sales day book and Cash Receipts Book are coded given the sales ledger code for each debtor.

In the main ledger there will be many, many ledger accounts and it will be normal practice to code each ledger account so that the correct ledger account can be found quickly and easily.

In general terms most businesses will probably wish to arrange their ledger accounts into groups representing the different accounting aspects of the business. For example the groups of accounts that may be required might be:

- income accounts

- expenses accounts

- asset accounts

- liability accounts

- capital accounts

Within each of the groups the ledger accounts may again be split into sub-groups, for example within asset accounts there might be fixed asset accounts and current (short-term) asset accounts.

There are many coding systems in practice and each organisation will choose one that suits its transactions and organisation. Probably the two most common methods are NUMERIC CODING and ALPHA-NUMERIC CODING.

A numeric coding system is where the code is entirely numerical. For example the main ledger codes might be set up as follows:

Income accounts	0001 – 0199
Expenses accounts	0200 – 0499
Asset accounts	0500 – 0699
Liability accounts	0700 – 0899
Capital accounts	0900 – 1000

There are potentially 1,000 ledger accounts here. They do not all have to be used but the coding system must be flexible enough to allow for new accounts to be opened up.

An alpha-numeric coding system uses a mixture of letters and numbers to code the ledger accounts. For example the main ledger account codes might alternatively be set up like this:

Income accounts	A001 – 100
Expenses accounts	B001 – 200
Asset accounts	C001 – 200
Liability accounts	D001 – 200
Capital accounts	E001 – 100

Once the coding system has been set up, when entries are made in the Cash Receipts Book and are referenced to the main ledger then the reference would include the account code for that ledger account.

POSTING SHEETS

As we have seen when considering the posting of the Cash Receipts Book the postings are becoming more complicated with more entries being made in more accounts. In many organisations the postings that are to be made by the bookkeeper from the books of prime entry are listed on a POSTING SHEET prior to the postings being made.

This is simply a list of all of the debit and credit entries to be made. It will include the name and code of the ledger accounts and the amounts to be entered.

HOW IT WORKS

A posting sheet for Southfield's Cash Receipts Book might look like this:

POSTING SHEET

Account name	Account code	Debit £	Credit £
VAT	0780		45.15
Sales	0010		258.00
Sales ledger control	0550		1,663.20
Disposals	0340		1,400.00
Discounts allowed	0260	53.32	
Sales ledger control	0550		53.32

Prepared by: .... **Date**: ....

Checked by: .... **Date**: ....

Posted by: .... **Date**: ....

CASH RECEIPTS IN COMPUTERISED SYSTEMS

A typical integrated accounting system will have a separate 'cash' or 'bank' module to carry out the various accounting tasks associated with cash.

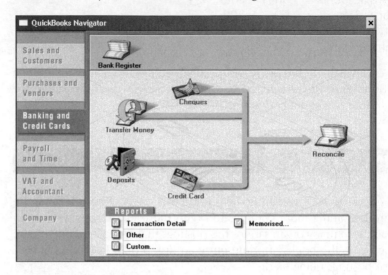

This does not mean that there is really a separate cash 'book' in a computerised system. Cash and bank accounts are simply main ledger accounts, but special processes are needed to record transactions because most cash received needs to be matched against the individual invoices posted to the sales ledger.

If you attempt to post a receipt to the bank account without allocating it to sales invoices you will probably get a warning.

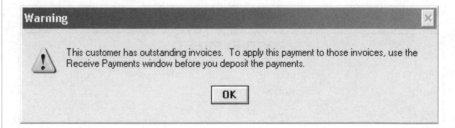

The customer receipts part of the system will automatically list all the outstanding invoices on a customer's account and will expect you to allocate the cash received accordingly, as in the following illustration.

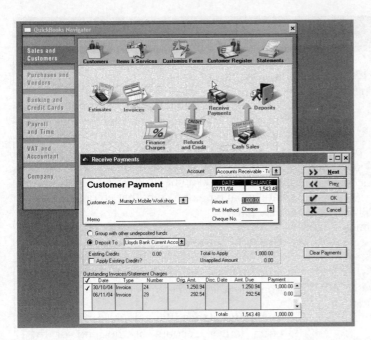

In this example the customer has paid a round sum amount of £1,000 and this is allocated to the first outstanding invoice in date order, leaving £250.94 outstanding on invoice number 24 and the whole of invoice number 29 outstanding.

In other circumstances this customer might have paid only £292.54, being the payment for the second invoice, but not have paid the first invoice at all, perhaps because it was in dispute. If that happens the £292.54 must be allocated to invoice number 29, not to invoice number 24.

CHAPTER OVERVIEW

- the book of prime entry used for entering money received into the accounting records is the Cash Receipts Book

- the Cash Receipts Book is normally not only a book of prime entry but is also part of the double entry system in the main ledger, being the debit side of the bank ledger account

- most businesses will use an analysed Cash Receipts Book with analysis columns for the main types of income as well as for VAT and discounts allowed

- the most common analysis columns are for cash sales and receipts from debtors or sales ledger customers

- VAT on income is only recorded in the Cash Receipts Book for cash sales. The VAT on credit sales has already been recorded from the Sales Day Book and therefore is not relevant when monies are received from those debtors

- receipts from credit customers are recorded in the sales ledger column of the Cash Receipts Book

- when the Cash Receipts Book is totalled and the totals are checked by cross-casting, the discount allowed column is not included as this is a memorandum column only

KEY WORDS

Cash receipts book the book of prime entry in which all receipts of money into the business are recorded

Analysed cash receipts book a cash receipts book with columns to separate out each individual type of receipt that an organisation may have

Discount allowed the settlement discount offered to a credit customer that the customer decides to accept by deducting it from the full invoice amount due

Opening balance the amount carried down on a ledger account at the end of the previous period and brought down on the account at the start of this period

Numeric coding a coding system that uses only numbers

Alpha-numeric coding a coding system that uses a mixture of letters and numbers

Posting sheet a written record of the postings that are to be made to the main ledger from the primary records

- the Cash Receipts Book is the debit side of the bank ledger account and as such no debit entries in the main ledger are required. Therefore the postings to the main ledger are the credit entries which are the totals of each of the remaining columns (other than the "discount allowed" column)

- ongoing ledger accounts will have opening balances being the balance at the end of the previous day or week, and therefore the balance at the start of the current day or week

- the total of the "discounts allowed" column does require full double entry with a debit to the discounts allowed account and a credit to the sales ledger control account

- once the postings have been made to the main ledger it is equally important to ensure that each receipt of money from a credit customer is recorded in the customer's individual account in the subsidiary (sales) ledger. These accounts are credited with both the cash received and any discount allowed

CHAPTER OVERVIEW cont.

- instead of making a payment by cheque a credit customer may automatically pay money into your organisation's bank account by bank giro credit. This must also be recorded in the Cash Receipts Book and should be included on the remittance list when a remittance advice is sent separately by the customer

- coding is an important part of the accounting process and is used in all aspects of accounting procedure. There are a variety of methods of coding and an organisation will choose that which is most appropriate to its own circumstances

- in many organisations a posting sheet will be drawn up to show the postings required from the primary records to the main ledger accounts

- in a computerised system the operations that the computer processes are the same as those in a manual system. Documents of similar types are input in batches in just the same way as the primary records would be written up

- the most important element in a computerised system is that the original data is input correctly. This will normally be done in batches with appropriate batch controls to pick up obvious errors. In a computerised system the aspect of correct coding becomes increasingly important as the computer relies on the codes input to process the transactions correctly

HOW MUCH HAVE YOU LEARNED?

1   Is the Cash Receipts Book a book of prime entry or a main ledger account, or is it both of these?

2   Explain how discounts allowed are entered into the main ledger accounts and the subsidiary (sales) ledger from the Cash Receipts Book.

3   Given below is the remittance list for an organisation (which is registered for VAT) for the week ended 30 June. You are also given the sales ledger codings for any credit customers.

REMITTANCE LIST	
	£
Cash sales	364.25
H Henry, cheque	146.79
P Peters, cheque	221.55 discount £6.85
K Kilpin, bank giro credit	440.30
Cash sales	294.50
B Bennet, cheque	57.80
S Shahir, cheque	114.68 discount £3.55

Sales ledger codings:

S Shahir	0106
H Henry	0115
K Kilpin	0128
B Bennet	0134
P Peters	0135

a)   Write up the Cash Receipts Book for the period.
b)   Show how the totals would appear in the main ledger accounts.
c)   Show how the individual debtor receipts would appear in the subsidiary (sales) ledger accounts.

4   Given below is a remittance list showing the receipts for an organisation (which is registered for VAT) for the week ending 20 May. You are also given the an extract from the main ledger coding manual.

REMITTANCE LIST	
	£
G Gonpipe, cheque, SL 55	332.67
Cash sales	658.00
J Jimmings, bank giro credit SL 04	127.37 discount £6.70
N Nutely, cheque SL 16	336.28 discount £17.70
T Turner, cheque SL 21	158.35
Cash sales	329.88
R Ritner, bank giro credit SL 45	739.10 discount £38.90

Main ledger coding manual (extract)

Sales	110
Discount allowed	280
Sales ledger control	560
VAT	710

a)   Write up the Cash Receipts Book for the week.

b)   Complete the posting sheet for the main ledger accounts for the week.

c)   Show how the individual receipts would appear in the debtors' accounts in the subsidiary (sales) ledger.

5   Briefly explain how the receipts of an organisation would be input into a computerised system and how the computer would then process them.

146

chapter 7:
THE BANKING SYSTEM

chapter coverage 📖

Having dealt with receiving money in a business and recording that money, it is now time to deal with paying the money into the bank. The topics that are to be covered are:

✍ banking services

✍ how the clearing system works

✍ completing a paying-in slip

✍ paying in credit card vouchers

✍ bank statements

KNOWLEDGE AND UNDERSTANDING AND PERFORMANCE CRITERIA COVERAGE

Unit 1

knowledge and understanding – the business environment

7 the use of banking documentation

knowledge and understanding – the organisation

27 banking and personal security procedures

Unit 3

knowledge and understanding – the business environment

3 general bank services and operation of bank clearing system
4 function and form of banking documentation

Performance criteria – element 1.2

C prepare paying-in documents and reconcile to relevant records

BANKING SERVICES

Due to immense competition between the high street banks in recent years they now offer a vast array of services to customers. These services fall into four main categories:

HOLDING money for customers	Making PAYMENTS for customers
Providing LOANS	OTHER services

Holding of money

Most banks now offer a variety of different types of bank account to suit all customers needs. The most commonly used is a CURRENT ACCOUNT whereby customers pay money into the account and can then draw on it by writing cheques or withdrawing cash from Automatic Teller Machines (cash points) or arranging other methods of payment from the account. Many of these current accounts also attract a low rate of interest on any balances.

A customer can also choose to save money at a higher interest rate by paying money into a DEPOSIT ACCOUNT. This will not normally have a cheque book but will generally pay a higher rate of interest than a current account. Some deposit accounts will pay even higher rates of interest but may have restrictions placed upon the movement of funds for example a withdrawal of money may require one month's notice.

Making payments

Banks have a duty to pay cheques correctly written out by customers provided that they have enough funds in their account. The banks also offer the service of making payments out of an account by other means such as standing orders, direct debits and BACS (these will be dealt with in more detail in a later chapter). The banks will also collect payments for cheques that the customer pays into the bank account, and will accept transfers from other bank accounts.

Providing loans

Banks will provide loans to customers, both personal and business customers, in a number of different ways.

Many current accounts will have an agreed OVERDRAFT FACILITY whereby a customer can write cheques for more than the balance on the account up to a certain amount and these cheques will still be paid. A fairly high rate of interest is usually charged for this facility.

A further method of providing short term loans to customers is by issuing CREDIT CARDS. These allow customers to make purchases and to defer payment until some future time. The balance on the credit card is not required to be paid off each month, only a minimum sum is necessary. Any outstanding balances on these credit card accounts usually attract a very high rate of interest.

Banks will also provide LOANS to both personal and business customers with various terms and conditions and repayment terms.

Banks will also provide MORTGAGES, which are long term loans (normally 25 years) in order to purchase a property with the mortgage being secured on the property. This means that if the loan is not repaid for some reason then the bank has the right to sell the property in order to get its money back.

Other services

Banks also provide a number of other services that can be of use to businesses:

- provision of a nightsafe;
- supplying foreign currency;
- safe deposit boxes;
- investment advice.

Activity 1

A sole trader is setting up in business with £50,000. He hopes that only £30,000 of this will be required initially for trading transactions and that the remainder can be saved for future growth. What types of bank account would be best suited for this trader?

THE CLEARING SYSTEM

If you write out a cheque then the eventual outcome of this is that the money will be paid out of your bank account by your bank and paid into the account of the payee. However in order for this to happen to the many thousands of cheques that are written each day a complex system is in operation. This system was set up by the major banks and is known as the CLEARING SYSTEM and it generally means that it takes three working days for a cheque paid into a bank account to clear into that account and therefore be available as funds that can be drawn on.

HOW IT WORKS

Southfield Electrical banks with the First National Bank in Benham. It has recently written and sent out two cheques to suppliers:

    Cheque number 100362 to Harris Enterprises
    Cheque number 100363 to Simons Bros

Day 1

Harris Enterprises pays cheque 362 into its own bank, the First National branch in Winnish.

Simons Bros pays cheque 363 into its own bank, the National Eastern Bank in Benham.

Each bank sorts all of the cheques paid in that day by bank, and they are processed and coded.

First National, Winnish sends all of the cheques paid in during the day, including 362, to the First National clearing department in London by courier.

National Eastern, Benham sends all of the cheques paid in during the day, including 363, to the National Eastern clearing department in London by courier.

Day 2

Both bank's clearing departments receive all of the cheques paid into to their branches the previous day and these are then sorted by bank.

The First National clearing department sends cheque 362 directly to the Benham branch of First National – this is known as interbank clearing.

However the National Eastern clearing department sends cheque 363 to the Central Clearing House, as it is cheque that has been written on another bank.

The Central Clearing House arranges for the banks to swap cheques and agree any differences in value to be paid over the following day, known as operational balances.

Cheque 363 is then sent to the clearing department of the First National Bank and the clearing department sends it by courier to the First National branch in Benham.

Day 3

The Benham branch of First National checks that cheques 362 and 363 are valid and then pays them out of Southfield's current account and the accounts of Harris Enterprises and Simons Bros are credited with cleared funds.

The head offices of First National and National Eastern banks clear any operational balances outstanding between the two banks.

To summarise this long and complex process lets look at the journey that cheque number 100363 made in those three days.

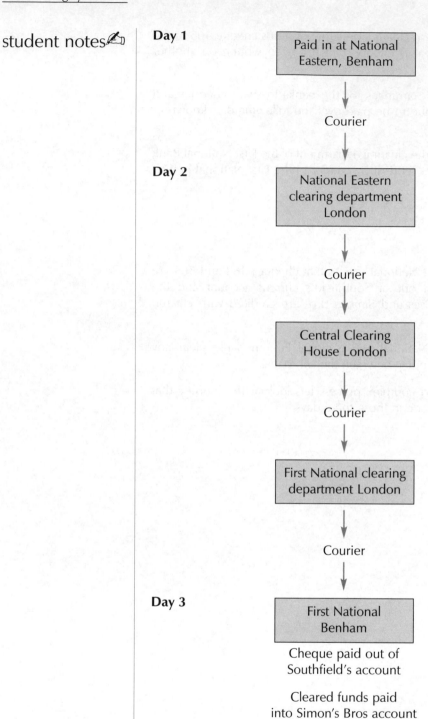

Day 1

Paid in at National
Eastern, Benham

Courier

Day 2

National Eastern
clearing department
London

Courier

Central Clearing
House London

Courier

First National clearing
department London

Courier

Day 3

First National
Benham

Cheque paid out of
Southfield's account

Cleared funds paid
into Simon's Bros account

Operational balances cleared

BANKING DOCUMENTATION

The three main documents that a business will be dealing with when dealing with its bank are:

- cheques;
- paying-in slips;
- bank statements.

Cheques were considered in detail in an earlier chapter and the other two will therefore be dealt with here.

Paying-in slips

When opening an account with a bank a business will be issued with a paying-in book which will contain probably 50 pre-printed, sequentially numbered PAYING-IN SLIPS. A typical paying-in slip is shown below – note how both sides are shown as both sides need to be filled in in detail.

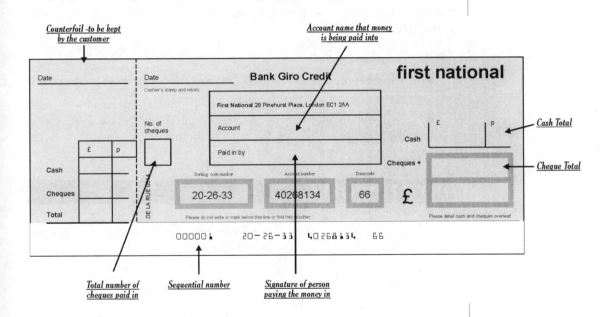

student notes

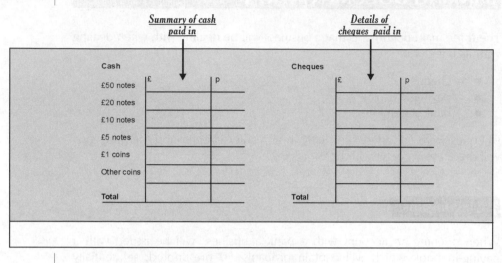

Summary of cash paid in

Details of cheques paid in

Cash	£	p		Cheques	£	p
£50 notes						
£20 notes						
£10 notes						
£5 notes						
£1 coins						
Other coins						
Total				**Total**		

How to complete the paying-in slip

When any cash takings and cheques received by a business are ready to be paid into the bank, the paying-in slip must be carefully and accurately completed.

Cash

- The cash must be first sorted into each denomination of notes and coins.

- Each denomination must then be counted and the total entered in the appropriate box on the back of the paying-in slip.

HOW IT WORKS

You are preparing the paying-in slip for your organisation and the following amounts of cash have been sorted and counted:

£50 notes	2
£20 notes	6
£10 notes	17
£5 notes	13
£1 coins	28
50p coins	16
20p coins	37
10p coins	18
5p coins	9
2p coins	25
1p coins	42

These amounts must now be entered onto the back of the paying-in slip.

Cash	£	p	Cheques	£	p
£50 notes	100	00			
£20 notes	120	00			
£10 notes	170	00			
£5 notes	65	00			
£1 coins	28	00			
Other coins	18	57			
Total	501	57	Total		

There are also three cheques to be paid in which have been checked as valid and correct and listed on the remittance list:

REMITTANCE LIST

Date	Sender	Amount £
21 October	C Kelly	157.80
21 October	L Clifton	85.69
21 October	F Gingham	142.74

These must now be summarised on the back of the paying-in slip.

Cash	£	p	Cheques	£	p	
£50 notes	100	00		157	80	C Kelly
£20 notes	120	00		85	69	L Clifton
£10 notes	170	00		142	74	F Gingham
£5 notes	65	00				
£1 coins	28	00				
Other coins	18	57				
Total	501	57	Total	386	23	

Now the front of the paying-in slip must be completed:

- fill in the date;

- enter the account name that the money is to be paid into;

- enter the amount of cash in total taken from the back of the paying-in slip;

student notes

- enter the total of the cheques taken from the back of the paying-in slip;

- total the cash and cheques;

- enter the number of cheques paid in in the box provided;

- complete the counterfoil with the same details;

- the person paying the money in must sign the paying-in slip.

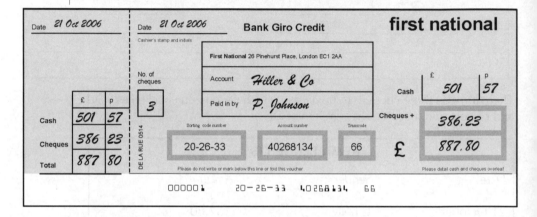

The paying-in slip is now complete and can be taken to the bank together with the cash and the cheques.

Security procedures

It is important that money received by a business is paid into the bank promptly. This is for two reasons:

- money kept on the premises is a security risk;

- money should be paid into the bank as soon as possible in order to increase the bank balance and earn more interest or reduce the overdraft and thereby the interest charged.

When actually transporting cash to the bank, personal security must be considered. It might be advisable for two members of staff to take the money together or to employ a security firm if the amount of cash is very large. It is advisable also to change the route and timing of the bank visits on a regular basis and, most importantly, the details of bank paying-in visits must be treated with the highest confidentiality.

Often a business, particularly a retail business, will need to pay money into the bank when the bank itself is shut. Many branches provide a nightsafe for such eventualities. A nightsafe is normally a hole in the wall of the bank where the money and paying-in slip can be placed in a special wallet. The wallet will then go down a chute into the bank itself.

Activity 2

Why is it important to maintain the highest levels of confidentiality about the banking process of your organisation?

PAYING IN CREDIT CARD VOUCHERS

When an organisation makes sales which are paid for by credit card and a mechanical imprinter is used, the vouchers must be paid into the bank in just the same way as cheques. If an electronic swipe machine is used for the credit card sales then normally the amount of the sale is automatically charged to the customer's credit card and credited to the retailer's account by EFTPOS, therefore there is no need to pay these vouchers into the bank.

Before entering any credit card voucher details on the bank's paying in slip a separate credit card voucher RETAILER SUMMARY must be completed. This is shown below:

- imprint the summary with the retailer's card;

- the back of the Summary must be completed first showing the amount of each voucher and these amounts are then totalled;

- the number and total of the sales vouchers is then entered onto the front of the Summary;

- the number and total of any refund vouchers is also entered on the front of the Summary;

- the Summary is then dated, totalled and signed;

- the Summary is a three part document and the top two copies are kept by the retailer, the bottom copy is placed in front of the sales vouchers and any refund vouchers and they are all placed in a clear plastic envelope;

- the vouchers are then paid into the bank by including the total as part of the cheques total on the paying-in slip. The total of the vouchers must also be included in the cheque details on the back of the paying-in slip.

student notes ✍

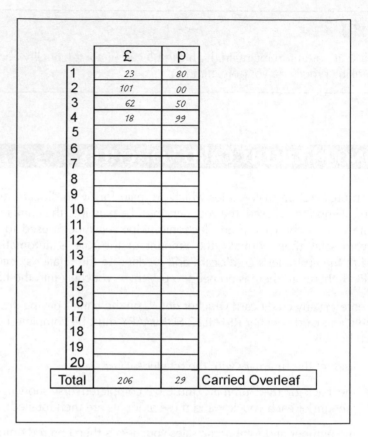

	£	p	
1	23	80	
2	101	00	
3	62	50	
4	18	99	
5			
6			
7			
8			
9			
10			
11			
12			
13			
14			
15			
16			
17			
18			
19			
20			
Total	206	29	Carried Overleaf

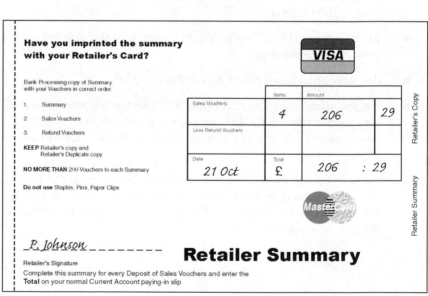

Have you imprinted the summary with your Retailer's Card?

Bank Processing copy of Summary with your Vouchers in correct order.

1. Summary
2. Sales Vouchers
3. Refund Vouchers

KEEP Retailer's copy and Retailer's Duplicate copy

NO MORE THAN 200 Vouchers to each Summary

Do not use Staples, Pins, Paper Clips

VISA

	Items	Amount	
Sales Vouchers	4	206	29
Less Refund Vouchers			
Date 21 Oct	Total £	206	: 29

Retailer's Copy

Retailer Summary

MasterCard

P. Johnson
Retailer's Signature

Complete this summary for every Deposit of Sales Vouchers and enter the **Total** on your normal Current Account paying-in slip

Retailer Summary

BANK STATEMENTS

At regular intervals an organisation's bank will send out a BANK STATEMENT showing movements on the bank account since the date of the last bank statement. A business cheque account which has many payments and receipts may require a weekly bank statement whereas a deposit account with less movement may only warrant a monthly statement.

A typical bank statement for Southfield Electrical is shown below.

There are various points to note about this bank statement:

STATEMENT

first national
30 High Street
Benham
DR4 8TT

SOUTHFIELD ELECTRICAL

Account number: 20-26-33 40268134

CHEQUE ACCOUNT

Sheet 023

Date	Sheet 023	Paid out	Paid in	Balance
2006				
17 Oct	Balance brought forward			2,595.23 CR
18 Oct	Cheque No 003067	424.80		
	Cheque No 003069	122.60		2,047.83 CR
19 Oct	DD Benham District Council	450.00		
	CR Paid in		1,081.23	2,679.06 CR
20 Oct	Cheque No 003073	1,480.20		
	Cheque No 003074	1,865.67		666.81 DR
21 Oct	CR Paid in		1,116.20	449.39 CR
	Balance carried forward			449.39 CR

- each sheet of a bank statement is sequentially numbered so an organisation can tell if any statements are missing.

- after each day's transactions the balance on the account is shown.

- each type of transaction is given a code – CHQ is a cheque being cleared, DD is a direct debit payment (see later chapter), SO is a standing order payment (see later chapter), CR is an amount paid into the account.

- note that on 20 October the account went into an overdraft balance which is denoted by DR standing for Debit.

You may have noticed something strange about the debit and credit terminology on the bank statement. Money paid into the bank account is deemed to be credited and payments are a debit as is an overdraft balance. This is the opposite way round to the way in which debits and credits are treated when writing up the bank account in the organisation's own books – money in is a debit and money out a credit!

The reason for this is that the bank is looking at the accounting from the opposite side to the organisation. To the bank, money paid into the account is an increase in the amount that the bank owes back to the customer eg, the bank's creditor, and cheques paid out of the account decreases the amount of the creditor, the customer.

Activity 3

If money is paid into a bank current account will this appear as a debit or a credit on the bank statement?

CHAPTER OVERVIEW

- banks provide a variety of different types of account that customers can use such as current accounts and deposit accounts

- banks have a duty to pay cheques that customers have correctly drawn up provided that there are enough funds in the customer's account

- banks provide overdraft facilities to customers, credit cards, loans and mortgages

- the clearing system is a system whereby all cheques paid into banks in a day are sorted by bank, swapped between the banks and any differences paid from bank to bank – the system means that it takes three working days for a cheque to clear after being paid into a bank

- the paying-in slip must be completed on both the front and the back

- the back of the paying-in slip should be completed first with details of the cash and cheques being paid in – these totals are then transferred to the front of the paying-in slip and the other details are also filled out

- great care must be taken when taking large amounts of cash to the bank – ideally two people should be taking the money and using different routes at different times of day

- credit card vouchers need to be paid into the bank on a paying-in slip but what is also required is the credit card voucher Retailer's Summary – the back of this should be completed first with the total of each credit card voucher, the final total is then transferred to the front of the summary and it is dated, signed and totalled

- a bank statement will be received regularly from the bank showing the balance at the end of the last bank statement, the movements on the account during the period and the balance on the last day of the statement

- on the bank statement, a credit is money paid into the bank account and a debit is money paid out – an overdraft is also known as a debit balance

KEY WORDS

Current account a bank account designed to have money withdrawn by cheque or other methods on a regular basis

Deposit account an account from which it is not intended to make regular withdrawals – a savings account

Overdraft facility an agreement that the customer can withdraw more money from the account than he has in it up to a certain limit

Credit card a card which allows the customer to purchase goods and services now but gives them flexibility as to when they repay the credit card company

Loan an advance from a bank on which interest will be charged and repayment conditions laid down

Mortgage a long term loan for purchase of a property under which the property serves as security for the loan

Clearing system the system set up by the major banks to deal with the payment of cheques

Paying-in slip a pre-printed document issued by the bank that must be completed each time money is paid into the bank

Retailer summary a pre-printed document that must be filled in on the front and back detailing the credit card vouchers that are being paid into the bank

Bank statement a statement issued on a regular basis by the bank showing the balance at the end of the last bank statement, the movements on the account during the period and the balance at the end of the current period

HOW MUCH HAVE YOU LEARNED?

1   What are the main differences between a current account and a deposit account?

2   What is an overdraft facility?

3   A cheque is written by F Harmer, whose bank is the Winchelsea branch of the First National Bank, to L Bridges, whose bank is the Winchelsea branch of the Northern Bank. Explain what happens to this cheque from when L Bridges pays it into his bank until it actually appears as cleared funds in his bank account.

4   You work for an organisation called Trefold Ltd and are dealing with the amounts to be paid into the bank today, 14 November 2006. The following items are to be banked:

Cash		*Cheques*	
£20 notes	2	£246.27	Hilders Ltd
£10 notes	5	£140.21	Farm Fields Ltd
£5 notes	6	£ 89.36	Gerald & Sons
£1 coins	20		
50p coins	16		
20p coins	25		
10p coins	61		
5p coins	18		
2p coins	24		
1p coins	10		

Complete the paying-in slip given below.

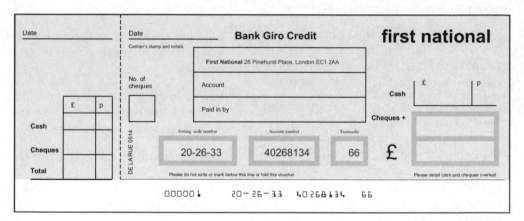

Cash	£	p		Cheques	£	p
£50 notes						
£20 notes						
£10 notes						
£5 notes						
£1 coins						
Other coins						
Total				Total		

5 You are Caroline Waters and you work for Thames Trading. You are required to fill out the credit card voucher Retailer Summary for today's takings. The credit card voucher details from the till for 14 November 2006 are as follows:

H James	£15.90
P Henry	£120.50
J Harrold	£56.75
B Percy	£25.99

Complete the Retailer Summary for the day given below.

	£	p	
1			
2			
3			
4			
5			
6			
7			
8			
9			
10			
11			
12			
13			
14			
15			
16			
17			
18			
19			
20			
Total			Carried Overleaf

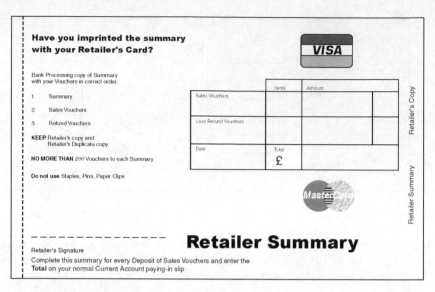

6   On a bank statement would each of the following be described as a debit or a credit entry or balance?

   a)   Money paid into the account
   b)   Cheques paid out of the account
   c)   An overdraft balance

chapter 8:
COMMUNICATION WITH CUSTOMERS

chapter coverage 📖

In the chapters so far in this Course Companion we have considered the operating cycle for sales on credit. This began with the ordering of the goods and their despatch and invoicing. We then considered the accounting procedures for and recording of credit sales. The income from sales was then considered, including the checks that should be made when money is received, the recording of receipts and the paying-in of monies to the bank. In this final chapter covering the Unit 1 performance criteria, we shall consider communication with the credit customers. The topics that are covered are:

✍ statements of account for customers

✍ credit control

✍ aged debtor analysis

✍ writing letters to customers

✍ writing a business letter in general

KNOWLEDGE AND UNDERSTANDING AND PERFORMANCE CRITERIA COVERAGE

Unit 1

knowledge and understanding – the business environment

9   credit limits

knowledge and understanding – the organisation

22   relevant understanding of the organisation's accounting systems and administrative systems and procedures

26   house style for correspondence

Performance criteria – element 1.1

F   produce statements of account for despatch to debtors

G   communicate politely and effectively with customers regarding accounts, using the relevant information from the aged debtors analysis

STATEMENTS OF ACCOUNT

It is common practice for a business to send out a reminder to customers of the amount owing on a regular, normally monthly, basis, in order to encourage payment. This reminder is usually in the form of a STATEMENT OF ACCOUNT. This shows the invoices sent out during the past month, any credit notes issued and any payments received from the customer during the month.

The statement will be prepared from the customer's account in the subsidiary (sales) ledger using all of the information that it contains. As with all the procedures we have seen so far, it can be done manually, or the statements can form part of the computer output.

HOW IT WORKS

Southfield Electrical has a policy of sending out statements to customers just after the end of each month showing how much was owing at the month end. The statement for Hilldon Sales Centre is currently being produced for the month ending 31 October 2006.

The sales ledger account for Hilldon Sales Centre has been accessed from the filing system and is shown below:

Hilldon Sales Centre		SL06	
	£		£
1 Oct Balance b/d	156.35	8 Oct SDB – CN2401	57.29
4 Oct SDB – 30253	147.35	15 Oct CRB	150.10
12 Oct SDB – 30287	117.46	15 Oct CRB – discount	6.25
21 Oct SDB – 30314	231.68	25 Oct SDB – CN2426	94.52
29 Oct SDB – 30361	169.35		

Step 1 Find the closing balance on this account at 31 October as this should agree with the final balance on the statement of account.

Hilldon Sales Centre		SL06	
	£		£
1 Oct Balance b/d	156.35	8 Oct SDB – CN2401	57.29
4 Oct SDB – 30253	147.35	15 Oct CRB	150.10
12 Oct SDB – 30287	117.46	15 Oct CRB – discount	6.25
21 Oct SDB – 30314	231.68	25 Oct SDB – CN2426	94.52
29 Oct SDB – 30361	169.35		
		31 Oct Balance c/d	514.03
	822.19		822.19

Step 2 Summarise these details on the pre-printed statement of account remembering to calculate a running balance after each entry has been shown.

STATEMENT

Southfield Electrical
Industrial Estate
Benham DR6 2FF
Tel 0308379 Fax 0303162
VAT Reg 0264 2274 49

To: Hilden Sales Centre

Account number: SL 06

Date: 31 Oct 2006

Date	Details	Debit	Credit	Balance
1 Oct	Balance b/d			156.35
4 Oct	Inv 30253	147.35		303.70
8 Oct	CN 2401		57.29	246.41
12 Oct	Inv 30287	117.46		363.87
15 Oct	Payment – thank you		150.10	
	Discount		6.25	207.52
21 Oct	Inv 30314	231.68		439.20
25 Oct	CN 2426		94.52	344.68
29 Oct	Inv 30361	169.35		514.03

Amount now due £514.03

Step 3 Send the statement out to the customer promptly.

Some statements of account include a remittance advice on the bottom of the statement that can be torn off by the customer and sent with their cheque. Other organisations will send two copies of the statement with a request that one is returned with the payment showing precisely which invoices (less credit notes) are being paid.

Activity 1

What is the purpose of sending a statement to a credit customer?

SLOW PAYMENT OF AMOUNTS DUE

Despite a policy of sending out regular statements to credit customers it will frequently be the case that some customers have large or longstanding balances outstanding. If credit customers take a long while to send your organisation the monies due, this will adversely affect the cash flow of the organisation. Therefore CREDIT CONTROL is an extremely important part of selling on credit.

Credit control begins when a new customer wishes to be allowed credit for their purchases. Thorough checks should be made on the customer's credit worthiness and references should be requested and followed up from the customer's bank and other traders with whom he trades on credit.

If the references are satisfactory then the next element of credit control is to set a CREDIT LIMIT for this customer. The credit limit is the maximum amount that should be owing from this customer at any point in time. Credit control is an on-going process and credit limits should generally not be exceeded. If a customer wishes to purchase more goods on credit then the amount currently outstanding should be compared to the credit limit. If the purchase would take the customer over the credit limit then authorisation for this sale must be sought from the appropriate person, which may involve a review and alteration of the customer's credit limit.

A further important part of credit control is the review of how long amounts have been outstanding from debtors. This is normally done by regularly reviewing the AGED DEBTOR ANALYSIS. This is a schedule showing, for each debtor, how long their balances have been outstanding. For Unit 1 you do not need to be able to prepare an aged debtor analysis, simply to understand how to use one.

HOW IT WORKS

Given below is an extract from the aged debtor analysis for Southfield Electrical at 31 October 2006.

```
                          AGED DEBTOR ANALYSIS

Date:   31 October 2006

Account Account         Credit  Balance  Current  > 30 days > 60 days > 90 days
number   name           limit      £        £         £         £         £
                          £
SL03    Polygon Stores 5,000.00 2,593.29 2,593.29    0.00      0.00      0.00
SL15    Dagwell Ent    2,000.00 2,254.67 1,356.26  898.41      0.00      0.00
SL18    Weller Ent     3,000.00 2,154.72 1,118.36  637.28    399.08      0.00
SL30    G Thomas & Co  6,000.00 3,425.47 3,116.35    0.00      0.00    309.12

                                10,428.15 8,184.26 1,535.69  399.08    309.12
```

The aged debtor analysis can be used to decide whether any action needs to be taken with each of these customers.

Polygon Stores – the entire balance is current which shows that Polygon are regular payers of the amounts due within the stated 30 day credit period.

Dagwell Enterprises – the balance owing from Dagwell is in excess of the credit limit and this might therefore need to be reviewed. Although most of the debt is current there is a large amount of £898.41 which has been outstanding for more than 30 days. It may be that Dagwell always pays in this manner or, if not, the 30 day plus amount might need to be investigated and a telephone call made or letter sent to Dagwell Enterprises.

Weller Enterprises – some of this balance is more than 60 days old and some more than 30 days old as well as the current element. The credit controller may decide that it is necessary to write to Weller Enterprises encouraging earlier payment.

G Thomas & Co – the vast majority of this balance is current with only a fairly small amount more than 90 days old. This old debt should be investigated as there may be a problem with this invoice or goods – perhaps G Thomas & Co returned these goods and are awaiting a credit note.

Activity 2

What is the purpose of an aged debtor analysis?

COMMUNICATION WITH CREDIT CUSTOMERS

The customers of an organisation are among its most vital assets, therefore it is important to remember that whenever dealing with customers, face to face, over the telephone or in writing, you should be polite and courteous. Having said this, if there is a problem with a customer then this must be dealt with effectively and firmly. This is often a difficult balance to achieve!

There are two main situations in which you might be expected to communicate directly with credit customers – when dealing with queries and when chasing payment. We will consider the general approach to take in each situation.

HOW IT WORKS

Some typical examples of queries that might need to be sorted out will be given and possible approaches considered.

Southfield's policy is that any error of less than £50 discovered on payments being received is adjusted for on the next statement and a telephone call is made to the customer to explain the problem. For amounts exceeding £50, a letter is sent to the customer explaining the situation and if further payment is required then this is requested in the letter.

Suppose that one of Southfield's customers, QQ Stores, has sent a payment and related remittance advice but the invoices being paid were incorrectly totalled and the cheque sent was for £200 less than the total of the invoices being paid. In this situation a letter must be written to QQ Stores – an example of the possible wording is given below.

Dear Sir

Underpayment of amount due

Thank you for your recent payment of £640.65. The payment however was incorrectly calculated and should have totalled £840.65. We enclose a statement showing how this figure was arrived at and would be grateful if the difference could be settled by return of post.

Another of Southfield's customers, G Bender & Sons, has sent a recent payment but the settlement discount that was deducted was invalid as the payment was received 15 days after the invoice date rather than the 10 days required for the discount to apply. The amount of the discount was £16.54.

In this case a polite telephone call should be made to the accounts department of G Bender & Sons explaining that the discount should not have been deducted and that the amount of £16.54 will be reinstated as owing on the next statement that is sent out.

Now suppose that it has been decided to chase payment from Weller Enterprises for the amount owing for more than 60 days shown on the aged debtor analysis, £399.08.

- The initial approach should be a polite letter requesting payment of this amount:

Dear Sir

Overdue account

It would appear from our records that an amount of £399.08 has been owing from you for more than 60 days. We have enclosed a current statement showing all amounts outstanding and would be grateful if this amount can be settled by return of post.

- If nothing is heard from the customer within say 7 days then a telephone call should be made to the accounts department. This should always be polite as there may well be a legitimate reason for the delay such as a dispute over the goods. However also be prepared for excuses such as "the cheque is in the post" which may simply be a method of playing for more time.

- The telephone reminder may be enough and payment is received. However if not, then a further, more strongly worded letter may be necessary:

Dear Sir

Overdue account

Further to our letter of 5 November and telephone call of 12 November we have still not received settlement of the £399.08 outstanding on your account for more than two months. If payment is not received within 7 days then this matter will be put into the hands of our solicitors.

- The threat of using a solicitor to send a formal demand for payment may now work – if not then there is an option to take the customer to court to obtain payment but as this is an expensive option then such decisions will be made at a high management level.

Activity 3

What are the key behavioural elements to consider when dealing with customers?

student notes✍

WRITING A BUSINESS LETTER

Most organisations will have a house style for letters and often a number of letters for specific purposes, such as chasing payment, will have a standard house wording. However you do need to appreciate the main elements of good business letter writing style.

The complete letter initially requesting payment from Weller Enterprises shown above will now be reproduced together with explanations of the key elements of the letter.

Letterhead

SOUTHFIELD ELECTRICAL
INDUSTRIAL ESTATE
BENHAM DR6 2FF
Tel 0303379 Fax 0303152
VAT Reg 02642274 49

Date

5 November 2006

References

Our ref: SH/RC/18

Recipient details

Purchase ledger manager
Weller Enterprises
Booker House
Industrial Estate
Benham DR6 2FH

Greeting

Dear Sir

Heading

Overdue account

Body of the letter

It would appear from our records that an amount of £399.08 has been owing from you for more than 60 days. We have enclosed a current statement showing all amounts outstanding and would be grateful if this amount can be settled by return of post.

We look forward to receiving your cheque.

Signing off

Yours faithfully

Simon Harris

Name
Title

Simon Harris
Credit control manager

Enclosure indicator

enc

Letterhead – this will normally be on standard pre-printed stationery showing the name, address and other relevant details of the organisation sending the letter.

Date – this is normally shown as in this letter – day, month then year.

Reference – this is the reference of the person sending the letter – in this case made up of the initials of the writer of the letter, Simon Harris, his secretary, Rita Cullen and the customer's sales ledger reference, 18. If replying to a letter then it is usual to also include 'Your reference' being the reference on the original letter received.

Recipient – it is usual to include here the name or title of the recipient plus the full postal address.

Greeting – if the name of the person is known then this should be used eg, Mr Grainger, Miss Temple etc – otherwise Sir or Madam.

Heading – a letter should always be given a heading in order to forewarn the reader of the content of the letter.

Body of the letter – the general rules for writing a good business letter are:

- use short, succinct sentences and paragraphs;

- set out the message of the letter in a logical manner;

- avoid use of technical jargon or slang;

- ensure the letter ends with a clear indication of what should happen next.

Signing off – the manner of signing off a letter will depend upon how it began:

- Dear Sir/ Dear Madam – Yours faithfully

- Dear Mr Grainger/ Dear Miss Temple – Yours sincerely

Name – the writer of the letter should sign the letter but also show his name underneath the signature.

Title – the reader of the letter should know the job title of the person sending it for any reply that is necessary.

Enclosure indicator – if anything is to be sent with the letter, in this case a statement, then this must be indicated by the abbreviation for enclosures.

CHAPTER OVERVIEW

- statements of account are normally sent out to credit customers monthly to inform them of the amount due – this will often include a tear off remittance advice designed to accompany the subsequent payment

- statements are prepared using the detailed information taken from the subsidiary (sales) ledger account for the customer

- the importance of credit control cannot be overstated

- when a new customer makes a purchase on credit, references must be sought, a credit limit set and then regular review of the account balance and movement

- an aged debtor analysis shows the breakdown of the amount owing by each customer according to the time the debt has been outstanding

- communication with customers should always be polite and courteous but at the same time firm and effective

- letters may be written to customers regarding queries on their account such as incorrect payments received, or to chase late payment of amounts due

- a business letter will be set out in the house style of the organisation but should have a number of important features

KEY WORDS

Statement of account a regular statement sent out to credit customers showing the invoices, credit notes and payments received during the period and a final closing balance or amount due

Credit control a system of monitoring credit customers' balances and accounts to ensure that credit limits are not exceeded and overdue accounts are chased

Credit limit the maximum amount that should be outstanding on a particular debtor's account

Aged debtor analysis an analysis of individual debtor balances according to how long they have been outstanding

HOW MUCH HAVE YOU LEARNED?

1   Given below is the sales ledger account for a customer of your organisation, Thames Trading. You are required to prepare a statement of account to be sent to this customer as at 31 October on the blank statement given below.

Middlesex Corporation			SL 23
	£		£
1 Oct Balance b/f	146.79	12 October – CN10046	56.89
7 Oct SDB – 10145	224.67	28 Oct CRB	298.84
15 Oct SDB – 10167	127.69	28 Oct CRB – discount	15.73
25 Oct SDB – 10180	201.84	31 Oct Balance c/f	329.53
	700.99		700.99

STATEMENT

Thames Trading
13 Putney Bridge
London SW14 3NT
Tel 0207 891 445 Fax 0207 891 446

To:

Account number:

Date:

Date	Details	Debit	Credit	Balance

Amount now due

2   Briefly explain the main elements involved in the process of credit control in an organisation.

3   Given below is an extract from an aged debtor analysis for an organisation. State any concerns that you might have about any of these credit customers, having studied the analysis.

AGED DEBTOR ANALYSIS

Date: 31 October 2006

Account number	Account name	Credit limit £	Balance £	Current £	> 30 days £	> 60 days £	> 90 days £
SL15	H Davids	1,000.00	879.46	761.46	0.00	118.00	0.00
SL27	E Craig	2,000.00	2,356.78	2,356.78	0.00	0.00	0.00
SL33	P Fisher	1,000.00	661.58	661.58	0.00	0.00	0.00
SL40	K Olsen	1,000.00	825.68	110.56	226.70	346.20	142.22
SL47	A Evans	2,000.00	506.37	0.00	0.00	0.00	506.37
			5,229.87	3,890.38	226.70	464.20	648.59

4   A customer of your organisation has an invoice that has been due for payment which was dated 15 August 2006, invoice number 20446 for a total of £358.39 . Today's date is 14 November and your department manager has asked you to draft a letter to this customer, G H Perkins on the pre-printed letterhead given below. You are Francis Hughes, credit controller and the reference for this letter is FH/TG/23.

THAMES TRADING
13 PUTNEY BRIDGE
LONDON SW14 3NT
Tel 0207 891445 Fax 0207 891446

chapter 9:
BUSINESS DOCUMENTS – PURCHASES

Unit 2

knowledge and understanding – the business environment

1 payment transactions including associated documentation
4 general principles of VAT regarding payments
5 types of discounts available from suppliers
8 different ordering systems: internet, verbal and written

knowledge and understanding – accounting methods

14 methods of coding data

knowledge and understanding – the organisation

24 relevant understanding of the organisation's accounting systems and administrative systems and procedures

25 the nature of the organisation's business transactions

26 organisational procedures for authorisation and coding of purchase invoices

28 organisational procedures for filing source information

Performance criteria – element 2.1

A check suppliers' invoices and credit notes against relevant documents for validity

B check calculations on suppliers' invoices and credit notes for accuracy

C identify and deduct available discounts

D correctly code invoices and credit notes

G identify discrepancies and either resolve or refer to the appropriate person if outside own authority

ORDERING THE GOODS

We have seen how the business document cycle works when looking at life from the viewpoint of the seller of goods. Now we will look at it in more detail from the purchaser's side.

The initial stage is that of ordering the goods. This can be done in a variety of different ways:

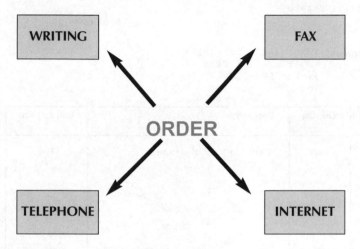

In writing

Perhaps still the most common way of ordering goods is in writing. This could be in the form of a letter but if many orders are placed with suppliers then it is more likely that the organisation will have pre-printed and sequentially numbered purchase order forms.

The PURCHASE ORDER used in an earlier chapter is given again below:

PURCHASE ORDER

WHITEHILL SUPERSTORES
28 Whitehill Park
Benham DR6 5LM
Tel 0303446 Fax 0303447

To: Southfield Electrical
Industrial Estate
Benham
DR6 2FF

Number: 32011

Date: 5 Sept 2006

Delivery address: Whitehill Superstores
28, Whitehill Park
Benham DR6 5LM

Product code	Quantity	Description	Unit list price £
4425	6	Zanpoint Dishwasher	200 (excluding VAT)

Authorised by: *P. Winterbottom* **Date:** *5 Sept 2006*

The purchase order is from Whitehill Superstores to Southfield Electrical and details the quantity, the specific item and the agreed price. The important issue from Whitehill's side is that it is properly authorised. Obviously it is necessary for any business to ensure that only goods that are absolutely necessary are purchased, and therefore there should be strict controls over who can authorise purchase orders.

By fax

The purchase order can be sent out by post or by fax but it is important that the accounts department keeps at least one copy of it for future reference.

Over the telephone

It is also possible to order goods by telephone. This is often the case where either the purchaser and seller are well known to each other or the purchases are of small quantities. If an order is placed over the telephone the most important issue is that a record is kept of what has been agreed in case of dispute in future. The purchaser might request from the seller a confirmation of the order that has been placed, or at the very least make a file note of the price and any other terms agreed over the telephone.

On the Internet

Finally, an increasingly popular method of purchasing goods is over the Internet. This should only be undertaken if it is an allowed method of ordering goods according to your organisation's policy manual, and if it has been authorised by an appropriate member of senior staff. Care should be taken with the choice of provider of the goods:

- preferably use a well-known, reputable seller;

- if the seller is unknown, at the very least ensure that they have a telephone number that can be called in order to check their authenticity.

When placing an order ensure that a copy is printed out to be placed on file.

Order details

Whatever method of ordering is used, it is important to ensure that a copy of the details of the order is kept in the filing system in the accounts department. Eventually this must be compared to the delivery note and sales invoice to ensure that only goods that have been properly authorised for ordering are received and paid for.

Activity 1

What must you check before placing an order on the Internet?

RECEIVING GOODS

Once the goods have been ordered, the next stage in the process is that they will be received. This will usually take place in the stores department or warehouse and an important part of the process takes place here.

When the goods arrive they will normally be accompanied by a delivery note. The DELIVERY NOTE used in an earlier chapter for the delivery from Southfield to Whitehill is reproduced below:

DELIVERY NOTE

Southfield Electrical
Industrial Estate
Benham DR6 2FF
Tel 0303379 Fax 0303152

Delivery address:

Whitehill Superstores
28, Whitehill Park
Benham DR6 5LM

Number: 34619

Date: 6 Sept 2006

Order number: 32011

Product code	Quantity	Description
4425	6	Zanpoint Dishwasher

Received by: [Signature] ....   **Print name:** ....

Date: ....

- this details the quantity and precise description of the goods using both the description in words and the stock code;
- there is no price as this is not relevant in the stores department;
- the delivery note will normally include the related purchase order number;
- the delivery note must be signed to evidence the fact that these goods have been delivered.

The signature of the stores personnel is extremely important. It proves that the carrier of the goods did indeed deliver these goods and that the purchaser actually received them.

The most important point that the stores personnel must check is that the quantity that has actually been delivered is that stated on the delivery note. In some cases it may be possible to check that none of the goods have any defects at the time of delivery but normally this will take place later. The initial signature from the stores manager on this delivery note is simply evidence that this number of these precise goods was delivered on this date.

student notes✐

GOODS RECEIVED NOTE

In many organisations, in addition to signing the delivery note, an internal document will also be filled out by the stores department. This is known as the GOODS RECEIVED NOTE. This is completed once there has been opportunity to examine the goods in more detail. A goods received note for the delivery to Whitehill from Southfield is shown below:

GOODS RECEIVED NOTE

Supplier: Southfield Electrical

GRN number:	47361
Date:	6 Sept 2006
Order number:	32011
Delivery Note No:	34619

Quantity	Description	Stock code
6	Zanpoint Dishwasher	4425

Received by: *L Daniels*

Checked by: *D Richards*

Comments: *1 damaged item. Dent in front door panel*

Note the main points:

- the goods received note (GRN) has its own sequential number;

- it is also referenced to the order number and delivery note number, both taken from the copy of the delivery note kept by the stores department;

- the quantity and precise detail of the goods received is noted;

- in order to ensure the security of the goods being received, the GRN is not signed by only one person but the goods are checked and signed by a second person;

- once there has been a chance to examine the goods in detail, any comments on their condition can then be added to the GRN. Note that in this case one of the machines is damaged and this has been noted.

Accounts department

Once the stores department have dealt with the checking of the goods all of the documentation is then passed over to the accounts department. At this stage the accounts department potentially have a purchase quotation, a purchase order, a delivery note and a goods received note.

The accounts department must check that the delivery note agrees to the purchase order so as to ensure that what was ordered has actually arrived. The details should then be compared with the goods received note to ensure that the goods that were actually delivered were of the correct quality and condition.

Debit notes

If on inspection the goods that have been supplied are not of the quality or in the condition expected they will be returned to the seller. Often the return of the goods will be accompanied by a DEBIT NOTE. This is a note detailing the goods returned and the reason for their return. The purpose of a debit note is formally to request a credit note from the supplier of the goods. A debit note from Whitehill to Southfield for the damaged item is shown below:

DEBIT NOTE

WHITEHILL SUPERSTORES
28 Whitehill Park
Benham DR6 5LM
Tel 0303446 Fax 0303447

To:	Southfield Electrical
	Industrial Estate
	Benham
	DR6 2FF

Debit note number: 0466
Date/tax point: 8 Sept 2006
Order number 32011
Delivery note number: 34619

Quantity	Description	Stock code	Unit amount £	Total £
1	Zanpoint Dishwasher	4425	200	200.00

Net total	200.00
VAT	35.00
Gross total	235.00

Reason: *Goods damaged. Dent in front door panel*

Authorised by: *N Jones*
Stores manager

Date: *7 Sept 2006*

- the debit note has a unique, sequential number;

- it shows the details of the goods returned ie, quantity, description and stock number;

- it also shows the price that was shown on the purchase order so that there is no disagreement concerning the price;

- most importantly, the reason for the return is shown and the return is authorised by a responsible official.

Activity 2

Is a debit note from the buyer or the seller?

RECEIVING THE INVOICE

The next item in the purchase cycle is the receipt of the INVOICE. This is the document that will eventually form the authorisation for payment of the amount due to the seller. Many checks must be carried out on this invoice before it is authorised for payment.

Step 1   Have the goods been received? First, the details of the invoice must be agreed to the purchase order, the delivery note and the goods received note. Do they all agree that the amount that was delivered of the correct quality is also the amount that was invoiced? In the scenario of Whitehill and Southfield the following invoice is received from Southfield:

INVOICE

Southfield Electrical
Industrial Estate
Benham DR6 2FF
Tel 0303379 Fax 0303152
VAT Reg 0264 2274 49

To: Whitehill Superstores
28, Whitehill Park
Benham DR6 5LM

Invoice number: 56314

Date/tax point: 7 Sept 2006

Order number: 32011

Account number: SL 44

Quantity	Description	Stock code	Unit amount £	Total £
6	Zanpoint Dishwasher	4425	200	1,200.00

Net total	1,200.00
VAT @ 17S%	210.00
Invoice total	1,410.00

Terms
Net 30 days
E & OE

This invoice is for the 6 dishwashers delivered although only 5 were of the acceptable quality. The delivery note shows that 6 dishwashers were delivered but the goods received note indicates that one was not of acceptable quality.

The accounts department would check that a debit note had been sent when the damaged dishwasher was returned and would not pay the invoice until the related credit note was received.

The CREDIT NOTE does then arrive and again is checked to the file of documentation on this purchase which now consists of (potentially):

- purchase quotation
- purchase order
- delivery note
- goods received note
- invoice

CREDIT NOTE

SOUTHFIELD ELECTRICAL
INDUSTRIAL ESTATE
Benham DR6 2FF
Tel 0303379 Fax 0303152
VAT Reg 0264 2274 49

Invoice to:

Whitehill Superstores
28, Whitehill Park
Benham DR6 5LM

Credit note number:	08641
Date/tax point:	12 Sept 2006
Order number	32011
Account number:	SL 44

Quantity	Description	Stock code	Unit amount	Total
			£	£
1	Zanpoint Dishwasher	4425	200.00	200.00

Net total	200.00
VAT	35.00
Gross total	235.00

Reason for credit note:

Damaged goods

The credit note will then be attached to the invoice and they will be passed for payment together.

DISCOUNTS AND VAT

<u>Step 2</u>   Are the calculations correct?

The invoice and credit note considered so far have been very uncomplicated. However when trade discounts and settlement discounts are introduced the checks that have to be made become more involved.

Given below is a more realistic invoice from Southfield Electrical to Whitehill Superstores:

INVOICE

Southfield Electrical
Industrial Estate
Benham DR6 2FF
Tel 0303379 Fax 0303152
VAT Reg 0264 2274 49

To: Whitehill Superstores
28, Whitehill Park
Benham DR6 5LM

Invoice number: 56483

Date/tax point: 8 Oct 2006

Order number: 32174

Account number: SL 44

Quantity	Description	Stock code	Unit amount £	Total £
4	Hosch Washing Machine	6160	300.00	1,200.00
9	Temax Mixer	3172	40.00	360.00
				1,560.00
Less:	10% discount			156.00

Net total	1,404.00
VAT @ 17½%	235.87
Invoice total	1,639.87

Terms
4% discount for settlement within 10 days of invoice date, otherwise 30 days net
E & OE
Carriage Paid

HOW IT WORKS

The checks that should be made on this invoice are as follows:

- compare the purchase order, delivery note and goods received note to the invoice to ensure that the correct quantity has been invoiced (this was covered earlier in the chapter);

- check that the unit prices are correct – this may be checked from a purchase quotation or from the price list or catalogue of the seller;

- check that the total price for each item has been correctly calculated by multiplying the unit price by the quantity eg, 4 x £300 = £1,200;

- check that the total of the goods price has been correctly added up eg, £1,200 + £360.00 = £1,560.00;

- check that the trade discount has been correctly calculated eg, £1,560 x 10/100 = £156. You should also check the suppliers' file to ensure that the correct trade discount has been deducted;

- check that the VAT is correct – remember that when a settlement discount is offered the VAT is calculated on the basis that the discount is actually taken:

	£
eg, net total	1,404.00
Less: settlement discount (£1,404.00 x 4/100)	56.16
	1,347.84
VAT £1,347.84 x 17.5/100.00	235.87

- check that the VAT has been correctly added to the net total eg, £1,404.00 + £235.87 = £1,639.87.

SUMMARY OF INVOICE CHECKS

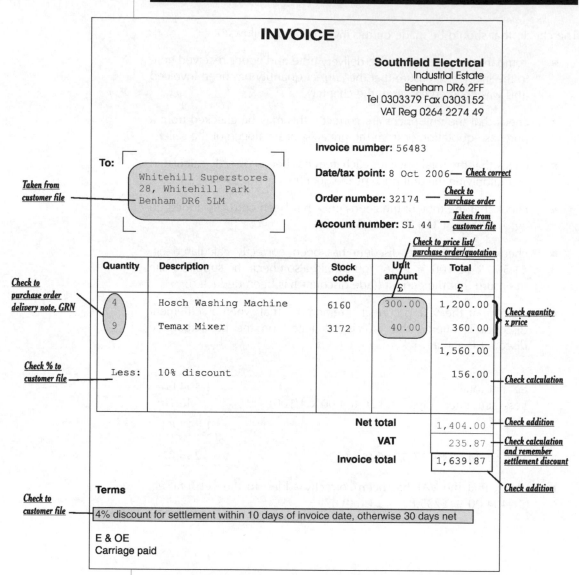

INVOICE

Southfield Electrical
Industrial Estate
Benham DR6 2FF
Tel 0303379 Fax 0303152
VAT Reg 0264 2274 49

To:

Whitehill Superstores
28, Whitehill Park
Benham DR6 5LM

Taken from customer file

Invoice number: 56483

Date/tax point: 8 Oct 2006 — *Check correct*

Order number: 32174 — *Check to purchase order*

Account number: SL 44 — *Taken from customer file*

Check to price list/purchase order/quotation

Quantity	Description	Stock code	Unit amount £	Total £
4	Hosch Washing Machine	6160	300.00	1,200.00
9	Temax Mixer	3172	40.00	360.00
				1,560.00
Less:	10% discount			156.00

Check to purchase order delivery note, GRN

Check quantity x price

Check % to customer file

Check calculation

Net total	1,404.00
VAT	235.87
Invoice total	1,639.87

Check addition

Check calculation and remember settlement discount

Check addition

Terms

Check to customer file

4% discount for settlement within 10 days of invoice date, otherwise 30 days net

E & OE
Carriage paid

Activity 3

The net total of goods purchased from a supplier is £1,478.60 and the supplier has offered a settlement discount of 5%. What is the correct amount of VAT to be charged on the invoice?

Bulk discounts

We have already come across trade discounts and settlement discounts. There is however potentially one other type of discount, the BULK DISCOUNT. This may be given by some suppliers if the purchase is for a large quantity. For example the normal list price for an item may be £18.00 per unit but if an order is placed for 400 or more of this item then the seller offers them at a price of £17.00 per unit.

Any such bulk discount should be documented on the purchase order and when the invoice is received it should be checked to ensure that the bulk discount price has been charged and not the normal list price.

Checking credit notes

When a credit note is received the same checks should be made as are made on the invoice. The credit note is reducing the amount that your organisation has to pay and therefore it is important that this is accurate and correct. Therefore all figures, calculations and additions should be checked in the same way as with the invoice.

Services received

One of the initial checks on goods is that they are actually received . This will be evidenced by a delivery note or goods received note. However with services there will not tend to be any physical goods.

However it is also important to check that the services that have been invoiced have been received. Typical invoices for services might include utilities such as electricity, gas and telephone bills. Such bills can usually be checked to meter readings and for reasonableness, for example each organisation should have an idea of the normal value of the telephone bill and therefore if a very different amount is billed then this should be investigated.

Other services that might be invoiced are items like cleaning contractors. There should be evidence of the hours that have been worked and billed, such as clock cards or time sheets. Alternatively service-providers such as the cleaning contractors or annual auditors may have already agreed a fee, so the documentation for that agreement should be checked upon receipt of the invoice.

AUTHORISATION OF INVOICES

When the accuracy of an invoice has been thoroughly checked then it is ready for payment at the appropriate time and will be passed to the person in the Accounts department who is responsible for making payments (this area will be dealt with in a later chapter).

There must be some evidence to show that the invoice has been checked and is therefore correct and authorised for payment. Each organisation will have different methods of indicating that an invoice has been checked and authorised. Some examples are given:

- the simplest method is for the invoice to be stamped or marked "pay" and signed by the checker;

- a more detailed method might be to stamp the invoice with a standard check list or attach such a checklist to the invoice to be marked off as each check is carried out.

Such a stamp or checklist might look like this:

INVOICE AUTHORISATION		
	Initials	**Date**
Checked to order		
Checked to delivery note/GRN		
Unit price checked		
Total price checked		
VAT checked		
Authorised by:	**Date:**	

Settlement discounts

Some authorisation stamps may also include space for the amount of any settlement discount that can be deducted. This should be calculated when checking the invoice and entered in this space.

The discount that can be deducted is the relevant percentage of the net total of goods, as the VAT calculation should have already taken the settlement discount into account.

An extract from an invoice where a 5% settlement discount has been offered is given:

	£
Net total of goods	1,427.63
VAT	237.34
Invoice total	1,664.97

The amount of settlement discount that could be deducted from the invoice total is 5% of the net total calculated as follows:

£1,427.63 x 5/100 = £71.38

This amount can then be entered onto the authorisation stamp and the payer can then decide whether or not to pay the invoice in time to claim the discount. Alternatively it might be the policy of the organisation that the discount is not calculated until the person responsible for paying the invoice deals with it.

Activity 4

An invoice for goods shows the net total of the goods as £650.30 and the VAT as £110.38 giving a gross total of £760.68. A settlement discount of 3% is offered. How much discount can be deducted?

Coding of invoices

The authorisation stamp or sheet may also have space for entries to be made to code the purchase invoice. The invoice will eventually have to be entered into the accounting records and the main codes that might be included on the authorisation stamp would be:

- a code for the particular supplier, probably his purchase ledger account number (see next chapter for more detail);

- a code for the type of goods or service that is being invoiced in order to aid recording in the accounting records.

SUPPLIERS' STATEMENTS

The final document that might be received by a buyer of goods from the seller is a statement of account. As we have already seen from the seller's side, this is produced by the seller of the goods on a regular basis and sent out to the buyer.

On receipt of a statement of account this should be checked for accuracy to the individual supplier's account in the subsidiary ledger, the purchases ledger (this will be dealt with in more detail in a later chapter).

In many cases a statement may include a tear off REMITTANCE ADVICE at the bottom which allows you to show which invoices from the statement are being paid. The remittance advice would then be returned to the supplier together with the payment.

A typical statement and remittance advice is shown below:

STATEMENT

Southfield Electrical
Industrial Estate
Benham DR6 2FF
Tel 0303379 Fax 0303152
VAT Reg 0264 2274 49

To: Whitehill Superstores
28, Whitehill Park
Benham
DR6 5LM

Account number: SL 44

Date: 31 Oct 2006

Date	Details	Debit	Credit	Balance
01.10.03	Balance b/f	1,483.29		1,483.29
02.10.03	Inv 56389	2,140.16		3,623.45
15.10.03	Inv 56436	1,118.23		4,741.68
18.10.03	CN 08662		123.80	4,617.88
28.10.03	Payment received		1,483.29	3,134.59

Amount now due	£3,134.59

REMITTANCE ADVICE

To: Southfield Electrical
Industrial Estate
Benham DR6 2FF

From: Whitehill Superstores
28 Whitehill Park
Benham DR6 5LM

Account no: SL 44

Please indicate items you are paying (✓) and
return with your cheque.

Detail	Debit	Credit	(✓)
Inv 56389	2,140.16		
Inv 56436	1,118.23		
CN 08662		123.80	

Cheque enclosed £

CHAPTER OVERVIEW

- the main methods of ordering goods are in writing, by fax, over the telephone and over the Internet

- whatever method of ordering is used, there must be some form of evidence of the goods ordered as this will be needed later when the goods and then the invoice are received

- when the goods are received they will normally be accompanied by a delivery note which must be checked and signed as evidence that the stated quantity of goods was delivered

- on receipt of goods many organisations complete an internal document, the goods received note, detailing the quantity and condition of the goods received

- the accounts department opens a file for each purchase which will include the purchase quotation, the purchase order, the delivery note and the goods received note

- if goods have to be returned to the supplier a debit note may be issued, formally requesting a credit note from the supplier for the returned goods

- when the invoice is received it must first be checked to the purchase order to ensure that the goods were ordered and to the delivery note and GRN to ensure that they were received

- when any related credit note is received then this should be filed with the invoice awaiting payment

- all of the calculations on a supplier's invoice should be checked including the deduction of trade discount, any bulk discount, the calculation of total price from quantity and unit price, the additions and the VAT calculation

- credit notes received should be checked in exactly the same manner

- when invoices for services are received there will be no delivery note or GRN but evidence must be sought that the service has been provided and that the amount charged is reasonable or the agreed amount

KEY WORDS

Purchase order the written document sent from the buyer to the seller detailing the goods that are being ordered and the agreed price

Delivery note the document sent by the seller with the goods detailing which goods, and in what quantities, are being sent

Goods received note an internal document completed by the buyer on receipt of the goods showing the quantity and condition of the goods received

Debit note a document sent by the buyer to the seller when returning goods to request a credit note for the goods returned

Invoice the document sent by the seller to the buyer requesting payment for the goods

Credit note the document sent by the seller to the buyer showing the amount that can be deducted from the related invoice for the goods that have been returned

Bulk discount a reduction from the list price given by a supplier if an order is placed for a large quantity of an item

Remittance advice a document often attached to any statement received from the supplier designed to be returned with any payment made, showing details of the invoices being paid

CHAPTER OVERVIEW cont.

- when all of the checks have been carried out and it has been determined that the invoice is correct then it must be authorised and passed for payment

- at this point it may be the organisation's policy for the amount of any settlement discount offered to be calculated – this is the given percentage of the net total of the invoice

- the invoice will probably be coded at this stage to indicate the supplier and the type of goods or services

- at regular intervals it is likely that the organisation may receive statements from suppliers showing the amount currently due – this may include a tear-off remittance advice which should be returned with the payment indicating which invoices have been paid

HOW MUCH HAVE YOU LEARNED?

1   Which type of document would be used for the following purposes?

a)   to accompany goods being returned to a supplier
b)   to record for internal purposes the quantity of goods received
c)   to request payment from a purchaser of goods
d)   to order goods from a supplier
e)   to accompany payment to a supplier

2   Explain the importance of the signature on a purchase order.

3   What is the main problem with placing an order for goods over the telephone and how can this be overcome?

4   Given below is an invoice received by Whitehill Superstores. You are also given the related purchase order, delivery note and GRN. You are required to check the invoice thoroughly and note any problems that you discover.

GOODS RECEIVED NOTE

Supplier: Southfield Electrical

GRN number: 47422
Date: 16 Sept 2006
Order number: 32103
Delivery Note No: 34660

Quantity	Description	Stock code
10	A3 Night Light	9116
6	Zanpoint Tumble Dryer	4560

Received by: L Daniels

Cheched by: D Richards

Comments: All in good condition

DELIVERY NOTE

Southfield Electrical
Industrial Estate
Benham DR6 2FF
Tel 0303379 Fax 0303152

Delivery address:

Whitehill Superstores
28, Whitehill Park
Benham DR6 5LM

Number: 34660
Date: 15 Sept 2006
Order number: 32103

Product code	Quantity	Description
9116	10	A3 Night Light
4560	6	Zanpoint Tumble Dryer

Received by: [Signature] *L Daniels*   **Print name:** *L DANIELS*
Date: *15 Sept 2006*

PURCHASE ORDER

WHITEHILL SUPERSTORES
28 Whitehill Park
Benham DR6 5LM
Tel 0303446 Fax 0303447

To: Southfield Electrical
Industrial Estate
Benham
DR6 2FF

Number: 32103

Date: 10 Sept 2006

Delivery address: As above

Product code	Quantity	Description	Price £
4560	7	Zanpoint Tumble Dryer	245.00
9116	10	A3 Night light	24.58

Authorised by: *P. Winterbottom*   **Date:** *10 Sept 2006*

INVOICE

Southfield Electrical
Industrial Estate
Benham DR6 2FF
Tel 0303379 Fax 0303152
VAT Reg 0264 2274 49

To:

Whitehill Superstores
28, Whitehill Park
Benham DR6 5LM

Invoice number: 56389

Date/tax point: 2 Oct 2006

Order number: 32103

Account number: SL 44

Quantity	Description	Stock code	Unit amount £	Total £
7	Zanpoint Tumble Dryer	4560	245.00	1,778.00
10	A3 Night lights	9116	24.58	245.80
				2,023.80
Less:	10% discount			202.38
	Net total			1,821.42
	VAT			318.74
	Invoice total			2,140.16

Terms
4% discount for settlement within 10 days, otherwise 30 days net
E & OE
Carriage paid

5   Given below is an invoice received by Dartmouth Supplies and the related purchase order and delivery note. The suppliers' file shows that a 10% trade discount is normally given but no settlement discount offered. You are required to check this invoice thoroughly and to note any problems that you discover.

INVOICE

Dan Industrials
Park Rise
Fenbridge DR2 7AD
Tel 0461222 Fax 461223
VAT Reg 0621 3384 20

To:
Dartmouth Supplies
Fenbridge Estate North
Fenbridge
DR2 6PQ

Invoice number: 77412

Date/tax point: 7 Oct 2006

Order number: 317428

Account number: SL 116

Quantity	Description	Stock code	Unit amount £	Total £
24	Regent Chair	C11	40.50	972.00
16	Imperial Desk	D46	96.00	1,536.00

Net total	2,535.00
VAT	443.62
Invoice total	2,978.62

Terms
Net 30 days
E & OE

PURCHASE ORDER

DARTMOUTH SUPPLIES
Fenbridge Estate North
Fenbridge DR2 6PQ
Tel 0461310 Fax 0461311

To: Dan Industrials
Park Rise
Fenbridge
DR2 7AD

Number: 317428

Date: 20 Sept 2006

Delivery address: As above

Product code	Quantity	Description	Price (£)
D46	16	Imperial Desk	96.00
C11	24	Regent Chair	40.50

Authorised by: *J. Sellers*   **Date:** *20 Sept 2006*

DELIVERY NOTE

Dan Industrials
Park Rise
Fenbridge DR2 7AD
Tel 0461222 Fax 461223

Delivery address:

Dartmouth Supplies
Fenbridge Estate North
Fenbridge
DR2 6PQ

Number: 62601

Date: 27 Sept 2006

Order number: 317428

Product code	Quantity	Description
D46	16	Imperial Desk
C11	24	Regent Chair

Received by: [Signature] *S. Simons*   **Print name:** *S. SIMONS*

Date: *27 Sept 2006*

6 Given below are an invoice and credit note received by A J Hammond and the related purchase order, delivery note and goods received note. Check the invoice and credit note thoroughly and note any problems that there might be.

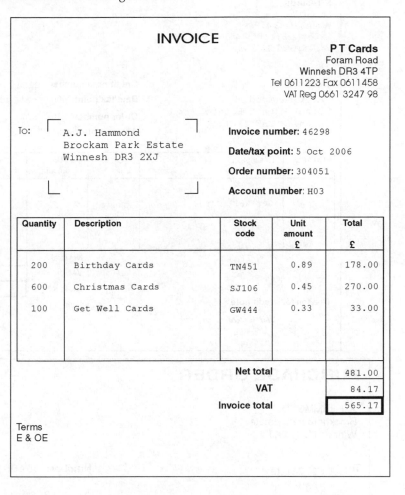

INVOICE

P T Cards
Foram Road
Winnesh DR3 4TP
Tel 0611223 Fax 0611458
VAT Reg 0661 3247 98

To:
A.J. Hammond
Brockam Park Estate
Winnesh DR3 2XJ

Invoice number: 46298

Date/tax point: 5 Oct 2006

Order number: 304051

Account number: H03

Quantity	Description	Stock code	Unit amount £	Total £
200	Birthday Cards	TN451	0.89	178.00
600	Christmas Cards	SJ106	0.45	270.00
100	Get Well Cards	GW444	0.33	33.00

Net total	481.00
VAT	84.17
Invoice total	565.17

Terms
E & OE

CREDIT NOTE

P T Cards
Foram Road
Winnesh DR3 4TP
Tel 0611223 Fax 0611458
VAT Reg 0661 3247 98

Credit note to:
A.J. Hammond
Brockam Park Estate
Winnesh DR3 2XJ

Credit note number: 31313
Date/tax point: 10 Oct 2006
Order number: 304051
Account number: H03

Quantity	Description	Stock code	Unit amount	Total
			£	£
30	Get Well Cards	GW444	0.25	7.50

Net total	7.50
VAT	1.31
Gross total	8.81

Reason for credit note:
Not ordered

PURCHASE ORDER

A J HAMMOND
Brockham Park Estate
Winnesh DR3 2XJ

To: P.T.Cards
Foram Road
Winnesh DR3 4TP

Number: 304051

Date: 13 Sept 2006

Delivery address: As above

Product code	Quantity	Description	Price (£)
SJ106	600	Christmas Cards	0.45
GW444	70	Get well Cards	0.33
TN451	200	Birthday Cards	0.89

Authorised by: *P T Thomas*   **Date:** *13 Sept 2006*

DELIVERY NOTE

P T Cards
Foram Road
Winnesh DR3 4TP
Tel 0611223 Fax 0611458

Delivery address:

A.J.Hammond
Brockham Park Estate
Winnesh DR3 2XJ

Number: 21690
Date: 20 Sept 2006
Order number: 304051

Product code	Quantity	Description
SJ106	600	Christmas Cards
GW444	100	Get Well Cards
TN451	200	Birthday Cards

Received by: [Signature] *J T Turner*   **Print name:** *J T TURNER*

Date: *20 Sept 2006*

GOODS RECEIVED NOTE

A J Hammond
Brockam Park Estate
Winnesh DR3 2XJ

Supplier:

GRN number: 27428
Date: 21 Sept 2006
Order number: 304051
Delivery Note No: 21690

Quantity	Description	Stock code
200	Birthday Cards	TN 451
100	Get Well Cards	GW 444
600	Christmas Cards	SJ 106

Received by: *P Darren*

Checked by: *D Gough*

Comments: *All in good condition*

chapter 10:
ACCOUNTING FOR CREDIT PURCHASES

KNOWLEDGE AND UNDERSTANDING AND PERFORMANCE CRITERIA COVERAGE

Unit 2

knowledge and understanding – accounting methods

11 double entry bookkeeping, including balancing accounts
15 operation of manual accounting systems
16 operation of computerised accounting systems, including output
19 relationship between accounting system and ledger
18 batch control

Performance criteria – element 2.1

E correctly enter invoices and credit notes into books of prime entry according to organisational procedures

F enter invoices and credit notes in the appropriate ledgers

BOOKS OF PRIME ENTRY

When we were considering the sales cycle in an earlier chapter we discovered that the transactions of a business are initially entered into BOOKS OF PRIME ENTRY. This is done by entering the details from the transaction documents into the appropriate books of prime entry. The entries in the books of prime entry are then posted to the ledger accounts.

For invoices received from suppliers and providers of services the relevant book of prime entry is the PURCHASES DAY BOOK.

A typical Purchases Day Book would look like this:

Date	Customer	Invoice number	Ref	Gross £	VAT £	Purchases £	Telephone £	Stationery £	Other £
2006									
1 May	Haley Ltd	33728	PL25	228.49	34.03	194.46			
1 May	JJ Bros	242G	PL14	372.70	55.50	317.20			
1 May	B Tel	530824	PL06	152.52	22.71		129.81		
2 May	Moss & Co	2574	PL33	84.00	12.51	71.49			
3 May	K T Trading	B295	PL16	227.98	33.95	194.03			
4 May	T W Jones	101893	PL05	60.45	9.00			51.45	

The writing up of the Purchases Day Book for the period would have the following steps:

Step 1   Find all of the invoices that have been checked and authorised for payment since the day book was last written up. All of the information that you require for writing up the purchases day book should be on the face of the invoice or the authorisation stamp or sheet.

Step 2   Enter the date of the invoice and the name of the supplier in the first two columns. The invoice number is then entered into the third column. This will normally be the invoice number that the supplier has assigned to the invoice when sending it out so there will be no sequence here. However some organisations apply a sequential number of their own to each invoice that is received from suppliers and if this is the case this should be recorded on the authorisation stamp or sheet and taken from there for entry into the day book.

Step 3 The reference column is also sometimes headed up 'folio'. In this column should be entered the supplier's account code number. This will be the account code from the subsidiary (purchases) ledger and as such often has the pre-fix "PL".

This code should have been entered onto the authorisation stamp or sheet and can be taken from there. The code is important as it will help with the eventual entry of these figures into the ledger accounts.

Step 4 Enter the invoice totals. The entry in the gross column is the final total on the invoice including any VAT. The VAT amount is entered into the VAT column. The net amount ie, the invoice total minus the VAT, is then entered into the appropriate analysis column. This is where the purchases day book differs from the sales day book in that there are likely to be different types of invoices being received and therefore an analysed purchases day book is normally used. Each invoice should have been analysed and coded when being checked and the authorisation sheet should show a code for the type of expense that the invoice was for.

The most common type of invoice will be for goods for resale in a retail environment or materials required in a manufacturing environment. These are known as PURCHASES and therefore the net amount of the invoice is entered into the purchases column. In practice there is likely to be a variety of analysis columns only a few of which have been illustrated here. The net amount of the telephone bill has been entered into the telephone column and the net amount of the invoice for stationery is in the stationery column.

Activity 1

An invoice for goods for resale has the following totals:

	£
Goods total	258.38
VAT	45.21
Invoice total	303.59

Which columns in the Purchases Day Book would each of these figures be entered into?

POSTING THE PURCHASES DAY BOOK

Once all of the details of the invoices received have been entered into the purchases day book then the next stage is to transfer the details to the accounting records.

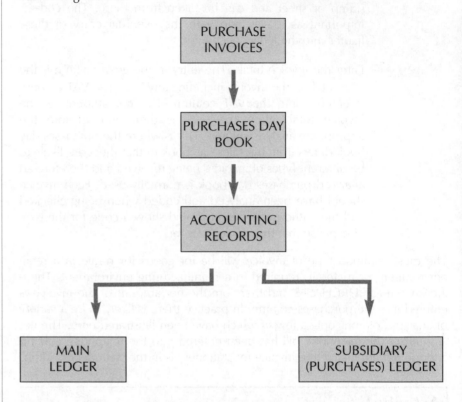

In order to post the figures to the ledger accounts the purchases day book must be cast. The day book illustrated before has now been cast.

Date	Customer	Invoice number	Ref	Gross £	VAT £	Purchases £	Telephone £	Stationery £	Other £
2006									
1 May	Haley Ltd	33728	PL25	228.49	34.03	194.46			
1 May	JJ Bros	242G	PL14	372.70	55.50	317.20			
1 May	B Tel	530824	PL06	152.52	22.71		129.81		
2 May	Moss & Co	2574	PL33	84.00	12.51	71.49			
3 May	K T Trading	B295	PL16	227.98	33.95	194.03			
4 May	T W Jones	101893	PL05	60.45	9.00			51.45	
				1,126.14	167.70	777.18	129.81	51.45	

Activity 2

Check that the Purchases Day Book has been correctly cast by cross-casting the column totals.

Entries in the main ledger

Remember that the main ledger is where the double entry takes place so let us now consider the double entry for each of the column totals.

Gross total the gross total is the amount that must eventually be paid to the supplier, the goods total plus the VAT. This is therefore the amount owing to the supplier, the creditor, and therefore it is a credit entry in the PURCHASES LEDGER CONTROL ACCOUNT.

VAT total the VAT total is input VAT and as such can be reclaimed back from HMRC. Therefore this is a debit entry in the VAT account.

Analysis column totals the total of each of the analysis columns is the actual amount of the expense of each type. The purchases total is therefore the total purchases cost for the period and as such is a debit entry in the purchases account. Similarly the telephone and stationery totals will be debit entries in their respective accounts.

This can be illustrated as follows:

Date	Customer	Invoice number	Ref	Gross £	VAT £	Purchases £	Telephone £	Stationery £	Other £
2006									
1 May	Haley Ltd	33728	PL25	228.49	34.03	194.46			
1 May	JJ Bros	242G	PL14	372.70	55.50	317.20			
1 May	B Tel	530824	PL06	152.52	22.71		129.81		
2 May	Moss & Co	2574	PL33	84.00	12.51	71.49			
3 May	K T Trading	B295	PL16	227.98	33.95	194.03			
4 May	T W Jones	101893	PL05	60.45	9.00			51.45	
				1,126.14	167.70	777.18	129.81	51.45	-

CREDIT   DEBIT

↓   ↓   ↓   ↓   ↓

Purchases ledger control   VAT   Purchases   Telephone   Stationery

So these totals must now be posted into the ledger accounts in the main ledger.

Main ledger

Purchases ledger control account

	£		£
		Purchases day book	1,126.14

VAT account

	£		£
Purchases Day Book	167.70		

Purchases account

	£		£
Purchases Day Book	777.18		

Telephone account

	£		£
Purchases Day Book	129.81		

Stationery account

	£		£
Purchases Day Book	51.45		

There are five entries here but as always the double entry is maintained and the credit entry equals the debit entries:

Debits £167.70 + £777.18 + £129.81 + £51.45 = £1,126.14
Credit   £1,126.14

Note that the reference for each transaction is to the primary record, the Purchases Day Book. This will often be shortened to PDB.

Activity 3

Name the accounts that each of the following totals from a purchases day book would be posted to, and whether they would be a debit or a credit entry:

a)   gross column total
b)   vAT column total
c)   purchases column total

Posting to the subsidiary ledger

The ledger account posting of course does not stop here as each individual invoice must be posted to the correct individual creditor account in the subsidiary (purchases) ledger.

Step 1   Find the individual supplier's account in the subsidiary (purchases) ledger using the account code in the reference column of the Purchases Day Book.

Step 2   Enter the gross total of the invoice, from the gross column, as this is the amount actually owed to the creditor on the credit side of his account.

Subsidiary (purchases) ledger

Haley Ltd		PL 25
£	PDB – 33728	£ 228.49

JJ Bros		PL 14
£	PDB – 242G	£ 372.70

B Tel		PL 06
£	PDB – 530824	£ 152.52

Moss & Co		PL 33
£	PDB – 2574	£ 84.00

K T Trading		PL 16
£	PDB – B295	£ 227.98

T W Jones		PL 05
£	PDB – 101893	£ 60.45

The reference for each entry is again the Purchases Day Book (PDB) but the invoice number is also entered as it can be useful when problems arise with a supplier's account or when dealing with statements received from suppliers.

PURCHASES RETURNS AND CREDIT NOTES

As we have already seen if goods are returned to a supplier then the supplier will in due course issue a credit note. Now we will consider how the credit notes received will be accounted for.

As with purchase invoices the credit notes will have their own book of prime entry known as the PURCHASES RETURNS DAY BOOK. This will look very similar to the purchases day book with the same details required to be entered into it. A typical example is given below:

Date	Customer	Credit note no	Ref	Gross £	VAT £	Purchases £	Telephone £	Stationery £	Other £
4 May	JJ Bros	371C	PL14	58.90	8.77	50.13			
5 May	Haley Ltd	C886	PL25	16.75	2.49	14.26			

The only difference here is that a credit note number replaces the invoice number. All of the other entries and details are exactly the same as for the Purchases Day Book and can all be found from the credit note itself and the authorisation stamp or sheet.

As with the Purchases Day Book the Purchases Returns Day Book must now be totalled and posted to the ledgers.

Date	Customer	Credit note no	Ref	Gross £	VAT £	Purchases £	Telephone £	Stationery £	Other £
4 May	JJ Bros	371C	PL14	58.90	8.77	50.13			
5 May	Haley Ltd	C886	PL25	16.75	2.49	14.26	—	—	—
				75.65	11.26	64.39	—	—	—

Activity 4

Check that the purchases returns day book has been correctly cast by cross-casting the column totals.

Now the purchases returns day book details must be entered into the accounting records.

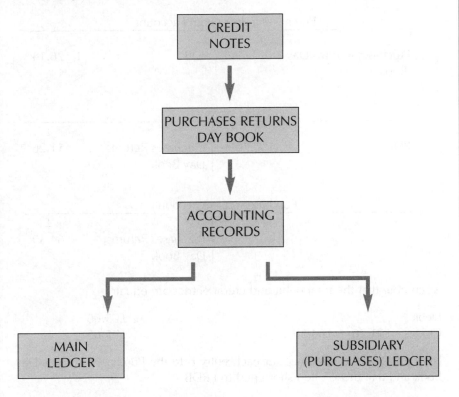

POSTING THE PURCHASES RETURNS DAY BOOK

In the main ledger the column totals must be entered into the ledger accounts. The double entry is effectively the reverse of the entries from the purchases day book and we will briefly consider each of these entries before making the postings.

Gross total – this is the total amount that will be deducted from what is owed to the supplier. You will no longer be required to pay this amount to the supplier so the entry is a **debit** entry in the purchases ledger control account.

VAT total – as these goods have been returned, the VAT on them can no longer be claimed back from HMRC so the original entry must be reversed by a **credit** entry to the VAT account.

Analysis column totals – it is likely that most returns of goods will be returns of 'purchases' and they have their own ledger account, the purchases returns account. The entry to this account is a **credit**. If however for example there were returns of stationery then the column total would be a **credit** entry to the stationery account.

Main ledger

Purchases ledger control account

	£		£
Purchases Returns Day Book	75.65	PDB	1,126.14

VAT account

	£		£
PDB	167.70	Purchases Returns Day Book	11.26

Purchases returns account

	£		£
		Purchases Returns Day Book	64.39

Again note that the total debit and credit entries are equal:

Debit		£75.65
Credits £11.26 + £64.39	=	£75.65

Note also that the reference for each entry is to the Purchases Returns Day Book and that this is often shortened to PRDB.

Now for the entries in the purchases ledger. Each individual credit note must be entered into the account of that supplier in the purchases ledger. The amount to be used is the gross total of the credit note and it is entered on the **debit** side of the supplier's account as this amount is no longer owed to the supplier.

JJ Bros   PL 14

	£		£
PRDB – 371C	58.90	PDB – 2426	372.70

Haley Ltd   PL 25

	£		£
PRDB – C886	16.75	PDB – 33728	228.49

Note that again the reference is to the Purchases Returns Day Book (PRDB) and the credit note number is also given as this may be useful information when dealing with this supplier.

| Activity 5 | student notes✍ |

Activity 5

A credit note is received for £40.00 plus VAT. Name the accounts in the main ledger and subsidiary ledger that would be debited and credited and state what amounts these debit and credit entries would be.

CREDIT NOTES AND THE PURCHASES DAY BOOK

Some organisations do not bother with a separate primary record for credit notes. Instead they are entered directly into the Purchases Day Book and shown as credit notes by putting brackets around all of the figures.

The Purchases Day Book used in this chapter is now shown again with the credit notes entered in this way as well:

Date	Customer	Invoice number	Ref	Gross £	VAT £	Purchases £	Telephone £	Stationery £	Other £
2006									
1 May	Haley Ltd	33728	PL25	228.49	34.03	194.46			
1 May	J J Bros	242G	PL14	372.70	55.50	317.20			
1 May	B Tel	530824	PL06	152.52	22.71		129.81		
2 May	Moss & Co	2574	PL33	84.00	12.51	71.49			
3 May	K T Trading	B295	PL16	227.98	33.95	194.03			
4 May	J J Bros	371C	PL14	(58.90)	(8.77)	(50.13)			
4 May	T W Jones	101893	PL05	60.45	9.00			51.45	
5 May	Haley Ltd	C886	PL25	(16.75)	(2.49)	(14.26)			
				1,050.49	156.44	712.79	129.81	51.45	

When casting the purchases day book care must be taken to ensure that each of the credit notes, in brackets, is deducted and not added in.

student notes✎ | The posting to the main ledger will be as follows:

Date	Customer	Invoice number	Ref	Gross £	VAT £	Purchases £	Telephone £	Stationery £	Other £
2006									
1 May	Haley Ltd	33728	PL25	228.49	34.03	194.46			
1 May	J J Bros	242G	PL14	372.70	55.50	317.20			
1 May	B Tel	530824	PL06	152.52	22.71		129.81		
2 May	Moss & Co	2574	PL33	84.00	12.51	71.49			
3 May	K T Trading	B295	PL16	227.98	33.95	194.03			
4 May	J J Bros	371C	PL14	(58.90)	(8.77)	(50.13)			
4 May	T W Jones	101893	PL05	60.45	9.00			51.45	
5 May	Haley Ltd	C886	PL25	(16.75)	(2.49)	(14.26)			
				1,050.49	156.44	712.79	129.81	51.45	-

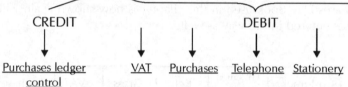

CREDIT ↓ Purchases ledger control

DEBIT

VAT Purchases Telephone Stationery

This time there is no posting to a separate purchases returns account as the returns have already been netted off from the purchases total in the purchases account.

When posting the individual amounts to the purchases ledger accounts it is necessary to remember that the invoices are posted to the credit side of the account and the credit notes to the debit side of the supplier's account.

COMPUTERISED CREDIT PURCHASES

Credit purchases in a computerised system work in much the same way as computerised credit sales. The package will hold data about suppliers and the products that are bought from them so all the operator needs to do normally is enter a series of codes and quantities. There is no need for day books because transactions are posted directly to the ledgers in one go.

If the business sells stocks of products credit purchasing may be managed by a Purchase Order Processing system such as the one illustrated below from the Sage line 50 package. Note that there are options for recurring transactions, so if you regularly order the same item from the same supplier the whole process can be speeded up even further.

A new order will be created using a screen such as the following. This will be printed and sent to the supplier.

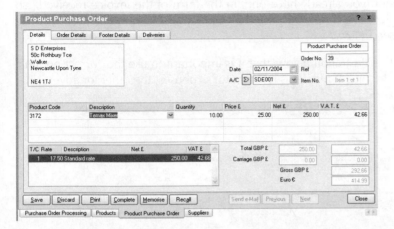

When the goods are received they will be placed into stock, simply by selecting the order from a list and clicking on the GRN button.

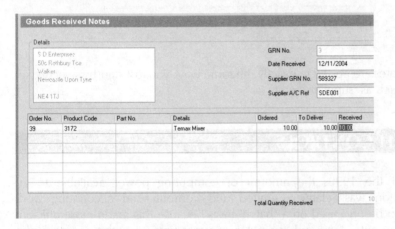

Finally, all the ledger will be updated at the click of a button.

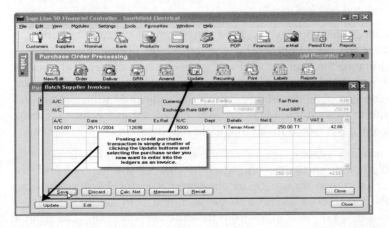

student notes ✍

Companies that do not deal in stocks can post supplier invoices directly, just by typing in a few codes and a brief description. There is no need to produce a document (you already have one, in the form of the invoice received), so such invoices can simply be posted on the same screen in batches, say once a week (see below).

Note, in the illustration below, that it is important to use the correct nominal ledger code: one of the items is for motor expenses, the other for advertising.

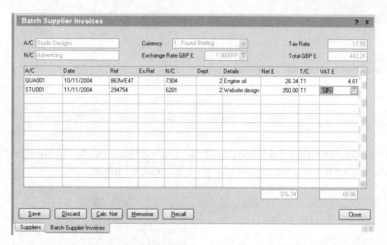

Credit notes are posted in exactly the same way: you just start by selecting an option such as 'supplier credit'.

BATCH CONTROLS

Up until the 1990s the amount of computing power available to an organisation was relatively limited and computerised accounting work tended to be organised on a 'batch' basis because this made more efficient use of computer time and computer operator time. In other words all the different types of transactions would be saved up for a period (a week, say) and then input in batches.

A by-product of this approach was the development of batch controls. A batch total of the documents to be entered would be calculated prior to input: for instance the total net, VAT and gross amounts of, say, 100 invoices would be calculated before they were input, and once inputting was complete the computer could add up all the individual values input and compare the result with the totals that were calculated in advance. If these was a difference this would mean that there had been an error in inputting.

Although modern systems are much more powerful, and it is perfectly possible to enter transactions as and when they occur, you may still find that organisations you work for use the batch approach, simply because they can then apply these extra controls over accuracy. In addition, smaller organisations may not be able to afford full-time accounts staff, and again it may be more convenient for them to save up transactions and enter them in batches once a week.

CHAPTER OVERVIEW

- all of the invoices received from suppliers of goods and services are initially entered into the Purchases Day Book

- the totals from the Purchases Day Book are then posted to the main ledger

- each individual invoice must also be entered into the individual supplier's account in the subsidiary (purchases) ledger

- credit notes that are received when goods are returned can be recorded in a separate primary record, the Purchases Returns Day Book

- the totals from the Purchases Returns Day Book are posted to the main ledger and each individual credit note is entered in the individual supplier's account in the subsidiary (purchases) ledger

- in some accounting systems the credit notes received by an organisation are recorded in the Purchases Day Book, with brackets to indicate a credit note, rather than in a separate book of prime entry

- a typical integrated computerised accounting system does not need books of prime entry for credit purchases, because all the ledger entries can be made in one go. The organisation may use a purchase order processing system if it sells stocks or it may simply enter supplier invoices in batches

KEY WORDS

Books of prime entry the initial records in the accounting system in which the details of each different type of transaction document is recorded

Purchases Day Book the book of prime entry in which all invoices from suppliers of goods and services are recorded

Purchases in a retail organisation these are goods which are purchased for resale – in a manufacturing organisation they are the materials required for the manufacturing process

Purchases ledger control account the ledger account which records the transactions with all of the organisation's creditors in total

Purchases Returns Day Book the book of prime entry in which all credit notes from suppliers are recorded

HOW MUCH HAVE YOU LEARNED?

1   Given below are three invoices received from suppliers by Whitehill Superstores.

An extract from the supplier code listing is given:

Bass Engineers	PL13
Southfield Electrical	PL20
Herne Industries	PL15

Today's date is 20 October and you are required to:

a)   record the invoice details in the Purchases Day Book
b)   post the totals of the day book to the main ledger
c)   post the individual invoices to the subsidiary (purchases) ledger

---

INVOICE

Herne Industries
Fuller House
Bean Park
Benham DR6 3PQ
Tel 0303226 Fax 0303582
VAT Reg 0624 3361 29

To: Whitehill Superstores
28, Whitehill Park
Benham DR6 5LM

Invoice number: 46121

Date/tax point: 16 Oct 2006

Order number: 32216

Account number: SL 23

Quantity	Description	Stock code	Unit amount £	Total £
3	Komax Camcorder	KC410	240.00	720.00

Net total	720.00
VAT	126.00
Invoice total	846.00

Terms
Net 30 days
E & OE

INVOICE

Southfield Electrical
Industrial Estate
Benham DR6 2FF
Tel 0303379 Fax 0303152
VAT Reg 0264 2274 49

To: Whitehill Superstores
28, Whitehill Park
Benham DR6 5LM

Invoice number: 56521

Date/tax point: 12 Oct 2006

Order number: 3226

Account number: SL 44

Quantity	Description	Stock code	Unit amount £	Total £
6	Zanpoint Freezer	6540	310.00	1,860.00
Less:	10% discount			186.00

Net total	1,674.00
VAT	281.23
Invoice total	1,955.23

Terms
4% discount for settlement within 10 days, otherwise 30 days net
E & OE

INVOICE

Bass Engineers
Bass House
Parrish DR3 2FL
Tel 0462333 Fax 0462334
VAT Reg 2016 2131 87

To: Whitehill Superstores
28, Whitehill Park
Benham DR6 5LM

Invoice number: 663211

Date/tax point: 15 Oct 2006

Order number: 32213

Account number: W15

Quantity	Description	Stock code	Unit amount £	Total £
16	Standard lamps	33116	24.00	384.00

Net total	384.00
VAT	67.20
Invoice total	451.20

Terms
Net 30 days
E & OE

2 Today's date is 20 October 2006. Given below are two credit notes received by Whitehill Superstores. Enter the details of these credit notes into the Purchases Returns Day Book – use the account references from the previous question. You are also required to post the credit notes to the main ledger and the subsidiary ledger, the purchases ledger.

CREDIT NOTE

SOUTHFIELD ELECTRICAL
INDUSTRIAL ESTATE
Benham DR6 2FF
Tel 0303379 Fax 0303152
VAT Reg 0264 2274 49

Invoice to:

Whitehill Superstores
28 Whitehill Park
Benham DR6 5LM

Credit note number: 08702

Date/tax point: 16 Oct 2006

Order number 32217

Account number: SL 44

Quantity	Description	Stock code	Unit amount	Total
			£	£
2	Temax Coffee maker	9130	50.00	100.00

Net total	100.00
VAT	17.50
Gross total	117.50

Reason for credit note:

Not ordered by customer

CREDIT NOTE

HERNE INDUSTRIES
Fuller House
Bean Park
Benham DR6 3PQ
Tel 0303226 Fax 0303582
VAT Reg 0624 3361 29

Invoice to:		**Credit note number:**	CN 4502
Whitehill Superstores		**Date/tax point:**	17 Oct 2006
28 Whitehill Park		**Order number**	32221
Benham DR6 5LM		**Account number:**	SL 23

Quantity	Description	Stock code	Unit amount	Total
			£	£
1	Kemax Camera	KC450	110.00	110.00
		Net total		110.00
		VAT		19.25
		Gross total		129.25

Reason for credit note:

....

3 Your organisation records both its purchases invoices received and credit notes received in the Purchases Day Book. The following documents must be recorded in the Purchases Day Book today, 5 June 2006.

1 June	Invoice 224363 from Y H Hill (PL16)	£158.38 + VAT
2 June	Invoice PT445 from Letra Ltd (PL24)	£227.39 + VAT
2 June	Invoice 77352 from Coldstores Ltd (PL03)	£157.38 + VAT
3 June	Invoice 17452 from H Hardcastle (PL07)	£269.30 + VAT
5 June	Credit note C7325 from Y H Hill (PL16)	£24.68 + VAT
5 June	Telephone bill 0174659 B Tel (PL 02)	£368.15 + VAT

You are required to:

a) enter these documents into the Purchases Day Book
b) post the Purchases Day Book to the main ledger
c) post the Purchases Day Book to the purchases ledger

226

chapter 11:
MAKING PAYMENTS TO CREDIT SUPPLIERS

chapter coverage 📖

Now that we have seen how invoices and credit notes should be checked and authorised for payment and initially recorded in the primary records and ledger accounts, we must consider how payment of these invoices is made to credit suppliers. The topics that are to be covered are:

✍ methods of determining when suppliers' invoices are to be paid

✍ determining the date of payment if a settlement discount is offered

✍ making payment using a remittance advice when the supplier's statement is received

✍ calculating the amount of settlement discount to be deducted

✍ totalling of remittance advices

✍ authorisation limits

✍ methods of payment - cheque, standing order, direct debit, bank giro credit, BACS, CHAPS, credit card

✍ cheque requisition forms

Unit 1

knowledge and understanding – the business environment

8   automated payments from customers

Unit 2

knowledge and understanding – the business environment

6   payment cheques, including crossings and endorsements
7   automated payments to suppliers
9   documentation for payments

Performance criteria – element 2.2

A   calculate payments from relevant documentation

B   schedule payments and obtain authorisation

C   use the appropriate payment method and timescale, in accordance with organisational procedures

E   identify queries and resolve or refer to the appropriate person

F   ensure security and confidentiality is maintained according to organisational requirements

TIMING OF PAYMENTS

Different organisations will have different methods and processes for ensuring that payments are made to suppliers on a timely basis. Some of the more common methods are:

- payment by invoice;
- payment by statement;
- payment on a regular timescale.

Each of these methods will be considered.

Payment by invoice

This system means that when each invoice is checked and authorised as ready for payment because it is correct and any related credit notes have been received then the precise payment date for this invoice is set.

The payment date will depend upon the payment terms of the invoice and whether or not any settlement discount is to be taken. If there is no settlement discount offered then most organisations are likely to take as much credit as possible in order to keep money in their own bank account for as long as possible, thereby earning interest or reducing overdraft interest.

Therefore when the invoice is passed for payment, the invoice date and terms should be checked in order to determine the latest date on which payment should be made. For example if an invoice dated 23 May is received on 26 May and the terms state that payment is due in 30 days then the payment date would be calculated as 22 June (as there are 31 days in May). Technically the payment should reach the supplier on this date so the day for writing the cheque may be 20 June. This payment date must then be recorded in a diary system which will show the precise invoices that are due to be paid each day.

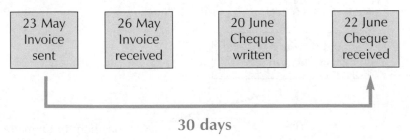

| 23 May Invoice sent | 26 May Invoice received | 20 June Cheque written | 22 June Cheque received |

30 days

Activity 1

Suppose that an invoice is received by your organisation on 14 July. The invoice is dated 9 July and the terms are stated as "net 30 days". Payment is to be made by cheque and posted and this takes three days from writing out the cheque to receipt by the supplier. When should the cheque be written?

Settlement discounts

If a settlement discount is offered on an invoice then there are further considerations that must be made in deciding when to make payment.

- Is it the organisation's policy to take settlement discounts? If a settlement discount is taken then obviously a smaller amount is paid to the supplier, but it is paid earlier, meaning that money leaves the organisation's bank account earlier. This reduces any interest receivable on the account or increases any overdraft interest.

- If the policy of the organisation is only to take settlement discounts from some suppliers, depending upon the terms that they offer, is this supplier one of those for which a settlement discount should be taken?

- If the settlement discount is to be taken, how much should the payment be and when should it be made?

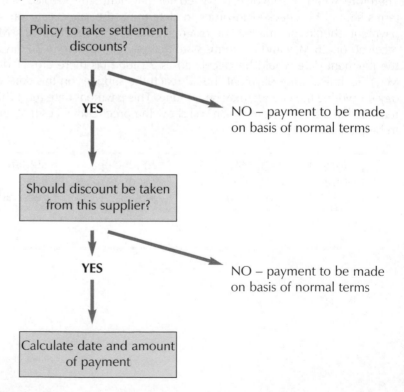

The amount of the payment will be considered later in the chapter. Here we will consider the timing of the payment.

HOW IT WORKS

An invoice is received on 10 December and was dated 8 December. The terms show that a settlement discount of 3.5% is offered for payment received within 14 days of the invoice date. Payment is to be made by cheque and posted, which takes two days. When should the cheque be written in order to take advantage of the discount?

The invoice is dated 8 December, so to take advantage of the settlement discount the payment must reach the supplier no later than 22 December. Therefore the cheque should be written on 20 December at the latest.

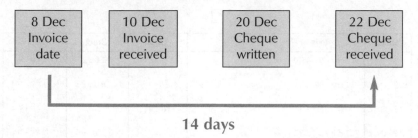

| 8 Dec
Invoice
date | 10 Dec
Invoice
received | 20 Dec
Cheque
written | 22 Dec
Cheque
received |

14 days

Activity 2

An invoice dated 23 November is received by your organisation on 25 November. The settlement discount of 4% for payment within 10 days of the invoice date is to be taken and the payment will be received by the supplier two days after the cheque is written. What is the latest date that the cheque should be written?

Payment by statement

In some organisations payment is only made upon receipt of a supplier's statement of account. Such statements are normally received just after the end of the month and will have been made up to the end of the month. Payment will then be made according to the supplier's terms. This means that all invoices, less credit notes, that are more than, say, 30 days old will be paid.

HOW IT WORKS

The following statement is received by Dagwell Enterprises from one of their suppliers Southfield Electrical on 4 December.

STATEMENT

Southfield Electrical
Industrial Estate
Benham DR6 2FF
Tel 0303379 Fax 030 31 52
VAT Reg 0264 2274 49

To: Dagwell Enterprises
J. D. House
High Street
Benham DR6 5TQ

Account number: SL 15

Date: 30 November 2006

Date	Details	Debit	Credit	Balance
8 Oct	Inv 56480		410.27	410.27
22 Oct	Inv 56531		386.33	796.60
28 Oct	CN 08723	68.40		728.20
29 Oct	Inv 56580		211.44	939.64
10 Nov	Inv 56629		268.93	1,208.57
27 Nov	Inv 56701		438.67	1,647.24

Amount now due	£ 1,647.24

REMITTANCE ADVICE

To: Southfield Electrical
Industrial Estate
Benham DR6 2FF

From: Dagwell Enterprises
J.D. House
High St.
Benham DR6 5TQ

Inv	Amount	(✓)
56480	410.27	
56531	386.33	
08723	(68.40)	
56580	211.44	
56629	268.93	
56701	438.67	

Cheque enclosed £

If Dagwell Enterprises' policy is to pay all of the invoices dated up to a month before the statement date, they would pay off the following invoices with one cheque:

	£
Invoice 56480	410.27
Invoice 56531	386.33
CN 08723	(68.40)
Invoice 56580	211.44
	939.64

The advantage of this method of payment is that only one payment is made each month. However the main disadvantage is that any settlement discounts offered would be lost, as any payment made would be too late to take advantage of the discount. It also means that a longer period of credit is being taken than the stated 30 days. For example the invoice dated 8 October is not being paid until early December, which is closer to 60 days of credit.

Payment on a regular timescale

In practice, many organisations may make payments on a weekly basis rather than a daily or monthly basis. So for example payments may be made every Friday instead of every day. In this case, when an invoice is passed for payment it must be determined which Friday the payment must be paid in order not to exceed the credit period.

HOW IT WORKS

An invoice dated Monday 7 August is received on Thursday 10 August. The stated credit terms are 30 days from the invoice date. With 30 days credit the payment should reach the supplier by Wednesday 6 September, so the cheque needs to be written on the previous Friday, 1 September.

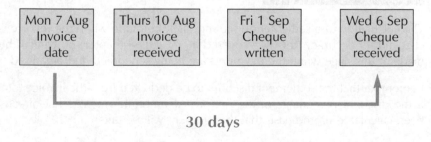

| Mon 7 Aug Invoice date | Thurs 10 Aug Invoice received | Fri 1 Sep Cheque written | Wed 6 Sep Cheque received |

30 days

student notes🖎

Activity 3

An invoice dated Monday 13 November is received on Wednesday 15 November. Payment terms are 30 days from the invoice date. Your organisation pays suppliers each Friday. On which Friday must this payment be made in order not to exceed the credit period?

If payment is made on a weekly basis and a settlement discount is offered, calculations should be made to determine in which week the payment must be made in order to be able validly to take the settlement discount. This must be done promptly or it is possible that the period in which the discount is valid will pass, no payment will be made and the discount will be lost.

Activity 4

An invoice dated Wednesday 23 November is received by your organisation on Friday 25 November. The settlement discount of 4% for payment within 10 days of the invoice date is to be taken and the payment will be received by the supplier two days after the cheque is written. If payment is made every Friday what is the latest date that the cheque should be written?

AMOUNT OF THE PAYMENT

As well as making sure that payments are made according to the organisational timescales that are set, the correct amount must also be made out for payment.

Settlement discounts

The calculation of a settlement discount might be made when the invoice is checked for accuracy (this was covered in an earlier chapter) or it might be made at this stage when the payments are being scheduled and organised.

Remember that the settlement discount to be deducted from the invoice total is the discount percentage of the net of VAT amount. The VAT has already been calculated on the basis that the discount will be taken.

HOW IT WORKS

Given below is an extract from one of Whitehill Superstores' invoices:

	£
Goods total	1,363.20
VAT	230.21
Invoice total	1,593.41

Terms: 3.5% settlement discount for payment received within 14 days of the invoice date

The payment that will be made if the discount is taken is calculated as follows:

Step 1   Calculate the discount to be deducted:

£1,363.20 x 3.5/100 = £47.71

Step 2   Deduct the discount from the invoice total to find the amount to be paid:

£1,593.41 – £47.71 = £1,545.70

Activity 5

An invoice is received by your organisation on which a settlement discount of 2.5% is offered. The invoice totals are given below. Calculate the amount of the payment required if the discount is taken.

	£
Goods total	582.65
VAT	99.41
Invoice total	682.06

Remittance advices

We saw in an earlier chapter that often when a statement of account is sent to a customer a tear-off REMITTANCE ADVICE is added to the bottom, for the payer to fill in showing the details and amounts of the invoices, less credit notes being paid. When filling in a remittance advice and totalling it to find the total payment, care should be taken to ensure that the total is correctly added up.

HOW IT WORKS

The statement of account received by Dagwell Enterprises earlier is now shown again.

STATEMENT

Southfield Electrical
Industrial Estate
Benham DR6 2FF
Tel 0303379 Fax 0303152
VAT Reg 0264 2274 49

To: Dagwell Enterprises
J. D. House
High Street
Benham DR6 5TQ

Account number: SL 15

Date: 30 November 2006

Date	Details	Debit	Credit	Balance
8 Oct	Inv 56480		410.27	410.27
22 Oct	Inv 56531		386.33	796.60
28 Oct	CN 08723	68.40		728.20
29 Oct	Inv 56580		211.44	939.64
10 Nov	Inv 56629		268.93	1,208.57
27 Nov	Inv 56701		438.67	1,647.24

Amount now due £ 1,647.24

REMITTANCE ADVICE

To: Southfield Electrical
Industrial Estate
Benham DR6 2FF

From: Dagwell Enterprises
J.D. House
High St.
Benham DR6 5TQ

Inv	Amount	(✓)
56480	410.27	✓
56531	386.33	✓
08723	(68.40)	✓
56580	211.44	✓
56629	268.93	
56701	438.67	

Please indicate items you are paying (✓) and return with your cheque.

Cheque enclosed £ 939.64

The invoices and credit notes that are being settled by this payment are ticked and then added up and the total entered in the "cheque enclosed" section. If the addition is incorrect then the amount paid will also be incorrect.

Authorisation limits

At this stage your responsibilities are to schedule and organise the payments that are to be made either today, at the end of the week or at the month end. Most organisations will have a system whereby different levels of employees and management deal with different amounts of payments. For example if you are in charge of scheduling payments to credit suppliers you might be set an authorisation limit of say £5,000. Therefore any payments to suppliers up to this amount can be arranged by you. If however in exceptional circumstances a payment is due to a supplier of £8,000 then a higher level of management will be required to authorise this amount for payment. When organising the payments for your organisation you should always be aware of your authorisation limits and know to whom to pass payments that exceed that limit.

METHODS OF PAYMENT

As well as ensuring that payments are made to credit suppliers at the correct time and for the correct amount you are also required to ensure that the most appropriate method of payment is used.

There are several different methods of payment that you should be aware of:

- cheque;
- standing order;
- direct debit;
- bank giro credit;
- BACS;
- CHAPS;
- credit card.

Each of these will be considered in turn.

student notes ✍

Cheques

Probably the most common method of paying credit suppliers is by cheque. The detailed legal rules regarding valid cheques were considered in an earlier chapter.

When writing out a cheque the same considerations should apply as when receiving a cheque from a customer – the following checks should be made:

- the date is correct as today's date;
- the name of the payee is correct;
- the amount in words and in figures are the same and are the correct amount;
- the cheque is signed either by you or another person in the organisation if this is not your responsibility.

When writing out a cheque a further consideration is the cheque counterfoil or cheque stub. This is the record that is kept by your organisation of the payment that is made and may well be used to enter the payment into the accounting records (see next chapter). Therefore it is also important that this is correctly written up. The details required are:

- date;
- payee;
- amount;
- often any discount taken is also recorded here in order to be entered into the accounting records at a later date.

HOW IT WORKS

Southfield Electrical is making a payment to a supplier, Grangemouth Supplies, of £783.60 after deducting a settlement discount of £23.50. The cheque and counterfoil are shown below:

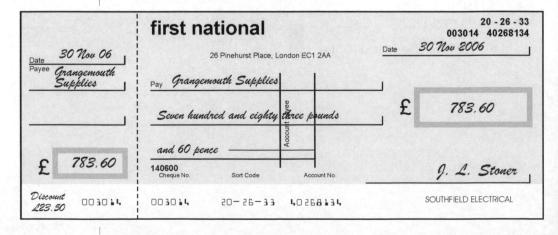

Note that where there are any blank spaces on the cheque, for example after the writing of the amount in words, a line is drawn through the space in order to minimise the chances of the cheque being fraudulently altered. If an error is made when writing out the cheque this should be altered and then initialled by an AUTHORISED SIGNATORY.

Authorised signatories

Authorised signatories are the people within the organisation that are authorised to sign the organisation's cheques. Most organisations will have a written agreement with their bank regarding who is allowed to sign the organisation's cheques. The bank will only accept cheques that have been signed by the correct people. In many organisations there will be monetary limits set on cheque signatures. For example, in a company the signature of just one director is required for cheques up to a value of £8,000 but if the cheque is for more than this amount then two directors' signatures are required.

Computer printed cheques

If the organisation has a computerised accounting system this often extends to the computer generation of authorised cheques. Obviously the data input to the computer system must be correct in order for the cheques to be printed for the correct amount. There should also be strict controls over this facility to prevent fraudulent payments being made.

Activity 6

What should normally be recorded on the cheque counterfoil?

Standing order

A STANDING ORDER is a method of making regular payments directly from your bank account to the bank account of a third party. This is organised through your bank by filling in a standing order form – an example is shown below:

STANDING ORDER

To: First National Bank

Please make the payments detailed below and debit my account:

Name of account to be debited _____

Account number _____

Payee details

Name of payee _____

Bank of payee _____

Sort code of payee _____

Account number of payee _____

Amount of payment (in words) _____ £ _____

Date of first payment _____

Frequency of payment _____

Continue payments until _____

Signature _____   Date _____

This standing order mandate is an order to the bank to make a payment of a fixed amount out of your bank account and into that of the payee on a regular basis.

You will note that the following details are included on the form:

- it is addressed to your bank;

- details of your bank account;

- details of the payee and his bank account ie, account number, sort code, bank;

- the amount of the payment;

- the date of the first payment;

- the frequency of the payment thereafter, usually monthly or quarterly;

- the date that the payments cease;

- the signature of the account holder.

As a standing order is for a fixed amount it is not particularly useful for paying credit suppliers, but can be of use for making fixed payments such as insurance premiums or loan repayments.

Direct debits

A DIRECT DEBIT is a further method of making a payment directly from your bank account to that of another party. However it operates in a different manner to a standing order.

HOW IT WORKS

Suppose that Southfield Electrical wish to pay National Water for its water rates by direct debit. The steps in the process are as follows:

Step 1   National Water sends Southfield Electrical a Direct Debit mandate which it has prepared – an example is given below:

NATIONAL
WATER

Please fill in the whole form including 'the official use' box using a ball point pen and send the form to us at the address below in the envelope provided. Please do not send this instruction direct to your bank.

National Water plc
PO Box 284
Donchurch
South Yorkshire
DN4 5PE

Name(s) of Account Holder(s)

Bank/Building Society account number

Branch Sort Code

Name and full postal address of your Bank or Building Society

To: The Manager	Bank/Building Society
Address	
	Postcode

Reference Number (as shown on your water services bill)

2	2	3	0	1	7	4	0	1	2	0	1	6

Instruction to your Bank or Building Society to pay by Direct Debit

DIRECT
Debit

Originator's Identification Number

6	2	4	8	3	2

FOR NATIONAL WATER PLC OFFICIAL USE ONLY
This is not part of the instruction to your Bank or Building Society
To be completed by customer
Please tick required option:

☐ Annually   ☐ Half Yearly   ☐ Monthly April to January

☐ 1st of the month   ☐ 15th of the month

Instruction to your Bank or Building Society

Please pay National Water plc Direct Debits from the account detailed in this Instruction subject to the safeguards assured by the Direct Debit Guarantee. I understand that this Instruction may remain with National Water plc and if so, details will be passed electronically to my Bank/Building Society.

Signature(s)

Date

Banks and Building Societies may not accept Direct Debit Instructions from some types of account

The Direct Debit Guarantee

DIRECT
Debit

- This Guarantee is offered by all Banks and Building Societies that take part in the Direct Debit Scheme. The efficiency and security of the Scheme is monitored and protected by your own Bank or Building Society.

- If the amounts to be paid or the payment dates change National Water plc will notify you 10 days in advance of your account being debited or as otherwise agreed.

- If an error is made by National Water plc or your Bank or Building Society, you are guaranteed a full and immediate refund from your branch of the amount paid.

- You can cancel a Direct Debit at any time by writing to your Bank or Building Society. Please also send a copy of your letter to us.

Step 2   Southfield Electrical completes the Direct Debit mandate instructing its bank to pay the amounts that National Water ask for on the dates that National Water requests payment.

Step 3   Southfield Electrical return the Direct Debit mandate to National Water who then send this to their bank.

Step 4   When a payment is required from Southfield Electrical to National Water this is requested by National Water and Southfield's bank will pay the amount requested.

The usefulness of a direct debit compared to a standing order is that it can be for variable rather than fixed amounts and can also be used for payments to be made at varying time intervals.

Activity 7

What is the essential difference between a standing order and a direct debit?

Bank Giro credit

A BANK GIRO CREDIT is a method of paying a cheque into another party's bank account directly rather than sending it to them through the post. Bank giro credit slips are often preprinted at the bottom of bills for telephone, electricity etc.

HOW IT WORKS

Southfield Electrical has received a telephone bill and wishes to pay this by bank giro credit.

Step 1   A cheque is written out for the amount of the bill.

Step 2   The bank giro credit slip at the bottom of the bill is detached and the amount of the cheque written in, together with the date and an authorised signature – the completed bank giro credit is shown below:

	Your Customer No ND 5534 2780	Bank Giro Credit

BT

Payment slip

Cashier's stamp and initials

Total amount due £ **300.96**

Dear Customer
- Please fill in parts 1 to 3 and insert a total next to the £ sign below.
- Details of how to pay are shown overleaf.
- Please do not send cash by post.

89440124 55342780 00317007

1 Signature *P. Watton*	3 Cash	—

Bank details
HSBC Bank plc
Head Office Collection Acct.

2 Date *10 Dec 2006*	or cheques	300	96

44 - 70 - 93

£	300	96

No cheques   Fee

Please do not fold, pin or staple this slip or write below this line.

03 ND 55342780 Q003   P F   300.96

<3ND55342780Q003< 447093+< 73   X

Step 3   The cheque and bank giro credit slip are paid into Southfield's bank and they then work through a three day clearing system after which Southfield's account is debited and that of British Telecom is credited.

BACS

BACS stands for Bankers Automated Clearing System. This is a system for making transfers between one bank account and another via the banks' computer systems, and unlike a bank giro credit means that to make a payment to another party's bank account there is no need to physically go to the bank itself with a cheque.

This system is often used for payment of wages and will be considered in more detail in a later chapter.

CHAPS

CHAPS stands for Clearing House Automated Payments System and is a system set up by the banks for payments from one bank account to another through the banks' computer networks. CHAPS is used for high value transfers and unlike other automatic transfer systems, the transfer takes place on the same day. In order to make a high value payment using CHAPS a form must be completed for the banks showing the details of the accounts to be debited and credited and the amount. Great care should be taken with this as once the money has been sent it cannot be recalled.

Credit card

This is not a method of paying a credit supplier but it is another type of payment that an organisation may have to make. Often organisations will issue employees such as travelling sales representatives with a corporate credit card. They will use this to pay for accommodation, food, fuel etc and the bill will be sent directly to the company. The company then pays the credit card company. This allows the organisation to monitor closely the expenses of the employees, and means that the employees do not have to pay these expenses themselves and then be reimbursed by the company.

CHEQUE REQUISITION FORM

So far in this chapter we have been considering methods of making regular payments to credit suppliers and providers of services. However on occasion a cheque might be required for a one-off payment for which there is no invoice as such. Most organisations will have pre-printed CHEQUE REQUISITION FORMS which are a formal request for a cheque for payment of a particular amount.

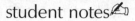

HOW IT WORKS

Ian Hamilton, one of the employees at Southfield Electrical has been asked to organise the Christmas party. He has booked caterers for the event but they require a deposit of £100. Ian must fill in a cheque requisition form giving details of the payment – his completed form is shown below:

CHEQUE REQUISITION FORM
Southfield Electrical

Requested by: *Ian Hamilton*   **Date:** *5 Dec 2006*

Payable to: *Clarke Caterers*

Amount: *£100*

Send to: *Clarke Caterers*

62, Westfield Road, Benham DR6 2QL

Reason: *Deposit for caterers for Xmas party*

Invoice/receipt attached: *None*

Other documentation: *None*

Authorised by: _____ **Date:** _____

This must then be signed as authorised by an appropriate member of the management team at Southfield. Once the appropriate authorisation has taken place the cheque will be written and sent out to Clarke Caterers.

In this instance there was no receipt or other documentation to evidence the payment, but in some cases an employee might have had to pay an expense himself that is to be reimbursed by the organisation. In this case the cheque would be made out to the employee himself and the receipt for the expense would be attached to the cheque requisition form as evidence of the original payment.

CHAPTER OVERVIEW

- different organisations will have different methods of organising the payment of their suppliers

- some organisations will consider each invoice as it arrives in the post and determine the date on which it is to be paid – this may be affected by the offer of a settlement discount

- an alternative method is to wait until the monthly statement is received from each supplier and then to pay the appropriate invoices, less credit notes, and to send details of the payment on the remittance advice attached to the statement

- another method is to make payments on a regular timescale, for example a particular day each week – each invoice must be examined to determine in which week it must be paid to either remain within the stated credit period or validly to take any settlement discount offered

- the amount of the payment must of course be correctly calculated – settlement discounts must be correctly calculated and deducted, remittance advices must be correctly totalled

- there are many methods of payment now available – the most common method of paying suppliers is to send a cheque in the post – the cheque must be properly prepared and the correct details also recorded on the cheque counterfoil

- each cheque must be signed by the appropriate authorised cheque signatory

KEY WORDS

Remittance advice a tear-off document, usually at the bottom of a supplier's statement, which allows the payer to indicate which invoices less credit notes are being paid

Authorised signatory those people within an organisation who are authorised to sign the organisation's cheques – the bank will only accept cheques signed by authorised signatories

Standing order a method of paying a fixed amount on fixed dates from one party's bank account to that of another

Direct debit a method of making payment from one party's bank account to that of another where the amount and timing of the payments can vary

Bank giro credit a method of paying a cheque directly into a supplier's bank account by paying the cheque in with a bank giro credit slip

BACS a method of making payments from one party's bank account to that of another through the banks' computer network

CHAPS a method of making high value, same day, transfers from the bank account of one party to that of another

Cheque requisition form a formal method of requesting a cheque for a one-off payment

- a standing order is a method of paying a third party a fixed amount on a regular basis directly from the organisation's bank account

- a direct debit is similar to a standing order but the amount of the payment can vary each time it is made and it can be made at varying intervals of time

- a cheque that is paid into a bank with a bank giro credit slip is then paid directly into the account of the payee after passing through the clearing system

- the Bankers Automated Clearing System (BACS) is a system used for making transfers from one bank account to another – often used for payment of wages

CHAPTER OVERVIEW cont.

- the Clearing House Automated Payments System (CHAPS) provides a method of making high value, same day transfers from one party's bank account to another's

- some organisations issue their employees with credit cards for their expenses which are then settled directly by the organisation with the credit card company

- if a cheque is required for a one-off payment for which there is no invoice then a cheque requisition form can be completed and authorised and the cheque then issued

HOW MUCH HAVE YOU LEARNED?

1   You are responsible for scheduling payments to suppliers and calculating the amount of the cheque that is to be made out to each supplier. You have in front of you a number of invoices the relevant details of which are summarised below:

	Invoice date	Payment terms	Invoice amount £
a)	6 May	30 days	356.90 + VAT
b)	6 May	3.5% settlement discount for receipt within 10 days	258.00 + VAT
c)	6 May	5% settlement discount for receipt within 7 days	111.60 + VAT
d)	8 May	30 days	263.57 + VAT
e)	9 May	2.5% settlement discount for receipt within 14 days	148.26 + VAT

When a cheque is written it is then posted to the supplier and generally takes two days to reach the supplier. Today's date is 12 May and you are required to prepare a schedule showing the date on which the cheque should be written and the amount of the cheque for each invoice. It is your organisation's policy to take advantage of settlement discounts wherever possible, but if a discount cannot be taken then the invoice is paid after 30 days. Your organisation's policy is take the longest period of credit allowed by suppliers.

2   Given below is a statement from one of your organisation's suppliers, an attached blank remittance advice and a blank cheque. You are instructed that all of the May invoices less credit notes are to be paid and that there is no settlement discount offered from this supplier. Today's date is 5 July 2006.

You are required to complete the remittance advice and the cheque (do not sign the cheque) and cheque counterfoil.

STATEMENT

Fishpool Supplies
280 Main Road
Winnish DR2 5TL
Tel 0411226 Fax 041126
VAT Reg 0611 2383 58

To: Tryprint Traders
Barnsgate Industrial Park
Fretton PT7 2XY

Account number: SL 48

Date: 30 June 2006

Date	Details	Debit	Credit	Balance
7 May	Inv 61234		401.23	401.23
14 May	Inv 61287		226.40	627.63
20 May	Inv 61299		106.68	734.31
28 May	CN C4361	16.48		717.83
6 June	Inv 61340		430.16	1,147.99
19 June	Inv 61388		269.73	1,417.72

Amount now due | £ 1,417.72

REMITTANCE ADVICE

To: Fishpool Supplies
280, Main Rd
Winnish DR2 5TL

From: Tryprint Traders
Barnsgate Ind Park
Fretton PT7 2XY

Invoices	Amount £

Cheque enclosed £

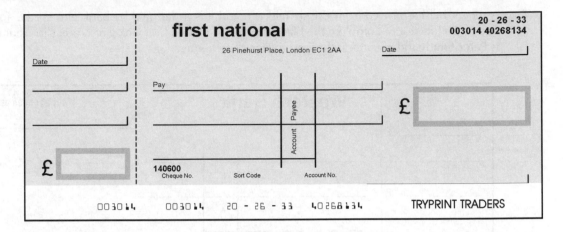

3 You are required to complete the blank cheque and cheque counterfoil given in order to pay one of your suppliers, Planet Earth Products. The goods total of the invoice was £230.00 and VAT was added of £38.64. A settlement discount of 4% was offered and the payment has been made in time to take advantage of this. Today's date is 16 July 2006.

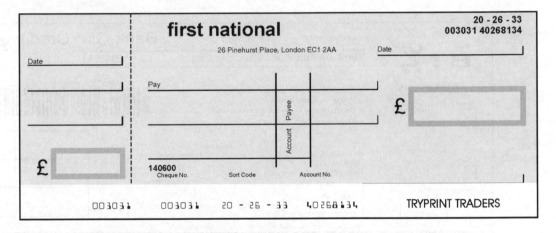

4 For each of the following transactions what would be the most appropriate method of payment?

a) Fixed repayments of a loan
b) Monthly salaries for 235 employees
c) Quarterly gas bills
d) Invoice from a credit supplier
e) Deposit on purchase of new factory that must reach the seller today

5 Why is it necessary for an organisation to complete a standing order mandate?

6 How does the system of direct debits work?

7 A recent bill has arrived from British Telecom and it is to be paid by bank giro credit. Today's date is 20 July 2006. Complete the blank cheque given and the bank giro credit slip. Your name is Peter Smith and you are authorised to sign this cheque.

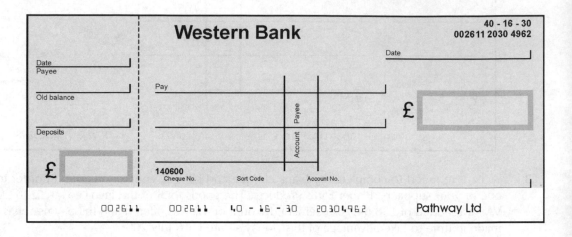

BT Payment slip			
Your Customer No ND 5534 2780		**Bank Giro Credit**	
Total amount due	£	512.63	

Dear Customer
- Please fill in parts 1 to 3 and insert a total next to the £ sign below.
- Details of how to pay are shown overleaf.
- Please do not send cash by post.

89440124 55342780 00317007

Cashier's stamp and initials

No cheques   Fee

Bank details
HSBC Bank plc
Head Office Collection Acct.

1 Signature

2 Date

3 Cash

or cheques

44 - 70 - 93

£

Please do not fold, pin or staple this slip or write below this line.

03 ND 55342780 Q003   P F   512.63

<3ND55342780Q003< 447093+< 73   X

8   Your name is Fred Barrett and you have spent £167.40 having a new clutch on your company car. This is reclaimable from your company and you are required to complete the following cheque requisition form for this amount. Today's date is 21 July 2006 and you do have a receipt from the garage.

CHEQUE REQUISITION FORM

Requested by: _____   **Date:** _____

Payable to: _____

Amount: _____

Send to: _____

_____

Reason: _____

Invoice/receipt attached: _____

Other documentation: _____

Authorised by: _____   **Date:** _____

---

chapter 12:
RECORDING PAYMENTS

chapter coverage 📖

Now that invoices from suppliers have been checked, accounted for, authorised and scheduled for payment, it is necessary to deal with entering the actual payment into the accounting records. The topics that are to be covered are:

✍ the layout of the cash payments book

✍ writing up the cash payments book

✍ totalling the cash payments book

✍ posting the cash payments book to the main ledger

✍ double entry for discounts received

✍ posting the cash payments book to the subsidiary ledger

✍ entering automated payments into the cash payments book

✍ capital and revenue expenditure

✍ checking suppliers' statements

✍ how this all works in a computerised accounting system

Unit 2

knowledge and understanding – accounting methods

11 double entry bookkeeping, including balancing accounts

12 accounting for payments to credit suppliers, and to suppliers where a credit account is not available

13 capital and revenue expenditure

15 operation of manual accounting systems

16 operation of computerised accounting systems, including output

17 the use of the cash book and petty cash book as part of the double entry system or as books of prime entry

19 relationship between the accounting system and the ledger

Performance criteria – element 2.1

H communicate appropriately with suppliers regarding accounts

Performance criteria – element 2.2

D enter payments into accounting records

BOOK OF PRIME ENTRY

When payments are made by a business, for any purpose, they are initially recorded in the CASH PAYMENTS BOOK. The Cash Payments Book is the mirror image of the cash receipts book. In just the same way as the cash receipts book, the Cash Payments Book normally performs the dual function of both a book of prime entry and part of the double entry system.

The entries made in the Cash Payments Book are the credit entries in the cash account in the main ledger, and therefore all that remains is for the debit entries to be made in the main ledger.

The cash payments book will normally be an ANALYSED CASH PAYMENTS BOOK as there will be different types of payments made by an organisation.

The cash payments book will be largely written up from the cheque counterfoils or stubs or from a listing of the cheques written each day or week.

The layout of a typical analysed Cash Payments Book is shown below:

Date	Details	Ref	Total £	VAT £	Cash purchases £	Purchases ledger £	Sundry £	Discounts received £

Date – the date will be the date on which the cheque was written or the date on which the cash book is written up, depending upon the organisation's policy.

Details – the details should be sufficient to describe the payment so that it can be easily analysed and checked at a later date – the usual details to enter will be the cheque number and the name of the payee.

Ref – the reference will depend upon the type of payment that is being made. If the payment is to a credit supplier then the reference will be the subsidiary (purchases) ledger account number for the supplier. If the payment is for cash purchases or to buy a fixed asset then the reference may be the main ledger code for that type of transaction, or simply a reference to the main ledger in order to distinguish it from the purchase ledger payments.

Total – the figure in the total column is the total value of the cheque.

student notes✍

VAT – when a payment is made to a creditor no VAT is recorded, as the VAT was recorded and posted to the VAT account when the original purchase invoice was entered into the purchases day book. However if other types of payment are made on which VAT is charged, the VAT element should be recorded in the VAT column.

Cash purchases – if the payment is for purchases of goods that are not bought on credit, the net amount of the purchase, the total minus the VAT, is entered in this column. Remember that a cash purchase is one that is not on credit – the actual purchase is being made not for cash but by cheque.

Purchases ledger – this column is used to record the payments made to credit suppliers. The details of VAT and net and gross amounts were recorded in the purchases day book when the invoice was received from the supplier. When the supplier is paid by cheque only the total amount of the actual payment need be recorded here. This amount will be the total of the cheque ie, after the deduction of any settlement discount (see below).

Sundry – this column is used for the net amount, ie, minus any VAT, for any other payments that are made by cheque. It is important that the "details" and reference coding are detailed enough for the payment to eventually be posted to the correct main ledger account.

Discount received – the DISCOUNT RECEIVED column is known as a "memorandum" column. What is recorded here is the amount of any settlement discount that was deducted before the payment was made. This can be taken from the note on the cheque stub or will be included on the list of cheque payments made. This column will be used when making the postings from the cash payments book to the main ledger and subsidiary ledger.

Activity 1

When should VAT be recorded in the cash payments book?

HOW IT WORKS

Southfield Electrical normally pays its credit suppliers by cheque once a week. The CHEQUE LISTING for this week is given below. The cheque listing is simply a list of the details of the cheques that were written out during the week. It will show the cheque number, the name of the payee, the subsidiary (purchases) ledger account number of the payee (taken from the invoice authorisation stamp or sheet) the total amount of the cheque and any settlement discount that was taken.

Cheque listing 28 September 2006

Cheque number	Payee	Purchases ledger code	Amount £	Discount £
003102	Seeban	PL46	1,284.90	67.62
003103	Elec. North Ltd	PL13	440.00	
003104	P J Harvey		268.50	
003105	Comtec Ltd	PL19	650.37	34.23
003106	Chiller Supplies	PL03	849.37	
003107	W G Supplies		500.00	

The cheque payments to payees without a purchase ledger code are payments for cash purchases on which VAT has been charged.

These payments must now be written up in the cash payments book.

Date	Details	Ref	Total £	VAT £	Cash purchases £	Purchases ledger £	Sundry £	Discounts received £
28/9	003102 Seeban	PL46	1,284.90			1,284.90		67.62
28/9	003103 Elec North Ltd	PL13	440.00			440.00		
28/9	003104 P J Harvey	ML	268.50	39.98	228.52			
28/9	003105 Comtec Ltd	PL19	650.37			650.37		34.23
28/9	003106 Chiller Supplies	PL03	849.37			849.37		
28/9	003107 W G Supplies	ML	500.00	74.46	425.54			

Reference – The reference for the payments to purchase ledger suppliers is their subsidiary (purchases) ledger account number, as eventually these amounts will need to be posted to their individual creditor accounts in the subsidiary (purchases) ledger. For the payments for cash purchases the reference ML refers to the main ledger, indicating that the only entries for these amounts will be in the main ledger.

Total and analysis columns – Each payment is entered in the total column and then in the appropriate analysis column – the payments to the credit suppliers are analysed into the purchases ledger column, and the cash payments are analysed out into the VAT column and the net amount into the cash purchases column.

VAT – when payment is made to credit suppliers there is no entry for VAT as this has already been accounted for in the purchases day book. However the payments for cash purchases include VAT that has not yet been accounted for – therefore the VAT element of the total payment must be calculated:

P J Harvey   VAT = $£268.50 \times 17.5/117.5$ =   £39.98
W G Supplies   VAT = $£500.00 \times 17.5/117.5$ =   £74.46

Discounts received – although it is the actual amount of the cheque total that is recorded in the cash payments book the amount of any discount taken must also be noted in the discount received column as this is important for the eventual posting of the payments.

Activity 2

If a cheque was written for £683.47 for cash purchases, what entries should there be in the cash payments book?

TOTALLING THE CASH PAYMENTS BOOK

Once the cash payments book has been written up for a period it must be totalled in order for the postings to the main ledger to take place.

Step 1   Each column of the cash payments book should be totalled.

Step 2   The casting should be checked by cross-casting the column totals to ensure that they add back to the "total" column total. Take care here as the discount received column should not be included in the cross-casting – this column is a memorandum column and does not form part of the total payments made.

HOW IT WORKS

Southfield's cash payments book will now be totalled and the totals checked by cross-casting.

Date	Details	Ref	Total £	VAT £	Cash purchases £	Purchases ledger £	Sundry £	Discounts received £
28/9	003102 Seeban	PL46	1,284.90			1,284.90		67.62
28/9	003103 Elec North Ltd	PL13	440.00			440.00		
28/9	003104 P J Harvey	ML	268.50	39.98	228.52			
28/9	003105 Comtec Ltd	PL19	650.37			650.37		34.23
28/9	003106 Chiller Supplies	PL03	849.37			849.37		
28/9	003107 W G Supplier	ML	500.00	74.46	425.54			
			3,993.14	114.44	654.06	3,224.64		101.85

Cross-cast check

	£
VAT	114.44
Cash purchases	654.06
Purchases ledger	3,224.64
	3,993.14

Remember not to include the discount received column in this cross-casting as this is not part of the payments made in total.

POSTING THE CASH PAYMENTS BOOK TO THE MAIN LEDGER

Now we must look at the posting of the column totals to the main ledger accounts in order to complete the double entry. Remember that the cash payments book is part of the main ledger as well as being a book of prime entry and therefore the "total" column is effectively the credit entry for each of these cash payments in the main ledger.

The postings that remain are the debit entries for each of the column totals:

	£
VAT account	114.44
Purchases account	654.06
Purchases ledger control account	3,224.64
	3,993.14

The total of these debit entries is equal to the credit entry, the total of the entries in the cash payments book.

HOW IT WORKS

Each of these totals will now be posted to the relevant ledger account in the main ledger. Remember that these accounts will have opening balances in them showing the amount of that type of transaction to date.

The opening balance on the VAT account shows the amount that at the start of today Southfield owe to HMRC – as an amount owing, a creditor, this is a credit balance.

VAT account			
	£		£
Cash payments book	114.44	Balance b/d	6,732.62

The opening balance on the purchases account shows the amount of purchases to date and, as an expense, is a debit balance.

Purchases account			
	£		£
Balance b/d	167,335.21		
Cash payments book	654.06		

The opening balance on the creditors control account shows the amount currently owing to credit suppliers – a credit balance as this is a liability.

Purchases ledger control account

	£		£
Cash payments book	3,224.64	Balance b/d	6,728.30

Note that each of the debit entries has been referenced to the cash payments book. In future this will be shortened to CPB.

Activity 3

Would a liability account in the main ledger have a debit or credit balance as its opening balance in normal circumstances?

DISCOUNTS RECEIVED

We have not quite completed the entries to the main ledger accounts as we still have to deal with the discounts received.

Both a debit and credit entry are required for the discounts received column total. The debit entry is to the purchases ledger control account as the discount received is effectively reducing the amount owed to the creditors.

The credit entry is to a discounts received account. Remember that a credit entry means either a liability or income. The discount received is a form of income as it is a reduction of the invoiced amount of the goods purchased.

HOW IT WORKS

The total of the discount received column from Southfield's cash payments book will now be posted:

Purchases ledger control account

	£		£
Cash payments book	3,224.64	Balance b/d	6,728.30
CPB – discount	101.85		

Discount received account		
£		£
	CPB	101.85

Activity 4

What are the two entries that must be made for discounts received in the main ledger?

POSTING THE CASH PAYMENTS BOOK TO THE SUBSIDIARY LEDGER

Every payment made to credit suppliers must be entered not only in the main ledger as part of the totals posted, but also in the subsidiary (purchases) ledger.

Therefore each item in the "purchases ledger" column must be entered into the individual creditors' accounts in the subsidiary (purchases) ledger. The entry for the payment will be on the debit side of the creditor's account as it is reducing the amount owed to the creditor.

Do not forget about the discounts received – just as in the main ledger any discount received from a supplier must also be debited to that supplier's individual account.

As in the main ledger each of the creditor accounts are now shown with an opening balance representing the amount owed to that creditor at the start of the day.

HOW IT WORKS

We will now post each entry from the 'purchases ledger' column to purchases ledger accounts for Southfield.

	Seeban		PL 46
	£		£
CPB	1,284.90	Balance b/d	2,573.28
CPB – discount	67.62		

	Elec. North Ltd		PL 13
	£		£
CPB	440.00	Balance b/d	440.00

	Comtec Ltd		PL 19
	£		£
CPB	650.37	Balance b/d	1,026.36
CPB – discount	34.23		

	Chiller Supplies		PL 03
	£		£
CPB	849.37	Balance b/d	2,958.08

Activity 5

The opening balance on a creditor's account, Hillside Enterprises, is £1,275.04. Show how this would appear in the purchases ledger account for this supplier.

student notes✎

AUTOMATED PAYMENTS

We saw in an earlier chapter that there are many ways in which payments can be organised directly out of the bank account without the need for writing a cheque. The most commonly used of these are likely to be standing orders and direct debits.

Standing orders and direct debits are payments and therefore should be recorded in the cash payments book. However as no cheque is written then there is no originating document that will allow the payment to be automatically written up in the cash payments book.

Standing order and direct debit mandates should be filed and this file should be checked frequently to ensure that all payments are recorded in the cash payments book.

As a standing order is for a fixed amount at a fixed time, there is no problem recording this as a payment on the due date. However some direct debits are of variable amounts and at variable times which means that although you know that a payment of some sort is due to leave the bank account at some point, you cannot be more specific than this. In these cases it is normal practice for the receiver of the money to send some sort of statement showing the amount that is to be paid and the date that it will leave your bank account. You should use this to write up the cash payments book.

HOW IT WORKS

You are writing up the cash payments book for Southfield Electrical on 28 September and as part of this process you check the automated payments file. In this file the following are noted:

25th of each month – standing order payment to Benham District Council – £400.00 – business rates – PL 12

27th of each month – direct debit payment to English Gas – currently £200.00 – gas bill on account – PL04

These must be entered into the cash payments book before it is totalled.

Date	Details	Ref	Total £	VAT £	Cash purchases £	Purchases ledger £	Sundry £	Discounts received £
28/9	003102 Seeban	PL46	1,284.90			1,284.90		67.62
28/9	003103 Elec North Ltd	PL13	440.00			440.00		
28/9	003104 P J Harvey	ML	268.50	39.98	228.52			
28/9	003105 Comtec Ltd	PL19	650.37			650.37		34.23
28/9	003106 Chiller Supplies	PL03	849.37			849.37		
28/9	003107 W G Supplier	ML	500.00	74.46	425.54			
28/9	BDC – SO	PL12	400.00			400.00		
28/9	English Gas – DD	PL04	200.00			200.00		
			4,593.14	114.44	654.06	3,824.64		101.85

In the purchases ledger there would then be two more entries:

Benham District Council		PL 12	
	£		£
CPB - SO	400.00	Balance b/d	2,400.00

English Gas		PL 04	
	£		£
CPB - DD	200.00	Balance b/d	400.00

Activity 6

Post the new column totals of the cash payments book to the relevant main ledger accounts.

CAPITAL AND REVENUE EXPENDITURE

Most of the payments that a business will make will be for goods for manufacture or to resell, or for expenses of the business. However on occasions there may be other types of payment.

In the first chapter of this Course Companion we saw that when a business buys assets which are for long term use in the business, such as machinery, property, cars, fixtures and fittings, these are known as fixed assets. The expenditure on fixed asset is known as CAPITAL EXPENDITURE. Payments for all other day to day running costs and purchases are REVENUE EXPENDITURE.

If the business does purchase a fixed asset by writing a cheque or making some other form of payment out of the bank account this capital expenditure must also be written up in the cash payments book. It may be included in the sundry expenditure column or in some businesses there may be a specific analysis column in the cash payments book for capital expenditure.

CASH PAYMENTS BOOK AND THE MAIN LEDGER

We have seen so far in this chapter that normally the cash payments book is not only a book of prime entry but also part of the main ledger. For this reason the only main ledger postings that are required are the debit entries for the total of each of the analysis columns. The credit entry is the total column in the cash payments book.

However in some accounting systems the cash payments book is only a book of prime entry, it is not part of the main ledger. In such an accounting system the total of the total column in the cash payments book must therefore be credited to the bank ledger account in order to complete the double entry.

SUPPLIERS' STATEMENTS

In earlier chapters it has been noted that it is common for sellers of goods to send out statements to each of their credit customers on a regular basis, showing the invoices and credit notes issued and any payments received.

When this statement is received by the buyer of the goods it should be checked carefully to the supplier's account in the buyer's subsidiary (purchases) ledger to ensure that it is correct. This is of particular importance if the payment to the supplier is to be based upon the information in the statement.

A statement from Southfield Electrical to Whitehill Superstores that was used earlier in this Companion is shown again below. Shown also is Southfield's creditor account in Whitehill's purchases ledger.

STATEMENT

Southfield Electrical
Industrial Estate
Benham DR6 2FF
Tel 0303379 Fax 0303152
VAT Reg 0264 2274 49

To: Whitehill Superstores
28, Whitehill Park
Benham
DR6 5LM

Account number: SL 44

Date: 31 Oct 2006

Date	Details	Debit	Credit	Balance
1 Oct	Balance b/d	1,483.29		1,483.29
2 Oct	Inv 56389	2,140.16		3,623.45
15 Oct	Inv 56436	1,118.23		4,741.68
18 Oct	CN 08662		123.80	4,617.88
28 Oct	Payment received		1,483.29	3,134.59

Amount now due | £3,134.59

Southfield Electrical

	£			£
		1 Oct Balance b/d		1,483.29
		2 Oct PDB – 56389		2,140.16
		15 Oct PDB – 56436		1,118.23
18 Oct PRDB – CN 08662	323.80			
23 Oct CPB	1,483.29			
Balance c/d	2,934.59			
	4,741.68			4,741.68
		Balance b/d		2,934.59

The statement and the creditor's account must be carefully compared:

- note that the debits and credits can be a bit confusing – remember that the statement is prepared by Southfield so when an invoice is sent out it is recorded as a debit – in Whitehill's account for Southfield however it will be recorded as a credit, being an invoice received;

- the first check that you would make would be if the balance carried down on the creditor's account agreed with the balance on the statement. In this case it does not, so check the statement entries carefully to the account entries to find the difference;

- in this case it is the credit note that is recorded as £123.80 on Southfield's statement and £323.80 in the creditor's account;

- when discovering a discrepancy such as this there should never be an immediate assumption that the supplier has made a mistake – instead the first reaction should be to check the original documentation – find the credit note 08662 from the filing system and check what amount it was for;

- if the error has been made by your own organisation, Whitehill, then a journal entry will be made to correct it (see later in this Course Companion);

- if the error has been made by Southfield then either a polite telephone call or letter to the sales manager at Southfield should mean that the error is rectified.

Whenever dealing with suppliers it is important that your information is always correct and that you have always checked any discrepancy to the original documentation. Provided this has been done then you are in a position to be firm and effective but, as always, remaining polite and courteous.

Timing differences

In the previous instance the difference between the statement balance and the creditor's account balance was due to an error having been made by either Southfield or Whitehill.

However the difference between the two balances might not be due to errors but due to timing differences.

HOW IT WORKS

Suppose that Southfield had not received the payment from Whitehill of £1,483.29 until 2 November, although Whitehill had entered it into the cash payments book on 25 October. This would have meant that the payment was in Whitehill's records on 31 October but not in Southfield's. Therefore Southfield's statement would have showed an amount of £4,617.88 being due.

Another example would have been if Southfield had sent more goods to Whitehill on 31 October but these were not entered into Whitehill's accounts until 1 November – these would have been recorded in Southfield's accounts but not in Whitehill's so again there would be a difference.

If such differences are identified then they should be dealt with courteously with the supplier in order to discover the reason for the difference, which may be a simple timing difference as illustrated here.

Discrepancies arising from supplier statements

As well as discrepancies arising from supplier statements due to timing differences, there are a number of other reasons for which there may be queries or discrepancies regarding the amounts owed to suppliers. The range statement for Unit 2 identifies four types of discrepancy.

Non delivery of goods charged

We saw in an earlier chapter that when a purchase invoice is authorised for payment it should be checked to supporting documentation. This will include checks to delivery documentation - delivery note and/or goods received note. If there is no internal evidence that the goods have actually been received then the invoice would not be authorised for payment and the supplier should be contacted.

Duplicated invoices

Again, during the authorisation process for the invoice the purchase invoice should be checked to the purchase order to ensure that the goods that were delivered and are being paid for are the goods that were actually ordered. The invoice should then be filed with the supporting documentation. Therefore if a further invoice is received for the same goods this will be identified as there will be no un-filed supporting documentation.

Incorrect calculations

Whilst checking the purchase invoice, basic checks should be carried out on all calculations and extensions on the invoice including additions, discounts and VAT calculations. If there are any incorrect calculations the supplier must be contacted and a credit note for the difference requested.

Incorrect discounts

When the authorisation checks are carried out on the invoice the supplier master file should be checked to ensure that the correct agreed trade and settlement discounts have been deducted by the supplier. If an incorrect discount has been applied to the invoice the supplier should be contacted and a credit note requested.

Communicating with the supplier

If any of the discrepancies above are noted on the invoice, a letter will normally be written to the supplier clearly explaining the problem and requesting rectification. If the problem is to do with the goods themselves then action will be required from the supplier to replace them. However in most cases the problem will be with the invoice itself and the normal procedure would be to request a credit note from the supplier in order to amend the original invoice so that the correct amount is payable.

COMPUTERISED PAYMENTS

As mentioned when dealing with cash receipts, a typical integrated accounting system will have special 'cash' or 'bank' options to carry out the various accounting tasks associated with cash.

Paying a supplier is a very similar process to receiving cash from a customer: you need to allocate the amount you intend to pay to outstanding invoices, as in the illustration below from the TAS Books package.

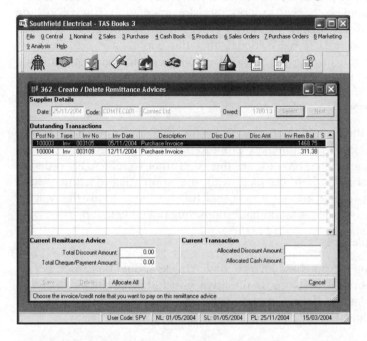

In this example you could either click on the Allocate All button or select one of the individual invoices and just pay that one.

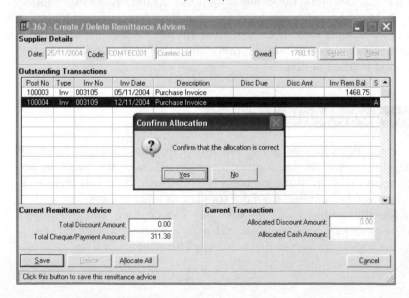

If you are using your package to produce the actual cheques (rather than writing them out by hand) the next step is to print them out. The accounting package can "translate" the figures into words for cheque writing purposes: you don't need to type the amount in words in yourself.

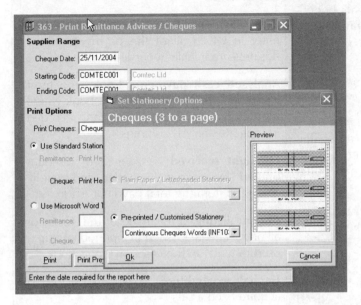

Finally you will post the details to the ledgers. Note that this stage is done last, to guard against errors in the printing process: for instance a paper jam might mean that a batch of pre-printed cheques are wasted and have to be printed again, so you will only know the actual cheque numbers when you are sure that they have been printed properly.

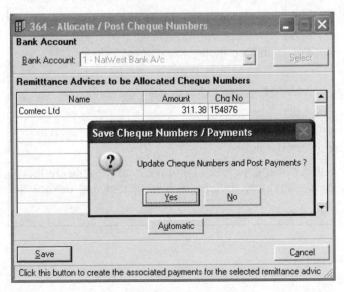

Clicking Yes here will post the necessary debit and credit entries to ALL the ledgers in one go, updating the individual supplier account and also the Creditors control account and the Bank account in the main ledger.

CHAPTER OVERVIEW

- the primary record for recording payments by an organisation is the cash payments book – this is normally not only a book of prime entry but also part of the main ledger being the credit entries in the cash account

- the main entries in the cash payments book are from the cheques written in the period

- when the cash payments book is totalled and the totals are checked by cross-casting the column totals, the discount received column total is not included as this is not part of the total payments

- when the cash payments book is posted to the main ledger the entries are to post the VAT and analysis column totals to the debit of the relevant main ledger accounts

- the discounts received column total is debited to the creditors control account and credited to a discounts received account

- the individual payments to credit suppliers must also be recorded in the subsidiary (purchases) ledger accounts by debiting each individual supplier's account with the total of the payment – the individual accounts must also be debited with the amount of any discount taken

- any standing order payments and direct debit payments must also be entered into the cash payments book and posted to the main ledger and subsidiary (purchases) ledger (if they are treated as credit suppliers)

- payments to be recorded in the cash payments book include capital expenditure as well as revenue expenditure

- if the cash payments book is not part of the double entry system a credit entry is required in the bank ledger account for the total payments for the period

- when a statement is received from a credit supplier it must be checked carefully to the creditor's account in the subsidiary (purchases) ledger and any differences investigated and dealt with appropriately

KEY WORDS

Cash payments book the book of prime entry in which all of the payments of the business are initially recorded

Analysed cash payments book the most common type of cash payments book where the different types of payment are recorded in separate analysis columns

Discount received a settlement discount offered by a credit supplier and validly deducted from the total payment made

Cheque listing a list made of the details of all of the cheques issued in a period and then used to write up the cash payments book

Capital expenditure payments made to acquire fixed assets

Revenue expenditure all payments other than capital expenditure

HOW MUCH HAVE YOU LEARNED?

1   Explain how the cash payments book is both a book of prime entry and part of the main ledger.

2   Why is it that the VAT is analysed out for payments for cash purchases but not for payments to credit suppliers?

3   Given below is a cheque listing for the week ending 22 October 2006 for your organisation.

Cheque listing 22 October 2006

Cheque number	Payee	Purchase ledger code	Amount £	Discount £
06273	P. Products Ltd	PL23	241.58	
06274	Jason Bros	PL36	336.29	6.86
06275	P Taylor		250.00	
06276	R R Partners	PL06	163.47	4.19
06277	Troyde Ltd	PL14	183.57	
06278	O L Simms		116.58	
06279	F Elliott	PL20	263.68	8.15

Any payment that does not have a purchase ledger code is a payment for cash purchases which include VAT at 17.5%.

You also discover from the file of standing order payments that there is a standing order payment of £200.00 on the 22nd of each month to G L Finance, being loan repayments.

You are required to write up the cash payments book using this information. At this stage you should total all of the columns and check that they are correct by cross-casting the column totals.

4   Using the cash payments book from the previous question, you are now required to enter the necessary totals in the main ledger accounts in order to complete the double entry.

5   Again using the cash payments book from the earlier question, you are now required to post the individual payments to creditors to the creditors' accounts in the subsidiary (purchases) ledger. These accounts are given below.

	R R Partners		PL 06
£			£
	Balance b/d		332.68

	Troyde Ltd		PL 14
£			£
	Balance b/d		183.57

	F Elliott		PL 20
£			£
	Balance b/d		558.93

	P Products Ltd		PL 23
£			£
	Balance b/d		724.02

	Jason Bros		PL 36
£			£
	Balance b/d		725.37

chapter 13:
PETTY CASH PROCEDURES

chapter coverage 📖

In the previous chapters we have learned how to check and account for receipts and payments. The payments that were considered were either cheque payments or automated payments and most of an organisation's payments will be of this type. However most organisations will on occasion require small amounts of cash for various types of payment or reimbursement of employees. This is known as petty cash and in this chapter we will consider the procedures necessary for dealing with, and accounting for, petty cash. The topics that are to be covered are:

✍ the need for petty cash in a business

✍ how a petty cash claim would be made

✍ the meaning of an imprest petty cash system

✍ the details of a petty cash voucher

✍ the layout of the petty cash book

✍ writing up the petty cash book

✍ totalling and balancing the petty cash book

✍ accounting for cash paid into the petty cash box

✍ posting the petty cash book payments

✍ non-imprest petty cash systems

Unit 2

knowledge and understanding – accounting methods

21 petty cash procedures: imprest and non imprest methods: analysis

17 the use of the cash book and petty cash book as part of the double entry system or as books of prime entry

Performance criteria – element 2.2

A calculate payments from relevant documentation

D enter payments into accounting records

THE NEED FOR PETTY CASH

Most business expenses will be paid for by cheque or other automated payment methods that have been considered in earlier chapters. However most organisations will find that they need small amounts of cash on the premises in order to make low value cash purchases and to reimburse employees for valid business expenses. Examples of typical reasons for needing cash might include:

- purchase of stationery or small items required in the office;

- postage payments;

- payment of casual wages, eg the window cleaner;

- reimbursement of travel expenses incurred by employees;

- reimbursement of other expenses of employees incurred on behalf of the organisation such as meals.

It would be inappropriate to require a cheque to be drawn up each time these types of expenses were incurred so instead a small amount of cash is kept for these purposes, known as the PETTY CASH FLOAT.

In outline, the way that it works is that a cheque is written out for a certain amount of cash and this is taken out of the bank and put into a lockable PETTY CASH BOX. This is then the responsibility of the PETTY CASHIER. The petty cashier will deal with all PETTY CASH CLAIMS and will ensure that every claim has a valid PETTY CASH VOUCHER. The petty cashier will also write up the PETTY CASH BOOK.

PETTY CASH SYSTEM

Before looking at the details of the recording and accounting for petty cash we will just consider the overall process of making a claim for petty cash.

You work in the accounts department of an organisation and you have been asked to go out to the local shop to buy more coffee for the office kitchen. This is how the petty cash system would work:

you go to the shop and buy a jar of coffee with your own money for £3.59

you return to the office with the coffee and a shop till receipt for £3.59

you go to the petty cashier and fill in a petty cash voucher with the shop receipt attached

you take the petty cash voucher to the person who told you to buy the coffee, for authorisation

you take the authorised petty cash voucher to the petty cashier and you are given £3.59 in return

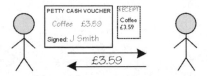

the petty cashier puts the petty cash voucher in the petty cash box and eventually records this in the petty cash book

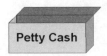

We will now consider this system in more detail.

AN IMPREST PETTY CASH SYSTEM

An IMPREST SYSTEM for petty cash is a common method of dealing with petty cash as it provides a fairly simple way of controlling the cash and payments.

The principle of an imprest system is that when the system is set up a certain sum of cash, say £100, is paid into the petty cash box. In order for any money to be paid out of the petty cash box a valid, authorised petty cash voucher must exist. These vouchers, once they have been paid are also kept in the petty cash box. Therefore at any point in time the amount of cash in the box plus the total of the vouchers should equal the imprest amount:

At the end of the week or month the cash in the petty cash box is topped up to the imprest amount by a withdrawal of cash, by writing a cheque, from the organisation's bank account. The amount needed to top up the petty cash box to the imprest amount is the total of the vouchers for the period:

	£
Imprest amount at start of week	100.00
Petty cash paid out = vouchers	64.00
Cash remaining	36.00
Cash withdrawn from bank to restore imprest	64.00
Cash at start of next week, imprest amount	100.00

PETTY CASH VOUCHER

The key internal document for the proper functioning of a petty cash system is the petty cash voucher. This must be completed and authorised before any cash can be paid out of the petty cash box.

The petty cash voucher for your coffee purchase is given below:

PETTY CASH VOUCHER

Number: *0463*   Date: *1 June 06*

Details	Amount
Coffee for office kitchen	*3 - 59*
Net	*3 - 59*
VAT	—
Gross	*3 - 59*

Claimed by: *P. Norris*

Authorised by: *J. Smith*

There are a number of important points to note about this petty cash voucher:

- it has a sequential number, which ensures that all petty cash vouchers are accounted for;

- the details of the expense are clear and wherever possible a receipt is attached;

- the amount of the expense is shown both net of VAT and gross, ie, the full cost – in this case there is no charge for VAT on food (see later in the chapter);

- the voucher is signed by the person claiming the petty cash;

- most importantly the voucher is authorised by an appropriate member of staff.

Activity 1

Write out a petty cash voucher for the purchase of stationery for £4.25 plus VAT on the blank voucher given below.

PETTY CASH VOUCHER

Number: *0464*   Date:

Details   *Amount*

Net	
VAT	
Gross	

Claimed by:

Authorised by:

PETTY CASH BOOK

Once payments have been made out of the petty cash box, they must be recorded in the petty cash book. The petty cash book will look very similar to the cash receipts and cash payments books already considered.

The difference is that whereas the cash receipts book and cash payments book were separate books with a page each, the petty cash book will generally show the receipts side and the payments side on one page.

The petty cash book is also similar to the cash receipts and payments books in that normally not only is it the book of prime entry for the petty cash vouchers but it is also part of the main ledger and therefore the double entry system.

A typical layout for a petty cash book is given next. Note that the payments side (credit side) is analysed as there are likely to be a number of different types of petty cash payment. However the receipts side (debit side) is much simpler as normally the only receipt into the petty cash box is the weekly or monthly top-up from the bank account.

This is what a typical petty cash book might look like:

RECEIPTS			PAYMENTS							
Date	Details	Amount £	Date	Details	Voucher number	Total £	VAT £	Travel £	Post £	Stationery £	Office supplies £

Note the following points about this layout:

- the receipts are recorded on the debit side as in the main cash account or cash book and the payments on the credit side;

- the receipts side of the petty cash book is not analysed as all that will be recorded here is the payment of cash into the petty cash box;

- the payments side is however analysed into the types of petty cash expenditure incurred by the organisation (there may well be more columns than illustrated here);

- the payments side includes a column for VAT as this must be analysed out if any of the payments include a VAT element (see below).

VAT

If a payment is made out of the petty cash box for an item that has had VAT charged on it, the VAT must be recorded in the VAT column and the net of VAT amount shown in the analysis column. The VAT laws are fairly complex but for the purposes of writing up the petty cash book the following guidelines should help. There is no VAT on:

- postage costs;
- bus or rail fares;
- food or drinks;
- taxi fares;

There is VAT on :
- restaurant meals;
- stationery.

When goods are purchased in a shop then a till receipt will be given to the customer. When a claim for petty cash is made this receipt should be attached to the petty cash voucher and will also be used to determine any VAT on the purchase. Very often this till receipt however shows only the total price of the goods and the VAT is not analysed out. A typical receipt for a pack of printer paper is shown:

```
F G SMITH
VAT 446 7265 31


PAPER        3.80

TOTAL        3.80


CASH         5.00
CHANGE       1.20


CASHIER 2
10:26AM 8/12/06
```

- the receipt shows the total cost of the paper as £3.80

- the cash given to pay for it was £5.00 and the change was £1.20

- the paper includes VAT but the amount of the VAT must be calculated:

  $£3.80 \times 17.5/117.5 = £0.56$
  (remember that VAT is rounded down to the nearest penny)

- the net cost of the paper is therefore:

  $£3.80 - 0.56 = £3.24$

Activity 2

A taxi fare is to be reimbursed of £9.00. Calculate the VAT included in this fare and the net amount of the fare.

WRITING UP THE PETTY CASH BOOK

At regular intervals the petty cashier will write up the petty cash book from the petty cash vouchers that have been kept in the petty cash box. As well as writing up the payments side of the petty cash book there should also be an entry in the receipts side of the book for any cash paid into the petty cash box.

HOW IT WORKS

One of your duties at Southfield Electrical is to write up the petty cash book each week. At the start of the week, 4 October, the petty cash box was empty and the imprest amount of £100.00 was withdrawn from the bank in cash and placed in the petty cash box.

The petty cash vouchers for the week show the following details:

Voucher 0465	Stationery costing £5.60 including VAT
Voucher 0466	Train fare of £15.80
Voucher 0467	Postage costs of £15.60
Voucher 0468	Coffee and biscuits for the office costing £3.85
Voucher 0469	Taxi fare £4.80 including VAT
Voucher 0470	Postage costs of £8.30
Voucher 0471	Envelopes costing £2.60 including VAT
Voucher 0472	Train fare of £12.30

The petty cash book will now be written up.

RECEIPTS			PAYMENTS								
Date	Details	Amount £	Date	Details	Voucher number	Total £	VAT £	Travel £	Post £	Stationery £	Office supplies £
4 Oct	Cash	100.00	8 Oct	Stationery	465	5.60	0.83			4.77	
			8 Oct	Train fare	466	15.80		15.80			
			8 Oct	Postage	467	15.60			15.60		
			8 Oct	Coffee	468	3.85					3.85
			8 Oct	Taxi fare	469	4.80	0.71	4.09			
			8 Oct	Postage	470	8.30			8.30		
			8 Oct	Envelopes	471	2.60	0.38			2.22	
			8 Oct	Train fare	472	12.30		12.30			

Once the petty cash vouchers have been written up in the petty cash book then the petty cash book must be totalled and balanced.

Step 1   Total the receipts column and underline it.

Step 2   Total the total payments column but do not underline the total.

Step 3   Total each of the payments analysis columns and rule them off. Cross-cast these totals to ensure that they add back to the total of the total column.

Step 4   Put the receipts total as the final total in the payments column and find the difference between the receipts total and the total payments total – the balance on the petty cash book that should be carried down.

RECEIPTS			PAYMENTS								
Date	Details	Amount £	Date	Details	Voucher number	Total £	VAT £	Travel £	Post £	Stationery £	Office supplies £
4 Oct	Cash	100.00	8 Oct	Stationery	465	5.60	0.83			4.77	
			8 Oct	Train fare	466	15.80		15.80			
			8 Oct	Postage	467	15.60			15.60		
			8 Oct	Coffee	468	3.85					3.85
			8 Oct	Taxi fare	469	4.80	0.71	4.09			
			8 Oct	Postage	470	8.30			8.30		
			8 Oct	Envelopes	471	2.60	0.38			2.22	
			8 Oct	Train fare	472	12.30		12.30			
						68.85	1.92	32.19	23.90	6.99	3.85
			Balance c/d			31.15					
		100.00				100.00					
Balance b/d		31.15									

The final stage in the process is to bring the petty cash box back to the imprest amount and to enter this into the petty cash book.

We have already seen that to bring the petty cash box back to the imprest amount the cash required is the total of all of the petty cash vouchers. Therefore in this case £68.85 in cash is required. This will normally be achieved by completing a CHEQUE REQUISITION FORM for this amount. This is shown below:

CHEQUE REQUISITION FORM

Southfield Electrical

Requested by:	*Petty cashier*	**Date:**	*8 Oct 2006*
Payable to:	*Cash*		
Amount:	*£68.85*		
Send to:	*Petty cashier*		

Reason: *Petty cash imprest*

Invoice/receipt attached: ....

Other documentation: ....

Authorised by: .... **Date:** ....

The cheque requisition form will now be authorised by a more senior person in the accounts department and a cheque will be written out for cash of £68.85.

When the cash is put into the petty cash box the petty cash book will be amended to show this receipt:

RECEIPTS			PAYMENTS								
Date	Details	Amount £	Date	Details	Voucher number	Total £	VAT £	Travel £	Post £	Stationery £	Office supplies £
4 Oct	Cash	100.00	8 Oct	Stationery	465	5.60	0.83			4.77	
			8 Oct	Train fare	466	15.80		15.80			
			8 Oct	Postage	467	15.60			15.60		
			8 Oct	Coffee	468	3.85					3.85
			8 Oct	Taxi fare	469	4.80	0.71	4.09			
			8 Oct	Postage	470	8.30			8.30		
			8 Oct	Envelopes	471	2.60	0.38			2.22	
			8 Oct	Train fare	472	12.30		12.30			
						68.85	1.92	32.19	23.90	6.99	3.85
			Balance c/d			31.15					
		100.00				100.00					
Balance b/d		31.15									
8 Oct	Cash	68.85									

The petty cash book now has an opening balance of £100.00, the imprest amount, ready for the start of the following week.

Double entry

We will now consider the double entry for this payment of cash into the petty cash box. Remember that both the petty cash book and the cash payments book are normally part of the main ledger as well as being books of prime entry.

When the cheque for £68.85 was written out it would have been entered into the cash payments book, a credit entry, along with all of the other cheque payments of the organisation. When the £68.85 was entered in the receipts column of the petty cash book that was the corresponding debit entry – so the double entry for the top-up of the petty cash box is complete.

Activity 3

A business has a petty cash system with an imprest amount of £50.00. During the week petty cash was paid out of the petty cash box totalling £41.30 and the remaining balance in the box was £8.70. How much cash is required to bring the petty cash box back to the imprest amount?

POSTING THE PAYMENTS SIDE OF THE PETTY CASH BOOK

Posting of the payments side of the petty cash book is very similar to posting the Cash Payments Book.

Remember that the petty cash book is normally part of the double entry system and therefore the total column represents the credit entry for each of the petty cash payments. All that remains is to post each of the analysis column totals to the debit side of their relevant accounts.

RECEIPTS			PAYMENTS								
Date	Details	Amount £	Date	Details	Voucher number	Total £	VAT £	Travel £	Post £	Stationery £	Office supplies £
4 Oct	Cash	100.00	8 Oct	Stationery	465	5.60	0.83			4.77	
			8 Oct	Train fare	466	15.80		15.80			
			8 Oct	Postage	467	15.60			15.60		
			8 Oct	Coffee	468	3.85					3.85
			8 Oct	Taxi fare	469	4.80	0.71	4.09			
			8 Oct	Postage	470	8.30			8.30		
			8 Oct	Envelopes	471	2.60	0.38			2.22	
			8 Oct	Train fare	472	12.30		12.30			
						68.85	1.92	32.19	23.90	6.99	3.85
						CREDIT	VAT	Travel		Stationery	Office supplies
									DEBITS		
			Balance c/d			31.15			Postage		
		100.00				100.00					
Balance b/d		31.15									
8 Oct	Cash	68.85									

student notes ✍

Main ledger

VAT account

	£		£
Petty cash book	1.92		

Travel expenses account

	£		£
Petty cash book	32.19		

Postage account

	£		£
Petty cash book	23.90		

Stationery account

	£		£
Petty cash book	6.99		

Office supplies account		
	£	£
Petty cash book	3.85	

Note that in each case the reference is to the petty cash book. This will normally be abbreviated to PCB and will include the precise page number of the petty cash book eg, PCB42.

NON IMPREST PETTY CASH SYSTEMS

We have concentrated so far on a petty cash system that has a fixed imprest amount. The petty cash box is always topped up to that amount at the end of each period. However it is also possible to run a petty cash system without an imprest amount.

For example, it might be the organisation's policy to pay £50 into the petty cash box at the start of each week as this is a good estimate of the value of petty cash claims there are each week.

There are two potential problems with this system:

- if the claims in a week are more than £50 then the petty cashier may run out of cash in the petty cash box;

- if the claims are substantially less than £50 for a number of weeks then the amount of cash being held in the petty cash box will accumulate – this cash would be of more use in the business bank account than sitting unused in the petty cash box.

PETTY CASH BOOK AND THE MAIN LEDGER

Throughout this chapter we have assumed, as is normal practice, that the petty cash book is not only the book of prime entry for petty cash vouchers but is also part of the double entry in the main ledger. This has meant that other than writing up the petty cash book the only necessary entries were to debit the various expense accounts with the totals of the analysis columns on the payments side of the petty cash book.

In some businesses the petty cash book is simply the book of prime entry and is not part of the double entry system in the main ledger. In such an accounting system there will be a separate main ledger account for petty cash. The total of the receipts into the petty cash box will be debited to this account and the total petty cash payments for the period, taken from the petty cash book, will be credited to the petty cash ledger account.

CHAPTER OVERVIEW

- most businesses will require small amounts of cash on the premises for the purchase of low value items and the reimbursement of employees for business expenses

- this cash is known as the petty cash float and is kept in the petty cash box by the petty cashier

- if an employee incurs a business expense and pays for it himself then this can be reclaimed by completing a petty cash voucher, attaching evidence of the expense, having the voucher authorised and then presenting this to the petty cashier for reimbursement of the amount spent

- an imprest system for petty cash is where the petty cash box is always topped up to the same amount, the imprest amount, at the end of each week or month

- claims can only be made from the petty cashier if they are supported by a properly authorised petty cash voucher

- the petty cash vouchers must then be written up in the petty cash book

- the petty cash book has a receipts side and a payments side and is normally part of the main ledger as well as being a book of prime entry – the payments side will be analysed into columns for VAT and all of the types of petty cash claim that the organisation normally deals with

- when the petty cash vouchers have been written up into the petty cash book it must then be totalled and balanced – finally the petty cash box must be reimbursed back to the imprest amount and this is recorded on the receipts side

- the double entry for the cash being paid into the petty cash box is a credit entry in the cash payments book and the debit entry in the petty cash book

- the payments side of the petty cash book is posted by debiting the VAT and analysis column totals to the relevant accounts in the main ledger

- other non-imprest petty cash systems may be used by some organisations where for example a fixed amount is paid into the petty cash box at the start of each week or month

- if the petty cash book is not part of the double entry system then a separate petty cash ledger account must be kept in the main ledger to record the receipt into the petty cash box and the total payments made

HOW MUCH HAVE YOU LEARNED?

1   Explain how an imprest petty cash system works.

2   Given below are details of three petty cash claims – write up the petty cash vouchers given below showing all of the details for these claims. The last petty cash voucher used was number 0623 and today's date is 20 October 2006.

For each claim state what documentation should be attached to the claim.

a)   A claim made by Trevor Forbes for postage for a parcel to a customer totalling £8.30

b)   A claim made by Janis Williams for the purchase of paper costing £4.80 and envelopes costing £2.40 for use in the office

c)   A claim made by Dan Granger for his train fare of £12.80 when visiting a customer

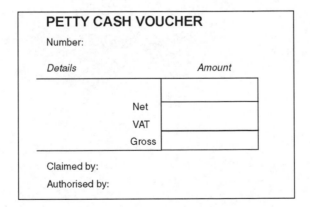

PETTY CASH VOUCHER

Number:

Details		Amount
	Net	
	VAT	
	Gross	

Claimed by:
Authorised by:

PETTY CASH VOUCHER

Number:

Details		Amount
	Net	
	VAT	
	Gross	

Claimed by:
Authorised by:

PETTY CASH VOUCHER

Number:

Details		Amount
	Net	
	VAT	
	Gross	

Claimed by:
Authorised by:

3   A petty cash system is run on the basis of £150 in the petty cash box at the start of each week. At the end of one week the total of the vouchers in the petty cash box was £89.46. How much should the cheque requisition form be made out for to restore the petty cash box to its imprest amount?

4   The petty cash system in your organisation is run on an imprest system with an imprest amount of £150.00. The petty cash float at the start of the week beginning 20 October was £150.00 and the 8 petty cash vouchers were completed, authorised and paid during the week. The petty cash book analyses payments into VAT, postage, travel, sundry office expenses, and miscellaneous expenses.

The details of the petty cash vouchers are given below:

Voucher 771   train fare £14.00
Voucher 772   postage £18.60
Voucher 773   taxi fare £15.00
Voucher 774   window cleaner £20.00
Voucher 775   pens and paper £14.83
Voucher 776   postage £5.46
Voucher 777   taxi fare £18.70
Voucher 778   computer discs £14.70

You are required to:

a)   write up the petty cash book for these vouchers

b)   total and balance the petty cash book

c)   post the payments side of the petty cash book to the main ledger

d)   account for the amount of cash paid into the petty cash box to restore it to the imprest amount

chapter 14:
PAYROLL ACCOUNTING PROCEDURES

chapter coverage 📖

The Unit 2 syllabus is not confined only to dealing with payments to credit suppliers. As we saw in the previous chapter you also need to be able to deal with and account for petty cash payments. In this chapter we will consider the final type of payment that must be dealt with for Unit 2 and that is the payment of, and accounting for, wages and salaries. The topics that are to be covered are:

- ✍ the UK income tax system

- ✍ PAYE

- ✍ National Insurance Contributions – employee and employer

- ✍ other non-statutory deductions

- ✍ calculating net pay from gross pay

- ✍ methods of paying employees

- ✍ the payslip

- ✍ double entry accounting for payroll payments

- ✍ the wages book

- ✍ the employer's payments to HM Revenue and Customs

- ✍ security and confidentiality

Unit 2

knowledge and understanding – accounting methods

11 double entry bookkeeping including balancing accounts

22 the processes and systems required to make and record internal and external payroll payments, excluding the use of tax and NI tables

23 methods of handling and storing money from a security aspect

Performance criteria – element 2.2

A calculate payments from relevant documentation

B schedule payments and obtain authorisation

C use the appropriate payment method and timsescale in accordance with organisational procedures

D enter payments into accounting records

F ensure security and confidentiality is maintained according to organisational requirements

THE UK TAX SYSTEM

In order to fully understand the payments that are made to employees for wages and salaries and the accounting procedures that are followed, it is necessary to have an outline understanding of the way in which individuals are taxed in the UK.

An individual is required to pay INCOME TAX to HM Revenue and Customs (HMRC) on all the types of income that he has. The only income that we are concerned about is the wage or salary that an employee earns.

This income tax is charged at different rates depending upon the amount of income that the person has. For 2007/2008 the rates of income tax are:

Up to £2,230	10%
£2,231 – £34,600	22%
Above £34,600	40%

However, not all income that a person receives is taxed, as each individual is allocated a PERSONAL ALLOWANCE. This personal allowance is the amount that can be earned before any income tax becomes payable. For 2007/08 the personal allowance for a person is £5,225. This means that a person can earn up to £5,225 before any tax is paid.

HOW IT WORKS

Ian works for Southfield Electrical and earns £24,000 in a year. His income tax payable can be calculated:

	£		Income tax payable £
Earnings	24,000		
Less: personal allowance	5,225		
Taxable income	18,775		
Starting rate tax	(2,230)	× 10%	223.00
Basic rate tax	16,545	× 22%	3,639.90
Total tax payable for the year			3,862.90

Activity 1

What is a personal allowance?

PAYE

Ian will pay the tax on his income under PAYE. PAYE stands for Pay As You Earn and in outline it means that Ian's personal allowance and different tax rates are spread over the entire tax year, 6 April to 5 April, meaning that he pays approximately the same amount of income tax each week or month.

The way in which the income tax is paid is that each time Ian is paid by his employer the income tax for that week or month is deducted from his salary by the employer and the employer then pays it over to the Inland Revenue on Ian's behalf.

The PAYE system is complicated but at this level you only need to have an outline understanding of how it works.

HOW IT WORKS

Let's suppose that Ian is employed and paid monthly by Southfield. Earning £24,000 a year means that each month his GROSS WAGE/SALARY is £2,000. Gross wage or salary is the amount an employee earns before any deductions.

Whether an employee's pay is described as a wage or a salary usually depends upon the frequency of payment – weekly payments are normally termed wages whilst monthly payments are described as salaries – otherwise the distinction is not of any relevance.

Each month Ian will not receive £2,000 as there will be a number of deductions made from this amount. Once all the deductions have been made the remainder that is paid to Ian is his NET WAGE/SALARY.

For the time being we will consider only the deduction for PAYE income tax. Each month the payroll department of Southfield must calculate the amount of income tax to be deducted from Ian's gross salary. This is a complicated process but is eased by the fact that the Inland Revenue provide tables to help employers calculate the correct figures.

The first thing that the payroll department will need to know is Ian's personal allowance. This is notified to Southfield by the Inland Revenue in the form of Ian's TAX CODE. Southfield will be sent a P6 Notice of coding which will state Ian's tax code. The tax code is basically the first three digits of his personal allowance followed by a letter that indicates his status for tax purposes ie, single or married, under or over 65. In the absence of any other complications Ian's tax code would be 522L. This tax code is the key to the employer's further calculations.

Once the tax code is known then the payroll department will be able to calculate the income tax that should be paid by Ian for this particular month of the tax year using the TAX TABLES provided by HMRC. These tables consist of Table A, Table LR and Tables B to D.

Although you need to be aware of the existence of these tax tables you do not need to be able to use them for Unit 30.

Using the tax tables, Southfield's payroll department calculate that the income tax due by Ian for this month, October, is £344.41.

When Ian is paid by Southfield this amount of tax will be deducted from his gross salary of £2,000 and paid over to HMRC by Southfield on Ian's behalf (see later in the chapter). This means that although Ian will receive a smaller amount each month than his gross salary he does not have to worry about paying any income tax as it has already been done on his behalf by Southfield.

Activity 2

What is the difference between a gross wage and a net wage?

NATIONAL INSURANCE CONTRIBUTIONS

Income tax in the form of PAYE is not the only STATUTORY DEDUCTION from gross pay that must be made by an employer. Employer's must also deduct NATIONAL INSURANCE CONTRIBUTIONS (NIC) from an employee's gross pay.

NIC deductions are also paid over to HMRC by the employer on behalf of the employee. For 2007/2008 the rates for an employee's NIC are:

Earnings below £5,225 per year	nil
Earnings from £5,225 to £34,840 per year	11%
Earnings above £34,840 per year	1%

There are tables provided in order to calculate easily the employee's NIC deduction for the week or month – again you do not need to know how to use these tables.

HOW IT WORKS

Let us suppose that the payroll department at Southfield use the NIC tables and calculate that Ian's NIC payment for the month should be £167.05. This will also be deducted from Ian's gross salary and will be paid over to HMRC by Southfield on Ian's behalf.

Therefore, so far, Ian's monthly net pay would be calculated as follows:

	£	
Gross salary	2,000.00	
PAYE Income tax	(344.41)	Paid to HMRC by Southfield
NIC	(167.05)	Paid to HMRC by Southfield
Net pay	1,488.54	

Employer's National Insurance Contributions

So we have seen that at each pay day the employee must pay NIC, these are known the EMPLOYEE'S NIC.

As well as this however the employer is also required to pay National Insurance Contributions for each employee, known as the EMPLOYER'S NIC. For the year 2007/2008 the rates for the employer are:

Earnings below £5,225 per year	nil
Earnings from £5,225 and above per year	12.8%

Again tables are provided to make the calculation of the amount easier.

HOW IT WORKS

When Southfield pay Ian each month they are also required to pay to the Inland Revenue, the employer's NIC, as well.

Suppose that the employer's NIC for Ian is calculated as £238.42. Southfield will be required to pay this over to HMRC together with the PAYE deducted of £344.41 and Ian's employee's NIC of £167.05.

NON-STATUTORY DEDUCTIONS

So far we have considered two deductions from an employee's pay which are both required by law, income tax and NIC. These are statutory deductions.

There may also be other types of deductions from an employee's pay which are not required by the law but have been chosen by the employee and employer. These are NON-STATUTORY DEDUCTIONS. The most common of these are:

- pension contributions;
- give as you earn;
- save as you earn;
- subscriptions, such as trade union subscriptions.

Each of these will be considered in turn.

Pension contributions

Many employees will be required by their contract of employment to pay a certain percentage of their gross salary into a pension scheme which will accumulate to provide a pension for the employee on his retirement. This amount will be deducted from the employee's gross salary by the employer and paid into the pension scheme on the employee's behalf. In some organisations the employer will also pay a certain percentage into the pension scheme for that employee on each pay day.

Give as you earn scheme – GAYE

Employees can choose to pay money to an approved charity directly from their gross salary under the Give As You Earn Scheme, GAYE. The employee is allowed to pay any amount without limit per tax year and the employer deducts the money from the employee's pay packet and pays it over to the stated charity.

Save as you earn – SAYE

Some employers offer their employees the chance to make regular savings each pay day by an agreed amount being deducted from the pay packet and invested by the employer. At an agreed date the amounts saved can be used to buy shares in the employer's company.

student notes✏

Other deductions

There are also other deductions that can be made from an employee's gross pay, for example the weekly or monthly subscription to the employee's trade union.

GROSS PAY TO NET PAY

Once all of the deductions, both statutory and non-statutory, have been made from an employee's gross pay, what is left is the amount that the employee will actually receive – the net pay.

HOW IT WORKS

When Ian joined Southfield Electrical it was agreed that each month he would pay 5% of his gross salary into the company pension scheme.

We will now see all the elements of Ian's monthly pay and see who pays what to whom:

	£	
Gross pay	2,000.00	
PAYE Income tax	(344.41)	➞ HMRC
Employee's NIC	(167.05)	➞ HMRC
Pension contribution	(100.00)	➞ Pension scheme
Net pay	1,388.54	

So of the original gross salary of £2,000.00 per month Ian only receives £1,388.54. However his income liability has been settled as has the amount of NIC due from him and an amount has been paid into his pension fund.

There is one further payment by Southfield to be made:

Employer's NIC   £238.42   ➞ HMRC

Activity 3

Joan also works for Southfield and is paid on a weekly basis. Her gross wage is £400 per week. The payroll department have calculated that for this week the PAYE income tax payable is £69.07 and Joan's NIC for the week is £33.60. Joan also pays a weekly subscription to her trade union through the payroll of £2.50.

What is Joan's net pay?

PAYING THE EMPLOYEES

Once the payroll department have made all of the calculations required for each employee for that payday then the employees must be actually paid.

Methods of payment

Cash

It is possible to pay employees in cash. However the practical and security arrangements required mean that this is very rarely done. If the employees were to be paid in cash then the factors that need to be considered are:

- withdrawing precisely the correct amount of notes and coins required to give each employee the correct net pay;

- arranging for this cash to be withdrawn from the bank, usually by a security firm;

- keeping the cash secure once it arrives in the payroll department – this must be kept in a safe;

- counting the correct amount of cash for each employee's net pay and placing it in an envelope for that employee;

- ensuring that each employee is given the correct envelope and that this is signed for;

- dealing with the pay envelopes for employees who are absent on pay day.

Cheque

It is also possible to pay each employee's net pay with a cheque. Again however this is a time consuming process as a cheque must be written out for each individual's net pay. The cheques should be crossed for security so that the pay can only be paid into that employee's bank account. Payment by this method would normally only be for an organisation with a small number of employees or for one-off payments for work carried out.

BACS

The most common method of making payroll payments is by BACS, Bankers Automated Clearing System. This is a method of paying the net pay for each employee directly into that employee's bank account.

The details of each employee's bank account and net pay are submitted to the BACS Clearing Centre by computer and the net pay is then directly credited to each employee's bank account and debited from the organisation's bank account.

PAYSLIP

Whatever method of payment is used for paying employees, each payday the employee must be supplied with a payslip showing the makeup of his net pay.

A typical BACS payslip is shown below and the main elements are highlighted:

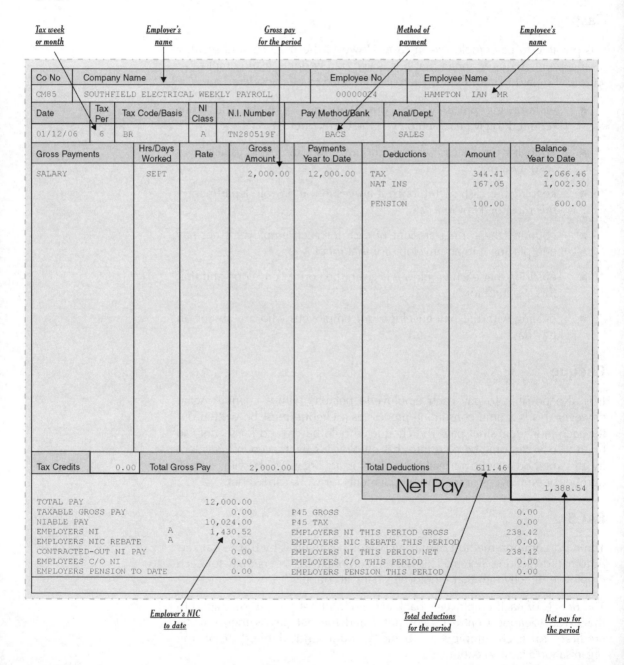

Tax week or month — *Employer's name* — *Gross pay for the period* — *Method of payment* — *Employee's name*

Co No	Company Name					Employee No		Employee Name	
CM85	SOUTHFIELD ELECTRICAL WEEKLY PAYROLL					00000024		HAMPTON IAN MR	

Date	Tax Per	Tax Code/Basis	NI Class	N.I. Number	Pay Method/Bank	Anal/Dept.
01/12/06	6	BR	A	TN280519F	BACS	SALES

Gross Payments	Hrs/Days Worked	Rate	Gross Amount	Payments Year to Date	Deductions	Amount	Balance Year to Date
SALARY	SEPT		2,000.00	12,000.00	TAX	344.41	2,066.46
					NAT INS	167.05	1,002.30
					PENSION	100.00	600.00

Tax Credits	0.00	Total Gross Pay	2,000.00		Total Deductions	611.46

Net Pay 1,388.54

TOTAL PAY	12,000.00		
TAXABLE GROSS PAY	0.00	P45 GROSS	0.00
NIABLE PAY	10,024.00	P45 TAX	0.00
EMPLOYERS NI	A 1,430.52	EMPLOYERS NI THIS PERIOD GROSS	238.42
EMPLOYERS NIC REBATE	A 0.00	EMPLOYERS NIC REBATE THIS PERIOD	0.00
CONTRACTED-OUT NI PAY	0.00	EMPLOYERS NI THIS PERIOD NET	238.42
EMPLOYEES C/O NI	0.00	EMPLOYEES C/O THIS PERIOD	0.00
EMPLOYERS PENSION TO DATE	0.00	EMPLOYERS PENSION THIS PERIOD	0.00

Employer's NIC to date — *Total deductions for the period* — *Net pay for the period*

ACCOUNTING FOR PAYROLL PAYMENTS

The entries into the ledger accounts for the payroll payments are fairly complex but if you bear in mind the system that has just been considered they can be followed through logically:

■ the full cost of employing an employee is:

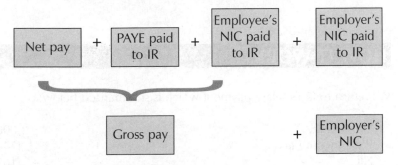

Therefore this cost, gross pay plus employer's NIC, must be what appears as the wages expense for the organisation.

■ the PAYE and NIC that is deducted from the employee's gross pay must be paid over to HMRC by the 19th of the following month (see later in the chapter). Therefore these amounts are creditors until they are paid and must appear in a creditors account.

The double entry reflects these two fundamental factors and uses three main accounts:

■ the gross wages control account;
■ the wages expense account;
■ the PAYE/NIC creditor account;

There are four double entries to be made:

■ gross wages:

   – **debit** entry in the wages expense account
   – **credit** entry in the gross wages control account

■ net wages paid to employee:

   – **debit** entry in the gross wages control account

   – **credit** entry to the cash payments book (the cash/bank account)

■ PAYE and employee's NIC deducted from gross wages

   – **debit** entry in the gross wages control account
   – **credit** entry in the PAYE/NIC creditor account

student notes✎

- employer's NIC

    - **debit** entry in the wages expense account
    - **credit** entry in the gross wages control account

    and

    - **debit** entry in the gross wages control account
    - **credit** entry in the PAYE/NIC creditor account

HOW IT WORKS

We return to Ian's salary payment which is summarised below:

	£
Gross salary	2,000.00
PAYE Income tax	(344.41)
NIC	(167.05)
Pension contribution	(100.00)
Net pay	1,388.54
Employer's NIC	238.42

The entries in the ledger accounts would be as follows:

- gross pay

Wages expense account

	£		£
Gross wages control	2,000.00		

Gross wages control account

	£		£
		Wages expense	2,000.00

- net wages

Gross wages control account

	£		£
Cash Payments Book	1,388.54	Wages expense	2,000.00

- **PAYE and NIC deducted**

Gross wages control account

	£		£
Cash Payments Book	1,388.54	Wages expense	2,000.00
PAYE/NIC creditor	511.46		

PAYE/NIC creditor account

	£		£
		Gross wages control	511.46

- **Pension contribution deducted**

Gross wages control account

	£		£
Cash Payments Book	1,388.54	Wages expense	2,000.00
PAYE/NIC creditor	511.46		
Pension contributions	100.00		

Pension contribution account

	£		£
		Gross wages control	100.00

- **Employer's NIC**

Gross wages control account

	£		£
Cash Payments Book	1,388.54	Wages expense	2,000.00
PAYE/NIC creditor	511.46	Employer's NIC	238.42
Pension contributions	100.00		
Employer's NIC	238.42		
	2,238.42		2,238.42

Wages expenses account

	£		£
Gross wages control	2,000.00	Profit and loss	2,238.42
PAYE/NIC creditor	238.42		
	2,238.42		2,238.42

PAYE/NIC creditor account

	£		£
		Gross wages control	511.46
Balance c/d	749.88	Wages expense	238.42
	749.88		749.88
		Balance b/d	749.88

Summary of double entry

- the gross wages control account shows how the total gross salary was broken down into net pay and deductions;

- the wages expense account shows the cost of employing Ian, ie, gross pay plus employer's NIC;

- the PAYE/NIC creditor account shows how much must be paid over to the creditor by the 19th of the following month;

- the pension contributions account shows how much should be paid into the pension scheme.

Activity 4

Joan works for Southfield and is paid on a weekly basis. Her gross wage is £400 per week. The payroll department have calculated that for this week the PAYE income tax payable is £69.07 and Joan's NIC for the week is £33.60. Joan also pays a weekly subscription to her trade union through the payroll of £2.50. Southfield's NIC contribution for Joan for this week is £41.20.

Enter the payroll transactions for Joan into the ledger accounts.

Wages book

In practice the double entry considered above would not be made for each individual employee. Instead the details of gross pay, deductions, net pay and employer's NIC for each employee would be recorded in a book of prime entry, the WAGES BOOK, on each payday. The columns of the wages book would be totalled and the totals would be posted to the ledger accounts as we have seen earlier.

PAYMENTS TO HMRC

The PAYE and NIC deducted from the employee's gross pay and the employer's NIC are required to be paid over to HMRC each month by the employer. The payment must be made within fourteen days of the tax month end which is the 5th of each month. So payment must reach HMRC by the 19th of each month.

The payment is accompanied by a P30B PAYSLIP.

A P30B payslip is a sort of bank giro credit which details how much is paid to the Collector of Taxes at the Accounts Office split between:

- Income tax;

- National Insurance.

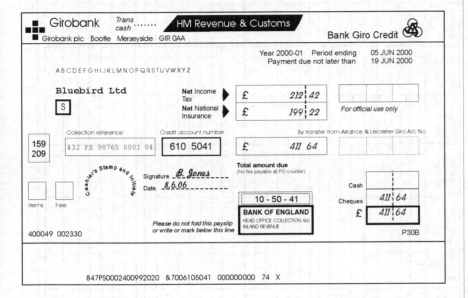

Step 1   Enter in the Net Income Tax box what is due from employees as PAYE.

Step 2   The Net National Insurance is the total of employees' NICs and employer's NICs.

You can use any of these methods for paying HMRC

- Cheque (payable to HMRC)
- Bank giro at the employer's bank
- Transfer from an Alliance & Leicester Giro account
- At a Post Office
- Direct Credit (BACS)

Every time you make a payment this should be recorded on Form P32 or in the Payslip Booklet P30BC. An example of a completed Form P32 is shown below.

HM Revenue & Customs

Employer's Payment Record

Employer's name

SOUTHFIELD ELECTRICAL LTD

Collection Office reference

P

Year ended 5 April — Enter year

You will need information about payments when you complete your form P35 (Employer's Annual Return).
Please enter the details requested each time you make a payment. For example, suppose you make quarterly payments. You would record the details every third month when you make the payment. Or if you enter details for each month (or week) and total them every third month.
Payments to last year's Class 1A National Insurance, unless paid by the Alternative Payment Method, should be included in column 5.

Period	Week no	Income Tax (Inc. outcomes x tax deductions) 1 £	Student Loan Deductions 2 £	Tax Credits Paid 3 £	Net Income Tax (1+2 minus 3) 4 £	Gross NIC 5 £	Statutory Sick Pay (SSP) recovered 6 £	Statutory Maternity Pay (SMP) recovered 7 £	NIC compensation on SMP (if due) 8 £	NIC Holiday claimed 9 £	NIC Rebate claimed 10 £	Total NIC deductions (6+7+8+9+10) 11 £	Net National Insurance (5 minus 11) 12 £	Total amount due (4+12) 13 £	Date paid 14	Tax Credit Funding Amount 15 £	Date received 16
6 April to 5 May	1	40,000 00															
	2																
	3																
Month 1	4																
	Total	40,000 00			40,000 00	21,000 00	-	-	-	-	-	-	21,000 00	61,000 00			
6 May to 5 June	5																
	6																
	7																
Month 2	8																
	Total																
6 June to 5 July	9																
	10																
	11																
	12																
Month 3	13																
	Total																
6 July to 5 Aug	14																
	15																
	16																
	17																
Month 4	Total																
6 Aug to 5 Sep	18																
	19																
	20																
	21																
Month 5	Total																
6 Sep to 5 Oct	22																
	23																
	24																
	25																
Month 6	26																
	Total																
Totals months 1-6																	

CONFIDENTIALITY

The issue of confidentiality has been addressed a number of times in this Course Companion. However nowhere is it more important to be aware of the confidentiality of the information that you are dealing with than when dealing with payroll activities. You are likely to come into contact with information for employees including their address, their bank account details as well as the details of how much they earn and how much tax they pay. Such information should never be passed onto another person either formally or informally.

CHAPTER OVERVIEW

- in the UK individuals pay income tax on all of their income at various rates depending upon the amount of that income

- each individual has a personal allowance which is the amount that they can earn before any income tax becomes payable

- if a person is employed then they will pay their income tax through the PAYE system

- the employer uses the HMRC tax tables and the employee's tax code to determine the amount of income tax that must be deducted from the employee's gross wage/salary each pay day

- a further statutory deduction from the employee's gross pay is the employee's National Insurance Contribution – again tables are provided to ease calculation of the deduction

- the employer must also pay National Insurance Contributions for each employee who earns more than a stated amount per year

- the PAYE deducted, the employee's NIC deducted and the employer's NIC will all be paid over to HMRC by the employer

- there are also other, non-statutory amounts, that may be deducted from an employee's gross pay – pension contributions, GAYE payments, SAYE payments, trade union subscriptions

- wages and salaries may be paid in cash or by cheque but the most common method is by BACS

- when each employee is paid they must be provided with a payslip showing details of the pay and deductions

- the ledger entries for payroll transactions take place in three main ledger accounts – the gross wages control account, the wages expense account and the PAYE/NIC creditor account

KEY WORDS

Income tax the UK tax payable by individuals on all of their income

Personal allowance the amount of income an individual is allowed to earn, given their personal circumstances, before they have to pay income tax

PAYE Pay As You Earn – a method of income tax being deducted from an employee's gross pay at each pay day and paid over to the Inland Revenue by the employer on behalf of the employee

Gross wage/salary the amount of wage or salary earned by an employee before any deductions

Net wage/salary the amount of wage or salary after all deductions have been made – the actual amount the employee is paid

Tax code the code allocated to each individual by HMRC which indicates that person's status for income tax purposes

Tax tables tables provided by HMRC to employers to enable them to calculate the amount of income tax to be deducted from an employee's gross pay each week or month

Statutory deductions the deductions from an employee's gross pay that are required by law – income tax and National Insurance Contributions

National Insurance Contributions an amount that must be paid over to HMRC by both the employee and employer

Employee's NIC the amount that must be deducted from the employee's gross pay and paid over to HMRC

Employer's NIC a further amount of NIC that must be paid by the employer for each employee earning more than a stated amount per year

CHAPTER OVERVIEW cont.

- in practice a wages book will be used as a form of book of prime entry – here the details of gross pay, deductions and net pay will be recorded for each employee – the columns will be totalled and the totals posted to the main ledger accounts

- each month payment of the PAYE and NIC due must be made to HMRC – this payment is accompanied by a completed P30B payslip

- when dealing with the payroll you are likely to come across detailed, personal information about employees – such information should always be treated with the highest level of confidentiality

KEY WORDS

Non-statutory deductions deductions from an employee's gross pay other than the statutory deductions of income tax and NIC

Wages book the book of prime entry for the details of gross pay, deductions and net pay

HOW MUCH HAVE YOU LEARNED?

1   Explain how the PAYE system works and why it is of benefit to employees.

2   When an employer pays a wage to an employee what other payments is the employer due to make?

3   State whether the following deductions from gross pay are statutory deductions or non-statutory deductions:

    a)   Pension contributions
    b)   Income tax
    c)   Employee's NIC
    d)   GAYE payments

4   An employee earns a gross salary of £27,000 and is paid on a monthly basis. For the month of October it has been calculated by the payroll department that the PAYE deduction is £418.16 and that the NIC contributions due are £189.00 from the employee and £274.50 from the employer.

    a)   What is the employee's net pay?
    b)   Record the payroll transactions for this employee in the ledger accounts.

chapter 15:
BANK RECONCILIATION STATEMENT

chapter coverage 📖

The cash book is one of the main books of prime entry and it is vital for any business to ensure control over its cash. The principal means of doing this is through the bank reconciliation statement. The topics that are to be covered are:

✍ writing up the cash receipts book

✍ writing up the cash payments book

✍ how debits and credits appear in the bank statement

✍ the procedure for comparing the cash books to the bank statement

✍ types of discrepancies between the cash books and the bank statement

✍ totalling and posting the cash books

✍ balancing the cash book

✍ preparing the bank reconciliation statement

Unit 3

knowledge and understanding – the business environment

3   general bank services and operation of the bank clearing system (Element 3.1)

knowledge and understanding – accounting methods

12   relationship between the accounting system and the ledger (Elements 3.1 and 3.2)

Performance criteria – element 3.1

A   record details from the relevant primary documentation in the cashbook and ledger
B   correctly calculate totals and balances of receipts and payments
C   compare individual items on the bank statement and in the Cash Book for accuracy
D   identify discrepancies and prepare a bank reconciliation statement

WRITING UP THE CASH BOOK

As we have seen in an earlier chapter the cash book is an unusual document within the accounting system as it is normally both a book of prime entry and part of the double entry system in the main ledger.

It is made up of a cash receipts book and a Cash Payment book.

HOW IT WORKS

We will use examples of receipts and payments that Southfield Electrical received and made during the week ended 28 September 2006.

The remittance list for the week showed the following:

REMITTANCE LIST	
	£
Dagwell Enterprises, cheque	336.50 – £14.02 discount taken
Polygon Stores, cheque	158.20
Peter Hayward, cheque	227.95 – cash sale
G Thomas & Co, cheque	269.43 – £11.23 discount taken
Whitehill Superstores, cheque	673.58 – £28.07 discount taken
Benham Garages, cheque	1,400.00 – sale of motor car
Weller Enterprises, cheque	225.49
John Cooper, cash	75.20 – cash sale

An extract from the sales account code listing is also given:

Polygon Stores	SL 03
Dagwell Enterprises	SL 15
Weller Enterprises	SL 18
Whitehill Superstores	SL 24
G Thomas	SL 30

student notes ✍

The cheque listing for the same week showing the cheque payments made is also given:

Cheque listing 28 September 2006

Cheque number	Payee	Purchase ledger code	Amount £	Discount £
003102	Seeban	PL46	1,284.90	67.62
003103	Elec. North Ltd	PL13	440.00	
003104	P J Harvey	Cash purchase	268.50	
003105	Comtec Ltd	PL19	650.37	34.23
003106	Chiller Supplies	PL03	849.37	
003107	W G Supplies	Cash purchase	500.00	

An extract from the STANDING ORDER SCHEDULE is also provided:

25th of each month   Benham District Council – business rates PL12
£400.00   SO

27th of each month   English Gas – gas bill PL04
£200.00   DD

We now need to write up the cash receipts book and cash payments book for the week:

Cash Receipts Book

Date	Details	Ref	Total £	VAT £	Cash sales £	Sales ledger £	Sundry £	Discounts allowed £
28/9	Dagwell Ent	SL15	336.50			336.50		14.02
28/9	Polygon Stores	SL03	158.20			158.20		
28/9	Peter Hayward	ML	227.95	33.95	194.00			
28/9	G Thomas & Co	SL30	269.43			269.43		11.23
28/9	Whitehill Superstores	SL24	673.58			673.58		28.07
28/9	Benham Garages – sale of car	ML	1,400.00				1,400.00	
28/9	Weller Ent	SL18	225.49			225.49		
28/9	John Cooper	ML	75.20	11.20	64.00			

Remember that when cash sales are made the VAT element must be analysed out:

Peter Hayward   VAT = £227.95 x 17.5/117.5 =   £33.95
John Cooper   VAT = £75.20   x 17.5/117.5 =   £11.20

Cash Payments Book

Date	Details	Ref	Total £	VAT £	Cash purchases £	Purchases ledger £	Sundry £	Discounts received £
28/9	003102 Seeban	PL46	1,284.90			1,284.90		67.62
28/9	003103 Elec North Ltd	PL13	440.00			440.00		
28/9	003104 P J Harvey	ML	268.50	39.98	228.52			
28/9	003105 Comtec Ltd	PL19	650.37			650.37		34.23
28/9	003106 Chiller Supplies	PL03	849.37			849.37		
28/9	003107 W G Supplies		500.00	74.46	425.54			
28/9	BDC – SO	PL12	400.00			400.00		
28/9	English Gas – DD	PL04	200.00			200.00		

There are a few points to note here:

student notes ✍

- the cash purchases will include VAT that must be analysed out into the VAT column:

  P J Harvey VAT = £268.50 x 17.5/117.5 = £39.98
  W G Suppliers VAT = £500.00 x 17.5/117.5 = £74.46

- the standing order schedules should be regularly examined in order to check that all standing order and direct debit payments are included in the cash payments book

- the cash receipts book and cash payments book have not yet been totalled – the reason for this is that the cash book is still to be checked in detail to the bank statement and there may be some additional entries into the cash book when this exercise has taken place.

Activity 1

If a cheque is written out for cash purchases for £640.89 in total, how should this appear in the cash payments book?

COMPARING THE BANK STATEMENT TO THE CASH BOOK

When all of the receipts for a period have been written up in the cash receipts book and all of the cheque payments, standing orders and direct debits have been entered into the cash payments book, it is necessary to carry out any further checks possible on the cash book. The most obvious check to make is to compare the entries in the cash receipts and payments book for the period to the entries on the bank statement, although some care does need to be taken here.

Debits and credits

One of the most obvious differences between the cash book and the bank statement is that the use of the terms debit and credit appear to be totally opposed to each other.

If cash is paid into the bank by a business then for the business this is a receipt and is entered in the cash receipts book as a debit entry. However in the bank statement this will be described as a credit and the balance will be a credit balance. This is due to the fact that if a business has money in the bank the bank effectively owes the money back to the business and therefore the business is a creditor of the bank.

Similarly, if the business writes a cheque out of the business bank account this will be entered in the cash payments book as a credit entry. From the bank's perspective however, this is known as a debit entry and any overdrawn balance is a debit balance.

Activity 2

A business's cash book shows that it has an overdrawn balance with the bank. Who would describe this as a debit balance, the business or the bank?

Procedure for checking the bank statement to the cash book

When the bank statement for the period is received then the following steps should be followed for comparison with the cash book:

Step 1 work through all of the receipts shown on the bank statement comparing each one to entries in the cash receipts book. When each receipt has been agreed to the cash receipts book the entry on the bank statement and in the cash receipts book should be ticked.

Step 2 work through all of the payments shown on the bank statement comparing each one to entries in the cash payments book. When each payment has been agreed to the cash payments book the entry on the bank statement and in the cash payments book should be ticked.

Step 3 any unticked items on the bank statement must then be used to adjust the cash receipts or payments book, whichever is relevant and eventually to prepare the bank reconciliation statement.

HOW IT WORKS

Southfield's bank statement for the week ending 28 September 2006 is shown below.

STATEMENT

first national
30 High Street
Benham
DR4 8TT

SOUTHFIELD ELECTRICAL LTD   **Account number:** 20-26-33 40268134

CHEQUE ACCOUNT

Date	Sheet 023	Paid out	Paid in	Balance
21.09.06	Balance b/f			3,884.21 CR
24.09.06	BGC - B.B. Berry Ltd		442.19	
				4,326.40 CR
25.09.06	SO-BDC	400.00		3,926.40 CR
26.09.06	Credit		336.50	
	Credit		158.20	
				4,421.10 CR
27.09.06	Credit		227.95	
	Cash		75.20	
	Bank charges	15.80		
	DD - English Gas	200.00		4,508.45 CR
28.09.06	Credit		269.43	
	Cheque No 003102	1,284.90		
	Cheque No 003104	268.50		
	BACS - Wages	1,804.80		1,419.68 CR

Now we need to compare the entries on the bank statement to the entries in the cash books.

Step 1   Comparing the cash receipts in the bank statement to the cash receipts book. As each entry on the bank statement (a further copy is shown after the cash books) is agreed to the cash receipts book then both the cash receipts book and the bank statement are ticked.

Remember that the receipts in the bank statement are shown in the credit column on the bank statement.

Cash Receipts Book

Date	Details	Ref	Total £	VAT £	Cash sales £	Sales ledger £	Sundry £	Discounts allowed £
28/9	Dagwell Ent	SL15	336.50 ✓			336.50		14.02
28/9	Polygon Stores	SL03	158.20 ✓			158.20		
28/9	Peter Hayward	ML	227.95 ✓	33.95	194.00			
28/9	G Thomas & Co	SL30	269.43 ✓			269.43		11.23
28/9	Whitehill Superstores	SL24	673.58			673.58		28.07
28/9	Benham Garages – sale of car	ML	1,400.00				1,400.00	
28/9	Weller Ent	SL18	225.49			225.49		
28/9	John Cooper	ML	75.20 ✓	11.20	64.00			

Step 2 Comparing the payments in the bank statement to the cash payments book. When each payment from the bank statement is agreed to the cash payments book tick the item in both the cash payments book and on the bank statement.

Remember that the payments are shown in the debit column on the bank statement.

Use the descriptions of the entries and any cheque numbers to help you locate the items in the cash book.

Cash Payments Book

Date	Details	Ref	Total £	VAT £	Cash purchases £	Purchases ledger £	Sundry £	Discounts received £
28/9	003102 Seeban	PL46	1,284.90✓			1,284.90		67.62
28/9	003103							
	Elec North Ltd	PL13	440.00			440.00		
28/9	003104							
	P J Harvey	ML	268.50 ✓	39.98	228.52			
28/9	003105							
	Comtec Ltd	PL19	650.37			650.37		34.23
28/9	003106							
	Chiller Supplies	PL03	849.37			849.37		
28/9	003107							
	W G Supplier		500.00	74.46	425.54			
28/9	BDC – SO	PL12	400.00 ✓			400.00		
28/9	English Gas – DD	PL04	200.00 ✓			200.00		

STATEMENT

first national
30 High Street
Benham
DR4 8TT

SOUTHFIELD ELECTRICAL LTD   **Account number:** 20-26-33 40268134

CHEQUE ACCOUNT

Date	Sheet 023	Paid out	Paid in	Balance
21.09.06	Balance b/f			3,884.21 CR
24.09.06	BGC - B.B. Berry Ltd		442.19	4,326.40 CR
25.09.06	SO-BDC	400.00 ✔		3,926.40 CR
26.09.06	Credit		336.50 ✔	
	Credit		158.20 ✔	4,421.10 CR
27.09.06	Credit		227.95 ✔	
	Cash		75.20 ✔	
	Bank charges	15.80		
	DD - English Gas	200.00 ✔		4,508.45 CR
28.09.06	Credit		269.43 ✔	
	Cheque No 003102	1,284.90 ✔		
	Cheque No 003104	268.50 ✔		
	BACS - Wages	1,804.80		1,419.68 CR

student notes ✍

Unticked items

We now need to consider the items on the bank statement that have remained unticked.

Starting with the receipts – there is a bank giro credit receipt from B B Berry Ltd of £442.19 on 24 September which, as it is not ticked, needs to be included in the cash receipts book. You discover that the sales ledger code for this customer is SL41 and, on contacting the customer, that no settlement discount was taken.

Cash Receipts Book

Date	Details	Ref	Total £	VAT £	Cash sales £	Sales ledger £	Sundry £	Discounts allowed £
28/9	Dagwell Ent	SL15	336.50 ✓			336.50		14.02
28/9	Polygon Stores	SL03	158.20 ✓			158.20		
28/9	Peter Hayward	ML	227.95 ✓	33.95	194.00			
28/9	G Thomas & Co	SL30	269.43 ✓			269.43		11.23
28/9	Whitehill Superstores	SL24	673.58		673.58		28.07	
28/9	Benham Garages – sale of car	ML	1,400.00			1,400.00		
28/9	Weller Ent	SL18	225.49		225.49			
28/9	John Cooper	ML	75.20 ✓	11.20	64.00			
28/9	B B Berry Ltd	SL41	442.19 ✓			442.19		

When this has been entered into the cash book both the cash book and the bank statement should be ticked.

Now for the cash payments – there are more unticked items here:

- 27/9 Bank charges – these have not yet been entered into the cash payments book as they would only have been known about when the bank statement was received. Therefore the cash payments book must be adjusted to show these bank charges.

- 28/9 BACS wages payment – there must have been an error in not entering this in the cash payments book. Southfield would have authorised and scheduled the wages payment through BACS and this should have been entered into the cash payments book. Again an adjustment must be made for this.

Cash Payments Book

Date	Details	Ref	Total £	VAT £	Cash purchases £	Purchases ledger £	Sundry £	Discounts received £
28/9	003102 Seeban	PL46	1,284.90✓			1,284.90		67.62
28/9	003103 Elec North Ltd	PL13	440.00			440.00		
28/9	003104 P J Harvey	ML	268.50✓	39.98	228.52			
28/9	003105 Comtec Ltd	PL19	650.37			650.37		34.23
28/9	003106 Chiller Supplies	PL03	849.37			849.37		
28/9	003107 W G Supplies		500.00	74.46	425.54			
28/9	BDC – SO	PL12	400.00✓			400.00		
28/9	English Gas – DD	PL04	200.00✓			200.00		
28/9	Bank charges	ML	15.80✓				15.80	
28/9	Wages – BACS	ML	1,804.80✓				1,804.80	

The bank charges and wages should be ticked in the cash book and on the bank statement when they have been entered into the cash payments book.

Every item on the bank statement will now be ticked.

You will note, however, that there are a number of unticked items in the cash receipts book and cash payments book.

In the cash receipts book these are receipts that have been paid into the bank account but have not yet cleared through the banking system. These are known as OUTSTANDING LODGEMENTS.

In the cash payments book they are cheques that have been written and sent out to suppliers but have either not yet been paid into the supplier's account or have not yet cleared through the banking system. These are known as UNPRESENTED CHEQUES.

These will be dealt with later in the chapter.

Activity 3

If a figure for bank interest appeared in the credit column of the bank statement would this be adjusted for in the cash receipts book or the cash payments book?

Other possible discrepancies

So far we have come across a bank giro credit receipt not recorded in the cash receipts book and bank charges and a BACS payment not recorded in the cash payments book.

There are a few other types of difference that might be discovered:

- **Bank interest received** – some cheque accounts earn interest when the account is in credit and therefore instead of bank charges there might be a receipt for bank interest being added to the balance on the bank account.

- **Standing order or direct debit** – we saw earlier how the standing order schedule should be consulted when writing up the cash payments book and any automated payments for the period put through – however if this procedure were omitted or a new standing order or direct debit not included in the schedule, then the bank statement would be the first evidence of the payment.

- **Bank errors** – on the whole it is more likely that any errors are made within the business's books rather than those of the bank. However banks do occasionally make errors and in particular you must check carefully the amount and date of payment of standing orders and direct debits, and the validity of any automated payments and receipts.

- **RETURNED CHEQUE** – when a cheque is received by a business it is written up in the cash receipts book and then paid into the business bank account. However sometimes the business will not actually receive the money from that cheque as it is returned by the drawer's bank. This might be either due to the fact that the drawer has "stopped" the cheque or because the cheque has "bounced" or been returned "refer to drawer". In either case the money will not be received on this cheque and an adjustment is required in the cash books. The adjustment is made by negating the cash receipt by showing it as a cash payment (credit entry).

The entries on the bank statement for a returned cheque would appear as follows:

STATEMENT

first national
30 High Street
Benham
DR4 8TT

CHEQUE ACCOUNT

Account number: 20-26-33 40268134

Date	Sheet 023	Paid out	Paid in	Balance
1/10	Credit		160.00	
3/10	Unpresented cheque	160.00		

Activity 4

If a standing order from the standing order schedule has been omitted from the cash books, should this be adjusted for in the cash receipts book or the cash payments book?

Alternative method of writing up the cash receipts book

In Southfield's cash receipts book each cheque or cash receipt was recorded separately and was clearly paid into the bank separately as this is how each one appeared on the bank statement.

However where there are a number of cheque receipts each day some organisations may pay all of these cheques and/or any cash into the bank on one paying in slip. The total of the paying in slip is what will appear on the bank statement. In such situations the cash receipts book may also be written up from the paying in slip and therefore it will be easy to match the totals from the bank statement to the cash receipts book.

However this method of including a paying in slip total in the cash receipts book rather than the total of each individual receipt makes the posting of the cash receipts book more complex. If only the total of the paying in slip is recorded in the cash receipts book, the details of the cheque receipts that make up the paying in slip must be recorded elsewhere in the accounting records in order for each individual debtor's account to be written up.

A more common method of writing up the cash receipts book is to enter each individual receipt into it. This means that it is more difficult to match up to the bank statement as the bank statement shows the paying in slip total. Normally this should not cause too many problems as the cheques that make up the paying in slip total will normally be recorded together in the cash receipts book.

HOW IT WORKS

A business records each individual receipt separately in the cash receipts book as follows:

Cash Receipts Book

Date	Details	Ref	Total £	VAT £	Cash sales £	Sales ledger £	Sundry £	Discounts allowed £
23/4	F Gibson	SL24	116.89			116.89		3.78
23/4	K Lipton	SL03	226.58			226.58		
23/4	J Freshman	ML	147.67	21.99	125.68			
24/4	C Vivien	SL28	368.34			368.34		
24/4	J Gillan	ML	108.45	16.15	92.30			
24/4	A Donner	SL14	285.37			285.37		

An extract from the bank statement is given below:

NATIONAL WESTERN BANK

CHEQUE ACCOUNT   30-46-26   0037583265

SHEET 134

		PAID OUT	PAID IN	BALANCE
26/4	Opening balance			589.30
26/4	Credit		491.14 ✓	
	Cheque no 103376	337.96		742.48
27/4	Credit		762.16 ✓	
	Cheque no 103372	569.23		935.41

student notes ✎

In order to check the bank statement to the cash receipts book the totals of the cheques and cash for each day in the cash receipts book must be calculated, so they can be compared.

This can be done as follows:

23/4	F Gibson	116.89
23/4	K Lipton	226.58
23/4	J Freshman	147.67
		491.14 ✓
24/4	C Vivien	368.34
24/4	J Gillan	108.45
24/4	A Donner	285.37
		762.16 ✓

Therefore the cash receipts book entries and the bank statement figures can be ticked as agreeing.

TOTALLING AND BALANCING THE CASH BOOK

Once the cash book entries have been checked to the bank statement then the business can be fairly certain that the cash book entries are correct.

Therefore at this stage the cash book should be totalled in order to post the totals to the main ledger.

The cash book must also be balanced in order to find the bank account figure that will appear in the trial balance.

Totalling the cash book

This area has been covered in an earlier chapter and therefore the amended cash receipts and payments book will simply be totalled here:

Cash Receipts Book

Date	Details	Ref	Total £	VAT £	Cash sales £	Sales ledger £	Sundry £	Discounts allowed £
28/9	Dagwell Ent	SL15	336.50			336.50		14.02
28/9	Polygon Stores	SL03	158.20			158.20		
28/9	Peter Hayward	ML	227.95	33.95	194.00			
28/9	G Thomas & Co	SL30	269.43			269.43		11.23
28/9	Whitehill Superstores	SL24	673.58			673.58		28.07
28/9	Benham Garages – sale of car	ML	1,400.00				1,400.00	
28/9	Weller Ent	SL18	225.49			225.49		
28/9	John Cooper	ML	75.20	11.20	64.00			
28/9	B B Berry Ltd	SL41	442.19			442.19		
			3,808.54	45.15	258.00	2,105.39	1,400.00	53.32
				VAT	Sales	CREDIT Sales ledger control	Disposals	

Remember that the cash receipts book total figure is the debit entry in the main ledger and therefore the only further postings required are the credit entries for each of the column totals. The only exception here is for the discounts allowed column for which the double entry is:

DR   Discounts allowed
CR   Sales ledger control account

student notes✍   **Cash Payments Book**

Date	Details	Ref	Total £	VAT £	Cash purchases £	Purchases ledger £	Sundry £	Discounts received £
28/9	003102 Seeban	PL46	1,284.90			1,284.90		67.62
28/9	003103 Elec North Ltd	PL13	440.00			440.00		
28/9	003104 P J Harvey	ML	268.50	39.98	228.52			
28/9	003105 Comtec Ltd	PL19	650.37			650.37		34.23
28/9	003106 Chiller Supplies	PL03	849.37			849.37		
28/9	003107 W G Supplies		500.00	74.46	425.54			
28/9	BDC – SO	PL12	400.00			400.00		
28/9	English Gas – DD	PL04	200.00			200.00		
28/9	Bank charges	ML	15.80				15.80	
28/9	Wages – BACS	ML	1,804.80				1,804.80	
			6,413.74	114.44	654.06	3,824.64	1,820.60	101.85

Bank charges
Wages

DEBIT

VAT — Purchases — Purchases ledger control

Remember that the cash payments book total is the credit entry in the main ledger and therefore the postings required are the debit entries for each of the column totals. In the sundry column there are two different types of transaction, bank charges and wages, and a separate debit must be made to each of these accounts.

Again the exception is the discounts received column total for which the double entry is:

DR   Purchases ledger control account
CR   Discounts received

Balancing the cash book

As the cash receipts and cash payments books are normally physically so large with so many analysis columns, it is not normal practice for a balance to be brought down and carried down as with a normal ledger account. Instead, at regular intervals a brief exercise will be carried out to find the balance on the bank account – this will normally take place when the cash books are being compared to the bank statement.

The procedure for finding the balance on the cash book is as follows:

Step 1   Find the balance on the bank account at the start of the current period – this will normally have been calculated when the bank statement and cash book were previously compared and will be filed with the bank statement at the end of the previous period.

Step 2   Add to the opening balance the total of the cash receipts book for the period and deduct the total of the cash payments book for the period – this gives the closing balance on the bank account.

Step 3   File this calculation with the bank statement at the end of the period.

HOW IT WORKS

Returning to Southfield Electrical Ltd, you discover from the filing system that the balance on the cash book at 21 September was £3,884.21.

Find the closing balance on the cash book at 28 September 2006.

	£
Opening balance	3,884.21
Add: total receipts for week (CRB)	3,808.54
Less: total payments for week (CPB)	(6,413.74)
	1,279.01

BANK RECONCILIATION STATEMENT

We now have the correct balance on the cash book at 28 September of £1,279.01. However if you return to the bank statement you will see that this does not agree with the bank's closing balance of £1,419.68.

This will often be the case and the reason for the difference is TIMING DIFFERENCES. Due to the operations of the banking system there will be an inevitable time lag between recording receipts and payments in the cash books and their appearance on the bank statement.

Cheques received will be recorded in the cash receipts book when they arrive through the post. Even if they are paid into the bank on the same day however there will be a three day delay, due to the clearing system (see chapter 7) before they appear on the bank statement. Such amounts are known as outstanding lodgements.

When cheques are written to suppliers they will be entered into the cash payments book immediately. The cheques must then be sent to the supplier, the supplier must take them to the bank and then there will be a three day clearing period before they appear on the bank statement. These cheque payments that are in the cash book but not on the bank statement yet are known as UNPRESENTED CHEQUES.

HOW IT WORKS

We can produce a BANK RECONCILIATION STATEMENT for Southfield which will reconcile the corrected cash book balance on 28 September with the bank statement balance on the same date.

We start with the bank statement balance.

Bank reconciliation statement at 28 September 2006

	£	£
Balance per bank statement		1,419.68

By examining the cash receipts book we can see that there are still three unticked items. These are receipts that have been recorded in the cash receipts book but have not yet appeared on the bank statement. These are outstanding lodgements which if they had cleared through the system would mean that the bank statement figure was larger. Therefore these are added into the bank statement balance.

Bank reconciliation statement at 28 September 2006

	£	£
Balance per bank statement		1,419.68
Outstanding lodgements		
Whitehill Superstores	673.58	
Benham Garages	1,400.00	
Weller Enterprises	225.49	
		2,299.07
		3,718.75

Now we turn to the cash payments book. There are still four unticked payments which are cheques which have not yet been paid into the bank by the recipients or have not yet cleared the banking system. These are unpresented cheques and if they had been presented they would make the bank statement figure smaller. Therefore we deduct these in the bank reconciliation statement in order to come back to the cash book balance of £1,279.01.

Bank reconciliation statement at 28 September 2006

	£	£
Balance per bank statement		1,419.68
Outstanding lodgements		
Whitehill Superstores	673.58	
Benham Garages	1,400.00	
Weller Enterprises	225.49	
		2,299.07
		3,718.75
Unpresented cheques		
003103	440.00	
003105	650.37	
003106	849.37	
003107	500.00	
		(2,439.74)
Amended cash book balance		1,279.01

SUMMARY

We will now just summarise the procedure for carrying out a bank reconciliation before working through a further example.

Step 1   Compare the cash receipts book to the receipts shown on the bank statement (the credits on the bank statement – for each receipt that agrees tick the item in both the cash book and the bank statement.

Step 2 Compare the cash payments book to the payments shown on the bank statement (the debits on the bank statement) – for each payment that agrees tick the item in both the cash book and the bank statement.

Step 3 Any unticked items on the bank statement (other than rare errors made by the bank) will be items that should have been entered into the cash books but have been omitted for some reason – these should be entered into the cash book and then the amended balance on the cash book can be found. To find the correct cash book balance a ledger account is used for the bank with the original cash book balance shown as the brought forward balance and any additional payments shown as credits and receipts as debits. This will be illustrated in the next example.

Step 4 Finally any unticked items in the cash book will be the timing differences – unpresented cheques and outstanding lodgements – these will be used to reconcile the bank statement closing balance to the corrected cash book closing balance.

HOW IT WORKS

Given below is a summary of a sole trader, Dawn Fisher's cash book for February 2006. The balance on the cash book on 1 February was £387.90.

Cash Receipts Book

Date	Details	£
2 Feb	G Hollings	1,368.48
7 Feb	S Dancer	368.36
14 Feb	K C Ltd	2,004.37
20 Feb	F W Painter	856.09
26 Feb	J J Hammond	648.34
28 Feb	L Minns	257.50
		5,503.14

Cash Payments Book

Date	Details	Cheque number	£
3 Feb	Long Associates	103567	1,007.46
5 Feb	Harland Bros	103568	524.71
5 Feb	L and P Timms	103569	1,035.76
8 Feb	Peter Thomas	103570	663.45
15 Feb	English Gas	103571	480.50
20 Feb	F P Travel	103572	1,233.80
24 Feb	K Riley	103573	246.58
26 Feb	Farman Ltd	103574	103.64
			5,295.90

Dawn has just received her bank statement for the month of February.

STATEMENT

first national
30 High Street
Benham
DR4 8TT

DAWN FISHER   **Account number:** 20-26-33 40268134

CHEQUE ACCOUNT   **Sheet 011**

Date		Paid out	Paid in	Balance
1 Feb	Balance b/f			387.90
6 Feb	Credit		1,368.48	1,756.38
9 Feb	Cheque No 103568	524.71		1,231.67
11 Feb	Credit		368.36	
	Bank giro credit		208.34	
	Cheque No 103567	1,107.46		700.91
13 Feb	Cheque No 103570	663.45		37.46
18 Feb	Credit		2,004.37	
	SO - FC Property	400.00		1,641.83
19 Feb	Cheque No 103571	480.50		1,161.33
24 Feb	Credit		856.09	
	Cheque No 103569	1,035.76		981.66
28 Feb	Bank interest		4.84	986.50
28 Feb	Balance c/f			986.50

student notes✍

The bank reconciliation will now be prepared:

- compare the receipts and payments in the cash book to the bank statement – for each one that agrees tick both the bank statement and the cash book entry.

Cash Receipts Book

Date	Details	£	
2 Feb	G Hollings	1,368.48	✓
7 Feb	S Dancer	368.36	✓
14 Feb	K C Ltd	2,004.37	✓
20 Feb	F W Painter	856.09	✓
26 Feb	J J Hammond	648.34	
28 Feb	L Minns	257.50	
		5,503.14	

Cash Payments Book

Date	Details	Cheque number	£	
3 Feb	Long Associates	103567	1,007.46	
5 Feb	Harland Bros	103568	524.71	✓
5 Feb	L and P Timms	103569	1,035.76	✓
8 Feb	Peter Thomas	103570	663.45	✓
15 Feb	English Gas	103571	480.50	✓
20 Feb	F P Travel	103572	1,233.80	
24 Feb	K Riley	103573	246.58	
26 Feb	Farman Ltd	103574	103.64	
			5,295.90	

STATEMENT

first national
30 High Street
Benham
DR4 8TT

DAWN FISHER

CHEQUE ACCOUNT

Account number: 20-26-33 40268134

Sheet 011

Date		Paid out	Paid in	Balance
1 Feb	Balance b/f			387.90
6 Feb	Credit		1,368.48 ✓	1,756.38
9 Feb	Cheque No 103568	524.71 ✓		1,231.67
11 Feb	Credit		368.36 ✓	
	Bank giro credit		208.34	
	Cheque No 103567	1,107.46		700.91
13 Feb	Cheque No 103570	663.45 ✓		37.46
18 Feb	Credit		2,004.37 ✓	
	SO - FC Property	400.00		1,641.83
19 Feb	Cheque No 103571	480.50 ✓		1,161.33
24 Feb	Credit		856.09 ✓	
	Cheque No 103569	1,035.76 ✓		981.66
28 Feb	Bank interest		4.84	986.50
28 Feb	Balance c/f			986.50

■ deal with each of the un-ticked items in the bank statement:

Payments

– cheque number 103567 has been recorded in the cash payments book as £1,007.46 whereas the bank statement shows it as an amount of £1,107.46 – if this is correct then the cash book must be corrected

– the standing order on 18 February has not been recorded in the cash payments book – the cash book must be corrected

Receipts

– the bank giro credit on 11 February has not been recorded in the cash receipts book – the cash book must be corrected

– on 28 February the account has been credited with bank interest – this must be entered into the cash book

- now the cash book must be amended to find the corrected cash book balance – we will do this in a summarised ledger account for the bank account:

Bank account

	£		£
Balance b/d	387.90	Cash payments book	5,295.90
Cash receipts book	5,503.14	Correction for cheque	
Bank giro credit	208.34	103567	100.00
Bank interest	4.84	Standing order	400.00
		Balance c/d	308.32
	6,104.22		6,104.22
Balance b/d	308.32		

Note that in practice the analysed cash book (the total and the analysis columns) would not be totalled until **after** all the adjustments had been put through. It would then be ruled off and a new balance brought down at the period end.

These totals would then be posted to the main ledger to complete the double entry.

- now the bank statement balance must be reconciled with this amended balance on the cash book – this is done by listing the un-ticked items in the cash book as the timing differences (remember however that cheque number 103567 was un-ticked because it was incorrect, not because it had not appeared on the bank statement)

Bank reconciliation statement at 28 February 2006

	£	£
Bank statement balance		986.50
Less: unpresented cheques		
103572	1,233.80	
103573	246.58	
103574	103.64	
		(1,584.02)
		(597.52)
Add: outstanding lodgements		
J J Hammond	648.34	
L Minns	257.50	
		905.84
Amended cash book balance		308.32

The bank statement and the cash book have now been reconciled and the figure that would appear in the trial balance for the bank account is the amended cash book balance of £308.32.

Activity 5

A cheque in the cash payments book is un-ticked after the bank statement and cash book have been compared.

How should this be dealt with in the bank reconciliation statement?

Completing the double entry

The corrections that were made to the cash book were only one side of the double entry – when preparing the accounts in practice the other side of the double entry must also be put through the ledger accounts:

- bank giro credit – this was from a credit customer and therefore the debtors control account should be credited with £208.34 as well as the debtors account in the subsidiary ledger, the sales ledger;

- the bank interest account must be credited with £4.84;

- the incorrect cheque payment must be adjusted by debiting the creditors control account with £100;

- the standing order is for the monthly rent payment – this must be debited to the rent account.

Opening balances on the cash book and bank statement

In both examples you may have noted that the opening balance on the cash book agreed with that of the bank statement – there were no unpresented cheques or outstanding lodgements at the end of the previous period.

This will not always be the case. If there were timing differences at the end of the previous period then a bank reconciliation statement should have been prepared. When comparing this period's bank statement and cash book you will need to have the previous period's bank reconciliation statement in order to be able to tick last period's timing differences when they appear on the bank statement this period.

HOW IT WORKS

When Dawn is preparing her bank reconciliation at the end of March 2006 she is likely to find that the unpresented cheques at the end of February, cheque numbers 103572 to 103574 do appear on the bank statement in March. When they are found on the bank statement in March then they should be ticked on the bank statement and on the opening bank reconciliation statement. The same will happen with the two outstanding lodgements at the end of February when they appear on the bank statement in March.

Activity 6

A business's bank statement shows bank interest as a payment. This has not been recorded in the cash payments book.

How would this be recorded in the ledger accounts?

Overdraft balances

Care should be taken with the calculation of the balance on the cash book to identify whether the opening balance on the cash book is a debit balance or an OVERDRAFT BALANCE.

HOW IT WORKS

Suppose that the opening balance on Southfield's cash book on 2 May was a credit balance of £225.68. The total receipts for the week ending 9 May are £4,246.73 and the total payments £4,114.98. What is the closing balance on the cash book?

This time as the opening balance is an overdraft the total payments should be added in, as these would increase the overdraft, and the total receipts would be deducted as they decrease the overdraft.

	£
Opening balance (credit balance)	(225.68)
Total payments for week	(4,114.98)
Total receipts for week	4,246.73
Closing balance (credit balance)	(93.93)

Activity 7

The opening balance on a business's cash book is £1,367.34 overdrawn. The total receipts for the period were £7,336.49 and the total payments for the period were £4,527.22.

What was the closing balance on the cash book?

Computerised bank reconciliation

Computerised packages offer the facility to reconcile what is recorded in the computerised banking records with your bank statements.

This is simply a matter of running the appropriate part of the program and "ticking" items off by clicking on them. Here is an illustration from the MYOB package.

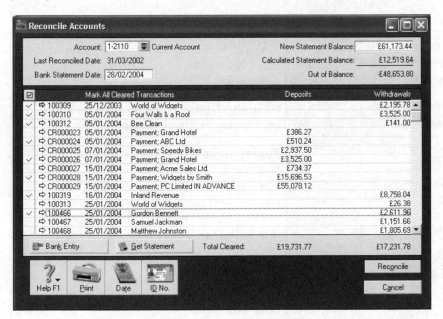

Here you enter the closing balance on the statement at the top of the screen and when you tick items to show that you have found them on the bank statement the "Out of Balance" amount will change accordingly until it is nil. If there are items on the bank statement that are not yet recorded in the accounting package, such as bank charges, you can enter them from this screen.

If you use Internet banking you can probably download your bank statements in a file. Some packages can use these files to do automatic comparisons with your accounting records, making the process of bank reconciliation even easier.

CHAPTER OVERVIEW

- the Cash Receipts Book is written up from the cheques and cash received, usually summarised in the remittance list

- the Cash Payments Book is written up from the cheque counterfoils or from the cheque listing

- the standing order schedule must also be consulted to ensure that all standing order and direct debit payments are recorded in the cash payments book on the correct date

- in order to check the accuracy of the cash receipts and payments books, they must be checked at regular intervals to the bank statements received

- the debit and credit entries and balances on the bank statement are the opposite to the entries in the ledger accounts as the bank is considering the accounting from its own perspective

- when checking the bank statement to the cash book, check each of the receipts and payments from the bank statement to the cash receipts and payment books and tick each agreed item in both the cash books and the bank statement

- any unticked items on the bank statement must be entered into the relevant cash book, either receipts or payments

- there will also be unticked items in the cash books which will be used to prepare the bank reconciliation statement

---

KEY WORDS

Standing order schedule listing showing all of the standing order and direct debit payments that a business has

Outstanding lodgements cheques that have been received and recorded in the Cash Receipts Book but do not yet appear on the bank statement

Returned cheque cheque that is paid into a business's bank account and then is returned by the drawer's bank unpaid

Timing differences the reason for the fact that the bank statement balance will rarely agree with the balance on the cash books, as receipts and payments recorded in the cash books will appear later in the bank statement due to the operation of the clearing system

Unpresented cheques cheque payments that have been recorded in the cash payments book but do not yet appear on the bank statement

Bank reconciliation statement a statement reconciling the bank statement balance to the corrected cash book balance

Overdraft balance This is where the business effectively owes the bank money – this appears as a debit balance in the bank statement and a credit balance in the cash book

---

- if a business has a number of cheques arriving each day then they will be paid into the bank account on a single paying in slip – this means that the checking to the cash receipts book can be more complex as cheques and cash will have to be totalled in order to agree back to the entry in the bank statement

- once the relevant corrections have been made to the cash receipts book and cash payments book they must be totalled and posted to the ledger accounts

- finally, in order to find the bank account total that is to be used in the trial balance the cash book must be balanced – this is done by taking the opening balance on the cash book at the start of the period, adding in the total receipts for the period and deducting the total payments for the period

CHAPTER OVERVIEW cont.

- if the opening balance on the cash book is an overdraft then the total payments are added and the total receipts deducted in order to find the closing balance on the cash book

- the closing balance on the bank statement is then reconciled to the corrected cash book balance in the bank reconciliation statement. The reconciling items will be the outstanding lodgements and the unpresented cheques

HOW MUCH HAVE YOU LEARNED?

1 You are the cashier for Thames Traders and you have on your desk the remittance list for the week ending 30 November 2006 showing the cash and cheques received, the cheque listing for the week and the standing order schedule. Each of these documents is reproduced below.

REMITTANCE LIST			
	SL code	Amount £	Discount taken £
Burser Ltd	SL14	147.89	6.49
Crawley Partners	SL23	448.36	18.79
Breon & Co	SL15	273.37	
Kogart Supplies	SL06	552.68	42.67
Alex & Bros	SL09	273.46	
Minicar Ltd	SL22	194.68	

Cheque listing

		PL code	Amount £	Discount received £
001367	Waterloo Partners	PL21	336.47	12.47
001368	Central Supplies	PL16	169.36	
001369	General London Trade	PL23	268.38	10.58
001370	Eye of the Tiger	PL19	84.50	
001371	Chare & Cope	PL27	447.39	19.86

Extract from standing order schedule

27th of each month – standing order to Loan Finance Repayment ML 23   £250.00

Write up the cash receipts book and the cash payments book.

2   You are now given the bank statement for Thames Traders for the week ending 30 November 2006. Compare this to the cash receipts book and cash payments book.

Make a note of the treatment required in either the cash book or the bank statement for any items that cannot be agreed.

STATEMENT

NATIONAL DIRECT

THAMES TRADERS

CHEQUE ACCOUNT

Account number: 15-20-40 10267432

Date	Sheet 136	Paid out	Paid in	Balance
23.11.06	Balance b/f			1489.65 CR
26.11.06	Bank Giro Credit - Burser Ltd		52.00	1541.65 CR
27.11.06	SO-Loan Finance Repayment	250.00		1291.65 CR
28.11.06	Cheque No 001367 Credit	336.47	147.89	1103.07 CR
29.11.06	Cheque No 001368 Credit	196.36	448.36	1355.07 CR
30.11.06	Credit Bank charges	34.53	552.68	1,873.22 CR

3   Adjust the cash receipts book and cash payments book for any items that appear to be relevant (assume that the bank statement is correct). Total the cash book.

4   You discover from the filing records showing the comparison of the cash book and the bank statement at 23 November that the balance on the cash book at that date was £1,489.65, a debit balance.

What figure will appear in the trial balance for the bank account at 30 November 2006?

5   Reconcile the closing bank statement balance to the corrected cash book balance.

6   Whilst comparing the cash book to the bank statement the following differences have appeared:

a)   a receipt from a debtor has been recorded in the Cash Receipts Book as £310.50 but appears correctly on the bank statement as £301.50

b)   bank charges on the bank statement are £15.80

c)   cheque number 10462 has not been ticked in the Cash Payments Book as it has not appeared on the bank statement

d)   a direct debit payment is in the bank statement to English Gas Co for £300.00 but has not been recorded in the Cash Payments Book.

What entries should be made in the ledger accounts or the bank reconciliation statement for each of these items?

7   Given below is a business's cash receipts and payments book for the week ending 8 March 2006, the bank statement for that week and the bank reconciliation statement for the week ended 1 March 2006.

You are required to prepare the bank reconciliation statement for the week ending 8 March 2006.

Cash Receipts Book

Date	Details	£
4 March	J Killick	365.37
	D Francis	105.48
5 March	I Oliver	216.57
6 March	L Canter	104.78
7 March	R Trent	268.59
8 March	P Otter	441.78
		1,502.57

Cash Payments Book

Date	Details	Cheque number	£
4 March	L L Partners	002536	186.90
	P J Parler	002537	210.55
5 March	J K Properties	002538	500.00
	Harmer & Co	002539	104.78
	Plenith Ltd	002540	60.80
7 March	Wessex & Co	002541	389.40
8 March	Filmer Partners	002542	104.67
			1,557.10

Bank reconciliation statement at 1 March 2006

	£	£
Balance per bank statement		835.68
Less: unpresented cheques		
002530	110.46	
002534	230.56	
002535	88.90	
		(429.92)
		405.76
Add: outstanding lodgement		102.45
Amended cash book balance		508.21

STATEMENT

first national
30 High Street
Benham
DR4 8TT

Account number: 20-26-33 3126897

CHEQUE ACCOUNT   **Sheet 023**

Date		Paid out	Paid in	Balance
1 Mar	Balance b/f			835.68
4 Mar	Cheque no 002534	230.56		
	Credit		102.45	707.56
5 Mar	DD - National Telephones	145.00		
	Bank charges	7.80		554.77
6 Mar	Cheque No 002530	110.46		
	BACS - J T Turner		486.20	930.51
7 Mar	Credit		470.85	
	Cheque No 002537	210.55		
	Cheque No 002536	186.90		
	Cheque No 002538	500.00		503.91
8 Mar	Cheque No 002535	88.90		
	Credit		216.57	
	Cheque No 002539	104.78		526.80
8 Mar	Balance c/f			526.80

chapter 16:
CONTROL ACCOUNT RECONCILIATIONS

chapter coverage 📖

In this chapter we will first revise the postings to the sales ledger and purchase ledger control accounts and to the relevant accounts in the subsidiary ledger. Then we will consider the checks that will be carried out to ensure that the debtors and creditors balances to be used in the trial balance are correct. Finally we shall consider the reconciliation of the petty cash account with the cash in hand. The topics that are to be covered are:

✍ revision of the accounting system for debtors

✍ revision of the accounting system for creditors

✍ the detailed entries to a sales ledger control account

✍ how to account for bad debts

✍ the detailed entries to a purchases ledger control account

✍ the reason for control account reconciliations

✍ the errors likely to affect the control accounts and the subsidiary ledger

✍ how to prepare a sales ledger control account reconciliation

✍ how to prepare a purchases ledger control account reconciliation

✍ non-trade debtors

✍ petty cash reconciliation

Unit 3

knowledge and understanding – accounting methods

5   double entry bookkeeping, including balancing accounts
11 identification of different types of errors
12 relationship between the accounting system and the ledger
14 methods of posting from primary records to ledger accounts
15 inter-relationship of accounts – double entry system
17 reconciling control accounts with memorandum accounts

knowledge and understanding – the organisation

19 relevant understanding of the organisation's accounting systems and administrative systems and procedures

21 organisational procedures for filing source information

Performance criteria – element 3.2

A   make and record authorised adjustments

B   total relevant accounts in the main ledger

C   reconcile control accounts with the totals of the balance in the subsidiary ledger

D   reconcile petty cash control account with cash in hand and subsidiary records

E   identify discrepancies arising from the reconciliation of control accounts and either resolve or refer to the appropriate person

F   ensure documentation is stored securely and in line with the organisation's confidentiality requirements

THE ACCOUNTING SYSTEM FOR DEBTORS AND CREDITORS

In earlier chapters we considered the accounting systems for debtors and creditors. This chapter will start by bringing together the operation of the whole system, and we will then move onto new areas.

Accounting system for debtors

The process of accounting for debtors goes like this:

- the sales invoices sent to debtors are recorded in the sales day book;

- the total of the sales day book is posted to the sales ledger control account;

- the individual invoices in the sales day book are posted to the individual debtors' accounts in the subsidiary (sales) ledger;

- the receipt of cash/cheques from debtors is recorded in the cash receipts book;

- the total of the cash receipts book is posted to the sales ledger control account;

- the individual receipts are posted to the individual debtors' accounts in the subsidiary (sales) ledger.

HOW IT WORKS

Ben Charles has recently set up in business and he currently has just three credit customers A , B and C. His sales day book and cash receipts book for the month of May 2006 are given:

student notes ✍️

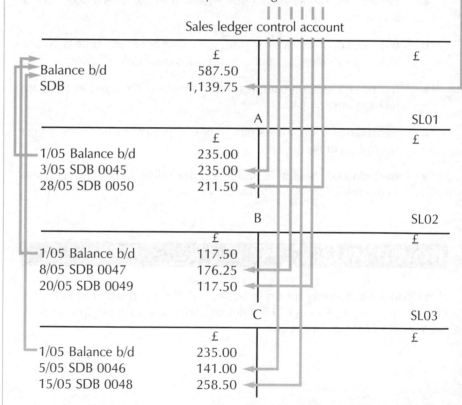

Sales Day Book

Date	Customer	Invoice no.	Ref	Gross £	VAT £	Net £
3/05	A	0045	SL01	235.00	35.00	200.00
5/05	C	0046	SL03	141.00	21.00	120.00
8/05	B	0047	SL02	176.25	26.25	150.00
15/05	C	0048	SL03	258.50	38.50	220.00
20/05	B	0049	SL02	117.50	17.50	100.00
28/05	A	0050	SL01	211.50	31.50	180.00
				1,139.75	169.75	970.00

This must be posted to the sales ledger control account and the individual debtors accounts in the subsidiary (sales) ledger:

Sales ledger control account

	£		£
Balance b/d	587.50		
SDB	1,139.75		

A   SL01

	£		£
1/05 Balance b/d	235.00		
3/05 SDB 0045	235.00		
28/05 SDB 0050	211.50		

B   SL02

	£		£
1/05 Balance b/d	117.50		
8/05 SDB 0047	176.25		
20/05 SDB 0049	117.50		

C   SL03

	£		£
1/05 Balance b/d	235.00		
5/05 SDB 0046	141.00		
15/05 SDB 0048	258.50		

Can you see how the totals of the opening balances on each individual account in the subsidiary (sales) ledger total up to the opening balance on the sales ledger control account?

Cash Receipts Book

Date	Details	Ref	Total	VAT	Cash sales	Sales ledger	Discounts allowed
			£	£	£	£	£
6/05	B	SL02	117.50			117.50	
10/05	A	SL01	225.60			225.60	9.40
13/05	C	SL03	200.00			200.00	
20/05	A	SL01	225.60			225.60	9.40
28/05	C	SL03	100.00			100.00	
30/05	B	SL02	176.25			176.25	
			1,044.95			1,044.95	18.80

This must now also be posted to the main ledger and the subsidiary (sales) ledger.

Sales ledger control account

	£		£
Balance b/d	587.50	CRB	1,044.95
SDB	1,139.75	CRB – discounts	18.80

A   SL01

	£		£
1/05 Balance b/d	235.00	10/05 CRB	225.60
3/05 SDB 0045	235.00	10/05 CRB – discount	9.40
28/05 SDB 0050	211.50	20/05 CRB	225.60
		20/05 CRB – discount	9.40

B   SL02

	£		£
1/05 Balance b/d	117.50	6/05 CRB	117.50
8/05 SDB 0047	176.25	30/05 CRB	176.25
20/05 SDB 0049	117.50		

C   SL03

	£		£
1/05 Balance b/d	235.00	13/05 CRB	200.00
5/05 SDB 0046	141.00	28/05 CRB	100.00
15/05 SDB 0048	258.50		

Finally at the end of May each of the accounts should be balanced:

Sales ledger control account

	£		£
Balance b/d	587.50	CRB	1,044.95
SDB	1,139.75	CRB – discounts	18.80
		Balance c/d	663.50
	1,727.25		1,727.25
Balance b/d	663.50		

A   SL01

	£		£
1/05 Balance b/d	235.00	10/05 CRB	225.60
3/05 SDB 0045	235.00	10/05 CRB – discount	9.40
28/05 SDB 0050	211.50	20/05 CRB	225.60
		20/05 CRB – discount	9.40
		Balance c/d	211.50
	681.50		681.50
Balance b/d	211.50		

B   SL02

	£		£
1/05 Balance b/d	117.50	6/05 CRB	117.50
8/05 SDB 0047	176.25	30/05 CRB	176.25
20/05 SDB 0049	117.50	Balance c/d	117.50
	411.25		411.25
Balance b/d	117.50		

C   SL03

	£		£
1/05 Balance b/d	235.00	13/05 CRB	200.00
5/05 SDB 0046	141.00	28/05 CRB	100.00
15/05 SDB 0048	258.50	Balance c/d	334.50
	634.50		634.50
Balance b/d	334.50		

Closing balances

Note how the total of each of the individual debtor balances equals the balance on the sales ledger control account.

	£
A	211.50
B	117.50
C	334.50
Sales ledger control balance	663.50

If the double entry has all been correctly carried out then the total of the list of debtor balances will always equal the balance on the sales ledger control account.

This whole process of accounting for credit sales in the main ledger and in the subsidiary ledger, the debtors ledger, can be illustrated in a diagram:

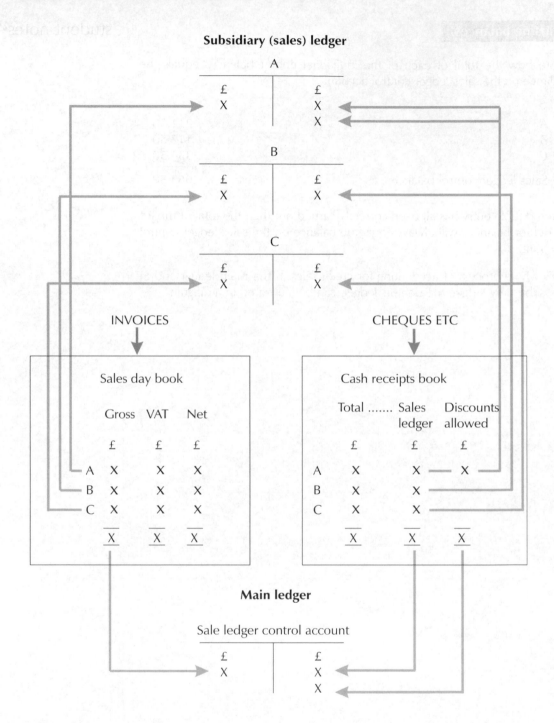

Subsidiary (sales) ledger

INVOICES

CHEQUES ETC

Sales day book

Cash receipts book

Main ledger

Sale ledger control account

Activity 1

What is the double entry in the main ledger for sales on credit?

Accounting for creditors

The accounting process for creditors is precisely the same as for debtors except that the entries in the accounts are the other way around.

- The purchase invoices received are recorded in the purchases day book.

- The total of the purchases day book is posted to the purchases ledger control account.

- The individual invoices in the purchases day book are posted to the individual creditors' accounts in the subsidiary (purchases) ledger.

- The payments to creditors are recorded in the cash payments book.

- The total of the cash payments book is posted to the purchases ledger control account.

- The individual payments are posted to the individual creditors' accounts in the subsidiary (purchases) ledger.

Again this can be shown in a diagram:

Subsidiary (purchases) ledger

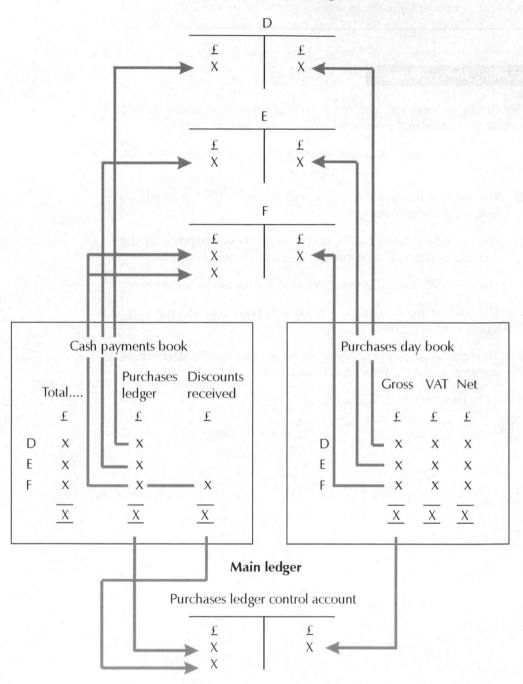

Main ledger

Purchases ledger control account

Closing balances

In just the same way as with the accounting system for debtors, if the double entry has been correctly performed then the closing balances on the individual creditor accounts in the subsidiary ledger should total back to the balance on the purchases ledger control account.

HOW IT WORKS

If Ben Charles has three credit suppliers, D, E and F then the sum of the final balances on their accounts should agree with the creditors control account:

D

	£		£
		Closing balance	115.60

E

	£		£
		Closing balance	220.00

F

	£		£
		Closing balance	150.00

Purchases ledger control account

	£		£
		Closing balance	485.60

	£
D	115.60
E	220.00
F	150.00
Purchases ledger control account balance	485.60

Activity 2

What is the double entry in the main ledger for purchases on credit?

CONTROL ACCOUNTS

We will now look in more detail at the figures that are likely to appear in the sales ledger control account and purchases ledger control account, as so far we have only considered the basic entries for invoices and cash.

Sales ledger control account

A typical sales ledger control account might have the following entries:

Sales ledger control account

	£		£
Balance b/d	X		
Credit sales	X	Sales returns	X
Returned cheques	X	Cash/cheques from debtors	X
		Discount allowed	X
		Bad debts written off	X
		Balance c/d	X
	X		X
Balance b/d	X		

These entries need a little more explanation:

Balances b/d the opening balance on the account is usually a large debit opening balance, although there can sometimes also be a smaller credit opening balance. Normally a debtor owes the business money. However in some circumstances debtors may have a credit balance at the start of the period.

Possible reasons for credit balances might be:

- if the customer paid too much for the goods owing, by mistake. This would then turn him from being a debtor into being a creditor ie, the business owes the money back to the customer;

- if the customer had returned goods after paying for them then again there would be a credit balance on the account, as the business owes the cost of the returned goods back to the customer.

There is only likely to be a small credit balance on the control account arising from transactions like that, but usually it is shown separately, rather than being netted off against the debit balance. This gives a more accurate overall picture.

Credit sales this is the figure that is posted from the gross column total in the sales day book.

Returned cheques if a customer has paid for goods then the entry to the sales ledger control account would be a credit entry. If the bank then returns the cheque as unpaid ie, the cheque has "bounced", the entry must be reversed by debiting the control account. The credit entry is in the cash payments book.

Sales returns this is the posting of the total of the gross column in the sales returns day book.

Cash/cheques from debtors this is the posting of the sales ledger or debtors ledger column total from the cash receipts book.

Discounts allowed this is the posting from the memorandum discount column in the cash receipts book.

Bad debts written off when a sale is made on credit to a customer it is assumed that the customer will eventually pay the amount due. However on occasion it may become clear that a debtor is not going to pay the amount due. This may be due to the fact that he has gone into liquidation or receivership or simply that he has disappeared. Whatever the reason, if it is thought that the debtor will not pay then this is known as a BAD DEBT.

The accounting treatment for a bad debt is that it must be removed from the accounting records as it is no longer a valid debtor. This is done by:

DR Bad debts expense account
CR Sales ledger control account

The debtor is removed by crediting the control account and this is treated as an expense of the business, the bad debts expense – a sale on credit was made but the cash not received.

The bad debt must also be removed from the individual account in the subsidiary (sales) ledger by crediting the individual debtor's account with the amount of the bad debt.

Activity 3

What is the double entry for writing off a bad debt?

Purchases ledger control account

A typical purchases ledger control account might look like this:

Purchases ledger control account

	£		£
		Balance b/d	X
Purchases returns	X		
Cash/cheques paid to creditors	X	Credit purchases	X
Discounts received	X		
Balance c/d	X		
	—		—
	X		X
	—		—
		Balance b/d	X

Balance b/d the large balance brought down will be on the credit side of the account. Occasionally there may be a small debit balance brought down to reflect items such as over-payment.

Purchases returns this is the posting from the gross column total of the purchases returns day book.

Cash/cheques paid to creditors this is the posting from the purchases ledger column total from the cash payments book.

Discounts received this is the posting from the memorandum discounts received column total from the cash payments book.

Credit purchases this is the posting from the gross column total of the purchases day book.

CONTROL ACCOUNT RECONCILIATIONS

We have seen that if all of the double entry in the main ledger, and entries in the subsidiary ledgers, are correctly carried out, then the totals of the balances on the subsidiary ledger should be equal to the balance on the control account.

Control account balances

The balances on the debtors' and creditors' control accounts are the figures that will appear in the trial balance for debtors and creditors. Therefore it is important to ensure that these figures are correct. This is done by carrying out a SALES LEDGER CONTROL ACCOUNT RECONCILIATION and a PURCHASES LEDGER CONTROL ACCOUNT RECONCILIATION.

The purpose of these reconciliations is to compare the balance on the control account to the total of the balances of the individual accounts in the subsidiary ledger. If the two totals do not agree then there have been errors made in either the control account or the subsidiary ledger. These errors must be investigated, discovered and corrected.

Some of the errors might have been made in the double entry in the main ledger therefore affecting the control account. Other errors might have been made when posting entries to the individual accounts in the subsidiary ledger or in listing the balances in the subsidiary ledger.

Errors affecting the control account

Typical types of errors that might have been made in the double entry in the main ledger, and therefore affect the control account balance, might include the following:

- the primary records may have been undercast or overcast therefore meaning that the incorrect total is posted to the control account;

- postings from the primary records may have been made to the wrong side of the control account;

- the discounts recorded in the cash book may be incorrectly treated;

- a bad debt may not have been entered into the main ledger although it was written off in the subsidiary ledger.

Errors affecting the list of balances

Some errors will not affect the double entry in the main ledger but will mean that the individual balances in the subsidiary ledger are not correct, or that these balances are listed and totalled incorrectly. Typical of these are the following:

- an entry from the primary records might be posted to the wrong account in the subsidiary ledger;

- entries from the primary records may be posted to the wrong side of the subsidiary ledger account;

- an entry from the primary records may be posted as the wrong amount to the subsidiary ledger account;

- a balance on an account in the subsidiary ledger may be included in the list of balances as the wrong amount or as the wrong type of balance eg, a debit rather than a credit.

Activity 4

If the sales day book total for a week is overcast by £1,000 would this affect the debtors control account or the individual debtors' accounts in the subsidiary (sales) ledger?

SALES LEDGER CONTROL ACCOUNT RECONCILIATION

A sales ledger control account reconciliation is a comparison of the balance on the sales ledger control account to the total of the list of debtor balances from the subsidiary (sales) ledger. This will be carried out on a regular basis, usually monthly.

HOW IT WORKS

Southfield Electrical is carrying out its sales ledger control account reconciliation at the end of October 2006. The balance on the sales ledger control account is a debit balance of £14,382. The total of the list of debtors' account balances from the subsidiary ledger comes to £13,777.

Step 1   Check whether the control account total agrees to the total of the subsidiary ledger balances.

	£
Control account total	14,382

As this does not agree to the total of the list of balances (£13,777) the difference of £605 must be investigated.

Step 2   The control account and the individual accounts and balances must be checked and any errors or omissions noted.

In Southfield's case the following errors were noted:

a)   a page of the cash receipts book had been overcast by £100;

b)   the total from the sales day book for a week had been posted as £3,675 instead of £3,765;

c)   a bad debt of £240 had been written off in the individual debtor's account but not in the main ledger;

d)   an invoice to Weller Enterprises for £478 had been entered into the account of Dagwell Enterprises instead;

e)   a cash receipt from B B Berry Ltd had been entered into the debtor's account in the subsidiary (sales) ledger as £256 instead of the correct figure from the sales day book of £265;

f)   a balance of £604 on one debtor's account had been omitted from the list of balances;

g)   a credit balance of £20 on a debtor's account had been included in the list of balances as a debit balance.

student notes✎

Step 3 The sales ledger control account must be adjusted for any errors that affect it:

Sales ledger control account

	£		£
Balance b/d	14,382		
a) Cash receipts book	100	c) Bad debt	240
b) Sales day book	90		
		Balance c/d	14,332
	14,572		14,572
Balance b/d	14,332		

a) the total from the cash receipts book would have been credited to the sales ledger control account. Therefore if it was overcast by £100 the account must be debited with £100, to reduce the amount of the entry;

b) the total from the sales day book is debited to the sales ledger control account. The original entry was for £90 too little (£3,675 instead of £3,765) so an extra debit entry of £90 is required to correct the error;

c) to write off a bad debt the sales ledger control account must be credited as the debt is no longer receivable.

Therefore the amended net balance on the control account is £14,332.

Step 4 Adjust the total of the list of balances from the subsidiary ledger by adding or deducting the errors that affect this total.

	£
Original total	13,777
Less: additional cash receipt (265– 256) (e)	(9)
Add: balance omitted (f)	604
Less: credit balance included as debit balance (g)	(40)
	14,332

d) the two debtor's accounts will need to be adjusted to reflect the error but this type of error does not affect the total of the balances on all of the debtor accounts;

e) the additional receipt of £9 that should have been recorded would reduce the total of the debtors balances;

f) the balance omitted must be added in to the total of the list of balances;

g) the £20 credit balance that was included as a debit balance would reduce debtors if it were correctly included – however twice the amount of the balance must be deducted as the balance has not been omitted but included on the wrong side which must be cancelled out.

student notes✍

The amended total of the list of balances now agrees to the amended sales ledger control account total and the main ledger and subsidiary ledger are now reconciled.

Activity 5

If the total of the discounts allowed column from the cash receipts book of £300 were not posted for a period how would this be adjusted for in the sales ledger control account reconciliation?

PURCHASES LEDGER CONTROL ACCOUNT RECONCILIATION

A purchases ledger control account reconciliation works in exactly the same manner as a sales ledger control account reconciliation with the entries on the opposite sides.

HOW IT WORKS

Whitehill Superstores is currently preparing its purchases ledger control account reconciliation at the end of October 2006. The balance on the purchases ledger control account was £17,240 and the total of the list of creditors' balances from the subsidiary ledger was £16,720.

The following errors and omissions were noted:

a) one page of the purchases day book has been overcast by £200;

b) an invoice has been posted to an individual creditor's account in the subsidiary ledger as £957 instead of the correct figure from the purchases day book of £597;

c) the total of discounts received of £250 was credited to the purchases ledger control account;

d) one of the balances in the subsidiary ledger was included in the total at a figure of £468 instead of £648.

student notes🖎

Step 1 Amend the control account balance for any errors that affect it.

Purchases ledger control account

	£		£
a) Purchases day book	200	Balance b/d	17,240
c) Discounts	500		
Balance c/d	16,540		
	17,240		17,240
		Balance b/d	16,540

a) the total from the purchases day book is credited to the purchases ledger control account, and therefore if it was overcast by £200 then the account must be debited by £200;

c) the discounts received should have been debited to the purchases ledger control account – instead they were credited and therefore not only should there be one debit of £250 but two, one to cancel out the credit and one to put the debit entry in, therefore a debit of £500.

Step 2 Amend the total of the list of balances to adjust for any errors that affect the individual balances or their total.

	£
Original total	16,720
b) Less: invoice misposting	
(957 – 597)	(360)
d) Add: balance misstated	180
	16,540

b) an invoice would be posted to the credit side of the creditor's account – in this case it was posted at a figure £360 too high and therefore the creditors' balances would be reduced when the account was amended;

d) the balance that was misstated was shown as £180 too little – therefore the balances need to be increased by £180.

Activity 6

An invoice for £200 was entered into the individual creditor's account in the subsidiary (purchases) ledger on the wrong side of the account. How should this be adjusted for in the purchases ledger control account reconciliation?

NON-TRADE DEBTORS

Most of the debtors of a business arise due to the fact that the business trades on credit, ie it sells its goods or services on credit. However it is possible for a business to have debtors other than for trading activities.

For example if the business rents out some of its warehouse space to another business and this rent is paid in arrears then there will be a debtor for the rent due. A further example might be if a business sold one of its delivery vans to a local garage and payment is due in three week's time.

HOW IT WORKS

Southfield Electrical have a large warehouse but not all of the space is required. Therefore a portion of it is rented out to Paul Evans at a quarterly rental of £400 paid on the last day of each quarter, ie 31 March, 30 June etc.

When Southfield prepare their accounts at 31 December 2006 they will have a rental income account with a credit balance of £1,600, the rental due for the four quarters of the year (this is a credit balance as it is income!).

Rental income account			
£			£
	31 Dec	Rental	1,600

However at 31 December Paul has not yet paid the final quarter's rent. Therefore during the year only £1,200 has been debited to the bank account and the final £400 of debit balance must be included in a debtor account.

Rental income due account			
		£	£
31 Dec	Paul Evans	400	

As this debtor is different in nature from the trade debtors of Southfield's business then it should not be recorded in the sales ledger control account but instead in a separate non-trade debtors control account. If there were a number of such debtors then the balance on the non-trade debtors control account should be reconciled to the totals of each of the individual non-trade debtors on a regular basis.

PETTY CASH RECONCILIATION

We have already seen in Chapter 13 that most businesses will hold some cash on the premises, known as petty cash. Even though the amount of petty cash will normally be quite small it is important that proper control is kept over this asset and that it is recorded as the correct amount of "cash in hand" in the trial balance.

Imprest system of petty cash

In an imprest system the petty cash box is maintained at a constant amount, the imprest amount. This means that each time the petty cash box is reimbursed then it is topped up to the imprest amount.

In theory, at any point in time, the amount of the cash in the petty cash box plus the total of the petty cash vouchers should be equal to the imprest amount.

CASH + VOUCHERS = IMPREST AMOUNT

This reconciliation of the amount of cash and vouchers in the petty cash box should take place on a regular basis to ensure that the petty cash system is working correctly.

HOW IT WORKS

Southfield Electrical has a petty cash box run on a £100 imprest system. At the end of the week beginning 25 October the following petty cash vouchers were found in the petty cash box:

PETTY CASH VOUCHER

Number: 0496

Details		Amount
Train fare		16 - 20
	Net	16 - 20
	VAT	—
	Gross	16 - 20

Claimed by: J. Goswell
Authorised by: M. Harris

PETTY CASH VOUCHER

Number: 0497

Details		Amount
Envelopes		2-50
Paper		2-06
	Net	4-56
	VAT	0-79
	Gross	5-35

Claimed by: T. Raine
Authorised by: M. Harris

PETTY CASH VOUCHER

Number: 0498

Details		Amount
Train fare		11-20
	Net	11-20
	VAT	—
	Gross	11-20

Claimed by: I. Hampton
Authorised by: M. Harris

PETTY CASH VOUCHER

Number: 0500

Details		Amount
Computer disks		11 - 65
	Net	11 - 65
	VAT	2 - 03
	Gross	13 - 68

Claimed by: I. Hampton
Authorised by: M. Harris

PETTY CASH VOUCHER

Number: 0499

Details		Amount
Taxi Fare		12 - 77
	Net	12 - 77
	VAT	2 - 23
	Gross	15 - 00

Claimed by: M. McCaul
Authorised by: M. Harris

PETTY CASH VOUCHER

Number: 0501

Details		Amount
Coffee for office kitchen		2 - 61
	Net	2 - 61
	VAT	—
	Gross	2 - 61

Claimed by: S. Stone
Authorised by: M. Harris

The following amounts of cash were also in the petty cash box:

£10 note	1
£5 note	1
£1 coin	14
50 pence coin	7
20 pence coin	9
10 pence coin	13
5 pence coin	3
2 pence coin	5
1 pence coin	11

You now need to reconcile the petty cash vouchers and the cash in the petty cash box.

The total of the vouchers is:

Voucher No.	£
0496	16.20
0497	5.35
0498	11.20
0499	15.00
0500	13.68
0501	2.61
	64.04

The total of the cash is:

		£
£10 note	1	10.00
£5 note	1	5.00
£1 coin	14	14.00
50 pence coin	7	3.50
20 pence coin	9	1.80
10 pence coin	13	1.30
5 pence coin	3	0.15
2 pence coin	5	0.10
1 pence coin	11	0.11
		35.96

These two totals together should be equal to the imprest amount of £100:

	£
Petty cash vouchers	64.04
Cash in petty cash box	35.96
	100.00

In this case the petty cash amount is reconciled. The procedures have been correctly carried out and if an amount were needed for cash in hand in the trial balance it would be £35.96.

Petty cash control account

In some businesses a petty cash control account will be included in the main ledger if the petty cash book is not treated as part of the main ledger. The petty cash control account would start with the imprest amount and show the total payments made out of the petty cash box. The remaining balance should be the actual amount of cash in the petty cash box.

HOW IT WORKS

If Southfield Electrical maintained a petty cash control account for the week commencing 25 October the account would be prepared like this:

Petty cash control account

	£		£
25 Oct Balance b/d	100.00	29 Oct Petty cash book	64.04
		29 Oct Balance c/d	35.96
	100.00		100.00

Discrepancies that arise

When the reconciliation of the cash in the petty cash box to the vouchers is carried out and the two amounts do not agree back to the imprest amount, it is clear that something has gone wrong with the system or procedure.

Too little cash in the petty cash box

If the reconciliation shows that there is not enough cash in the petty cash box then there are a number of possible reasons for this:

- probably the most obvious is that cash has been removed from the petty cash box without being supported by an authorised petty cash voucher;

- too much cash might have been given to a petty cash claimant and not noticed by either the petty cashier or the claimant;

- a petty cash voucher may be missing – this can be checked as the petty cash vouchers should be sequentially numbered.

Too much cash in the petty cash box

If the reconciliation shows that there is more cash in the petty cash box than there should be, this could also be for a number of possible reasons:

- too little cash may have been given to a petty cash claimant and not noticed by either the petty cashier or the claimant;

- a petty cash voucher has been placed in the petty cash box but no cash has yet been paid out;

- the amount paid into the petty cash box at the start of the period brought it up to an amount that was greater than the imprest amount.

Activity 7

The petty cash box is totalled and reconciled at the end of the week and it is discovered that there are petty cash vouchers totalling £103.69 and actual cash of £36.31. The imprest amount is £150. Does the petty cash reconcile with the vouchers? If not, suggest possible reasons why not.

CHAPTER OVERVIEW

- the sales ledger control account is debited with the sales invoices from the sales day book and credited with cash receipts and discounts from the cash receipts book

- the individual accounts for each debtor in the subsidiary (sales) ledger are also debited with each invoice total and credited with the cash and discounts

- if all of the entries are correctly carried out then the total of the closing balances on the individual debtors accounts from the subsidiary (sales) ledger should agree to the balance on the sales ledger control account

- the same system applies to accounting for creditors although the entries are all on the opposite sides

KEY WORDS

Bad debt a debt which it is believed will never be recovered

Sales ledger control account reconciliation an exercise which agrees the balance on the sales ledger control account to the total of the list of balances in the subsidiary (sales) ledger

Purchases ledger control account reconciliation an exercise which agrees the balance on the purchases ledger control account to the total of the list of balances in the subsidiary (purchases) ledger

- the sales ledger control account will also potentially have entries for sales returns, returned cheques and bad debts written off as well as the basic entries for invoices, cash and discounts

- the double entry for writing off a bad debt is to debit the bad debts expense account and credit the sales ledger control account

- the purchases ledger control account will also potentially have entries for purchases returns as well as the basic entries for invoices, cash and discounts

- when all of the entries in the main ledger and subsidiary ledger have not been properly performed then the subsidiary ledger balances total will not agree to the balance on the control account – in which case the causes of the difference must be discovered

- a sales ledger control account reconciliation compares the balance on the sales ledger control account to the total of the debtors' account balances in the subsidiary (sales) ledger – both are amended for any errors that have been made and the total and balance should agree after putting through the amendments

- a purchases ledger control account reconciliation works in exactly the same way as the debtors' reconciliation although all of the entries and balances are on the opposite sides.

- if a business has any non-trade debtors these should be accounted for separately in a non-trade debtors control account

- in an imprest petty cash system, at any point the amount of cash in the petty cash box plus the total of the petty cash vouchers in the box should equal the imprest amount

- a reconciliation of the petty cash and vouchers should be carried out at regular intervals

- if the petty cash book is not part of the main ledger double entry system then a petty cash control account will be in operation. The balance on this account should be equal to the amount of cash in the petty cash box

HOW MUCH HAVE YOU LEARNED?

1   DP Printing is a small company that has currently only four credit customers. The opening balances on their debtor's account in DP's subsidiary (purchases) ledger at the start of May 2006 were as follows:

	£
Virgo Partners	227.58
McGowan & Sons	552.73
J J Westrope	317.59
Jacks Ltd	118.36

The opening balance on the sales ledger control account at the start of May was £1,216.26.

The sales day book and cash receipts book for May are given below:

Sales day book

Date	Customer	Gross £	VAT £	Net £
3 May	J J Westrope	163.90	24.41	139.49
10 May	Virgo Partners	94.70	14.10	80.60
12 May	Jacks Ltd	105.47	15.70	89.77
15 May	J J Westrope	271.57	40.44	231.13
20 May	McGowan & Sons	582.69	86.78	495.91
23 May	Jacks Ltd	173.99	25.91	148.08
30 May	Virgo Partners	210.00	31.27	178.73
		1,602.32	238.61	1,363.71

Cash receipts book

Date	Details	Total	VAT	Cash sales	Debtors ledger	Discounts allowed
			£	£	£	£
3 May	Cash sales	476.90	71.02	405.88		
4 May	Virgo Partners	117.38			117.38	
10 May	Cash sales	442.38	65.88	376.50		
12 May	J J Westrope	308.86			308.86	8.73
15 May	McGowan & sons	552.73			552.73	
17 May	Cash sales	501.67	74.71	426.96		
20 May	Jacks Ltd	100.00			100.00	
30 May	Cash sales	557.50	72.26	485.24		
		3,057.42	283.87	1,694.58	1,078.97	8.73

Write up the sales ledger control account for the month and the individual debtors' accounts in the subsidiary (sales) ledger. Agree the control account balance to the total of the subsidiary account balances at the end of the month.

2 DP Printing has three credit suppliers and the opening balances on their creditor accounts in the subsidiary (purchases) ledger at the start of May 2006 were:

	£
Jenkins Suppliers	441.56
Kilnfarm Paper	150.00
Barnfield Ltd	247.90

The opening balance on the purchases ledger control account at the start of May was £839.46.

The purchases day book and cash payments book for the period are given below:

Purchases day book

Date	Supplier	Gross £	VAT £	Net £
5 May	Kilnfarm Paper	150.00	22.34	127.66
10 May	Jenkins Suppliers	215.47	32.09	183.38
12 May	Barnfield Ltd	310.58	46.25	264.33
20 May	Kilnfarm Paper	150.00	22.34	127.66
27 May	Jenkins Suppliers	441.90	65.81	376.09
30 May	Barnfield Ltd	305.77	45.54	260.23
		1,573.72	234.37	1,339.35

Cash payments book

Date	Details	Total	VAT £	Cash purchases £	Creditors ledger £	Discount received £
5 May	Cash purchases	225.68	33.61	192.07		
10 May	Jenkins Suppliers	423.89			423.89	17.67
12 May	Kilnfarm Paper	150.00			150.00	
15 May	Cash Purchases	315.22	46.94	268.28		
20 May	Barnfield Ltd	235.50			235.50	12.40
27 May	Kilnfarm Paper	150.00			150.00	
30 May	Cash purchases	210.44	31.34	179.10		
		1,710.73	111.89	639.45	959.39	30.07

Write up the purchases ledger control account for May and the individual creditors' accounts in the subsidiary (purchases) ledger. Agree the control account balance at the end of May to the total of the list of individual balances in the subsidiary (purchases) ledger.

3   Write up the sales ledger control account for the month of July 2006 from the following information:

	£
Opening balance 1 July	16,339
Credit sales for the month	50,926
Cash sales for the month	12,776
Sales returns (all for credit sales) for the month	3,446
Cash received from debtors in the month	47,612
Settlement discounts allowed to debtors in the month	1,658
Bad debt to be written off	500
Cheque returned by the bank "refer to drawer"	366

4   Write up the purchases ledger control account for the month of July 2006 from the following information:

	£
Opening balance 1 July	12,587
Cash purchases for the month	15,600
Credit purchases for the month	40,827
Purchases returns (all for purchases on credit)	2,568
Cheques paid to creditors in the month	38,227
Settlement discounts received from supplier in the month	998

5 The balance on a business's sales ledger control account at the end of June 2006 was £41,774 and the total of the list of debtor balances from the subsidiary (sales) ledger came to £41,586.

The following errors were discovered:

a)   the sales day book was undercast by £100 on one page

b)   a page from the sales returns day book with a total of £450 had not been posted to the control account although the individual returns had been recorded in the subsidiary (sales) ledger

c)   an invoice from the sales day book had been posted to the individual account of the debtor as £769 instead of the correct figure of £679

d)   a discount allowed to one customer of £16 had been posted to the wrong side of the customer's account in the subsidiary (sales) ledger

e)   a bad debt of £210 had been written off in the debtor's individual account in the subsidiary (sales) ledger but not in the main ledger

f)   a credit balance in the subsidiary (sales) ledger of £125 had been included in the list of balances as a debit balance

Reconcile the sales ledger control account to the total of the list of balances from the subsidiary (sales) ledger after taking account of the errors noted.

6 The balance on a business's purchases ledger control account at the end of June 2006 is £38,694 and the total of the list of balances in the subsidiary (purchases) ledger came to £39,741.

The following errors were noted for the month:

a)   a page in the purchases returns day book was overcast by £300

b)   a total from the cash payments book of £3,145 was posted in the main ledger as £3,415

c)   settlement discounts received from suppliers of £267 were omitted from both the main ledger and the subsidiary (purchases) ledger

d)   a credit note from a supplier for £210 was entered into the supplier's account in the subsidiary (purchases) ledger as £120

e)   a debit balance on a creditor's account in the subsidiary (purchases) ledger of £187 was omitted from the list of balances

f)   a credit balance in the subsidiary (purchases) ledger should have been included in the list as £570 but instead was recorded as £770

Reconcile the balance on the purchases ledger control account to the total of the list of balances in the subsidiary (purchases) ledger after taking account of these errors.

7 Your organisation has an imprest petty cash system with an imprest amount of £120. Today is the 30 November 2006 and you are required to reconcile the petty cash in the petty cash box and the petty cash vouchers.

You have already determined the denominations of the cash in the box:

£10 note	1
£5 note	2
£2 coin	1
£1 coin	5
50p coin	3
20p coin	15
10p coin	8
5p coin	11
2p coin	14
1p coin	6

You have also summarised the petty cash vouchers in the box:

Voucher No.	£
1256	14.67
1257	6.30
1258	10.00
1259	4.47
1260	13.80
1261	15.90
1263	8.95
1264	7.45

Carry out the necessary checks to ensure that the petty cash system has operated correctly and that the amount of cash in hand can be recorded in the trial balance as the total of the petty cash in the box.

chapter 17:
PREPARING AN INITIAL TRIAL BALANCE

chapter coverage 📖

For the purposes of Unit 3 you are required to draft an initial trial balance. Therefore in this chapter we will consider the process of preparing a trial balance and the information that you will require. The topics that are to be covered are:

✍ the nature and purpose of the trial balance

✍ balancing ledger accounts

✍ preparing a trial balance

✍ determining whether account balances are debits or credits

✍ additional information required when preparing a trial balance

---

KNOWLEDGE AND UNDERSTANDING AND PERFORMANCE CRITERIA COVERAGE

Unit 3

knowledge and understanding – accounting methods

5 double entry bookkeeping, including balancing accounts
18 function and form of the trial balance

knowledge and understanding – the organisation

19 relevant understanding of the organisation's accounting systems and administrative systems and procedures

21 organisational procedures for filing source information

Performance criteria – element 3.3

A prepare the draft initial trial balance in line with the organisation's policies and procedures

THE TRIAL BALANCE

A simple TRIAL BALANCE was prepared in an earlier chapter and in this chapter we will consider the process of preparing a trial balance in more detail.

The trial balance is a list of all of the balances in the main ledger. The debit balances are listed in one column and the credit balances in a second column. The two columns are then totalled and if the double entry has been correctly carried out then the debit total should be equal to the credit total.

The purpose of the trial balance

The purpose of a trial balance is two fold:

- the trial balance is part of the control process in the accounting system because if the debit and credit columns are not equal then this indicates that there have been errors made or omissions in the accounting process (errors identified and not identified by the trial balance process will be considered further in the next chapter);

- the trial balance also serves as the starting point for the eventual preparation of the financial statements of the business: the profit and loss account and the balance sheet (not required at the Foundation level).

Closing balances

The starting point for the preparation of the trial balance is to find the closing balance on each of the main ledger accounts at the date that the trial balance is being prepared.

So let's have a quick reminder of how to determine the closing balance on a ledger account.

HOW IT WORKS

Given below is a sales ledger control account for the month of November 2006:

Sales ledger control account

	£		£
Opening balance	14.623	Sales returns	1,446
Sales	58,993	Cash received	52,689
		Discounts allowed	2,017
		Bad debt written off	1,637

Now we will find the closing balance on this account.

Sales ledger control account

	£		£
Opening balance	14,623	Sales returns	1,446
Sales	58,993	Cash received	52,689
		Discounts allowed	2,017
		Bad debt written off	1,637
		Balance c/d	15,827
	73,616		73,616
Balance b/d	15,827		

This account would be said to have a debit balance of £15,827 as the balance b/d below the total is on the debit side of the account.

Activity 1

Find the closing balance on the following account and state whether it is a debit balance or a credit balance.

Purchases ledger control account

	£		£
Purchase returns	3,669	Opening balance	24,578
Cash paid	86,338	Purchases	89,451
Discounts received	3,698		

student notes✎

Accounts with a single entry

Some ledger accounts may only have one entry in them for the period – in these cases this entry is the balance on the account.

HOW IT WORKS

A business took out a loan of £10,000 from the bank during the accounting period – the loan account is shown below:

Loan account			
	£		£
		Cash received	10,000

The balance on this account is a credit balance of £10,000 as this single entry is on the credit side of the account.

Activity 2

State whether the balance on the following account is a debit balance or a credit balance.

Motor vehicles account			
	£		£
Cash payments book	15,600		

PREPARING A TRIAL BALANCE

In the assessments it is likely that you will only be given some of the main ledger accounts in full. The balances on the other accounts will be given to you in a list. The problem here is to determine whether the balance is a debit balance or a credit balance.

Rules

There are some rules that can help:

- asset accounts will normally have a debit balance;
- liability accounts will normally have a credit balance;
- expense accounts will normally have a debit balance;
- income accounts will normally have a credit balance.

HOW IT WORKS

Given below are the balances in the main ledger of a small business:

	£
Motor vehicles	15,600
Stock	2,100
Bank balance (debit balance)	9,130
Sales ledger control account	4,400
Purchases ledger control account	3,200
Capital	40,000
Sales	65,000
Sales returns	5,000
Purchases	42,000
Purchases returns	2,700
Bank charges	100
Discounts allowed	900
Discounts received	600
Wages and salaries	21,800
Rent and rates	6,200
Telephone	1,020
Electricity	2,550
Bad debts written off	700

student notes ✍

Now we have to determine whether each balance is a debit or a credit and then list it in the appropriate column of the trial balance.

Motor vehicles	15,600	– an asset, therefore a debit balance
Stock	2,100	– an asset, therefore a debit balance
Bank balance (debit balance)	9,130	– this can be either a debit or a credit balance (see later in the chapter) but in this case we are told that it is a debit
Sales ledger control account	4,400	– an asset, therefore a debit balance
Purchases ledger control account	3,200	– a liability, therefore a credit balance
Capital	40,000	– a special liability – the amount owed back to the owner – a liability, therefore a credit balance
Sales	65,000	– income, therefore a credit balance
Sales returns	5,000	– the opposite of sales, therefore a debit balance
Purchases	42,000	– an expense, therefore a debit balance
Purchases returns	2,700	– the opposite of purchases, therefore a credit balance
Bank charges	100	– an expense, therefore a debit balance
Discounts allowed	900	– an expense, therefore a debit balance
Discounts received	600	– similar to income, therefore a credit balance
Wages and salaries	21,800	– an expense, therefore a debit balance
Rent and rates	6,200	– an expense, therefore a debit balance
Telephone	1,020	– an expense, therefore a debit balance
Electricity	2,550	– an expense, therefore a debit balance
Bad debts written off	700	– an expense, therefore a debit balance

Trial balance

	Debits £	Credits £
Motor vehicle	15,600	
Stock	2,100	
Bank	9,130	
Sales ledger control	4,400	
Purchases ledger control		3,200
Capital		40,000
Sales		65,000
Sales returns	5,000	
Purchases	42,000	
Purchases returns		2,700
Bank charges	100	
Discounts allowed	900	
Discounts received		600
Wages and salaries	21,800	
Rent and rates	6,200	
Telephone	1,020	
Electricity	2,550	
Bad debts written off	700	
	111,500	111,500

Note how the total of the debit balances is equal to the total of the credit balances, indicating that if there are errors in the ledger they are not of the type that will be identified by a trial balance (see next chapter).

Activity 3

Is the balance on a discounts received account a debit balance or a credit balance?

CHAPTER OVERVIEW

- a trial balance is a list of all of the balances in the main ledger shown in two columns, the debit balances and the credit balances

- the purpose of the trial balance is to check on the accuracy of the accounting records and to serve as a basis for the eventual preparation of the financial statements

- the trial balance is prepared by listing the closing balance on each account at the trial balance date

- when the balances on the ledger accounts are given in a list, it is necessary to determine whether the balance is a debit or a credit balance – assets and expenses will normally be debit balances and liabilities and income will normally be credit balances

HOW MUCH HAVE YOU LEARNED?

1   Calculate the closing balances on each of the following accounts.

VAT account

	£		£
Input VAT	3,778	Opening balance	2,116
Cash paid	2,116	Output VAT	6,145

Sales account

	£		£
		Opening balance	57,226
		Debtors' control	23,512

Sales ledger control account

	£		£
Opening balance	4,689	Cash received	20,963
Sales	23,512	Discounts allowed	2,019
		Bad debt written off	542

Purchases ledger control account

	£		£
Purchases returns	1,334	Opening balance	2,864
Cash paid	13,446	Purchases	14,552
Discounts received	662		

2   Determine whether each of the following balances would be shown as a debit balance or a credit balance in the trial balance.

	£
Discounts allowed	1,335
Discounts received	1,013
Purchases returns	4,175
Sales returns	6,078
Carriage inwards	2,114
Carriage outwards	1,478
Bank interest received	328
Bank charges	163

3 Given below are the balances on the ledger accounts of Thames Traders at 30 November 2006. Prepare the trial balance as at 30 November 2006.

	£
Motor vehicles	64,000
Office equipment	21,200
Sales	238,000
Purchases	164,000
Bank overdraft	1,680
Petty cash	30
Capital	75,000
Sales returns	4,700
Purchases returns	3,600
Sales ledger control	35,800
Purchases ledger control	30,100
VAT (credit balance)	12,950
Stock	19,200
Telephone	1,600
Electricity	2,800
Wages	62,100
Loan	30,000
Discounts allowed	6,400
Discounts received	3,900
Rent	12,000
Bad debts written off	1,400

chapter 18:
ERRORS AND THE TRIAL BALANCE

— chapter coverage 📖 —

In the previous chapter, you saw how to prepare a trial balance. This chapter considers a trial balance that does not balance. For element 3.3 you are expected to identify and rectify discrepancies and create a suspense account where necessary. In order to identify the errors you will need to be aware of the different types of error that exist, both those that are shown up by the trial balance and those that are not. The topics that are to be covered are:

✍ types of errors that lead to an imbalance in the trial balance

✍ types of errors that do not cause an imbalance in the trial balance

✍ the procedure to follow to try to determine the error or errors made when the trial balance does not balance

✍ creation and clearing of a suspense account

KNOWLEDGE AND UNDERSTANDING AND PERFORMANCE CRITERIA COVERAGE

Unit 3

knowledge and understanding – accounting methods

5   double entry bookkeeping, including balancing accounts (Elements 3.1, 3.2 and 3.3)
8   operation of manual accounting systems (Elements 3.1, 3.2 and 3.3)
11   identification of different types of errors (Element 3.1)
16   use of journals (Elements 3.2 and 3.3)
18   function and form of the trial balance (Element 3.3)

Performance criteria – element 3.3

B   identify discrepancies in the balancing process
C   identify reasons for imbalance and rectify them
D   balance the trial balance

TYPES OF ERROR

In a manual accounting system there are several types of error that can be made when making entries to the ledger accounts. Some of these errors will be identified when a trial balance is extracted but a number of types of error can take place and the trial balance will still balance.

Errors leading to an imbalance on the trial balance

There are a number of types of errors that will mean that the debit balances on the trial balance will not equal the credit balances.

Single entry – if only one side of the double entry has been made in the ledger accounts, eg, the debit and not the credit, then the trial balance will not balance

Transposition error – a transposition error is where the digits in a number are transposed (swapped round), eg, a transaction for £435 is recorded correctly as a debit but is recorded as a credit of £345. It is also possible for the balance on an account to be transposed when it is taken to the trial balance eg, a balance of £1,268 is recorded in the trial balance as £1,628. This will also mean that the trial balance will not balance. If a transposition error has been made and is the only error then the difference between the debits and the credits will be divisible by 9. This is often useful when trying to track down errors made.

Balancing error – if a ledger account has not been correctly balanced and the incorrect balance has been included in the trial balance, it will not balance.

Balance omission – if a balance on a ledger account is omitted from the trial balance then again this means that the debits will not equal the credits.

Activity 1

A sales invoice recorded in the sales day book at £1,678 has been correctly recorded in the sales ledger control account but has been entered into the sales account as £1,768. What type of error is this?

Errors which do not cause an imbalance on the trial balance

Unfortunately there are also some types of error that will not cause a difference on the trial balance and therefore cannot be shown up through the trial balance process.

Error of original entry – here both entries into the main ledger, debit and credit, have been made using the wrong amount. This may be due to the fact that the transaction was recorded in the primary record at the incorrect amount or that the wrong figure was picked up from the primary record (eg a transposition error) and this incorrect figure was used for both the debit and the credit entry. However as long as both the debit and the credit entry are equal this error will not cause an imbalance in the trial balance.

Error of omission – an entry is completely omitted from the ledger accounts. If the transaction is not recorded as either a debit or a credit then it will not affect the trial balance.

Error of reversal – this type of error is where the correct figure has been used and a debit and a credit entry made but the debit and the credit are on the wrong side of the respective accounts. The trial balance will still balance but the two accounts will have incorrect balances.

Error of commission – the double entry is arithmetically correct but a wrong account of the **same type** has been used. For example if the telephone bill is paid the bank account will be credited and an expense account, the telephone account, should be debited. If instead the electricity account is debited this is an error of commission. It does not affect the trial balance but it does mean that both the telephone account and electricity account show the wrong balance.

Error of principle – an error of principle is similar to an error of commission in that the double entry is arithmetically correct but with an error of principle the **wrong type** of account has been used. For example if computer disks are purchased, the bank account should be credited and the computer expenses or office expenses account debited. If instead the cost of the disks is debited to the computer fixed asset account, this is an error of principle but again will not affect the balancing of the trial balance.

Compensating errors – these are probably rare in practice but it is where two errors are made which exactly cancel each other out. For example if the debtors control account is entered at £100 too high an amount (a debit balance) and the purchases returns (a credit balance) is also entered at £100 too high an amount, the two errors will cancel each other out. The errors are unrelated but the fact that they both occurred will mean that there is no imbalance in the trial balance.

Activity 2

A sales invoice to J K Reynolds was recorded in the subsidiary ledger for debtors in the account of T M Reynolds. What type of error is this?

Computerised accounting systems

In a computerised accounting system the number of types of different errors that can occur are limited as the computer system will not allow many of them to take place.

Where the accounting system is computerised the following types of error will not occur:

- single entries – the computer will not accept a debit without a credit and vice versa;

- transposition errors – these are human errors that are not made by a computer;

- balancing errors – again these are addition errors that will not be made by a computer;

- extraction errors – the computer will ensure that all balances are correctly included in the trial balance.

However even in a computerised system the data has to be input by human hand and this is where certain errors do creep in:

- errors of original entry;
- errors of commission;
- errors of principle;
- compensating errors.

IMBALANCE ON THE TRIAL BALANCE

If the trial balance does not balance then the reason or reasons for this have to be discovered. As we have seen in the previous paragraph there are many types of error that could cause the total of the debits not to equal the total of the credits. Rather than going back to each ledger account and checking each entry to find the cause of the imbalance it makes sense, both in practice and in assessments, to take a logical approach to finding the causes of any imbalance.

The problem might be arithmetical or to do with the double entry but it makes sense to check the more obvious and simple errors before getting involved with detailed checking of the ledger accounts.

Procedure for finding the error/errors

Step 1 Check the totalling of the debit column and the credit column. it is very easy to make an error when totalling a large column of figures therefore this is an obvious place to start.

Step 2 Calculate the difference between the debit and credit total as this may come in useful later in the checking exercise if the difference cannot be found easily.

Step 3 Check that each balance in the trial balance has been correctly copied into the trial balance and that each has been included on the correct side, debit or credit.

Step 4 Check that all of the balances in the main ledger have been included in the trial balance. In particular ensure that the bank balance and petty cash balances have been included as these are generally kept physically separate from the main ledger.

Step 5 Check that the calculation of the balance on each ledger account is correct.

Step 6 Look in the ledger accounts for any entry that is for the same amount as the difference on the trial balance and, if it is found, check that the double entry for this transaction has been correctly carried out.

Step 7 Look in the ledger accounts for any entry that is for half the amount of the difference on the trial balance and, if it is found check that the double entry for this transaction has been correctly carried out

If all else fails resort to:

Step 8 Checking all of the bookkeeping entries since the date of the last trial balance. This will entail following through each transaction from the primary records to the ledger accounts.

Number tricks to look out for

If the difference on the trial balance is divisible exactly by nine then the error is likely to be a transposition error. This means that two digits in a figure have been reversed, eg £654 is entered as £564 – the difference of £90 is exactly divisible by 9.

If the difference on the trial balance is a round number eg; £10, £100, £1,000 etc then it is likely that the error that has been made is arithmetical rather than a double entry error. Therefore take great care when checking account balance calculations.

Finding the error

When the reason for the imbalance of the trial balance is discovered it must be rectified. Each error or omission must be corrected and this is done using a JOURNAL ENTRY.

Journal entries

A journal is another type of book of prime entry. A journal entry is a written instruction to the bookkeeper to enter a double entry into the main ledger. The journal is used to record transactions that do not appear in any of the other books of prime entry and in particular to record the double entry necessary to correct any errors.

HOW IT WORKS

Suppose that the sales day book for a period had been undercast by £1,000. This means that both the sales ledger control account and the sales account have been understated by £1,000. Both accounts must have additional entries made into them and the way this is done is to write out a journal entry for the correcting double entry.

Date 2006	Ref	Debit	Credit
		£	£
Sales ledger control account		1,000	
Sales account			1,000

being correction of the undercasting of the sales day book

CREATION OF A SUSPENSE ACCOUNT

When the trial balance is initially drafted it is possible that the debit total does not equal the credit total. When this happens the reasons for this must be investigated. However until the reasons for the imbalance on the trial balance have been discovered a SUSPENSE ACCOUNT is opened in order to make the trial balance totals equal.

HOW IT WORKS

When a business drafted its initial trial balance the totals of the debit and credit columns were as follows:

	Debit £	Credit £
Total	157,600	157,900

The difference of £300 is initially dealt with by opening a suspense account in order to make the trial balance balance.

	Debit £	Credit £
	157,600	157,900
Suspense account	300	
	157,900	157,900

The trial balance now balances but there is also a new main ledger account, the suspense account, with a debit balance.

Suspense account		
	£	£
Balance b/d	300	

This balance must not remain in the ledger accounts. The reasons for the imbalance on the trial balance must be investigated and the corrections made using journal entries. Once the corrections have been put through the suspense account should be cleared to a balance of zero.

Correcting errors

In an assessment you will be told of any errors that have been made and will have to draft the journal entries to correct them. The procedure to follow is to work out what the incorrect double entry was and then to determine what double entry is required to correct the error.

Bear in mind that, as we have already seen in this chapter, not all errors affect the balancing of the trial balance. Therefore when drafting journals to correct errors there will not always be an entry to the suspense account. The only time that there will be a suspense account entry will be if the double entry has broken down in some way, so that there is only one correcting entry to the other ledger accounts rather than a double entry. In these situations the other side of the entry will be to the suspense account.

HOW IT WORKS

Continuing with the previous example remember that there is a debit balance of £300 on the suspense account. The following errors have been discovered:

1) Discounts received of £175 have been omitted from the main ledger accounts

2) Sales returns were correctly recorded as £1,500 in the sales returns account but as only £1,000 in the sales ledger control account

3) When the rent account was balanced it was undercast by £1,000

4) A purchase invoice for £460 was omitted from the purchases day book

5) Purchases returns of £580 were recorded in the main ledger as £850

6) Discounts allowed of £200 were only entered in the discount account

7) A receipt from a debtor of £140 was entered on the wrong side of the debtor's account in the subsidiary (sales) ledger

We will deal with each of these errors in turn.

1) Discounts received of £175 have been omitted from the main ledger accounts

As this has been omitted from the main ledger totally then the double entry is the full double entry for discounts received

		£	£
Debit	Purchases ledger control account	175	
Credit	Discounts received account		175

2) Sales returns were correctly recorded as £1,500 in the sales returns account but as only £1,000 in the sales ledger control account

The sales ledger control account must be credited with a further £500 but as there is no other entry to be made then the other side of the entry must be to the suspense account.

		£	£
Debit	Suspense account	500	
Credit	Sales ledger control account		500

	Suspense account		
	£		£
Balance b/d	300		
Sales ledger control	500		

3) **When the rent account was balanced it was undercast by £1,000**

The rent balance in the trial balance has to be increased by £1,000 in the trial balance but as this is the only entry required the other side of the entry must be to the suspense account.

		£	£
Debit	Rent account	1,000	
Credit	Suspense account		1,000

Suspense account			
	£		£
Balance b/d	300	Rent	1,000
Sales ledger control	500		

4) **A purchase invoice for £460 was omitted from the purchases day book**

As the invoice has not been entered into the purchases day book then it will not have been entered into the main ledger. Therefore the full double entry is required.

		£	£
Debit	Purchases account	460	
Credit	Purchases ledger control account		460

5) **Purchases returns of £580 were recorded in the main ledger as £850**

Both sides of the entry for purchases returns are too high by £270 therefore this element of the double entry must be reversed.

		£	£
Debit	Purchases returns account	270	
Credit	Purchases ledger control account		270

6) **Discounts allowed of £200 were only entered in the discount account**

If the discount was only entered in the discount account then the credit entry to the sales ledger control account is missing. As this is the only missing entry then the other side of the entry must be to the suspense account.

		£	£
Debit	Suspense account	200	
Credit	Sales ledger control account		200

Suspense account			
	£		£
Balance b/d	300	Rent	1,000
Sales ledger control	500		
Sales ledger control	200		

student notes✍

7) A receipt from a debtor of £140 was entered on the wrong side of the debtors' account in the subsidiary ledger

As this error has been made in the subsidiary ledger (so it has not affected the double entry) then there is no requirement for any alteration to the main ledger accounts.

Clearing the suspense account

Once all of the errors have been dealt with then the entries in the suspense account should be such that there is no remaining balance.

Suspense account

	£		£
Balance b/d	300	Rent	1,000
Sales ledger control	500		
Sales ledger control	200		
	1,000		1,000

Activity 3

A receipt from a debtor of £1,250 was entered on the debit side in both the cash book and the sales ledger control account. What is the journal entry required to correct this?

CHAPTER OVERVIEW

- some errors in the accounting records will result in an imbalance on the trial balance – these include single entry rather than double entry, a transposition error, a balancing error and a balance being omitted from the trial balance

- there are other errors in the accounting records which will not cause an imbalance on the trial balance – error of original entry, error of omission, error of reversal, error of commission, error of principle, compensating error

- in a computerised accounting system many of these errors will not be able to happen as the computer system will not allow them however, as the data is input there can still be errors of original entry, commission, principle and compensating error

- in order to find the error or errors if the debit total does not agree with the credit total carry out the basic arithmetical checks before checking the detailed double entry

- calculate the difference on the trial balance and look for this amount or half this amount in the ledger accounts and check the double entry of this transaction

- if the trial balance does not balance then a suspense account will be initially set up to make the debits equal to the credits

- once the errors have been determined, journal entries to correct them must be drafted and the suspense account cleared

KEY WORDS

Error of original entry both the debit and credit entries in the ledgers have been made at the wrong amount

Error of omission both the debit and credit have been omitted from the ledger accounts

Error of reversal the debit and credit entries have been reversed in the ledger accounts

Error of commission the double entry is largely correct but one of the entries has been made to the wrong account but an account of the correct type

Error of principle the double entry is largely correct but one of the entries has been to the wrong type of account

Compensating error two separate errors that completely cancel each other out

Journal entry a written instruction to the bookkeeper to make a double entry into the main ledger

1   Consider the account below and note any errors that you can find.

Purchases ledger control account

	£		£
Purchases returns	2,456	Opening balance	13,476
Cash paid	11,335	Purchases	15,778
Balance c/d	15,890	Discounts received	1,427
	30,681		30,681

2   A payment for rent of £4,300 has been entered into the cash payments book and the rent account as £3,400. What type of error is this?

3   The sales returns for a period of £1,276 have been entered into the ledger accounts as:

DR   Sales ledger control
CR   Sales returns

Is this correct? If not what type of error has taken place?

4   A credit note from supplier Hamish & Co has been debited to the account of C Hamish. What type of error is this?

5   The total of the debit balances on a trial balance are £325,778 and the total of the credit balances are £326,048. What would be one of the first types of error that you might look for?

6   The total of the debit balances on a trial balance was £452,362 and the credit side totalled £450,241. What is the balance on the suspense account?

7   The total of the debit balances on a trial balance was £184,266 and the credit side totalled £181,278. The following errors were discovered:

a)   a receipt of £3,250 from a customer was recorded in the cash receipts book correctly but in the sales ledger control account as £2,350;

b)   when the discount allowed account was being balanced prior to its entry in the TB it was overcast by £1,000;

c)   discounts received of £450 were debited to the discounts received account and credited to the purchases ledger control account;

d)   purchases returns of £1,088 had been correctly entered in the purchases ledger control account but had been omitted from the purchases returns account.

Draft journal entries for each of these errors and show how the suspense account is cleared.

chapter 19:
BUSINESS TRANSACTIONS AND THE LAW

chapter coverage 📖

For Units 1 and 2 you are required to have some basic knowledge of the law relating to general business transactions. In this chapter we will briefly consider the law of contract and the law relating to the sale of goods. The topics that are to be covered are:

✍ the required elements of a valid contract

✍ the offer

✍ an invitation to treat

✍ the duration of an offer

✍ the acceptance

✍ consideration

✍ intention to create legal relations

✍ breach of contract

✍ Sale of Goods Act 1979

✍ Data Protection Act 1998

✍ document retention policies

KNOWLEDGE AND UNDERSTANDING AND PERFORMANCE CRITERIA COVERAGE

Units 1 and 2

knowledge and understanding – the business environment

2 basic contract law regarding income and receipts and payments; Sale of Goods Act
3 document retention policies for income and receipts and for payments
10 basic law relating to data protection

CONTRACT LAW

What is a CONTRACT? – a legally binding agreement enforceable in a court of law.

As an individual you will enter into contracts every day – when you buy goods in a shop, when you place an order for goods over the telephone, when you hire a car. These contracts are made orally but contracts can also be in writing. For example if you take out a loan from your bank there will be a written contract.

When you are at work you will also be part of the process of contracts being made by your organisation with its customers and suppliers.

The importance of contract law

The importance of contract law is that if a contract is validly made between two parties and if one party does not satisfactorily carry out their side of the agreement, then the other party can take the defaulting party to court for BREACH OF CONTRACT.

How is a contract formed?

For a valid contract to be formed there must be three main elements:

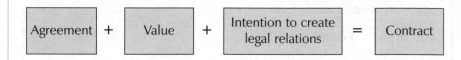

Agreement + Value + Intention to create legal relations = Contract

THE AGREEMENT

In legal terms, for there to be a valid agreement there must be a valid offer and a valid acceptance of that offer.

There will be two parties to a contract – the OFFEROR and the OFFEREE. The offeror is the person making the offer and the offeree is the person to whom the offer is made.

The offer

- The offer may be verbal or in writing.

- The offer can be made to one specific person, to a specific group of persons such as the employees of an organisation, or even to the whole world, ie anyone who decides to accept the offer.

- An offer must be communicated to the offeree, so if an offer is posted it will not become a valid offer until it reaches the offeree.

HOW IT WORKS

Southfield Electrical send out a purchase quotation to Whitehill Superstores for 6 Zanpoint dishwashers at a price of £200 plus VAT each.

This will become a valid offer from Southfield to Whitehill when Whitehill receive the purchase quotation in the post. Therefore obviously it is important that the price quoted is correct, as otherwise the contract could be based on the wrong price.

Remember also that an offer can be made verbally so if quoting a price to a customer over the telephone ensure that it is the correct price as this will be a valid offer to sell.

An invitation to treat

Care must be taken to distinguish between an offer and an INVITATION TO TREAT. An invitation to treat is an invitation by the seller of goods for the buyer to make an offer to buy them at that price. Example of invitations to treat are advertisements for goods, catalogues and price tickets on goods.

HOW IT WORKS

Southfield issues a catalogue to potential and existing customers twice a year listing the goods available and their prices. This is an invitation to treat and not an offer, so Southfield is not necessarily tied to the prices quoted in the catalogue. If a customer enquires about purchasing goods from the catalogue then they are making an offer to buy the goods at the catalogue price. It is then up to Southfield to decide whether or not to accept this offer by selling to the customer at the published price or changing the price if circumstances have changed.

If Whitehill Superstores have a washing machine on the shop floor with a price ticket mistakenly showing a price of £10 they are not legally bound to sell the machine at that price. The price ticket is an invitation to treat. The offer is made by the customer who wishes to buy the machine at this price. Whitehill can reject the offer and subsequently sell the washing machine at the correct price.

Activity 1

Ben answers an advertisement in his local paper for the sale of a car for £2,000. The seller is Bill. They agree on the price of £2,000.

a)   Who is the offeror and who is the offeree?

Now suppose that when Ben answers the advertisement he discovers from Bill that there was a misprint and the cost of the car is actually £20,000.

b)   Can Ben insist on buying the car for £2,000? If not why not?

Duration of an offer

If an offer is made then it does not have to remain in place indefinitely. There are a number of ways in which an offer can be brought to an end:

- if there is a set time period for an offer, the offer will lapse at the end of that time period. If there is no express time period set then the offer will lapse after a reasonable period of time;

- an offer can be REVOKED by the offeror at any point before it has been accepted – this means that the offer is cancelled;

- an offer comes to an end if it is REJECTED. Care must be taken here as rejection need not only be by the offeree specifically saying no to the offer. An offer is also rejected by a COUNTER-OFFER. For example if an offer is made to sell an item for £1,000 and the offeree replies to say that he will buy it at a price of £900 this is rejection of the original offer to sell. The offeree is making a new offer to buy for £900, which the original offeror may either accept or reject;

- the offer also comes to an end when a valid ACCEPTANCE is made.

Activity 2

Bill offers to sell his car to Ben for £2,000. Ben says that he will think about it and telephones two days later to say that he will buy the car for £1,800. Bill refuses.

Can Ben then insist that the car is sold to him for £2,000? Explain the reason for your answer.

student notes

The acceptance

The acceptance of an offer must be an absolute and unqualified acceptance. If not this will amount to a rejection of the offer.

- Acceptance can be in words or in writing.

- Acceptance cannot be in the form of silence – for example if an offer is made to "sell my car for £1,000 and I will assume this is a deal if I have not heard from you by Friday" – if the offeree does not reply by Friday there is no valid acceptance and therefore no contract.

- If an offer requires a particular form of acceptance (verbal, in writing, by fax) then this is the form in which the acceptance must be made.

- If an acceptance is sent by post then the date of the acceptance is the date that the letter was posted (provided that it was properly addressed, stamped and actually put into the post box) not the date on which the acceptance is received by the offeror.

- The acceptance must be unqualified – if any additional qualifications or terms are included in an acceptance then this takes the form of a counter-offer which rejects the original offer.

HOW IT WORKS

When Southfield sent the purchase quotation to Whitehill for the 6 Zanpoint dishwashers at £200 plus VAT each this was an offer. If Whitehill replies that it will buy the dishwashers at this price but they must be delivered tomorrow then this is a counter-offer which rejects Southfield's original offer. It is then up to Southfield to determine whether or not to accept this new counter-offer and sell the goods to Whitehill under these terms (ie to sell at £200 plus VAT with delivery on the next day).

Activity 3

Bill offers to sell his car to Ben for £2,000. Ben says that he will think about it and telephones Bill two days later to say that he will pay £2,000 for the car provided that it is cleaned and valeted.

Bill then sells the car to Fred.

Is Bill entitled to do this? Explain the reason for your answer.

VALUE

The basis of contract law is that we are dealing with a bargain of some sort, not just a promise by one of the parties to a contract to do something.

What is required for there to be a valid contract is known in legal terms as CONSIDERATION. Consideration can be thought of as something given, promised or done in exchange for the action of the other party.

In terms of business transactions the consideration given for a sale of goods is either the money paid now or the promise of a debtor to pay at a later date.

The existence of consideration

For there to be a valid contract consideration must exist and must have some value. In addition, to use a legal phrase "consideration cannot be past".

To explain this, suppose that James helped his neighbour, Dan, with his car when it had broken down, with no mention of any payment being required. Three days later Dan promised to pay James £50 for his help. If Dan did not pay the £50 James would have no recourse in law as the consideration (James' help with the car) was past and there is therefore no contract.

The value of consideration

Consideration must be 'sufficient' but it need not be 'adequate'.

This means that the consideration must have some monetary value ('sufficient') but it need not be the true value of the item or service that is the subject of the contract ('adequate').

INTENTION TO CREATE LEGAL RELATIONS

Remember that a contract is a legally binding agreement which means that if one party does not fully play their part in the contract the other party can take them to court for breach of contract. However many agreements that are made are never intended to be legally binding.

In general, agreements of a social nature with friends and family are presumed not to have any intention to create legal relations.

In contrast, business agreements are presumed to be intended to create legal relations and therefore can be enforced by the law.

HOW IT WORKS

If someone answers your advert to sell your sofa and a price is agreed, then there is an invitation to treat, an offer of price from you and an acceptance from the purchaser. The law will treat this as a contract as there will be a strong presumption that there was an intention to create legal relations.

If you offer to take a friend to the cinema and then do not turn up, there has been an offer and acceptance but no intention to create legal relations. Therefore your friend would have no recourse to the law because you didn't perform your part of the bargain ie, turning up.

BREACH OF CONTRACT

In a number of instances in this chapter we have mentioned one party taking the other to court for BREACH OF CONTRACT. Breach of contract is where one party to the contract does not fulfil his part of the agreement. Most contracts will have certain terms that must be fulfilled in order for the contract to be carried out.

HOW IT WORKS

If Southfield agrees to supply the 6 Zanpoint dishwashers tomorrow and then fails to do so, then they will be in breach of contract and it would be possible for Whitehill to take Southfield to court to claim damages for any losses due to this breach of contract.

Equally, on supply of the goods to Whitehill on time Southfield would expect Whitehill to pay for the goods within the stated credit period. If Whitehill does not pay then they will be in breach of contract and can in turn be taken to court for damages.

Terms in a contract

We have seen that if the terms of a contract are not fulfilled then one party will be in breach of contract. Legally, different terms of a contract have different effects.

EXPRESS TERMS are terms that are specifically stated in the contract and are binding on both parties.

CONDITIONS are terms that are fundamental to the contract and if they are broken then the party will be in breach of contract and can sue for damages.

WARRANTIES are less important terms in a contract. If any of these are not fulfilled then there is no breach of contract and the contract remains in force. However the injured party can still claim damages from the court for any loss suffered.

IMPLIED TERMS are terms of a contract which are not specifically stated but are implied in such a contract either by trade custom or by the law (see below).

SALE OF GOODS ACT 1979

If you are working in a retail environment then you will need to understand the basic outline of the law relating to retail sales which comes from the SALE OF GOODS ACT 1979.

The Act sets out a number of implied terms in a retail sale. The main ones are:

- Title – the seller has a right to sell these goods – this means that there is an implied term in the sale that the seller owns the goods and therefore has the right to sell them;

- Description – any goods sold will comply with any description of them – the goods are what they are described to be;

- Satisfactory quality – this means that the goods must be fit for the purpose for which such goods are normally used – therefore if food is purchased there is an implied condition that it is fit for eating.

As these are all implied conditions, if any are broken there is a breach of contract and the purchaser is entitled to a full refund. The purchaser can accept a replacement if this is acceptable to him, but he does not have to accept a credit note. He can insist on a refund.

Some shops will put up notices stating that "no refunds are given". However if the goods are returned because of a breach of any of these implied conditions, the shop must give a refund despite the notice.

DATA PROTECTION ACT

The Data Protection Act 1998 came into force on 1 March 2000 and affords protection to individuals over personal data that is held about them. The Act applies to records held on computer as well as records held in a manual system. The Act covers PERSONAL DATA which is data relating to an individual and that individual is known as the DATA SUBJECT.

Every organisation holding personal data must register the organisation with the Data Protection Commission and must appoint a DATA CONTROLLER who is the person in the organisation who is responsible for overseeing the processing of the data.

Principles of good information handling

The data controller should follow the eight guiding principles given in the Act requiring personal data to be handled properly. These principles state that personal data must be:

- fairly and lawfully processed;

- processed for limited purposes;

- adequate, relevant and not excessive;

- accurate;

- not held for longer than is necessary;

- processed in line with the data subject's rights;

- kept securely;

- not transferred to countries outside the European Union unless there is adequate protection in those countries.

Individuals have a legal right to know what information is held about them and they can apply in writing for a copy of the information that is held on file about them by the organisation.

DOCUMENT RETENTION POLICIES

As well as ensuring that documents and files are kept accurately and securely all business records must also be stored for six years. The reasons for keeping accounting records for six years is in case they need to be examined by HM Revenue and Customs or in case they are needed as evidence in any legal action.

CHAPTER OVERVIEW

- a contract is a legally binding agreement enforceable in a court of law

- for a valid contract to exist there must be agreement, value and an intention to create legal relations

- for an agreement to exist there must be a valid offer and acceptance

- an invitation to treat is an invitation to make an offer – advertisements, catalogues and price labels in shops are examples

- an offer may lapse, be revoked, be expressly rejected, be rejected by a counter-offer or accepted

- acceptance may be verbal or in writing but cannot be in the form of silence – if it is posted then it is valid from the date that it is posted

- the acceptance must be unqualified – if a qualification or additional term is introduced then this is deemed to be a counter-offer and the original offer is therefore rejected

- a valid agreement must also be supported by consideration – the consideration must be sufficient but it need not be adequate – the consideration must not be past

- for an agreement to be enforceable in law there must have been an intention to create legal relations when the contract was made – normally in business agreements there is a presumed intention to create legal relations

- if any terms of a contract are not fulfilled then the injured party can sue for damages for breach of contract

- the Sale of Goods Act 1979 deals with retail sales – there are three main implied terms as to title, description and satisfactory quality – if any of these implied terms is broken then the purchaser is entitled to a full refund

KEY WORDS

Contract a legally binding agreement enforceable in a court of law

Breach of contract if one party does not carry out the terms of the contract then that party is in breach of contract

Offeror the person making an offer in the hope of an acceptance

Offeree the person to whom the offer has been made

Invitation to treat an invitation to another party to make an offer

Revocation of an offer an offer is revoked if the offeror removes the offer before it is accepted

Rejection of an offer an offer is rejected if the offeree declines the offer

Counter-offer if an acceptance is made by an offeree which contains a new term or condition then this is deemed to be a counter-offer which in turn may be accepted by the original offeror

Acceptance where the offeree accepts the offer

Consideration something given, promised or done in exchange for the action of the other party

Express terms terms that are specifically stated in the contract

Conditions terms that are fundamental to the contract

Warranties less important terms in the contract

Implied terms terms of a contract that are not specifically stated but are implied by trade custom or law

Sale of Goods Act 1979 the statute that deals with transactions in a retail environment

CHAPTER OVERVIEW cont.

- the Data Protection Act is concerned with providing individuals with protection over personal data that is held by organisations about them

- organisations must keep all of their accounting records for six years for a number of tax and legal reasons

KEY WORDS

Personal data data relating to an individual

Data subject the individual on whom information is held

Data controller the person in the organisation who is responsible for overseeing the processing of data

HOW MUCH HAVE YOU LEARNED?

1   What are the three necessary elements for a valid contract?

2   i)   You are the buyer for your organisation. You order some goods from a supplier over the telephone and a price is agreed. Is there a contract?

    ii) Would your answer be different if you had sent a purchase order to the supplier?

3   A customer wishes to purchase an item from your shop which has a price attached to it of £15.99. The till price is shown as £20.99 as the lower price offer has now ended. Can the customer insist on only paying £15.99 for the item? Explain the reason for your answer.

4   You are the buyer for your organisation and on 15 November you telephone a supplier for a price quotation for some goods. The quotation is received on 20 November and you post a purchase order on 21 November which is received by the supplier on 23 November.

    On what date is the contract formed?

5   You agree to help a friend with his accounting records and he agrees to pay you £100 for this job. Later he refuses to pay. Is there a valid contract?

6   You agree to help a friend with his accounting records as a favour. Later he says that he will give you £100 for your help. Is there a valid contract?

7   You buy a clock/radio from a shop but when you get it home find that the radio works but not the clock. You return it to the shop and are told that the policy is only to give credit notes for returned goods. What are your rights?

8   You buy a leather coat from a catalogue but when you receive it you discover that it is actually plastic not leather. You wish to return the coat. What are your rights?

9   What are the eight principles of good information handling in the Data Protection Act?

chapter 20:
INTRODUCTION TO MANAGEMENT INFORMATION

chapter coverage 📖

This chapter serves as an introduction to Unit 4, Supplying Information for Management Control. It will introduce you to the concept of management information and accounting and some of the terminology that is used. The topics that are to be covered are:

✍ the role of management – decision making, planning and control

✍ cost centres

✍ profit centres

✍ investment centres

✍ service industries and cost centres

✍ the relationship between financial and management accounting

---

KNOWLEDGE AND UNDERSTANDING AND PERFORMANCE CRITERIA COVERAGE

Unit 4

knowledge and understanding – the business environment

1   types of cost centres, including profit centres and investment centres

knowledge and understanding – accounting methods

3   identifying cost centres
4   the purpose of management information: decision making; planning and control
6   the relationship between financial and management accounting
10 the role of management information in the organisation
11 awareness of the relationship between financial and management accounting

knowledge and understanding – the organisation

13 the nature of the organisation's business transactions
14 the goods and services produced, bought and delivered by the organisation
15 the cost centres within the organisation

MANAGEMENT INFORMATION

In the chapters of the Course Companion so far, we have considered the accounting entries for the transactions of a business. These transactions were all recorded in the main ledger and the next stage would be to take the trial balance and from that prepare a set of financial statements for the business (although this is not required for Foundation level).

This accounting all took place within the FINANCIAL ACCOUNTING SYSTEM of the business and its main aim is to provide the information necessary eventually to prepare a profit and loss account and balance sheet for the business at the end of each accounting period, normally a year.

However the management of the business will require other financial information on a more regular basis in order to run the business efficiently on a day to day basis. This will be provided by the MANAGEMENT ACCOUNTING SYSTEM.

The role of management

The management of a business must ensure that the business is run as well and efficiently as possible. There are three main elements involved in this:

- decision making
- planning
- control

Decision making

The management of a business will be constantly making decisions about how the business is operated. These will range from long-term strategic decisions through to short term day to day decisions.

Here are a few examples of the type of long-term decisions that might be made:

- which markets to operate in – the UK, Europe, worldwide etc
- how to organise the business – on a centralised basis or a divisional basis
- where to locate factories, warehouses etc
- how many employees and in what locations
- whether or not to expand the business

Other decisions might be classed as medium-term decisions:

- whether to fund the business by taking out a further loan;
- how to advertise and market the products;
- which products to continue making and which to discontinue, if any.

Yet more decisions will be of a short-term nature:

- how many raw materials or goods for resale to buy;
- which suppliers to use;
- how much overtime work is required;
- whether to rent more warehouse space;
- how many products to produce.

As you can see there are many aspects to the DECISION MAKING role of the management, and in order to make informed decisions management will need detailed, relevant and up to date information.

HOW IT WORKS

If the management of a manufacturing organisation are trying to decide which products to continue to produce for the following year, they will need information about the profitability of each product line:

- what does each product cost to make?
- how much is each product sold for?
- how many of each product is sold?
- how many man hours does each product require etc?

This type of information is not available from the financial accounting records. Although, for example, all of the purchases of raw materials are recorded in a purchases account in the main ledger, they are not split into which products they are used to make. This is the purpose of management information – to provide the type of detailed cost and income information that management need.

Planning

If a business is to operate efficiently then there is a great deal of forward planning required. In a similar manner to the decisions that have to be made, these plans will range from the long-term strategic plans to much shorter-term operational plans.

The long-term strategy of the business will include plans of the markets where the products are to be sold, the development and improvements of products, the expansion or contraction plans of the business.

In the shorter term the plans that must be made will include:

- how many products to produce;

- what materials are required for this production and what they will cost;

- how many employees are required for the production and how much will they be paid;

- how many machines are required for the production;

- what the advertising costs will be;

- what the administration costs are.

These plans are produced as BUDGETS. Budgets are normally produced for the next year. The budget process will normally start with determining the demand for each product in that year and therefore the number of products to be produced. Then there will be a variety of budgets produced, some in terms of number of products or hours to be worked and some in terms of costs and income. Typical budgets might include:

- sales budget – the number and price of the products expected to be sold;

- a production budget – number of products to be produced;

- a materials usage budget – number of units of raw materials required;

- a materials cost budget – cost of the raw materials required;

- labour hours budget – number of employee hours required for production;

- labour cost budget – cost of these labour hours;

- production expenses budget – cost of the expenses involved in the manufacturing of the products;

- selling costs budget – the costs involved in selling the products;

- administration costs budget – the administration costs necessary to support the production.

All of these budgets are required to ensure that the business runs efficiently, that there are enough materials for the production and enough employees to make the products etc.

The budgetary process is a large part of the role of management. In order to be able to estimate the figures for these future production requirements and costs, management will need detailed information about the current materials usage, labour hours, costs and so forth.

Control

When the plans for a business have been made and the decisions taken, the management must ensure that these plans are followed and that the decisions taken were the correct ones. In order to do this they must have control over all aspects of the business.

The system of control usually works by regular comparison of the actual production, sales, costs and income of the business to the plans or budgets. In practice there are likely to be differences between what actually happens and what was planned in the budget, and these differences are known as VARIANCES.

In order to control the business, management will regularly need to be made aware of any significant variances from the budgeted figures. Armed with this information they may change the plans or make different decisions. Therefore it is important that these variances are accurately reported on a regular basis.

Activity 1

What are the three main roles of management in an organisation?

COST CENTRES

In a manufacturing organisation, it is likely that the organisation will naturally split into a variety of different areas or departments. Typical examples might be:

- cutting;
- assembling;
- finishing;
- packing;
- warehouse;
- stores;
- maintenance;
- administration;
- selling and distribution.

The precise split of an organisation will depend upon its nature and the nature of its activities and transactions. However the business is split up, management will need to know the costs and/or income of each of these departments in order to be able to make decisions, plan operations and control the business.

Therefore each area or department will be known as a COST CENTRE. All of the costs incurred by that department will be collected together and it will then be possible to determine the costs incurred by each of these cost centres for a period.

Some of these cost centres are areas of the business that actually produce the products that the business sell – cutting, assembling, finishing, packing etc. These are known as PRODUCTION COST CENTRES.

Other cost centres do not actually produce the goods but they are necessary in order to ensure that the production and sales take place – warehouse, stores, maintenance etc. These cost centres are known as SERVICE COST CENTRES as they provide a necessary service to the production cost centres.

Activity 2

What possible cost centres might there be in an organisation that makes wooden furniture?

Profit centres

We have seen that cost centres are areas of the business for which the costs incurred are all collected together. Some areas of a business incur costs but also earn revenues.

HOW IT WORKS

In a retail organisation, each individual shop will produce revenue as well as incurring costs. If both the costs and revenues of an area of a business are to be gathered together then this is known as a PROFIT CENTRE as when the revenue and the costs are compared the final result will be the profit or loss made by the profit centre.

Investment centres

An INVESTMENT CENTRE is an area of a business that not only earns revenue and incurs costs but is also responsible for its own assets and liabilities. In an investment centre, management will not only need details of the profit but also the assets and liabilities, the investment, that is being used to produce this profit.

Activity 3

What is the essential difference between a profit centre and an investment centre?

SERVICE INDUSTRIES

So far in this chapter we have concerned ourselves mainly with manufacturing organisations. However the Unit 4 syllabus makes it clear that the unit not only relates to manufacturing but also to SERVICE INDUSTRIES. A service industry is an organisation that provides a service rather then producing a product, such as a firm of accountants, a painter and decorator or a transport organisation.

Service industries will divide their businesses into cost centres in a similar manner to a manufacturing organisation.

HOW IT WORKS

A firm of accountants might have the following cost centres:

- audit;
- tax;
- consultancy;
- administration;
- personnel;
- marketing.

It is also possible that the audit, tax and consultancy departments might be designated as profit centres rather than cost centres and the revenue they earn will be collected as well as the costs.

RELATIONSHIP BETWEEN FINANCIAL AND MANAGEMENT ACCOUNTING

You should now be able to see that the management of a business need particular types of information about the activities of the business which they cannot necessarily get from the financial accounting records.

It is important to realise however that the information they require will come from the same source as the information in the ledger accounts – it is simply classified and collected in a different manner.

HOW IT WORKS

A batch of purchase invoices from credit suppliers is received by a manufacturing organisation. They will be entered into the purchases day book and referenced to the correct credit supplier. The total of the purchase day book will be posted to the main ledger accounts and the individual invoices posted to the individual creditor accounts in the subsidiary (purchases) ledger. This is all done within the financial accounting system.

However the information from the purchase invoices will also be recorded for management accounting purposes. Each invoice will be analysed to determine whether it is for materials or expenses and which cost centre it relates to, and will be added to the costs already collected for that cost centre. This will take place in the management accounting records.

In the financial accounting system we are concerned with:

- the fact that these are purchases on credit;
- which credit supplier the invoice is from.

In the management accounting system we are concerned with:

- the type of cost (see next chapter);
- the cost centre the cost relates to.

CHAPTER OVERVIEW

- management have three main roles in an organisation – decision-making, planning and control – they need relevant, up to date information in order to carry out these roles

- decision-making covers long-term strategic decisions, medium term decisions and short term day to day decisions

- planning is also both long range and shorter range – the plans for the next year are set out in budgets which can be in terms of physical resources that are expected to be required, and in financial terms

- control is where the actual results of the organisation are compared to the budgeted figures and significant variances reported to management

- organisations will tend to be split up into cost centres for management accounting purposes and the costs of each cost centre collected together

- profit centres are areas of the business where not only the relevant costs are collected together but also the revenues of this area of the business

- an investment centre is similar to a profit centre but it is an area of the business that also has control of its own assets and liabilities. Management will wish to compare the profit for the period to the assets that have been used

- service industries will also split their organisations into cost centres and/or profit centres for management accounting purposes

- the financial accounting system and management accounting system use the same transactions but analyse and classify them in a different manner

KEY WORDS

Financial accounting system the recording of the transactions of the organisation in the main and subsidiary ledgers in order to prepare financial statements

Management accounting system the recording of the transactions of the organisation in order to provide useful information for management

Decision making the management role of making both long and short-term decisions regarding the operations of the organisation

Budgets the plans of the organisation for the next year set out in terms of resources required or in monetary terms

Variances the differences that arise when the actual results of the organisation differ from the budgeted results

Cost centre an area of the organisation for which costs are collected together for management accounting purposes

Production cost centres cost centres that actually produce the products that are to be sold

Service cost centres cost centres that provide support services to the production cost centres

Profit centre an area of the organisation for which costs and revenues are collected together for management accounting purposes

Investment centre an area of the organisation for which costs and revenues and the assets and liabilities that have earned those revenues are collected together for management accounting purposes

Service industries organisations that do not produce a product but instead provide a service

HOW MUCH HAVE YOU LEARNED?

1   If the management of a manufacturing organisation were considering whether or not to continue producing a particular product what type of information would they need?

2   The management of a retail organisation is considering the closure of one of its shops. What type of information would they require?

3   Explain what might appear in the following budgets:

  ■   a sales budget
  ■   a production budget
  ■   a materials cost budget
  ■   a labour hours budget

4   Explain what is meant by a variance? Why are variances important to management?

5   What types of cost centres might you find in an organisation which makes decorative pottery? Distinguish between the production cost centres and service cost centres.

6   What types of cost centres might you find in an organisation that delivers parcels by both van and motorbike?

chapter 21:
ELEMENTS OF COST

chapter coverage 📖

In this chapter we will consider the manner in which costs are analysed and classified for management accounting purposes and the different types of cost that an organisation will incur. The topics that are to be covered are:

- ✍ analysing materials costs
- ✍ the elements that make up gross pay
- ✍ basic pay
- ✍ overtime
- ✍ bonus payments
- ✍ employer's NIC
- ✍ direct expenses
- ✍ joint expenses
- ✍ service industries and cost analysis

KNOWLEDGE AND UNDERSTANDING AND PERFORMANCE CRITERIA COVERAGE

Unit 4

knowledge and understanding – the business environment

2   costs, including wages, salaries, services and consumables

knowledge and understanding – accounting methods

5   the make up of gross pay

knowledge and understanding – the organisation

13   the nature of the organisation's business transactions
14   the goods and services produced, bought and delivered by the organisation

Performance criteria – element 4.1

A   recognise appropriate cost centres and elements of cost
B   extract income and expenditure details from the relevant sources

CLASSIFICATION OF COSTS

In the financial accounting system costs are classified as:

- purchases;
- wages;
- various expenses – rent, telephone, electricity etc.

In the management accounting system the classification of costs is rather more detailed, as the information required by management is more detailed. The basic classification of costs is between materials, labour and expenses. However for management accounting purposes the costs need to be analysed further.

MATERIALS

In a manufacturing organisation materials costs will often be the most significant cost involved in making the products. The cost of the raw materials used in the production process will be taken from the purchase invoice or from details of any cash purchases of raw materials that are made.

Analysing the materials costs

When an invoice arrives from a supplier of raw materials it must be studied carefully as it needs to be analysed in a number of ways for management accounting purposes.

Step 1   Determine the quantity and cost of each type of material purchased as this will be required for the stores records.

Step 2   Determine the cost of the materials being used by each cost centre.

HOW IT WORKS

You work in the accounts department of Wilmshurst Furniture Makers, an organisation that makes good quality wooden furniture – tables, chairs, desks, wardrobes etc.

The manufacturing process is split into three separate cost centres:

- cutting;
- assembly;
- polishing.

The cutting department takes the wood and cuts it to the right size for each piece of furniture. The assembly department puts all of the pieces of wood together to form the finished item using glue, nails, screws etc. The polishing department prepares the furniture for eventual sale.

Given below is an invoice that has just been received from one of Wilmshurst's suppliers.

INVOICE

J J Supplies
Park Road
Benham DR6 2PQ
Tel 0303413 Fax 0303414
VAT Reg 0611 3987 24

To: Wilmshurst Furniture Makers
Industrial Estate
Benham DR6 2FF

Invoice number: 361120

Date/tax point: 29 Dec 2006

Order number: P049681

Account number: W49

Quantity	Description	Stock code	Unit amount £	Total £
20m	Solid Oak Panel - 40cm	41992	30.20 per m.	604.00
2 litre	Beeswax Polish	73126	22.00 per litre	44.00
		Net total		648.00
		VAT		113.40
		Invoice total		761.40

Terms
Net 30 days
E & OE

A number of pieces of information are required from this invoice:

- the stores department must update its records for the receipt of 20 metres of solid oak panel and 2 litres of beeswax polish. Often the stores records are kept in terms of quantity only and the price is dealt with in the accounting department. However if the stores records are also kept using price the unit prices of £30.20 per metre and £22.00 per litre must also be noted;

- the wood will be used by the cutting department, so the cost (net of VAT) of £604.00 must be charged to the cutting cost centre;

- the polish will be used by the polishing department and therefore its cost of £44.00 must be charged to the polishing cost centre.

Activity 1

Why are the costs charged to the cost centres net of VAT?

LABOUR

In the financial accounting records we saw that the cost of wages and salaries was the gross pay of the employees together with the employer's National Insurance Contributions.

For management accounting purposes it is often necessary to analyse the gross pay of the employees in more detail.

Gross pay

The gross pay of employees can be made up of a number of different elements:

- basic pay;
- overtime;
- bonus.

We shall look at each element in turn.

Basic pay

BASIC PAY is the amount that an employee is paid for the normal hours of work. Most employees will be employed on the basis that they are paid a certain rate for a certain number of hours a week, and then if they work for more hours than this in the week overtime payments are made.

The hours that an employee works must be recorded in some manner. The most common methods are clock cards, time sheets and job cards.

A CLOCK CARD is a mechanical device, normally on the factory floor, by which the time when an employee arrives for work and leaves work is recorded. The clock card will also record non-working hours such as lunch and tea breaks. In this way it can be determined precisely how many hours an employee has actually worked in the week.

A TIME SHEET is a method of the employee recording for himself the hours that have been worked in a week and the precise work that has been done in those hours. Time sheets are often used in service industries and this will be considered later in the chapter.

A JOB CARD is used in manufacturing organisations that produce large individual products such as aeroplanes or buildings. A job card relates to one of these large individual products and each employee that works on that job records the number of hours spent on it.

HOW IT WORKS

Jim Tyler works in the factory at Wilmshurst Furniture Makers. The terms of his employment are that his basic working week is 35 hours and his basic rate of pay is £8.60 per hour. For any hours over and above 35 a week he is paid overtime at time and a half (see later in the chapter).

For week 23 Jim's clock card shows that he has worked 35 hours in the week.

Therefore his gross pay for the week is made up solely of his basic pay and is calculated as:

35 hours @ £8.60 = £301.00

Analysis by cost centre

Many employees will work for only one cost centre in the hours that they work in which case the whole of their basic pay is collected as a cost for that cost centre.

However some employees may have a variety of skills which mean that they work for a number of different cost centres in a week. The clock card will show which cost centres the employee has worked for and how many hours for each – the basic pay must then be split between each of the cost centres.

HOW IT WORKS

Suppose that Jim's clock card shows that he worked in the cutting department for 24 hours during the week and in the assembly department for the remaining 11 hours.

His basic pay would be split between the two cost centres:

Cutting cost centre	24 hours @ £8.60	£206.40
Assembly cost centre	11 hours @ £8.60	£ 94.60

OVERTIME

OVERTIME is paid for the hours that employees work that is over and above the normal hours of work stated in their employment contract.

Overtime payments are normally expressed in terms of the basic pay – the most common are:

Time and a half – this means that any overtime hours are paid at one and half times the basic hourly rate;

Double time – overtime hours are paid at twice the basic hourly rate.

HOW IT WORKS

In week 39 Jim works for 29 hours in the cutting department and 12 hours in the assembly department. He has therefore worked not only the 35 hour basic week but 6 hours of overtime which were due to the amount of work in the cutting department.

First we must calculate Jim's pay for the week:

	£
35 hours @ £8.60	301.00
6 hours @ £8.60 x 1.5	77.40
	378.40

The figure of £77.40 is the overtime payment to Jim – the full cost of working for the additional 6 hours at a rate of £12.90 (1.5 x £8.60).

For management accounting purposes however the total pay for Jim would be expressed in a different manner in order to show the OVERTIME PREMIUM. The overtime premium is the additional payment over and above the basic rate for the overtime hours.

	£
Basic pay 41 hours @ £8.60	352.60
Overtime premium 6 hours x £8.60 x 0.5	25.80
	378.40

The overtime premium is the extra amount per hour that is being paid for the overtime hours. This is £4.30 (£8.60 x 0.5) per hour.

In most organisations the basic pay will be charged to the cost centres as a labour cost and the overtime premium charged to the cost centres as an expense.

Therefore the way in which Jim's week 39 wage will be charged to the cost centres is:

	£
Cutting cost centre – labour cost 29 hours @ £8.60	249.40
Assembly cost centre – labour cost 12 hours @ £8.60	103.20
Cutting cost centre – expense 6 hours @ £4.30	25.80
	378.40

Activity 2

Jan Simms works in the polishing department of Wilmshursts and her terms of employment are a 35 hour basic week with a basic rate of pay of £9.20 per hour and overtime paid at time and a half. In week 32 she worked for 43 hours in total.

How would her labour cost for the week be charged to the cost centre?

Bonus payments

In order to increase the productivity of employees often an employer will set up a bonus scheme whereby the employee can earn additional income over and above his basic pay if he works more efficiently. Bonus schemes may be on an individual basis or for a group of employees if they all work together on a particular task.

The bonus payment is usually charged to the relevant cost centre as an expense although some organisations include it as part of the labour cost for the cost centre.

Employer's National Insurance Contribution

Remember that the wages cost of an employee is made up of the gross pay plus the employer's NIC. Therefore the employer's NIC must also be charged to the relevant cost centre – sometimes this will be part of the labour cost but other organisations may include it as an expense.

HOW IT WORKS

As we have seen, Jim's gross pay for week 39 was £378.40. The employer's NIC is calculated as £36.02.

This figure of £36.02 will be charged to the relevant cost centres normally as an expense. In this case Jim worked for 29 hours in the cutting department and 12 hours in the assembly department therefore the Employer's NIC will be split in this ratio:

Cutting cost centre – expense £36.02 × 29/41	£25.48
Assembly cost centre – expense £36.02 × 12/41	£10.54

EXPENSES

As well as using materials and labour, each cost centre may also incur some expenses. Some of these expenses will be incurred specifically by the cost centre and others may be incurred jointly by a number of cost centres.

Specific expenses

Examples of expenses that might be incurred by a single cost centre directly might be:

- cleaning of machinery costs;
- repair of machinery costs;
- lubricants for machinery.

The details of these expenses will be taken from the invoice for the expense or other documentation that is associated with the expense.

HOW IT WORKS

The following two invoices have just been received by Wilmshurst Furniture Makers:

INVOICE

D. P. Repairs Ltd
High Street
Benham DR6 4MS
Tel 0303610 Fax 0303611
VAT Reg 4321 1168 22

To: Wilmshurst Furniture
     Makers

Invoice number: 46123

Date/tax point: 28 Dec 2006

Order number: -

Account number: SL 043

	Total £
Repair of X5461 Polishing machine	106.40
Net total	106.40
VAT	18.62
Invoice total	125.02

Terms
Net 30 days
E & OE

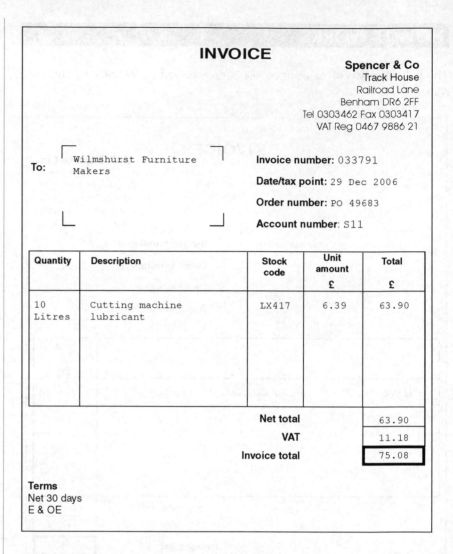

INVOICE

Spencer & Co
Track House
Railroad Lane
Benham DR6 2FF
Tel 0303462 Fax 0303417
VAT Reg 0467 9886 21

To: Wilmshurst Furniture Makers

Invoice number: 033791

Date/tax point: 29 Dec 2006

Order number: PO 49683

Account number: S11

Quantity	Description	Stock code	Unit amount £	Total £
10 Litres	Cutting machine lubricant	LX417	6.39	63.90

Net total	63.90
VAT	11.18
Invoice total	75.08

Terms
Net 30 days
E & OE

These expenses would be allocated to the cost centres as follows:

Cutting cost centre – expenses	£63.90
Polishing cost centre – expenses	£106.40

Note that, as with the materials cost, it is always the net of VAT amount that is charged to the cost centre.

Joint expenses

Often the expenses of an organisation are incurred by a number of cost centres jointly. For example when the rent is paid for the factory then this will be an expense of all of the cost centres that are housed in the factory. In these cases the expense must be split between the relevant cost centres and this is known as APPORTIONMENT OF COSTS.

The manner is which the expense is split between the cost centres that have incurred it will depend upon the policies of the organisation, but usually some fair basis is used to determine the split. For example with the rent expense this might be apportioned between the factory cost centres according to the amount of floor space that each cost centre uses.

HOW IT WORKS

Wilmshurst Furniture Makers have recently incurred the following expenses:

Factory rent	£6,000.00
Factory power	£2,200.00

All three manufacturing departments are housed within the factory and the rent is apportioned according to the floor space occupied:

Cutting	6,000 sq metres
Assembly	4,000 sq metres
Polishing	2,000 sq metres

It is estimated that the 60% of the power is used by the cutting department, 15% by the assembly department and 25% by the polishing department.

The apportionment of the expenses would be:

Factory rent £6,000   Total floor area   12,000 sq metres

Cutting	£6,000 x 6,000/12,000	£3,000
Assembly	£6,000 x 4,000/12,000	£2,000
Polishing	£6,000 x 2,000/12,000	£1,000

Factory power £2,200

Cutting	£2,200 x 60%	£1,320
Assembly	£2,200 x 15%	£330
Polishing	£2,200 x 25%	£550

SERVICE INDUSTRIES

In the previous chapter it was noted that service industries, although not producing a product, will also normally split the operations into cost centres or profit centres.

The largest type of cost for most service industries is likely to be the labour cost. It was mentioned earlier in the chapter that the recording of employees' working hours in a service industry is often by use of time sheets. For example, in a firm of accountants each employee would complete a weekly or monthly time sheet showing how many hours were worked not just in total, but the hours spent on each particular job in each department or cost centre. In a transport company, logs of some sort would be kept for the hours driven by each driver.

In a service industry a service is being provided rather than a product made and therefore it is unlikely that there are raw materials as such. However materials are used such as stationery, computer disks etc and these are often termed as CONSUMABLES. They would be charged to the cost centres as they are used.

Again, as with a manufacturing organisation, there will also be a wide variety of expenses incurred which must be charged directly to each cost centre or apportioned between the cost centres.

Activity 3

A delivery business has the following cost centres:

- vehicle deliveries
- motor bike deliveries
- bookings
- administration

The bookings and administration cost centres share the same building and use approximately half the space each. How would the following expenses be charged to the cost centres?

Rent and rates	£1,200.00
Repairs to motorbike	£240.00
Diesel for vans	£310.00

CHAPTER OVERVIEW

- for management accounting purposes, costs are classified as materials, labour and expenses

- the invoices for materials purchases must be analysed to determine the quantity and price of the particular raw material and which cost centre the material is to be used in

- the total labour cost is gross pay plus the employer's NIC – gross pay can be made up of basic pay, overtime and a bonus

- in order to determine the basic pay and any overtime, the actual hours that each employee works must be recorded – this will be done on a clock card, a time sheet or a job card

- the basic pay must be charged to the cost centre where the employee has worked during the period – if the employee has worked for more than one cost centre then each cost centre will be charged with the hours worked in the period

- if an employee works for longer than the basic hours in a week set out in his employment agreement, he will be paid overtime for the additional hours

- the basic pay for all of the hours that the employee works will be charged as a labour cost to the relevant cost centre – the overtime premium is charged to the relevant cost centre as an expense

- if a bonus is earned, this will be included as part of the gross pay – organisational policy will determine whether this is treated as a labour cost or an expense

- Employer's NIC is part of the cost of labour and therefore must be charged to the relevant cost centre – again organisational policy will determine whether this is treated as part of the labour cost or as an expense

- expense invoices should be analysed to determine which cost centre the expense relates to and charged to that cost centre

- some expenses relate to a number of different cost centres and need to be apportioned on an appropriate basis

KEY WORDS

Basic pay the amount paid to employees for their normal hours of work as agreed in the employment agreement

Clock card a mechanical device on the factory floor that records the precise hours that the employee works for

Time sheet a record of hours worked kept by the employee himself

Job card a document on which is recorded all of the hours that each employee works on a particular job

Overtime payment for the hours an employee works in a period over and above the agreed basic hours for the period

Overtime premium the additional payment over and above the basic pay rate for the overtime hours

Apportionment of costs the splitting of joint expenses amongst the relevant cost centres on an appropriate basis

Consumables materials that are used within a service industry although not used to make a product

CHAPTER OVERVIEW cont.

- service industries will also classify their costs and charge them to the relevant cost centre – the main category of cost for most service industries will be labour

- service industries will not have raw materials purchases but they will use materials in the business and these are known as consumables

HOW MUCH HAVE YOU LEARNED?

1   You work in the accounts department of Pole Potteries, a business that makes decorative pottery. The cost centres in your business are:

- throwing (making the item from clay)
- baking
- painting
- packaging
- stores
- maintenance
- selling and distribution
- canteen
- administration

The two invoices given below are on your desk and you need to decide which cost centres the costs relate to.

INVOICE

Purbeck Clay
Granite Yard
Compston BH3 4TL
Tel 01929 464810
VAT Reg 1164 2810 67

To: Pole Potteries

Invoice number: 36411

Date/tax point: 16 Nov 2006

Order number: 11663

Account number: SL 42

Quantity	Description	Stock code	Unit amount £	Total £
50 kg	Throwing clay	TC412	6.80	340.00
10 litres	Paint - Fuchsia	PF67	2.80	28.00
			Net total	368.00
			VAT	64.40
			Invoice total	432.40

Terms
Net 30 days
E & OE

INVOICE

IndCan Suppliers
High Street
Hamware BH3 7SP
Tel 01929 432432
VAT Reg 221 4 6182 93

To: Pole Potteries

Invoice number: 61212

Date/tax point: 17 Nov 2006

Order number: 11668

Account number: PP 02

Quantity	Description	Stock code	Unit amount £	Total £
100kg	Frozen chips	46112	1.20	120.00
48	Chicken pies	61297	0.90	43.20

Net total	163.20
VAT	28.56
Invoice total	191.76

Terms
Net 30 days
E & OE

2   Lara Binns works for Pole Potteries in both the throwing department and the baking department. Her employment agreement is that her basic week is 38 hours at a rate of £9.60 per hour. Any overtime is at double time.

During week 39 Lara worked for 26 hours hours in the throwing department and 15 hours in the baking department. All of the overtime hours were due to a backlog in the throwing department. The policy of Pole Potteries is to charge the basic pay for all hours as the labour cost and the overtime premium as an expense.

Show how the cost of employing Lara for week 39 would be analysed for management accounting purposes.

3   Pole Potteries have recently received invoices for the following expenses:

Factory rent	£15,000
Warehouse rent	£5,000
Head office rent	£3,000
Cleaning of the throwing department	£200
Servicing of baking ovens	£600
Advertising	£400

The factory houses the following departments with the approximate percentage of floor space:

Throwing	15%
Baking	40%
Painting	15%
Maintenance	10%
Canteen	20%

The warehouse holds the stores and packaging departments and the stores use approximately 80% of this area.

The head office is small and consists of only selling and distribution (one cost centre) and administration, using equal amounts of space.

Show the expenses to be collected for each of the cost centres.

4   An accountancy firm has four functions or cost centres, an audit function, tax function, consultancy function and administration function. All are computerised and the latest purchase of computer disks total £489.00 net of VAT. The estimated usage of computer disks is:

Audit	30%
Tax	40%
Consultancy	20%
Administration	10%

How would the cost of these consumables be allocated to the cost centres?

chapter 22:
CODING

chapter coverage 📖

We have seen how the elements of cost should be collected by each cost centre. In this chapter we shall see how this is done by coding the invoices and payroll information in order to achieve the accurate collection of these costs. The topics that are to be covered are:

- ✍ coding systems
- ✍ coding materials costs
- ✍ coding labour costs
- ✍ coding expense costs
- ✍ coding sales income
- ✍ updating cost and profit centre balances
- ✍ computer spreadsheets

KNOWLEDGE AND UNDERSTANDING AND PERFORMANCE CRITERIA COVERAGE

Unit 4

knowledge and understanding – accounting methods

7   methods of analysing information in spreadsheets

knowledge and understanding – the organisation

16   organisational coding structures

Performance criteria – element 4.1

C   code income and expenditure correctly
D   refer any problems in obtaining the necessary information to the appropriate person
E   identify and report errors to the appropriate person

METHODS OF CODING

In the previous chapter we saw how each cost incurred by the organisation must be analysed and then charged to the correct cost centre as materials, labour or an expense. In order for this to happen the expense must be coded to show what type of cost it is and which cost centre it is to be charged to.

Each organisation will have its own coding structure. In chapter 6 of this Companion the various methods of coding, NUMERIC CODING systems and ALPHA-NUMERIC coding systems, were considered in the context of the financial accounting system. A similar system of coding will be used for the management accounting system.

CODING THE ELEMENTS OF COST

Materials

We have already seen in the previous chapter that each purchase invoice that arrives must be analysed to determine the type of cost and the cost centre to which it should be charged. Each element of the invoice must then be coded to ensure that the cost is collected for the correct cost centre.

HOW IT WORKS

Wilmshurst Furniture Makers has a management accounting coding system that uses a six digit code. All cost centre codes begin with the digits 01. The second two digits in the code then denote the precise cost centre to which the cost relates as follows:

- cutting cost centre   01
- assembly cost centre   02
- polishing cost centre   03

The final two digits represent the type of cost:

- materials   01
- labour   02
- expenses   03

Given below is a purchase invoice that was used and analysed in the previous chapter. Each element of it must now be coded to show the type of expense – materials – and the cost centre to which they relate.

INVOICE

J. J. Supplies
Park Road
Benham DR6 2PQ
Tel 0303413 Fax 0303414
VAT Reg 0611 3987 24

To: Wilmshurst Furniture
Makers
Industrial Estate
Benham
DR6 2FF

Invoice number: 361120

Date/tax point: 29 Dec 2006

Order number: PO 49681

Account number: W49

Quantity	Description	Stock code	Unit amount £	Total £
20m	Solid oak panel 40cm	41992	30.20 per m.	010101 604.00
2 litre	Beeswax polish	73126	22.00 per litre	010301 44.00
			Net total	648.00
			VAT	113.40
			Invoice total	761.40

Terms
Net 30 days
E & OE

The solid oak panel is coded as follows;

| 0   1 | 0   1 | 0   1 |
| cost centre | cutting | material |

The polish is coded as:

| 0   1 | 0   3 | 0   1 |
| cost centre | polishing | material |

Labour

As with the materials so the labour costs from the payroll must also be coded. Remember that some elements of the labour cost may be charged as an expense rather than labour.

HOW IT WORKS

Wilmshurst's policy is to charge any overtime premium as an expense together with the employer's NIC.

Remember Jim? In week 39 he worked for 29 hours in the cutting department and 12 hours in the assembly department. His 6 hours of overtime were due to the amount of work in the cutting department. The employer's NIC is calculated as £36.02.

His basic pay was analysed as:

Cutting cost centre – labour cost 29 hours @ £8.60	249.40
Assembly cost centre – labour cost 12 hours @ £8.60	103.20
Cutting cost centre – expense 6 hours @ £4.30	25.80
Cutting cost centre – expense NIC £36.02 x 29/41	25.48
Assembly cost centre – expense NIC £36.02 x 12/41	10.54

This must now be coded:

Cutting cost centre – labour cost 29 hours @ £8.60	249.40 – 010102
Assembly cost centre – labour cost 12 hours @ £8.60	103.20 – 010202
Cutting cost centre – expense 6 hours @ £4.30	25.80 – 010103
Cutting cost centre – expense NIC £36.02 x 29/41	25.48 – 010103
Assembly cost centre – expense NIC £36.02 x 12/41	10.54 – 010203

The first two digits are always 01 as these are cost centres. The second pair of digits should be 01 for cutting and 02 for assembly. The final digits are 02 for the labour cost element and 03 for the expense element.

Activity 1

Jan Simms works in the polishing department of Wilmshurst's and has a 35 hour basic week with a basic rate of pay of £9.20 per hour and overtime paid at time and a half. In week 32 she worked for 43 hours in total. The employer's NIC is £42.55.

Show how the labour cost is made up and how it would be coded for this employee.

Expenses

The expense costs must also be coded.

HOW IT WORKS

The factory rent and power costs were apportioned to the three production cost centres in the previous chapter and must now be coded:

Factory rent –	cutting	£3,000	–	010103
	assembly	£2,000	–	010203
	polishing	£1,000	–	010303
Factory power –	cutting	£1,320	–	010103
	assembly	£330	–	010203
	polishing	£550	–	010303

The first two digits are 01 as these are cost centres. The second two digits represent the cost centre itself. The final two digits, 03, show that these are expenses.

Sales income

So far we have only concerned ourselves with costs. However the sales income must also be recognised in the management accounting records. This is done by analysing the sales invoices to the correct profit centre and coding them appropriately.

HOW IT WORKS

Wilmshursts makes its sales through three outlets: Dopham, Nutley and Jenson. The coding for sales is as follows:

first two digits	02 represents a PROFIT CENTRE	
second two digits	Dopham profit centre	10
	Nutley profit centre	11
	Jenson profit centre	12
third two digits	this depends upon the type of sale	
	– 5ft dining table	11
	– 6ft dining table	12
	– round coffee table	13
	– square coffee table	14
	– dining chair	15
	– 2 drawer chest	16
	– 3 drawer chest	17
	– 5ft wardrobe	18
	– 6ft wardrobe	19

Given below are two sales invoices that have to be coded.

INVOICE

Wilmshurst Furniture Makers
Retail Park
Jenson
DR2 4XK

To: Drayton Ltd

Invoice number: 42116

Date/tax point: 24 Dec 2006

Order number: 62113

Account number: SL 47

Quantity	Description	Stock code	Unit amount £	Total £
2	6ft wardrobe	WR12	260.00	021219 520.00
1	6ft dining table	DT47	310.00	021212 310.00
8	Dining chair	DC06	56.00	021215 448.00

Net total	1,278.00
VAT	223.65
Invoice total	1,501.65

Terms
Net 30 days
E & OE

INVOICE

Wilmshurst Furniture Makers
Retail Park
Nutley
DR5 2XJ

To:

Hoopers Stores Ltd

Invoice number: 42117

Date/tax point: 24 Dec 2006

Order number: WFM 317

Account number: SL 02

Quantity	Description	Stock code	Unit amount £	Total £
8	Round coffee table	RC11	130.00	021113 1,040.00
6	3 drawer chest	CD03	210.00	021117 1,260.00
6	2 drawer chest	CD02	160.00	021116 960.00

Net total	3,260.00
VAT	570.50
Invoice total	3,830.50

Terms
Net 30 days
E & OE

The coding of each item is:

6ft wardrobe	0 2	1 2	1 9
	profit centre	Jenson	6ft wardrobe

6ft dining table	0 2	1 2	1 2
	profit centre	Jenson	6ft dining table

Dining chair	0 2	1 2	1 5
	profit centre	Jenson	Dining chair

Round coffee table	0 2	1 1	1 3
	profit centre	Nutley	Round coffee table

3 drawer chest	0 2	1 1	1 7
	profit centre	Nutley	3 drawer chest

2 drawer chest	0 2	1 1	1 6
	profit centre	Nutley	2 drawer chest

Activity 2

Given below is a further sales invoice for Wilmshurst. Enter the correct coding.

INVOICE

Wilmshurst Furniture Makers
Retail Park
Dopham
DR3 4ZJ

To: Bots & Co

Invoice number: 42118

Date/tax point: 5 Dec 2006

Order number: P04662

Account number: SL 17

Quantity	Description	Stock code	Unit amount £	Total £
6	Dining chair	DC08	56.00	336.00
1	5ft dining table	DT31	270.00	270.00
	Net total			606.00
	VAT			106.05
	Invoice total			712.05

Terms
Net 30 days
E & OE

UPDATING THE COST CENTRE BALANCES

Once the invoices and payroll details have been analysed and coded, the amounts to be charged for each cost to each cost centre, or the income to be credited to a profit centre, must be added to the current balance for that account. This will give the total to date for each cost/profit centre and each type of cost/income.

HOW IT WORKS

All of the costs coded for Wilmshurst in this chapter so far are now summarised below:

Code	£
010101	604.00
010102	249.40
010103	25.80
010103	25.48
010103	3,000.00
010103	1,320.00
010202	103.20
010203	10.54
010203	2,000.00
010203	330.00
010301	44.00
010303	1,000.00
010303	550.00

An extract from the cost centre list of balances is also given. Each balance must be updated using the figures above to show the total for each cost.

Code	Opening balance	Update	Closing balance 31 Dec 2006
	£	£	£
010101	37,886.98		
010102	86,779.20		
010103	23,556.90		
010201	9,667.23		
010202	93,674.55		
010203	25,634.01		
010301	10,356.35		
010302	68,362.00		
010303	12,563.98		

student notes✍

Step 1 Find the total cost to be added to each code.

Code	£	
010101	604.00	
010102	249.40	
010103	25.80	
010103	25.48	£4,371.28
010103	3,000.00	
010103	1,320.00	
010202	103.20	
010203	10.54	
010203	2,000.00	£2,340.54
010203	330.00	
010301	44.00	
010303	1,000.00	
010303	550.00	£1,550.00

Step 2 Enter the new costs coded above into the update column to be added into the opening balance.

Code	Opening balance	Update	Closing balance 31 Dec 2006
	£	£	£
010101	37,886.98	604.00	
010102	86,779.20	249.40	
010103	23,556.90	4,371.28	
010201	9,667.23		
010202	93,674.55	103.20	
010203	25,634.01	2,340.54	
010301	10,356.35	44.00	
010302	68,362.00		
010303	12,563.98	1,550.00	

Step 3 Total the opening balance and the new costs to find the closing balance.

Code	Opening balance	Update	Closing balance 31 Dec 2006
	£	£	£
010101	37,886.98	604.00	38,490.98
010102	86,779.20	249.40	87,028.60
010103	23,556.90	4,371.28	27,928.18
010201	9,667.23		9,667.23
010202	93,674.55	103.20	93,777.75
010203	25,634.01	2,340.54	27,974.55
010301	10,356.35	44.00	10,400.35
010302	68,362.00		68,362.00
010303	12,563.98	1,550.00	14,113.98

Activity 3

Given below is a summary of all of the income coded in this chapter so far:

021113	1,040.00
021116	960.00
021117	1,260.00
021212	310.00
021215	448.00
021219	520.00

You are also given the opening balances on the profit centre accounts:

Code	Opening balance	Update	Closing balance 31 Dec 2006
	£	£	£
021113	21,056.00		
021116	96,100.00		
021117	22,650.00		
021212	53,682.00		
021215	3,480.00		
021219	12,420.00		

Enter the new income into the update column and find the closing balance on each of the profit centre product accounts.

COMPUTER SPREADSHEETS

SPREADSHEETS are computer packages that can be used to help in the tabulation of data and calculation of figures.

What is a spreadsheet?

Many of you will have come across computer spreadsheet packages either at work or on your own personal computer. As we saw in an earlier chapter, in essence a spreadsheet is a number of columns and rows and might typically look like this.

	A	B	C	D	E	F	G
1							
2							
3							
4							

Each column and each row will represent different factors so the column may be the opening balances, update figures and closing balances and the rows may represent each of the cost or profit centres.

Each cell can be defined in terms of its column heading (A, B, C etc) and its row number, Therefore the top left cell is A1 and the bottom right cell is G4.

The point of a computer spreadsheet is that it can be used to make large numbers of calculations very rapidly providing that the package is programmed by the use of formulae to make the correct calculations.

HOW IT WORKS

We will now set up a computer spreadsheet to calculate the updated balances for the cutting and assembly cost centres. This can be done by listing the cost centre codes in the first column, followed by the opening balance and then the update for the month. Formulae will then be inserted in order that the spreadsheet package automatically calculates the closing balances for each cost centre code.

	A	B	C	D
1	010101	37,886.98	604.00	
2	010102	86,779.20	249.40	
3	010103	23,556.90	4,371.28	
4	010201	9,667.23	-	
5	010202	93,674.55	103.20	
6	010203	25,634.01	2,340.54	

In the final column we need to enter the updated closing balance which is made up of the opening balance plus the update figure. This can be done using a SUM formula as follows.

	A	B	C	D
1	010101	37,886.98	604.00	=SUM(B1:C1)
2	010102	86,779.20	249.40	=SUM(B2:C2)
3	010103	23,556.90	4,371.28	=SUM(B3:C3)
4	010201	9,667.23	-	=SUM(B4:C4)
5	010202	93,674.55	103.20	=SUM(B5:C5)
6	010203	25,634.01	2,340.54	=SUM(B6:C6)

The final completed spreadsheet would look like this:

	A	B	C	D
1	010101	37,886.98	604.00	38,490.98
2	010102	86,779.20	249.40	87,028.60
3	010103	23,556.90	4,371.28	27,928.18
4	010201	9,667.23	-	9,667.23
5	010202	93,674.55	103.20	93,777.75
6	010203	25,634.01	2,340.54	27,974.55

This could then be continued month after month by continuing the columns and entering the update figure for each month.

Activity 4

How could this spreadsheet be improved?

CHAPTER OVERVIEW

- there are many methods of coding and each organisation will devise its own system

- each purchase invoice will be analysed and coded as to the type of cost, materials or expense, and the cost centre that it relates to

- the payroll details should also be coded to indicate the elements of gross pay that are treated as labour and the elements treated as an expense, and the cost centres they relate to

- the expenses must also be coded to show the cost centre that they relate to

- sales invoices must also be analysed to indicate that they are sales, the profit centre they relate to and in some systems also the product that is being sold

- once all of the costs and income have been collected for a period then the balance in the cost/profit centre account must be updated to show the additional costs/income collected for that cost/profit centre - this can be done using a computer spreadsheet

KEY WORDS

Numeric coding a coding system that uses numbers only

Alpha-numeric coding a coding system that uses letters and numbers

Profit centre an area of the business for which sales income is collected as well as costs

HOW MUCH HAVE YOU LEARNED?

1 Pole Potteries have a three digit coding system for their cost centres:

Digit one   1   means that this is a cost centre

Digit two   denotes the actual cost centre:

–	throwing	1
–	baking	2
–	painting	3
–	packaging	4
–	stores	5
–	maintenance	6
–	selling and distribution	7
–	canteen	8
–	administration	9

Digit three   denotes the type of cost

–	materials	1
–	labour	2
–	expenses	3

You are given the following purchase invoices and are required to code them.

INVOICE

Purbeck Clay
Granite Yard
Compston BH3 4TL
Tel 01929 464810
VAT Reg 1164 2810 67

To: Pole Potteries

Invoice number: 36411

Date/tax point: 16 Nov 2006

Order number: 11663

Account number: SL 42

Quantity	Description	Stock code	Unit amount £	Total £
50 kg	Throwing clay	TC412	6.80	340.00
10 litres	Paint - Fuchsia	PF67	2.80	28.00

Net total	368.00
VAT	64.40
Invoice total	432.40

Terms
Net 30 days
E & OE

INVOICE

IndCan Suppliers
High Street
Hamware BH3 7SP
Tel 01929 432432
VAT Reg 221 4 6182 93

To: Pole Potteries

Invoice number: 61212

Date/tax point: 17 Nov 2006

Order number: 11668

Account number: PP 02

Quantity	Description	Stock code	Unit amount £	Total £
100kg	Frozen chips	46112	1.20	120.00
48	Chicken pies	61297	0.90	43.20

Net total	163.20
VAT	28.56
Invoice total	191.76

Terms
Net 30 days
E & OE

2 Lara Binns works in the throwing department and baking department of Pole Potteries and her gross pay for week 39 has been analysed:

Throwing cost centre – labour 26 hours @ £9.60	249.60
Baking cost centre – labour 15 hours @ £9.60	144.00
Throwing cost centre – expense – overtime premium	28.80
Throwing cost centre – expense – employer's NIC	26.42
Baking cost centre – expense – employer's NIC	15.25

These are to be correctly coded.

3 The expenses of Pole Potteries for the period have been analysed and summarised below – they must now be coded.

Throwing cost centre – expense – rent £15,000 x 15%	2,250
Throwing cost centre – expense – cleaning	200
	2,450
Baking cost centre – expense – rent £15,000 x 40%	6,000
Baking cost centre – expense – servicing	600
	6,600
Painting cost centre – expense – rent £15,000 x 15%	2,250
Packaging cost centre – expense – rent £5,000 x 20%	1,000
Stores cost centre – expense – rent £5,000 x 80%	4,000
Maintenance cost centre – expense – rent £15,000 x 10%	1,500
Selling and distribution cost centre – expense – rent £3,000 x 0.5	1,500
Selling and distribution cost centre – expense – advertising	400
	1,900
Canteen cost centre – expense – rent £15,000 x 20%	3,000
Administration cost centre – expense – rent £3,000 x 0.5	1,500

chapter 23:
COMPARISON OF COSTS AND INCOME

chapter coverage 📖

In this final chapter we will be considering the ways in which the cost and income information collected can be compared to previous periods' figures and to budgeted figures in order to provide useful information for management. The topics that are to be covered are:

✍ the types of comparison required for Unit 4

✍ comparison of actual results to the results of the previous period

✍ comparison of actual results to those of the same period in the previous year

✍ comparison of actual results to budgeted figures

✍ calculation and reporting of variances

✍ methods of reporting

✍ confidentiality

Unit 4

knowledge and understanding – accounting methods

8   methods of presenting information, including word-processed documents
9   handling confidential information
10   the role of management information in the organisation

knowledge and understanding – the organisation

17   the organisation's confidentiality requirements
18   house style for presentation of different types of documents, including word-processed documents

Performance criteria – element 4.2

A   clarify information requirements with the appropriate person
B   compare information extracted from a particular source with actual results
C   identify discrepancies
D   provide comparisons to the appropriate person in the required format
E   follow organisational requirements for confidentiality strictly

TYPES OF COMPARISON

In an earlier chapter we considered the role of management in an organisation and that one of the key elements of this role was control. One way in which the costs and income of an organisation can be controlled is by comparing actual figures to either earlier period's figures or budgeted figures.

For Unit 4 three comparisons are required:

- to previous period's data – this means comparing the current month's figures to those of the previous month;

- to corresponding period's data – comparing the current month's figures to those of the same month in the previous year;

- to forecast data – comparison of actual figures to the budgeted figures.

When you are asked to provide one of these comparisons it is important that you are quite clear about precisely what is required. The exercise may well be time-consuming and therefore you should ensure that the precise requirements are clarified with the person requesting the comparison.

PREVIOUS PERIOD COMPARISON

In order to compare the current period's figures to those of the previous period you need to be able to access both sets of information from the organisation's ledgers and filing systems.

The current period's figures will be the latest in the management accounting records but they may need totalling. The previous period's figures will normally be kept in the ledger which records costs and income for management accounting purposes or they may be kept in the filing system.

HOW IT WORKS

You have been asked by your manager at Wilmshursts to provide a report showing a comparison of the costs for each of the production cost centres for the month of December 2006 to the same costs in November 2006.

As we know there are three production cost centres – cutting, assembly, polishing. However you must first clarify whether the cost centre costs are to be shown in total or whether they are to be split into the different elements of cost.

Your manager shows you the form of report that has been used for this exercise in the past in order to clarify exactly what information is required:

	Current month £	Previous month £
Cutting cost centre		
Materials		
Labour		
Expenses		
Total		
Assembly cost centre		
Materials		
Labour		
Expenses		
Total		
Polishing cost centre		
Materials		
Labour		
Expenses		
Total		

__Step 1__ Find the December figures for these costs from the coding listing that has been used previously.

Code	Opening balance	Update	Closing balance 31 Dec 2006
	£	£	£
010101	37,886.98	604.00	38,490.98
010102	86,779.20	249.40	87,028.60
010103	23,556.90	4,371.28	27,928.18
010201	9,667.23		9,667.23
010202	93,674.55	103.20	93,777.75
010203	25,634.01	2,340.54	27,974.55
010301	10,356.35	44.00	10,400.35
010302	68,362.00		68,362.00
010303	12,563.98	1,550.00	14,113.98

__Step 2__ Decipher the coding system. Remember that the middle two digits denote the cost centre:

01	cutting
02	assembly
03	polishing

The final two digits denote the type of cost:

01	materials
02	labour
03	expenses

__Step 3__ Enter the correct totals in the report and find the total cost for each cost centre.

	Current month December 2006 £	Previous month November 2006 £
__Cutting cost centre__		
Materials	38,490.98	
Labour	87,028.60	
Expenses	27,928.18	
Total	153,447.76	
__Assembly cost centre__		
Materials	9,667.23	
Labour	93,777.75	
Expenses	27,974.55	
Total	131,419.53	
__Polishing cost centre__		
Materials	10,400.35	
Labour	68,362.00	
Expenses	14,113.98	
Total	92,876.33	

student notes✍

Step 4   Find the totals for the month of November from the filing system.

Code	Total cost month of November 2006 £
010101	41,835.27
010102	86,145.64
010103	26,532.90
010201	8,274.23
010202	95,667.33
010203	26,285.37
010301	11,036.35
010302	69,661.29
010303	14,653.89

Step 5   Enter these figures into the report and find the totals for each cost centre.

	Current month December 2006 £	Previous month November 2006 £
Cutting cost centre		
Materials	38,490.98	41,835.27
Labour	87,028.60	86,145.64
Expenses	27,928.18	26,532.90
Total	153,447.76	154,513.81
Assembly cost centre		
Materials	9,667.23	8,274.23
Labour	93,777.75	95,667.33
Expenses	27,974.55	26,285.37
Total	131,419.53	130,226.93
Polishing cost centre		
Materials	10,400.35	11,036.35
Labour	68,362.00	69,661.29
Expenses	14,113.98	14,653.89
Total	92,876.33	95,351.53

Activity 1

Given below is a summary of the total income of each of Wilmshurst's three profit centres for the month of December 2006.

	Total income month of December 2006 £
Dopham	185,213.00
Nutley	167,232.00
Jenson	113,415.00

You find from the filing system the figures for total income for each of the profit centres for November 2006:

	Total income month of November 2006 £
Dopham	172,586.00
Nutley	178,353.00
Jenson	110,200.00

Prepare a comparison of the income of the three profit centres for the two months.

CORRESPONDING PERIOD COMPARISON

Just as it may be useful for management to monitor the costs and income of the business month by month it is also often useful to compare costs and income to the same month of the previous year.

Many types of business have SEASONAL BUSINESS. This means that in some months of the year production and sales of their products are higher than in other months. For example, sales of barbecue equipment are likely to be considerably higher in the spring and summer months than the autumn and winter. Therefore comparison of figures to the same month in the previous year may be more useful than comparison to earlier months in the current year.

Finding the information

The current period's figures will be found as before in the current management accounting records.

In practice however, it may be harder to find the figures for the previous year than for the previous month as they will no longer be in current use and will probably have been filed. If in doubt ask the appropriate person in the organisation rather than spending excessive time searching.

HOW IT WORKS

Again you are given the total costs of Wilmshurst's three cost centres in December 2006.

Code	Opening balance	Update	Closing balance 31 Dec 2006
	£	£	£
010101	37,886.98	604.00	38,490.98
010102	86,779.20	249.40	87,028.60
010103	23,556.90	4,371.38	27,928.28
010201	9,667.23		9,667.23
010202	93,674.55	103.20	93,777.75
010203	25,634.01	2,340.59	27,974.60
010301	10,356.35	44.00	10,400.35
010302	68,362.00		68,362.00
010303	12,563.98	1,550.00	14,113.98

Now the same figures for December 2005 must be found. They are given below in summary form as they were used in the same comparison in the previous year.

Code		Total costs month of December 2005
		£
Cutting –	materials	34,824.03
	labour	78,937.83
	expenses	21,567.27
Assembly –	materials	7,932.03
	labour	87,578.02
	expenses	25,376.36
Polishing –	materials	9,432.37
	labour	62,374.98
	expenses	12,582.09

Now prepare a report comparing the costs for December in 2006 and 2005.

Comparison of cost centre costs – December 2006 to December 2005

	December 2006 £	December 2005 £
Cutting		
Materials	38,490.98	34,824.03
Labour	87,028.60	78,937.83
Expenses	27,928.28	21,567.27
Total	153,447.86	135,329.13
Assembly		
Materials	9,667.23	7,932.03
Labour	93,777.75	87,578.02
Expenses	27,974.60	25,376.36
Total	131,419.58	120,886.41
Polishing		
Materials	10,400.35	9,432.37
Labour	68,362.00	62,374.98
Expenses	14,113.98	12,582.09
Total	92,876.33	84,389.44

Activity 2

Given again is the summary of the income of Wilmshurst's profit centres for December 2006 and also for December 2005. Prepare a comparison of these figures.

	Total income month of December 2006 £
Dopham	185,213.00
Nutley	167,232.00
Jenson	113,415.00

	Total income month of December 2005 £
Dopham	163,780.00
Nutley	159,885.00
Jenson	102,478.00

COMPARISON TO BUDGET

The BUDGETS of an organisation are the formal financial plans of the business. The budgets are set for future periods and show the anticipated levels of production and sales and the anticipated costs and income associated with the production and sales levels. Budgets will normally be prepared on a monthly basis, so for each month's actual figures there will be budgeted or expected figures to compare to.

Variances

Comparison of budgeted figures to actual figures is an extremely important tool for management in their control of the organisation. The difference between the actual costs and income and the budgeted costs and income are known as VARIANCES.

Any significant variances should be reported to management, as the reasons for them must be investigated and corrective action taken.

Adverse and favourable variances

ADVERSE VARIANCE –   where the actual cost is greater than the budgeted cost

where the actual income is less than the budgeted income

FAVOURABLE VARIANCE – actual cost is less than budgeted cost

actual income is greater than budgeted income

Management will want to be aware of significant variances both adverse and favourable. You might think that they are only concerned with adverse variances but a favourable variance might be an indication of a job well done by a department manager or the fact that the budget is not a fair reflection of the cost or income anticipated.

HOW IT WORKS

Again we have Wilmshurst's cost centre costs for December 2006.

Code	Opening balance	Update	Closing balance 31 Dec 2006
	£	£	£
010101	37,886.98	604.00	38,490.98
010102	86,779.20	249.40	87,028.60
010103	23,556.90	4,371.38	27,928.28
010201	9,667.23		9,667.23
010202	93,674.55	103.20	93,777.75
010203	25,634.01	2,340.59	27,974.60
010301	10,356.35	44.00	10,400.35
010302	68,362.00		68,362.00
010303	12,563.98	1,550.00	14,113.98

You also find from the filing system the budgeted costs for December 2006:

Budgeted costs – production cost centres – December 2006

Code	£
010101	37,200.00
010102	86,770.00
010103	23,550.00
010201	9,600.00
010202	99,540.00
010203	32,600.00
010301	10,350.00
010302	74,300.00
010303	10,560.00

Now we need to compare the actual costs to the budgeted costs and to calculate the variances.

Comparison of actual to budget for December 2006

		Actual £	Budget £	Variance £
Cutting –	materials	38,490.98	37,200.00	1,290.98 adv
	labour	87,028.60	86,770.00	258.60 adv
	expenses	27,928.28	23,550.00	4,378.28 adv
Assembly –	materials	9,667.23	9,600.00	67.23 adv
	labour	93,777.75	99,540.00	5,762.25 fav
	expenses	27,974.60	32,600.00	4,625.40 fav
Polishing –	materials	10,400.35	10,350.00	50.35 adv
	labour	68,362.00	74,300.00	5,938.00 fav
	expenses	14,113.98	10,560.00	3,553.98 adv

student notes✍

Reporting of variances

Normally the management of an organisation will only wish to be informed about significant or material variances.

The significance of a variance cannot be determined simply by its size – the size of the variance must be compared to the budgeted amount. For example a variance of £10,000 is tiny if the budgeted amount is £1,000,000 but is huge if the budgeted amount is only £15,000.

Therefore the significance of a variance will often be determined by measuring it as a percentage of the budgeted figure. If it is more than say 5% or 10% of the budgeted amount then the policy may be that it is reported to management.

HOW IT WORKS

We will now calculate the percentage that each variance is of the budgeted amount:

Cutting –	materials	1,290.98/37,200	x	100	=	3.5%
	labour	258.60/86,770	x	100	=	0.3%
	expenses	4,378.28/23,550	x	100	=	18.6%
Assembly –	materials	67.23/9,600	x	100	=	0.7%
	labour	5,762.25/99,540	x	100	=	5.8%
	expenses	4,625.40/32,600	x	100	=	14.2%
Polishing –	materials	50.35/10,350	x	100	=	0.5%
	labour	5,938.00/74,300	x	100	=	8.0%
	expenses	3,553.98/10,560	x	100	=	33.7%

If Wilmshurst's policy is to report any variances over 5% of the budgeted amount then the following would be reported:

Cutting –	expenses	£4,378.28 adverse
Assembly –	labour	£5,762.25 favourable
	expenses	£4,625.40 favourable
Polishing –	labour	£5,938.00 favourable
	expenses	£3,553.98 adverse

If the policy had been to report only variances greater than 10% of budget then the only variances reported would have been the three expenses variances.

Computer spreadsheet

Again a computer spreadsheet can be used to calculate the variances from budget and also to determine the percentage of budget represented by each variance in order to speed up the calculations.

HOW IT WORKS

We will illustrate this using the actual and budgeted figures for Wilmshurst for December 2006.

First set up the spreadsheet with the actual and budgeted figures for the month.

	A	B	C	D	E	F
1	Cost centre	Cost	Actual	Budget	Variance	% of budget
2	Cutting	Materials	38490.98	37200.00		
3	Cutting	Labour	87028.60	86770.00		
4	Cutting	Expenses	27928.28	23550.00		
5	Assembly	Materials	9667.23	9600.00		
6	Assembly	Labour	93777.75	99540.00		
7	Assembly	Expenses	27974.60	32600.00		
8	Polishing	Materials	10400.35	10350.00		
9	Polishing	Labour	68362.00	74300.00		
10	Polishing	Expenses	14113.98	10560.00		

Then we insert formulae into the variance column in order for the spreadsheet to calculate the variance. Take care with this. In order for adverse variances to be shown as negative figures and favourable variances to be shown as positive figures then the actual figure must be deducted from the budgeted figure.

Therefore for Cutting – materials   =   D2 – C2

Cutting – labour   =   D3 – C3 etc

Finally formulae must be inserted in the final column to calculate what percentage each variance is of the budget figure.

Cutting – materials   =   (E2/D2)*100

Cutting labour   =   (E3/D3)*100 etc

The final completed spreadsheet would appear as follows:

	A	B	C	D	E	F
1	Cost centre	Cost	Actual	Budget	Variance	% of budget
2	Cutting	Materials	38490.98	37200.00	=D2-C2	=(E2/D2)*100
3	Cutting	Labour	87028.60	86770.00	=D3-C3	=(E3/D3)*100
4	Cutting	Expenses	27928.28	23550.00	=D4-C4	=(E4/D4)*100
5	Assembly	Materials	9667.23	9600.00	=D5-C5	=(E5/D5)*100
6	Assembly	Labour	93777.75	99540.00	=D6-C6	=(E6/D6)*100
7	Assembly	Expenses	27974.60	32600.00	=D7-C7	=(E7/D7)*100
8	Polishing	Materials	10400.35	10350.00	=D8-C8	=(E8/D8)*100
9	Polishing	Labour	68362.00	74300.00	=D9-C9	=(E9/D9)*100
10	Polishing	Expenses	14113.98	10560.00	=D10-C10	=(E10/D10)*100

Activity 3

Given below are the actual sales for each of Wilmshurst's profit centres for December 2006 and the budgeted figures for the month.

Total income
month of December 2006
£

Dopham	185,213.00
Nutley	167,232.00
Jenson	113,415.00

Budgeted income
month of December 2006
£

Dopham	175,000.00
Nutley	170,000.00
Jenson	120,000.00

Compare the actual and budgeted figures and determine the variances. Calculate what percentage of the budgeted amount each variance is.

METHODS OF REPORTING

Each of the comparisons considered above will be reported to the appropriate person within the organisation – normally whoever asked you to prepare the comparison. When receiving instructions regarding the information and comparison that is required, you will normally also be told what format the comparison should be in. For example:

"send me a report ...."

"write me a memo ......"

"send me an e-mail ....."

If a particular format is requested then the comparison must be in this format.

In many cases, instead of producing a hand written document, you will need to word-process the document, particularly if it is to be sent by e-mail. When word-processing a document you may be able to make use of the facilities of the computer, for example using the table function when setting out data in a table.

House style of documents

Each organisation will have its own detailed styles for various methods of communication. Some of these will be pre-printed such as memo pads and letter heads.

However as well as following the house style you do also need to be aware of the general style and content of the most common forms of reporting.

A note

A NOTE is simply what the name implies – an informal note to a colleague or superior noting the details of the information that has been requested.

A note will often only be appropriate when a small, simple item of information is required.

"Please drop me a note letting me know the total materials cost of the cutting cost centre for December."

A memo

A MEMO is slightly more formal than a note but is still a fairly informal method of communication. Often an organisation will have pre-printed memo pads – the key elements of a memo are:

- the name of the person it is being sent to;
- the date;
- the subject;
- the name of the person it is from.

However, as it is an informal method of communication the style of the contents of the memo will not be particularly important as long as it is clear and understandable.

Again a memo will normally be required if information is required by a superior within the organisation about a relatively small matter.

"Please send me a memo about the coding of the enclosed sales invoices as I do not think they are correct".

student notes

student notes✎

An e-mail

An E-MAIL is essentially an electronic version of a memo.

However it is entirely possible that you could be asked to communicate a full, formal report (see below) by e-mail.

A report

A REPORT is a more formal method of providing information and is normally required for detailed information that is to be used by the managers of the organisation.

A report therefore will have a more formal layout and content than the other methods of communication discussed so far.

Your organisation may have a house style for reports but the typical heading will be something along these lines:

REPORT	
To:	Name and title of person to whom the report is to be sent
From:	Your name and title
Date:	Today's date
Subject:	A title that summarises the content of the report

The body of the report should also have the following typical structure:

- Introduction – briefly setting out the reasons for the report and the information that is contained in it;

- Body – the main details of what has been asked for (but normally excluding any calculations – these are shown in the appendix (see below));

- Conclusion – any conclusions or summaries that you have been asked to make on the information that is the subject of the report;

- Appendix – the calculations or numerical comparisons that form the subject of the report.

A letter

The subject of business letters was covered in Chapter 8 of this Course Companion. A letter is normally only required for someone external to the organisation, and when dealing with management information it would be unusual to be writing to someone outside the organisation about this. Therefore it would be rare for a letter to be required in the management accounting context.

Confidentiality

As an accountant dealing with the details of management accounting information, you are likely to have access to a range of confidential information.

For example you may well have access to the precise cost of producing the products that your organisation makes, which would obviously be of great interest to any competitors. On a more personal note you may have access to details of employees' pay, overtime and bonuses – again this is information that should not be widely known.

Whenever dealing with business information it is vital that confidentiality is always at the forefront of your mind. Your organisation will have a policy concerning confidentiality of information and this should always be fully adhered to.

Word-processing

The range statement for element 4.2 specifies word-processed documents. Further guidance from the AAT indicates that students should be able to produce a short informal report using the following word-processing features:

- different font sizes;
- bold type;
- italics;
- tables.

Microsoft Word is one of the most commonly used word processors. There is little difference between the main competitors these days: manufacturers are quick to copy each others' good features, and it is in their interests that users find it easy to transfer from another system to the one that they make.

If you start up Word you will be presented with a window like this.

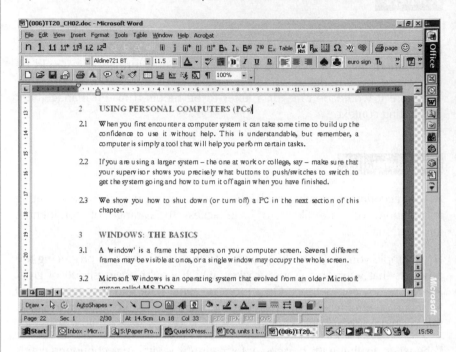

The main part of the screen is the area where you type, of course. At the top of the screen there is a bank of buttons and arrows that do useful things like **embolden** or *italicise* a word or words that you have selected, change the FONT STYLE or size of selected text, or place text in the centre of the page, or set it to one side of the page. A host of other things can be done and you can create your own customised buttons to do them if you like. Highlight the area you want to affect by left clicking the mouse on it and then click the relevant button.

In recent versions of Word, if you let the mouse pointer linger over a particular button (without clicking on it) a little label soon pops up telling you what it does. This is more fun than reading a book about it so we won't describe the buttons further.

The ruler below the buttons is used to set the left and right margins of the page and to indent paragraphs. You do this by dragging and dropping the triangular markers that you can see at either end of the ruler.

Tables

Some information to be included in a report, letter, memo or other document may best be presented in a table. We will briefly explain how to create and format a table using menu items. As with many Microsoft Word functions, the same process could be performed using toolbar buttons (if you wish to experiment using toolbar buttons, activate the Tables and Borders toolbar by selecting View, Toolbars, Tables and Borders from the main menu).

To create a simple table follow the following steps.

- Click where you want to create a table within your document.

- From the main menu select, Table, Insert, Table.

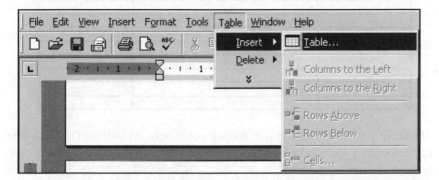

- The Insert Table dialogue box will appear as shown (if you are using an earlier version of Word the box will appear slightly different). Enter the required number of vertical columns and the number of horizontal rows (don't worry if you are not 100% sure as these options may be changed later). Accept the column width default setting of Auto.

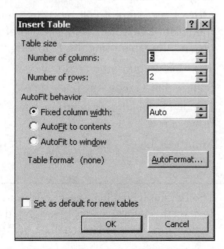

- Click OK.

You should now have a Table in your document. For example, if you had chosen 4 Columns and 10 rows, you would have the table shown.

The table you have created is a starting point only. As you add data to your table you may decide to format the contents of particular cells in a certain way, or to insert or delete columns or rows. Instructions for some useful actions associated with tables are shown in the table below.

Table action	Explanation
Entering text and moving around the table	Click into the appropriate cell (individual area of the table) and start typing. When you reach the end of the cell the text will continue on the next line, and the cell height will adjust automatically. Move to a different cell by using your mouse to click the cursor in the new cell. If you prefer, you can move around the table using the following keys. Tab - takes you to the next cell. Shift + Tab - takes you 'back' a cell. Up or Down direction arrow key - takes you up or down a row. Return or Enter - takes you to a new line within the same cell.
Aligning text	The default is to align text in tables to the left. To align text in the centre or to the right, use the alignment buttons on the standard toolbar.
Formatting text	You format text in a table just as you would format normal text - by selecting it then using toolbar buttons or the Format menu.
Selecting rows	Position the cursor to the left of the row you wish to select. The cursor will become an arrow pointing towards the top of the row. Click to select the row. If you prefer, click into the row you wish to select, then choose Table, Select, Row from the menu.

Table action	Explanation
Selecting columns	Position the cursor just above the column you wish to select. The cursor will become a black, downward pointing arrow. Click to select the column. If you prefer, click into the column you wish to select, then choose Table, Select, Column from the menu.
Selecting a single cell	Position the cursor just inside the left border of the cell you wish to select. The cursor will become a black arrow pointing towards the top of the cell. Click to select the cell. If you prefer, click into the row you wish to select, then choose Table, Select, Cell from the menu.
Selecting the entire table	Click in any cell in the table. Choose Table, Select, Table from the menu.
Deleting rows and columns	Select the row or column as above. Then chose Table, Delete, Rows or Table, Delete, Columns from the menu.
Deleting the contents of rows and columns	To clear the contents of a row or column select the area to be cleared then press the Delete key.
Adding rows and columns	To add an extra row, select the row below where you wish the new row to be then chose Table, Insert, Rows from the menu.To add an extra column, select the column to the right of where you wish the new column to be then chose Table, Insert, Columns from the menu.
Changing row height and column width	Move the cursor over the border you wish to move until it becomes two lines with arrows pointing up and down (rows) or left and right (columns). Hold down the mouse button and drag the boundary to the required height or width.
Merging cells	Joining two cells together to contain text that spans two or more columns is called merging cells. This is useful, for example, to provide a cell at the top of a table suitable for a heading that spans across all columns.To merge cells, you must first select the cells you wish to merge - then choose Table, Merge Cells from the menu.
Borders and shading	Word inserts a simple line border around all cells in a new table. You may change some or all borders, or add shading, or remove all border lines, by using the options available under Format, Borders and Shading. You should experiment with these options.

student notes✍

CHAPTER OVERVIEW

- one of the key roles of management is control – this can be helped by constant comparison of actual results to the previous periods' results and budgeted figures

- comparison to a previous period is comparison to the previous month's figures – the current costs/income can be found from the current management accounting ledgers or balances – the previous month's figures may still be active or may have been filed

- many businesses are seasonal and therefore comparison to the previous month may not be particularly useful – what may be more useful is comparison to the same period in the previous year

- a key element in management control of a business is the budgetary system – actual results should be compared to the expected or budgeted figures and the differences, called variances, reported to management when significant

- it is important that both adverse and favourable variances are reported

- there are a variety of methods of reporting the comparisons that have been outlined – the method required will depend upon the complexity of the information and the recipient

- the main methods of reporting are a note, a memo, e-mail, a report or a letter

- when dealing with management information a great deal of confidential information is accessed which should not be disclosed either within the organisation or outside it

KEY WORDS

Seasonal business a business whose sales and production fluctuate during the year as demand for their goods fluctuates

Budgets formalised financial plans of the future operations of the organisation

Variances the difference between the budgeted cost/income and the actual cost/income

Adverse variance the actual result is worse than the budgeted result

Favourable variance the actual result is better than the budgeted result

Note the most informal method of internal written communication

Memo a slightly more formal method of internal communication than a note

E-mail an electronic version of a memo

Report a formal, internal method of communication with a standardised format

HOW MUCH HAVE YOU LEARNED?

1   Given below are the total costs of the production cost centres for Pole Potteries for November 2006.

		£
Throwing –	materials	12,145.76
	labour	7,442.46
	expenses	6,335.49
Baking –	materials	1,336.48
	labour	2,447.28
	expenses	10,492.43
Painting –	materials	4,263.98
	labour	13,572.41
	expenses	2,684.50

You are also given the comparable costs for October 2006.

		£
Throwing –	materials	11,374.83
	labour	6,526.46
	expenses	6,103.78
Baking –	materials	1,263.78
	labour	1,984.05
	expenses	10,145.83
Painting –	materials	3,982.56
	labour	11,457.20
	expenses	2,155.83

Prepare a comparison of the two months' figures.

2 Given below are the production cost centre costs for Pole Potteries for November 2005.

		£
Throwing –	materials	12,672.84
	labour	6,627.31
	expenses	6,301.83
Baking –	materials	1,382.14
	labour	1,646.23
	expenses	10,646.29
Painting –	materials	3,896.22
	labour	12,118.29
	expenses	2,375.08

i) Explain why some organisations may find a comparison of the current month's costs to those of the same month a year ago more useful than a month to month comparison for the current year.

ii) Prepare a comparison of the November 2006 costs (from task 1) and the November 2005 costs.

3 Given below are the budgeted costs for the production cost centres for Pole Potteries for November 2006.

		£
Throwing –	materials	11,202.67
	labour	6,158.20
	expenses	7,135.52
Baking –	materials	1,505.60
	labour	2,490.82
	expenses	11,356.50
Painting –	materials	3,660.30
	labour	11,240.25
	expenses	2,800.00

Produce a comparison of actual costs for November 2006 to budgeted costs for the month and show the variances. The policy of Pole Potteries is to report any variances that are more than 10% of the budgeted amount to management. Indicate which variances would be reported.

CHAPTER 1 Introduction to business

1   Credit transaction

2   Capital transaction

CHAPTER 2 Business documents – Sales

1   The buyer

2   The delivery note is proof that the carrier did actually deliver the goods and that the customer actually received them.

3   A debit note is issued by the buyer of goods requesting a credit note from the seller. The seller then issues the credit note.

4   Output VAT is VAT on sales. Input VAT is VAT on purchases and expenses.

5   VAT $=$ £337.58 x 17.5/100 $=$ £59.07

6   VAT $=$ £442.68 x 17.5/117.5 $=$ £65.93

     Net price of goods $=$ £442.68 – £65.93 $=$ £376.75

7

	£
List price	2,450.00
Less: discount £2,450.00 x 15/100	(367.50)
	2,082.50
VAT	364.43
	2,446.93

8

	£
Goods total	368.40
Less: settlement discount	(11.05)
	357.35
Goods total	368.40
VAT £357.35 x 17.5/100	62.53
Invoice total	430.93

9 A credit note is the reversal of a sales invoice and therefore represents a loss of income. Therefore it is important to check that the credit is valid and that the amount of the credit is correct.

10 The main difference is that the customer discount is not shown separately: in this example it would have been calculated using a special customer price list, which has to be set up separately (but it only has to be set up once, and it can then automatically be applied to all customers who get 10% discount).

Another difference is that the computerised system numbers the invoice automatically: it will look up the last invoice number and add one, so you'll never need to look this up again, and you'll never accidentally issue two invoices with the same number. The date will be 'today's' date according to the computer's internal clock, unless you wish to change this.

You may also have spotted that then computerised system can calculate Euro amounts automatically, provided the correct exchange rate has been entered in another part of the program. The account number is also different.

CHAPTER 3 Double entry bookkeeping

1   a) Purchases of goods for resale have been made
A creditor (a liability) has been incurred

b) Sales have been made
A debtor has been created

c) Cash increases
The amount owed by the debtor decreases

d) Cash decreases
The amount owed to the creditor decreases

2   a) Debit   Purchases
Credit   Creditors

b) Debit   Debtors
Credit   Sales

c) Debit   Cash
Credit   Debtors

d) Debit   Creditors
Credit   Cash

3

Debtors account

	£		£
Sales	2,600	Bank	1,800
Sales	1,400	Bank	1,200
Sales	3,700	Bank	2,000
Sales	1,300	Balance c/d	4,000
	9,000		9,000
Balance b/d	4,000		

The balance represents the amount owing from debtors.

4

James Daniels

	£		£
Sales	1,000	Bank	800
		Balance c/d	200
	1,000		1,000
Balance b/d	200		

CHAPTER 4 Accounting for credit sales

1

Goods total	£1,235.57	–	net column
VAT	£216.22	–	VAT column
Invoice total	£1,451.79	–	Gross column

2

Total	–	debit to sales ledger control account
VAT	–	credit to VAT account
Net	–	credit to sales account

3 Main ledger:

Debit	–	Sales returns account
Debit	–	VAT account
Credit	–	Sales ledger control account

Subsidiary (sales) ledger:

Credit	–	individual debtor's account

4 Sales day book:

Date	Customer	Invoice number	Ref	Gross £	VAT £	Computers £	Printers £	Scanners £
				1,527.50	227.50	800.00	300.00	200.00

5   No. You are NOT connected directly into an organisation's accounting system computers when you complete a transaction with the organisation on the Internet. You will be connected to a computer known as a 'web server' and the web server's job is simply to deliver web pages and pass on messages, both to the organisation's computers and back to your computer. The whole process may indeed be fully automated - handled without human intervention - but you cannot hack into Amazon's accounting records directly via the website!

There will be many computerised checks along the way. For instance the web server will contact your bank's computer to make sure you have enough money available, and Amazon's computers will also make sure the transaction is reasonable (e.g. their systems will not let you place an order for a million copies without at least alerting a human operator that the transaction is a bit unusual, and needs to be verified).

CHAPTER 5   Receiving money

1   A crossed cheque must be paid directly into a bank account and cannot be exchanged for cash in a bank.

2   Provided that the correct procedures have been followed and the cheque guarantee card is valid, then the retailer is guaranteed that the cheque will be paid by the bank.

3   When a credit card is used for payment the customer has the purchase amount added to what is already owing to the credit card company. The retailer is then paid by the credit card company, and the customer pays some or all of his credit card bill. When payment is made by a debit card the funds are automatically debited from the customer's bank account and credited to the retailer's account.

4   Payment received £418.06 therefore discount of (£430.99 – 418.06) £12.93 has been taken.

Correct discount should have been £368.45 x 3/100 = £11.05. Therefore the payment that should have been received is (£430.99 – £11.05) = £419.94.

The error made was to calculate the discount on the gross invoice value: £430.99 x 0.03 = £12.93.

CHAPTER 6   Recording receipts

1   VAT should only be recorded in the Cash Receipts Book for receipts that have not come from credit customers. This will normally mean that the only entries for VAT are the VAT amounts on cash sales.

2   VAT on cash sales = £893.00 x 17.5/117.5 = £133.00

Entries in the Cash Receipts Book:

Total column	£893.00
VAT column	£133.00
Cash sales column	£760.00

3   Debit   Discount allowed account
      Credit   Sales ledger control account

4

J Thomlinson		
	£	£
Opening balance	146.78	

CHAPTER 7 The banking system

1   A current account for the £30,000 to be used for trading and a deposit account for the £20,000 to be saved for future use.

2   If confidentiality is not maintained about the banking process for your organisation, it would be possible for villains to attempt to seize the money being banked, thereby endangering a member or members of staff as well as risking the loss of cash and cheques belonging to the organisation.

3   A credit entry

CHAPTER 8 Communication with customers

1   A statement of account shows the customer how the balance due is made up and serves as a reminder to the customer to pay the amount due.

2   An aged debtor analysis assists in the credit control process by highlighting credit customers with balances that have been outstanding for more than the stated credit period.

3   Be polite, courteous, effective and firm.

CHAPTER 9 Business documents – Purchases

1   ■   that purchasing over the Internet is allowed organisational policy

      ■   this method has been authorised by an appropriate person

      ■   there is certain security about the provider of the goods and their existence and reputation is checked out

2   The buyer

3

		£
Net total		1,478.60
Less discount 5/100 x 1,478.60		73.93
		1,404.67
VAT £1,404.67 x 17.5/100		245.81

4   Discount = £650.30 x 3/100 = £19.50

CHAPTER 10 Accounting for credit purchases

1   Goods total £258.38 = purchases column
VAT total £45.21 = VAT column
Invoice total £303.59 = total column

2

	£
VAT	167.70
Purchases	777.18
Telephone	129.81
Stationery	51.45
	1,126.14

3

a)	Gross total	–	credit to purchases ledger control account
b)	VAT total	–	debit to VAT account
c)	Purchases total	–	debit to purchases account

4

	£
VAT	11.26
Purchases	64.39
	75.65

5   Main ledger:

Purchases ledger control account – debit entry £47.00

Purchase returns account – credit entry £40.00

VAT account – credit entry £7.00

Subsidiary (purchases) ledger:

Supplier's account – debit entry £47.00

CHAPTER 11 Making payments to credit suppliers

1 5 August (9 + 30 – 3 – 31)

2 1 December (23 + 10 – 2 – 30)

3 Friday before 13 December

4 Friday before 1 December

5 Discount = £582.65 x 2.5/100 = £14.56
Payment = £682.06 – 14.56 = £667.50

6 Date
Payee
Amount
Discount taken

7 A standing order is only for fixed payments at fixed time intervals. A direct debit is for payments that can vary as to amount and time interval.

CHAPTER 12 Recording payments

1 VAT should be recorded on any payments that are not payments to purchase ledger suppliers.

2 VAT = £683.47 x 17.5/117.5 = £101.79
Net amount = £683.47 – 101.79 = £581.68

Entries in the cash payments book:

Total column £683.47
VAT column £101.79
Cash purchases column £581.68

3 Credit balance

4 A debit entry to the purchases ledger control account

A credit entry to the discount received account

5

Hillside Enterprises			
	£		£
		Balance b/d	1,275.04

6

VAT account

	£		£
CPB	114.44		

Purchases account

	£		£
CPB	654.06		

Purchases ledger control account

	£		£
CPB	3,824.64		
CPB – discounts	101.85		

Discounts received account

	£		£
		CPB – discount	101.85

CHAPTER 13 Petty cash procedures

1

```
PETTY CASH VOUCHER

Number: 0464                    Date: 24 Jan 2006

Details                        Amount

Stationery                          4 - 25
                    Net             4 - 25
                    VAT             0 - 74
                    Gross           4 - 99

Claimed by:      A. Student
Authorised by:
```

2 VAT   = £9.00 x 17.5/117.5 = £1.34
Net amount = £9.00 – 1.34   = £7.66

3 £41.30

CHAPTER 14 Payroll accounting procedures

1 A personal allowance is the amount of income that an individual can earn, given their individual circumstances, before they are liable to pay income tax on those earnings.

2 Gross wage is the amount the person earns before any deductions have been made. The net wage is the final amount the person will receive after all deductions for tax, NIC and any other non-statutory deductions.

3

	£
Gross wage	400.00
PAYE income tax	(69.07)
NIC	(33.60)
Trade union subscription	(2.50)
Net pay	294.83

4

Gross wages control account

	£		£
CPB – net pay	294.83	Wages expense	400.00
PAYE/NIC creditor		Employer's NIC	41.20
(69.07 + 33.60)	102.67		
Trade union subscriptions	2.50		
Employer's NIC	41.20		

Wages expense account

	£		£
Gross wages control	400.00		
PAYE/NIC creditor	41.20		

PAYE/NIC creditor account

	£		£
		Gross wages control	102.67
		Wages expense	41.20

Trade Union Subscriptions

	£		£
		Gross wages control	2.50

CHAPTER 15 Bank reconciliation statement

1   Total column   £640.89
    VAT column   £640.89 x 17.5/117.5 =   £95.45
    Cash purchases column   £640.89 – 95.45   =   £545.44

2   The bank

3   Cash Receipts Book

4   Cash Payments Book

5   As an unpresented cheque

6   Debit bank interest
        Credit cash payments book

	£
7   Opening balance – overdraft (credit balance) | (1,367.34) |
        Payments | (4,527.22) |
        Receipts | 7,336.49 |
        Closing balance (debit balance) | 1,441.93 |

CHAPTER 16 Control account reconciliations

1   DR   Sales ledger control account
        CR   Sales account
        CR   VAT

2   DR   Purchases account
        DR   VAT
        CR   Purchases ledger control account

3   DR   Bad debts expense account
        CR   Sales ledger control account

4   The sales ledger control account but not the individual balances in the subsidiary ledger.

5   DR   Discount allowed account
        CR   Sales ledger control account

6   If the invoice was entered on the wrong side of the account then it was debited to the account. To correct this the creditor's account must be credited with twice the amount of the invoice in order to remove the debit and put in place the credit. Therefore the list of creditors' balances would increase by £400.

7
	£
Vouchers	103.69
Petty cash	36.31
	140.00

The petty cash does not reconcile with the petty cash vouchers as there is £10 of cash missing. This could be due to a mistake such as £10 too much being paid out on a petty cash voucher, or £10 having been removed from the petty cash box without a supporting voucher.

CHAPTER 17 Preparing an initial trial balance

1

Purchases ledger control account

	£		£
Purchase returns	3,669	Opening balance	24,578
Cash paid	86,338	Purchases	89,451
Discounts received	3,698		
Balance c/d	20,324		
	114,029		114,029
		Balance b/d	20,324

This is a credit balance.

2 Debit balance

3 Credit balance

CHAPTER 18 Errors and the trial balance

1 A transposition error

2 An error of commission

3 Debit   Suspense account   £2,500

Credit   Sales ledger control account   £2,500

CHAPTER 19 Business transactions and the law

1 a) Offeror – Ben
Offeree – Bill

b) No. The advertisement is an invitation to treat. When answering the advertisement Ben is making an offer of £2,000 – Bill is perfectly within his rights to reject that offer.

2 No. By changing the price to £1,800 Ben has made a counter-offer which has rejected the initial offer. It is then up to Bill to accept or reject this counter-offer which he chooses to reject.

3 Yes. The acceptance that Ben made was conditional and therefore there is no valid contract between Bill and Ben.

CHAPTER 20 Introduction to management information

1
- decision making
- planning
- control

2
- cutting
- assembly
- polishing
- packaging
- selling and distribution
- administration
- stores
- maintenance
- canteen

3 A profit centre is where the costs and revenues, therefore profit, are collected. In an investment centre this profit is also compared to the assets and liabilities used to earn the profit.

CHAPTER 21 Elements of cost

1 VAT is not a cost of a VAT registered business as it is reclaimed from HM Revenue and Customs. Therefore it should not be included as part of the cost of materials or expenses.

2	£
Polishing cost centre – labour 43 x £9.20	395.60
Polishing cost centre – expenses 8 x (£9.20 x 0.5)	36.80

3	£
Vehicle deliveries cost centre	310.00
Motorbike deliveries cost centre	240.00
Bookings cost centre	600.00
Administration cost centre	600.00

CHAPTER 22 Coding

1

	£		Code
Basic pay 43 x £9.20	395.60	–	010302
Overtime premium 8 x £4.60	36.80	–	010303
Employer's NIC	42.55	–	010303

2

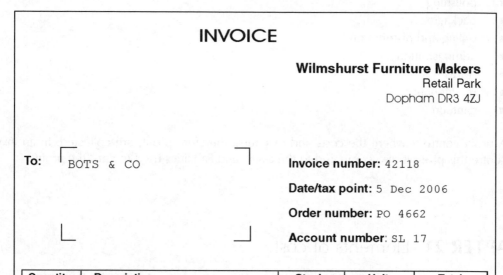

INVOICE

Wilmshurst Furniture Makers
Retail Park
Dopham DR3 4ZJ

To: BOTS & CO

Invoice number: 42118

Date/tax point: 5 Dec 2006

Order number: PO 4662

Account number: SL 17

Quantity	Description	Stock code	Unit amount £	Total £
6	Dining Chairs	DC 08	56.00	021015 336.00
1	5ft Dining Table	DT 31	270.00	021011 270.00

Net total	606.00
VAT	106.05
Invoice total	712.05

Terms
Net 30 days
E & OE

3

Code	Opening balance £	Update £	Closing balance £
021113	21,056.00	1,040.00	22,096.00
021116	96,100.00	960.00	97,060.00
021117	22,650.00	1,260.00	23,910.00
021212	53,682.00	310.00	53,992.00
021215	3,480.00	448.00	3,928.00
021219	12,420.00	520.00	12,940.00

4   The spreadsheet columns should have headings, as in the manual version.

CHAPTER 23 Comparison of costs and income

1

	Current month December 2006 £	Previous month November 2006 £
Dopham	185,213	172,586
Nutley	167,232	178,353
Jenson	113,415	110,200
	465,860	461,139

2

	December 2006 £	December 2005 £
Dopham	185,213	163,780
Nutley	167,232	159,885
Jenson	113,415	102,478
	465,860	426,143

3

	Actual Dec 2006 £	Budget Dec 2006 £	Variance £
Dopham	185,213	175,000	10,213 fav
Nutley	167,232	170,000	2,768 adv
Jenson	113,415	120,000	6,585 adv

Variance percentage of budgeted amount

Dopham	10,213/175,000 x 100	=	5.8%
Nutley	2,768/170,000 x 100	=	1.6%
Jenson	6,585/120,000 x 100	=	5.5%

HOW MUCH HAVE YOU LEARNED? – ANSWERS

CHAPTER 1 Introduction to business

1   Limited liability means that if the company is declared bankrupt then the shareholders cannot be asked to contribute any more money to pay off creditors than the amount that they agreed to pay for their shares. Therefore the maximum that the shareholders can lose is the amount that they paid for their shares.

2   a)   Credit transaction
     b)   Cash transaction
     c)   Cash transaction
     d)   Credit transaction
     e)   Cash transaction

3   a)   Revenue transaction
     b)   Capital transaction
     c)   Revenue transaction
     d)   Capital transaction

4   Income or revenue
     Expenses
     Profit or loss

5   Fixed assets and current assets

6   Capital represents the amount initially paid into the business by the owners plus any accumulated profits less any amounts taken out of the business by the owners in the form of drawings or dividends.

CHAPTER 2 Business documents – Sales

1 a) Sales invoice
   b) Purchase order
   c) Debit note or goods returned note
   d) Delivery note
   e) Credit note

2 A delivery note is a document sent by the seller of the goods to the customer when the goods are delivered. It shows the quantity of each type of goods that are being delivered. It should be signed by an employee of the customer after that employee has checked that the quantity delivered agrees with the quantity on the delivery note. The deliverer keeps one copy as proof that he did deliver these goods and a further copy is returned to the seller as proof that the goods were delivered and accepted.

3 ▪ seller's name, address and VAT registration number
   ▪ the name and address of the customer
   ▪ the invoice number
   ▪ the date
   ▪ the related purchase order number
   ▪ the customer's account number
   ▪ the quantity of goods
   ▪ description and product code of the goods
   ▪ any trade discount
   ▪ the net total
   ▪ VAT total
   ▪ the gross invoice total
   ▪ any terms of payment

4 a) VAT = £288.59 x 17.5% (17.5/100) = £50.50

   b) VAT = £288.59 x $\dfrac{17.5}{117.5}$ = £42.98

       Net amount = £288.59 – 42.98
                  = £245.61

5 a) VAT $= £3,152.90 \times \dfrac{17.5}{117.5} = £469.58$

Net amount $= £3,152.90 - 469.58$
$= £2,683.32$

b) VAT $= £446.28 \times \dfrac{17.5}{117.5} = £66.46$

Net amount $= £446.28 - 66.46$
$= £379.82$

c) VAT $= £168.35 \times \dfrac{17.5}{117.5} = £25.07$

Net amount $= £168.35 - 25.07$
$= £143.28$

6 a)

	£
Cost before discount 23 × £56.00	1,288.00
Trade discount 15% × £1,288.00	193.20
Net of discount price	1,094.80
VAT 17.5% × £1,094.80	191.59
Total cost	1,286.39

b)

	£
Cost before discount 23 × £56.00	1,288.00
Trade discount 15% × £1,288.00	193.20
Net of discount price	1,094.80
VAT 17.5% × (1,094.80 – (3% × 1,094.80))	185.84
or 1,094.80 × 0.97 × 0.175	
Total cost	1,280.64

7 The invoice is for 15 toasters whereas the delivery note shows that only 12 were delivered – the invoice should be amended to show only 12 toasters and the reason for the short delivery should be investigated.

The invoice is charging the vacuums at £220 each whereas the purchase order shows a unit price of £210 – this difference should be investigated – was it agreed in a price quotation to Whitehill that the price would be only £210?

8 Errors on the invoice:

- it is not dated
- there is no customer account code
- the calculation of the total cost of the tumble dryers is incorrect
- the calculation of the trade discount is incorrect
- the VAT has been calculated without taking account of the cash discount offered

Corrected figures:

	£
Tumble dryers 21 x £180	3,780.00
Mixers	400.00
	4,180.00
Less: 15% discount	627.00
	3,553.00
VAT 17.5% x (3,553 – (5% x 3,553))	590.68
	4,143.68

9   Errors on the credit note:

- the calculation of the total for the whisks is incorrect
- the trade discount has been omitted
- the VAT has been rounded up not down
- the VAT has been deducted rather than added

Corrected figures:

	£
Fridges	660.00
Whisks 2 x 6.99	13.98
	673.98
Less: 20% discount	134.80
	539.18
VAT	94.35
	633.53

CHAPTER 3 Double entry bookkeeping

1 a) increase in cash and increase in capital
   b) increase in purchases and increase in creditors
   c) increase in fixed assets and decrease in cash
   d) increase in sales and increase in debtors
   e) decrease in cash and increase in drawings

2

Bank account

		£			£
	Capital	25,000	a)	Delivery van	8,000
h)	Sales	1,200	b)	Purchases	6,000
m)	Debtors control	3,600	c)	Rent	2,400
			e)	Stationery	100
			i)	Telephone	140
			k)	Creditors control	2,500
			l)	Drawings	1,200

Capital account

	£			£
		Bank		25,000

Delivery van account

		£		£
a)	Bank	8,000		

Purchases account

		£		£
b)	Bank	6,000		
f)	Creditors control	4,500		

Rent account

		£		£
c)	Bank	2,400		

Sales ledger control account

		£			£
d)	Sales	2,700	m)	Bank	3,600
g)	Sales	5,200			
j)	Sales	3,000			

Sales account

	£			£
		d)	Debtors control	2,700
		g)	Debtors control	5,200
		h)	Bank	1,200
		j)	Debtors control	3,000

Stationery account

		£		£
e)	Bank	100		

Purchases ledger control account

		£			£
k)	Bank	2,500	f)	Purchases	4,500

Telephone account

		£		£
i)	Bank	140		

Drawings account

		£		£
i)	Bank	1,200		

3

Bank account

		£			£
Capital		25,000	a)	Delivery van	8,000
h)	Sales	1,200	b)	Purchases	6,000
m)	Debtors control	3,600	c)	Rent	2,400
			e)	Stationery	100
			i)	Telephone	140
			k)	Creditors control	2,500
			l)	Drawings	1,200
				Balance c/d	9,460
		29,800			29,800
Balance b/d		9,460			

Capital account

	£			£
		Bank		25,000

Delivery van account

		£		£
a)	Bank	8,000		

Purchases account

		£		£
b)	Bank	6,000		
f)	Creditors control	4,500	Balance c/d	10,500
		10,500		10,500
Balance b/d		10,500		

Rent account

		£		£
c)	Bank	2,400		

Sales ledger control account

		£			£
d)	Sales	2,700	m)	Bank	3,600
g)	Sales	5,200			
j)	Sales	3,000		Balance c/d	7,300
		10,900			10,900
	Balance b/d	7,300			

Sales account

	£			£
		d)	Sales ledger control	2,700
		g)	Sales ledger control	5,200
		h)	Bank	1,200
Balance c/d	12,100	j)	Sales ledger control	3,000
	12,100			12,100
			Balance b/d	12,100

Stationery account

		£		£
e)	Bank	100		

Purchases ledger control account

		£			£
k)	Bank	2,500	f)	Purchases	4,500
	Balance c/d	2,000			
		4,500			4,500
				Balance b/d	2,000

Telephone account

		£		£
i)	Bank	140		

Drawings account

		£		£
i)	Bank	1,200		

Trial balance

	Debits £	Credits £
Bank	9,460	
Capital		25,000
Delivery van	8,000	
Purchases	10,500	
Rent	2,400	
Sales ledger control account	7,300	
Sales		12,100
Stationery	100	
Purchases ledger control account		2,000
Telephone	140	
Drawings	1,200	
	39,100	39,100

4   The main ledger is the ledger which holds all of the ledger accounts of the business. There will be ledger accounts for income, expenses and all assets and liabilities. The main ledger is where the double entry bookkeeping takes place.

The subsidiary ledgers are supporting ledgers or memorandum ledgers. There is a subsidiary (sales) ledger and a subsidiary (purchases) ledger. The subsidiary (sales) ledger has an account for each individual debtor and the subsidiary (purchases) ledger has an account for each individual creditor.

CHAPTER 4 Accounting for credit sales

1   When a sale is made on credit the two effects on the business are that sales increase and that a debtor is set up or increased.

Income, ie sales, is a credit entry, therefore the sales account is credited. The amount of the credit is the net amount of the sale. The reason for this is that the business makes no profit out of VAT as it simply pays it over to HMRC; therefore the VAT is not included in sales.

The VAT however is owed to HMRC and, as a creditor, this is therefore a credit entry in the VAT account.

The sales ledger control account is debited with the gross amount of the sale (including VAT) as this is the amount that the customer is due to pay.

The accounting for sales returns is effectively the reverse of accounting for credit sales. As the goods have been returned they are no longer a sale and therefore are debited to the sales returns account. Again the net amount is used here, as with the original sale. The VAT is no longer due to HMRC so the VAT account is debited and the customer no longer owes the money to the business so the sales ledger control account is credited with the gross amount of the return.

2 a) and b)

Date	Customer	Invoice number	Ref	Gross £	VAT £	Net £
21/9	Dagwell Enterprises	56401	SL 15	928.83	138.33	790.50
21/9	G Thomas & Co	56402	SL 30	3,443.26	495.26	2,948.00
22/9	Polygon Stores	56403	SL 03	1,924.65	286.65	1,638.00
23/9	Weller Enterprises	56404	SL 18	1,121.28	161.28	960.00
				7,418.02	1,081.52	6,336.50

c) **Main ledger**

Sales ledger control account

	£		£
SDB	7,418.02		

Sales account

	£		£
		SDB	6,336.50

VAT account

	£		£
		SDB	1,081.52

Subsidiary (sales) ledger

Dagwell Enterprises   SL 15

	£		£
SDB - 56401	928.83		

G Thomas & Co   SL 30

	£		£
SDB - 56402	3,443.26		

Polygon Stores   SL 03

	£		£
SDB - 56403	1,924.65		

Weller Enterprises   SL 18

	£		£
SDB - 56404	1,121.28		

3   a) and b)

Date	Customer	Credit note number	Ref	Gross £	VAT £	Net £
21/9	QQ Stores	08660	SL 37	348.97	51.97	297.00
23/9	Dagwell Enterprises	08661	SL 15	239.70	35.70	204.00
				588.67	87.67	501.00

c)   **Main ledger**

Sales ledger control account

	£			£
		SRDB		588.67

Sales Returns account

	£		£
SRDB	501.00		

VAT account

	£		£
SRDB	87.67		

Subsidiary (sales) ledger

QQ Stores   SL 37

	£		£
		SRDB – 08660	348.97

Dagwell Enterprises   SL 15

	£		£
		SRDB - 08661	239.70

4

Date	Customer	Invoice number	Ref	Gross £	VAT £	Net £
1 June	J Jepson	44263	SL 34	138.65	20.65	118.00
2 June	S Beck & Sons	44264	SL 01	370.12	55.12	315.00
2 June	Scroll Ltd	CN3813	SL 16	(21.73)	(3.23)	(18.50)
3 June	Penfold Ltd	44265	SL 23	193.52	28.82	164.70
4 June	S Beck & Sons	44266	SL 01	301.27	44.87	256.40
4 June	J Jepson	44267	SL 34	169.20	25.20	144.00
5 June	Penfold Ltd	CN3814	SL 23	(19.74)	(2.94)	(16.80)
				1,131.29	168.49	962.80

Main ledger

Sales ledger control account

	£		£
SDB	1,131.29		

Sales account

	£		£
		SDB	962.80

VAT account

	£		£
		SDB	168.49

Subsidiary (sales) ledger

J Jepson   SL 34

	£		£
SDB – 44263	138.65		
SDB – 44267	169.20		

S Beck and Sons   SL 01

	£		£
SDB – 44264	370.12		
SDB – 44266	301.27		

Scroll Ltd   SL 16

	£		£
		SDB - 3813	21.73

Penfold Ltd   SL 23

	£		£
SDB - 44265	193.52	SDB - 3814	19.74

CHAPTER 5 Receiving money

1. a) The drawer is K Filmer, the person writing the cheque in order to make a payment

    b) The drawee is Western Bank who are the bank that will be required to pay the cheque

    c) The payee is F Robertson, the person being paid by the cheque

2. Cheque from P Barret – the words and figures do not agree

    Cheque from A Peters – the cheque is out of date and no longer valid as it is dated more than 6 months ago

    Cheque from F Pilmer – not signed

3. The blank crossing simply means that the cheque must be paid into a bank account.

    The special crossing means that the cheque can only be paid into the Main branch of the Western Bank

    The account payee crossing means that this cheque can only be paid into the account of the payee of the cheque and cannot be endorsed to a third party.

4. The first endorsement means that the cheque should be paid into the account of Fiona Fisher.

    The second endorsement means that the cheque is now a bearer cheque and can be paid into the account of anyone in possession of the cheque.

5.
    - check that the guarantee card has not been tampered with
    - check that the guarantee card has not expired
    - check that the amount of the purchase does not exceed the guarantee amount on the card
    - check that the account name and number on the card are the same as those on the cheque
    - ensure that the cheque is signed in your presence and the signature is the same as that on the card.
    - ensure that you (and not the customer) write the card number on the reverse of the cheque.

6. a) If you do accept the cheque it will not be guaranteed to be paid by the bank

    b) Again the guarantee would only cover one of the cheques. Therefore there is no guarantee that the other cheque would be paid.

7.
    - that the card had not been tampered with
    - that the card has not expired
    - that the card has not been stolen
    - that the purchase does not exceed the floor limit and if it does seek an authorisation code from the credit card company
    - that the signature on the credit card voucher is the same as that on the card.

8 A credit card allows a customer to make purchases now and then to pay the credit card company the amount outstanding at a later date. A debit card is a method of paying for goods directly out of the customer's bank account without writing a cheque. When the debit card is accepted the customer's account will be automatically debited and the retailer's account automatically credited.

9 Electronic Funds Transfer at Point of Sale – this means that the customer's account is debited directly for the amount of the purchase and the retailer's account is credited.

10

REMITTANCE LIST		
Date	Sender	Amount £
15 October	B Bourne & Co	321.43
15 October	Hoppers Ltd	400.00
15 October	Tykes Ltd	654.80

11 Cheque from Quinn Ltd – the remittance advice has been correctly cast but there has been an error made in writing the cheque as the cheque is for £770.80 rather than £770.08.

Cheque from T T Peters – the remittance advice has been incorrectly cast and the cheque total should have been for £1,191.02.

12 Cheque from Hayworth Ltd – the settlement discount should not have been taken as the cheque arrived 13 days after the invoice date even though it was written only 9 days after the invoice date.

Cheque from Harper & Sons – a discount of £28.97 has been taken. The discount is valid but has been incorrectly calculated. The correct discount is £620.00 x 4/100 = £24.80. Therefore the cheque should have been made out for £724.16 – £24.80 = £699.36.

13 By a process of trial and error you can find the invoices and credit note that total to £226.79.

	£
30234	157.35
30239	85.24
CN2381	(15.80)
	226.79

CHAPTER 6 Recording receipts

1   The Cash Receipts Book is both a book of prime entry and the debit side of the bank account in the main ledger.

2   The discount allowed column in the Cash Receipts Book is a memorandum column used as a reminder to put through the double entry for the discounts. In the main ledger the sales ledger control account is credited with the discount as the discount is reducing the amount that the debtor owes. The discount allowed account is debited as the discount is an expense of the business. In the subsidiary (sales) ledger the discounts are entered on the credit side of the individual debtors' accounts.

3   a)

Date	Details	Ref	Total	VAT	Cash sales	Sales ledger	Discounts allowed
			£	£	£	£	£
30/6	Cash sales	ML	364.25	54.25	310.00		
30/6	H Henry	0115	146.79			146.79	
30/6	P Peters	0135	221.55			221.55	6.85
30/6	K Kilpin	0128	440.30			440.30	
30/6	Cash sales	ML	294.50	43.86	250.64		
30/6	B Bennet	0134	57.80			57.80	
30/6	S Shahir	0106	114.68			114.68	3.55
			1,639.87	98.11	560.64	981.12	10.40

VAT calculations for cash sales:

364.25 x 17.5/117.5 = £54.25
294.50 x 17.5/117.5 = £43.86

b)   **Main ledger**

VAT account

£		£
	CRB	98.11

Sales account

£		£
	CRB	560.64

Sales ledger control account

	£		£
		CRB	981.12
		CRB – discounts	10.40

Discounts allowed account

	£		£
CRB	10.40		

c) **Subsidiary ledger – sales ledger**

H Henry   0115

	£		£
		CRB	146.79

P Peters   0135

	£		£
		CRB	221.55
		CRB - discount	6.85

K Kilpin   0128

	£		£
		CRB	440.30

B Bennet   0134

	£		£
		CRB	57.80

S Shahir   0106

	£		£
		CRB	114.68
		CRB - discount	3.55

4 a)

Date	Details	Ref	Total	VAT	Cash sales	Sales ledger	Discounts allowed
			£	£	£	£	£
20/5	G Gonpipe	SL55	332.67			332.67	
20/5	Cash sales	110	658.00	98.00	560.00		
20/5	J Jimmings	SL04	127.37			127.37	6.70
20/5	N Nutely	SL16	336.28			336.28	17.70
20/5	T Turner	SL21	158.35			158.35	
20/5	Cash sales	110	329.88	49.13	280.75		
20/5	R Ritner	SL45	739.10			739.10	38.90
			2,681.65	147.13	840.75	1,693.77	63.30

VAT calculations for cash sales:

658.00 x 17.5/117.5 = £98.00
329.88 x 17.5/117.5 = £49.13

b)

POSTING SHEET			
Account name	Account code	Debit £	Credit £
VAT	710		147.13
Sales	110		840.75
Sales ledger control	560		1,693.77
Discount allowed	280	63.30	
Sales ledger control	560		63.30

Prepared by: .... **Date**: ....

Checked by: .... **Date**: ....

Posted by: .... **Date**: ....

c)   **Subsidiary (sales) ledger**

G Gonpipe		SL 55
£		£
	CRB	332.67

J Jimmings		SL 04
£		£
	CRB	127.37
	CRB - discount	6.70

N Nutely		SL 16
£		£
	CRB	336.28
	CRB - discount	17.70

T Turner		SL 21
£		£
	CRB	158.35

R Ritner		SL 45
£		£
	CRB	739.10
	CRB - discount	38.90

5   In a computerised accounting system the details of the receipts for the period would be batched. The totals that are to be input would be listed and totalled and will be checked with the final totals that are input into the system. Each receipt must be coded to reflect what type of receipt it is, ie, cash sales or receipts from credit customers. If the receipt is from a credit customer then the sales ledger code of the customer code must also be input.

Once the details have been input the computer system will automatically post the totals to the main ledger accounts. It will also post the individual receipts to the individual debtor accounts in the subsidiary (sales) ledger.

CHAPTER 7 The banking system

1 A current account with a bank is an account that is intended to have payments in and regular payments out in the form of written cheques and other forms of payment such as direct debits and standing orders. A cheque book is routinely issued with a current account.

A deposit account is an account whereby the intention is to largely pay money into the account and not to withdraw money from it on a regular basis. A cheque book is therefore not normally issued with a deposit account and indeed there may be restrictions on the withdrawals from the account.

2 An overdraft facility is something that is granted to some customers with a current account. It is an agreement with the bank that the customer can withdraw more funds than it has in its current account in the form of cheques or cash up to a certain limit. When the account does become a debit balance or an overdraft then the bank will charge interest on this balance.

3
- L Bridges pays the cheque into the Winchelsea branch of the Northern Bank.
- sent to the Northern Bank clearing department
- sent to the Central Clearing House
- sent to First National Bank clearing department
- sent to Winchelsea branch of First National Bank
- if the cheque is correctly written out it is debited from F Harmer's account and credited to L Bridges account

4

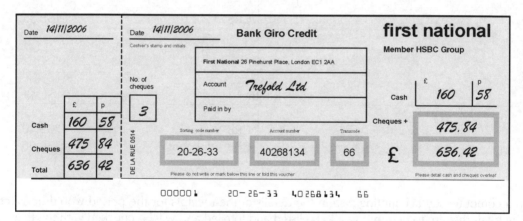

5

	£	p	
1	15	90	
2	120	50	
3	56	75	
4	25	99	
5			
6			
7			
8			
9			
10			
11			
12			
13			
14			
15			
16			
17			
18			
19			
20			
Total	219	14	**Carried Overleaf**

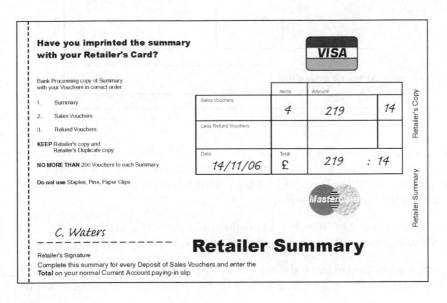

Have you imprinted the summary with your Retailer's Card?

VISA

Bank Processing copy of Summary with your Vouchers in correct order.

1. Summary
2. Sales Vouchers
3. Refund Vouchers

KEEP Retailer's copy and Retailer's Duplicate copy

NO MORE THAN 200 Vouchers to each Summary

Do not use Staples, Pins, Paper Clips

	Items	Amount	
Sales Vouchers	4	219	14
Less Refund Vouchers			
Date 14/11/06	Total £	219	: 14

MasterCard

Retailer's Copy

Retailer Summary

C. Waters

Retailer's Signature

Complete this summary for every Deposit of Sales Vouchers and enter the **Total** on your normal Current Account paying-in slip

Retailer Summary

6 a) credit entry
  b) debit entry
  c) debit balance

CHAPTER 8 Communication with customers

1

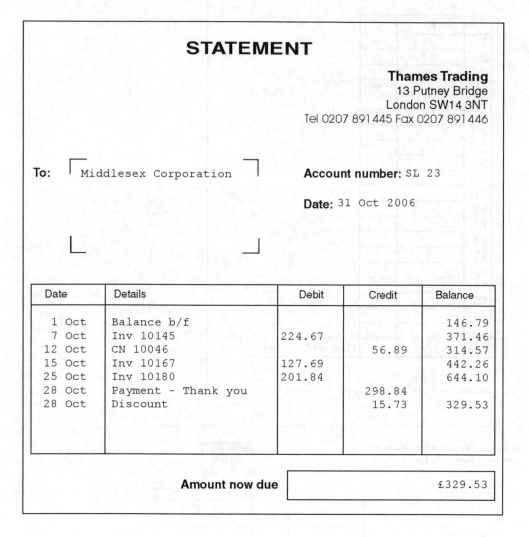

STATEMENT

Thames Trading
13 Putney Bridge
London SW14 3NT
Tel 0207 891 445 Fax 0207 891 446

To: Middlesex Corporation

Account number: SL 23

Date: 31 Oct 2006

Date	Details	Debit	Credit	Balance
1 Oct	Balance b/f			146.79
7 Oct	Inv 10145	224.67		371.46
12 Oct	CN 10046		56.89	314.57
15 Oct	Inv 10167	127.69		442.26
25 Oct	Inv 10180	201.84		644.10
28 Oct	Payment - Thank you		298.84	
28 Oct	Discount		15.73	329.53

Amount now due	£329.53

2   Credit control is an on going process once a customer has been allowed to purchase goods on credit. When the customer first wishes to purchase goods on credit then it is important that reasonable credit checks are made. This will normally mean following up at least two references, one of which should be the customer's bank.

Once the credit record of the customer has been determined then a credit limit must be set dependent upon the amount of custom that the customer is likely to be supplying.

Thereafter the credit control department should ensure that the customer is not exceeding the credit limit and that invoices are being paid according to the specified credit terms of the invoice.

3
- H Davids – an investigation of the £118.00 might be advisable as other balances have been paid off and there may be a problem with this particular amount

- E Craig – the credit limit has been exceeded. However there are no debts later than the current period. Therefore maybe the credit limit should be reviewed

- K Olsen – there are a lot of outstanding amounts from periods from 30 days onwards – this account would be particularly worrying as there is a trend of non-payment

- A Evans – this debt has been outstanding for more than 90 days. This must be investigated and payment encouraged from the customer.

4

THAMES TRADING
13 PUTNEY BRIDGE
LONDON SW14 3NT
Tel 0207 891445 Fax 0207 891446

14 November 2006

Our ref: FH/TG/23

Purchase ledger manager
G H Perkins

Dear Sir

Invoice number 20446

Invoice 20446, for £358.39, has been outstanding since 15 August 2006. A copy of the invoice is enclosed. As our trading terms are 30 days of credit we would be grateful if payment were made by return of post.

We look forward to receiving your cheque.

Yours faithfully

Francis Hughes

Francis Hughes
Credit Controller

enc

CHAPTER 9 Business documents – Purchases

1   a)   debit note
    b)   goods received note
    c)   invoice
    d)   purchase order
    e)   remittance advice

2   Purchases of any sort should only be made in an organisation if they are expressly required and have been thoroughly investigated to ensure that the best price and terms have been found. Therefore it is important that any purchase order is authorised by an appropriate person who can verify that the order is necessary and this is the best deal that can be secured.

3   If an order is placed over the telephone then the immediate problem is that there is no documentary evidence for that order. Some form of documentary evidence will be required when the goods are received, in order to check that they were actually ordered, and when the invoice is received to check that it is for the correct quantity. This can be solved ideally by requesting of the supplier a confirmation of the order. If that is not possible then a written note of all of the order details should be made and filed.

4   ■   the invoice quantity agrees to the purchase order but the delivery note and GRN show that only 6 tumble dryers were delivered

    ■   the calculation of the total cost of the tumble dryers is incorrect. It should be £1,715 (7 x £245) not £1,778

    ■   the VAT calculation is incorrect – it should be:

	£
Net total	1,821.42
Less: settlement discount (£1,821.42 x 4/100)	72.85
	1,748.57
VAT £1,748.57 x 17.5/100	305.99

5   ■   no trade discount has been deducted despite the fact that the supplier's file shows that a trade discount of 10% is normally deducted

    ■   the net total of the goods is incorrect and should total £2,508 not £2,535

6   ■   the invoice does not agree to the purchase order as only 70 Get Well cards were ordered. However when the credit note is taken into account the invoice quantity is correct minus the credit note quantity

    ■   the unit price on the credit note is only £0.25 whereas the invoice price is £0.33

CHAPTER 10 Accounting for credit purchases

1

Date	Customer	Invoice number	Ref	Gross £	VAT £	Purchases £	Telephone £	Stationery £	Other £
20 Oct	Herne Industries	46121	PL15	846.00	126.00	720.00			
20 Oct	Southfield Electrical	56521	PL20	1,955.23	281.23	1,674.00			
20 Oct	Bass Engineers	663211	PL13	451.20	67.20	384.00			
				3,252.43	474.43	2,778.00			

Main ledger

Purchases ledger control account

	£			£
		PDB		3,252.43

Purchases account

	£		£
PDB	2,778.00		

VAT account

	£		£
PDB	474.43		

Subsidiary (purchases) ledger

Herne Industries   PL 15

	£		£
		PDB – 46121	846.00

Southfield Electrical　　　　　　　　PL 20

	£		£
		PDB – 56521	1,955.23

Bass Engineers　　　　　　　　　PL 13

	£		£
		PDB – 663211	451.20

2

Date	Customer	Credit note no	Ref	Gross £	VAT £	Purchases £	Telephone £	Stationery £	Other £
20 Oct	Southfield Electrical	08702	PL20	117.50	17.50	100.00			
20 Oct	Herne Industries	CN4502	PL15	129.25	19.25	110.00			
				246.75	36.75	210.00			

Main ledger

Purchases ledger control account

	£		£
PRDB	246.75		

Purchases returns account

	£		£
		PRDB	210.00

VAT account

	£		£
		PRDB	36.75

Subsidiary (purchases) ledger

	Southfield Electrical		PL 20
	£		£
PRDB – 08702	117.50		

	Herne Industries		PL 15
	£		£
PRDB – CN4502	129.25		

3

Date	Customer	Invoice number	Ref	Gross £	VAT £	Purchases £	Telephone £	Stationery £	Other £
5 June	YH Hill	224363	PL 16	186.09	27.71	158.38			
5 June	Letra Ltd	PT445	PL 24	267.18	39.79	227.39			
5 June	Coldstores	77352	PL 03	184.92	27.54	157.38			
5 June	H Hardcastle	17452	PL 07	316.42	47.12	269.30			
5 June	YH Hill	C7325	PL 16	(28.99)	(4.31)	(24.68)			
5 June	B Tel	0174659	PL 02	432.57	64.42		368.15		
				1,358.19	202.27	787.77	368.15		

Main ledger

	Purchases ledger control account		
£			£
	PDB		1,358.19

	VAT account		
	£		£
PDB	202.27		

Purchases account

	£		£
PDB	787.77		

Telephone account

	£		£
PDB	368.15		

Subsidiary (sales) ledger

Y H Hill   PL 16

	£		£
PDB – C7325	28.99	PDB – 224363	186.09

Letra Ltd   PL 24

	£		£
		PDB – PT445	267.18

Coldstores Ltd   PL 03

	£		£
		PDB – 77352	184.92

H Hardcastle   PL 07

	£		£
		PDB – 17452	316.42

B Tel   PL 02

	£		£
		PDB – 0174659	432.57

CHAPTER 11 Making payments to credit suppliers

1

	Cheque to be written on:	**Amount**
		£
a)	3 June	419.35 (356.90 + 62.45)
b)	14 May	292.53 (Working 1)
c)	3 June	130.15 (111.60 + 18.55) (The VAT is calculated net of the 5% discount)
d)	5 June	309.69 (263.57 + 46.12)
e)	21 May	169.85 (Working 2)

Note that invoice (c) should have been paid on 11 May if the discount were to be taken and therefore it must be paid in full after 30 days.

Working 1

Invoice for £258.00 + VAT

Discount amount	=	£258.00 x 3.5/100	=	£9.03
VAT	=	(£258.00 – 9.03) x 17.5/100	=	£43.56
Invoice total	=	£258.00 + 43.56	=	£301.56
Payment	=	£301.56 – 9.03	=	£292.53

Working 2

Invoice for £148.26 + VAT

Discount amount	=	£148.26 x 2.5/100	=	£3.70
VAT	=	(£148.26 – £3.70) x 17.5/100	=	£25.29
Invoice total	=	£148.26 + 25.29	=	£173.55
Payment	=	£173.55 – 3.70	=	£169.85

2

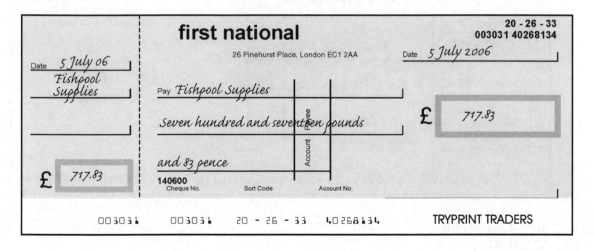

**REMITTANCE
ADVICE**

To:
Fishpool Supplies
280, Main Rd
Winnish DR2 5TL

From:
Tryprint Traders
Barnsgate Ind Park
Fretton PT7 2XY

Invoice	Amount £
61234	401.23
61287	226.40
61299	106.68
CN 4361	(16.48)

Cheque enclosed £ 717.83

3 Discount = £230.00 x 4/100 = £9.20
Payment = £230.00 + 38.64 – 9.20 = £259.44

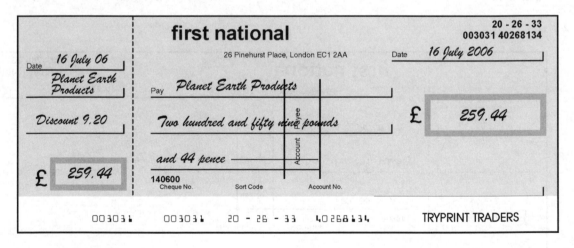

4 a) standing order
b) BACS
c) direct debit
d) cheque
e) CHAPS transfer

5   A standing order mandate is the instruction to your bank to pay a particular amount, starting on a particular date for a period of time at regular intervals. Without this written instruction the bank could not go ahead with the payments.

6   A direct debit is initiated by the party who will be receiving payment by sending the payer a direct debit mandate form. The payer fills this in with his bank details and then sends it back to the receiver who passes it on to his bank. The receiver's bank then requests payment from the payer's bank of the relevant amount at the relevant time.

7

8

```
┌─────────────────────────────────────────────────────────┐
│                                                           │
│            CHEQUE REQUISITION FORM                        │
│                                                           │
│                                                           │
│   Requested by:   F. Barrett        Date:   21 July 2006  │
│                                                           │
│   Payable to:     F. Barrett                              │
│                                                           │
│   Amount:         £167.40                                 │
│                                                           │
│   Send to:        Employee                                │
│                                                           │
│                                                           │
│                                                           │
│   Reason:         New clutch on company car               │
│                                                           │
│   Invoice/receipt attached:   ✓                           │
│                                                           │
│   Other documentation:                                    │
│                                                           │
│   Authorised by:                    Date:                 │
│                                                           │
└─────────────────────────────────────────────────────────┘
```

CHAPTER 12 Recording payments

1   The cash payments book is the book of prime entry for recording all of the cheque and automated payments that a business makes. It also serves a secondary purpose in that it is the credit side of the cash or bank ledger account therefore making it part of the double entry in the main ledger. The only further requirement then to complete the double entry is to post all of the relevant debit entries.

2   When a cheque is written for the cash purchase of goods then when the cheque is written into the cash payments book this is the first time that this transaction has been recorded in the accounting records. Therefore the VAT must be accounted for at this stage.

However when a cheque is written to a credit supplier and entered into the cash payments book this is not the first time that the transaction has been recorded. The transaction would initially have been recorded when the invoice was received from the credit supplier and it was recorded in the purchases day book. When it was written into the purchases day book the VAT was analysed out and posted to the VAT account. Therefore there is no requirement to do this again when recording the payment.

3

Date	Details	Ref	Total £	VAT £	Cash purchases £	Purchases ledger £	Sundry £	Discounts received £
22 Oct	06273 P Products Ltd	PL23	241.58			241.58		
22 Oct	06274 Jason Bros	PL36	336.29			336.29		6.86
22 Oct	06275 P Taylor	ML	250.00	37.23	212.77			
22 Oct	06276 R R Partners	PL06	163.47			163.47		4.19
22 Oct	06277 Troyde Ltd	PL14	183.57			183.57		
22 Oct	06278 O L Simms	ML	116.58	17.36	99.22			
22 Oct	06279 F Elliott	PL20	263.68			263.68		8.15
22 Oct	SO G L Finance	ML	200.00				200.00	
			1,755.17	54.59	311.99	1,188.59	200.00	19.20

Cross-cast:

	£
VAT	54.59
Cash purchases	311.99
Purchases ledger	1,188.59
Sundry	200.00
	1,755.17

4

VAT account

	£		£
CPB	54.59		

Purchases account

	£		£
CPB	311.99		

Purchases ledger control account

	£		£
CPB	1,188.59		
CPB	19.20		

Loan account

	£		£
CPB	200.00		

Discount received

	£		£
		CPB	19.20

5

R R Partners   PL 06

	£		£
CPB – 06276	163.47	Balance b/d	332.68
CPB – discount	4.19		

Troyde Ltd   PL 14

	£		£
CPB – 06277	183.57	Balance b/d	183.57

F Elliott			PL 20
	£		£
CPB – 06279	263.68	Balance b/d	558.93
CPB – discount	8.15		

P Products Ltd			PL 23
	£		£
CPB – 06273	241.58	Balance b/d	724.02

Jason Bros			PL 36
	£		£
CPB – 06274	336.29	Balance b/d	725.37
CPB – discount	6.86		

CHAPTER 13 Petty cash procedures

1   An imprest petty cash system is one where the amount of petty cash float at the start of the week or month is always the same. Claims are made with petty cash vouchers and at the end of the week or month the total of the vouchers is the amount needed to restore the petty cash box to the imprest amount. This sum is then withdrawn from the bank and paid into the petty cash box to start the following week or month with the same amount.

2

PETTY CASH VOUCHER		
Number: *0624*	Date: *20 Oct 2006*	
Details	Amount	
Postage		*8 - 30*
	Net	*8 - 30*
	VAT	*-*
	Gross	*8 - 30*
Claimed by: *Trevor Forbes*		
Authorised by:		

PETTY CASH VOUCHER

Number: *0625*   Date: *20 Oct 2006*

Details		Amount
Paper		*4 - 09*
Envelopes		*2 - 05*
	Net	*6 - 14*
	VAT	*1 - 06*
	Gross	*7 - 20*

Claimed by: *Janis Williams*

Authorised by:

Paper VAT = 4.80 x 17.5/117.5	=		0.71
Envelopes VAT = 2.40 x 17.5/117.5	=		0.35
Total VAT			1.06
Paper net = 4.80 – 0.71	=		4.09
Envelopes net = 2.40 – 0.35	=		2.05

PETTY CASH VOUCHER

Number: *0626*   Date: *20 Oct 2006*

Details		Amount
Train fare		*12 - 80*
	Net	*12 - 80*
	VAT	*-*
	Gross	*12 - 80*

Claimed by: *Dan Granger*

Authorised by:

The documentation required for each claim would be:

i)   a receipt from the post office
ii)   a sales receipt
iii) the rail ticket or a receipt

3   £89.46

4

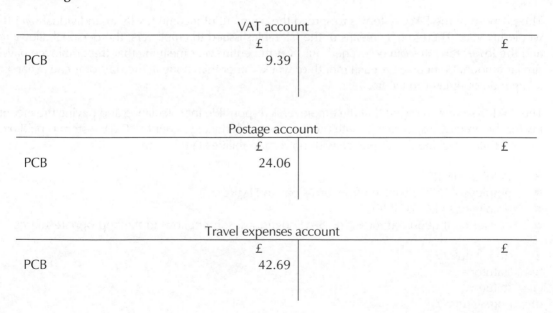

RECEIPTS			PAYMENTS								
Date	Details	Amount £	Date	Details	Voucher number	Total £	VAT £	Post £	Travel £	Sundry office £	Misc £
20 Oct	Cash	150.00	24 Oct	Train fare	771	14.00			14.00		
			24 Oct	Postage	772	18.60		18.60			
			24 Oct	Taxi fare	773	15.00	2.23		12.77		
			24 Oct	Window cleaner	774	20.00					20.00
			24 Oct	Pens/paper	775	14.83	2.20			12.63	
			24 Oct	Postage	776	5.46		5.46			
			24 Oct	Taxi fare	777	18.70	2.78		15.92		
			24 Oct	Computer disks	778	14.70	2.18			12.52	
						121.29	9.39	24.06	42.69	25.15	20.00
				Balance c/d		28.71					
		150.00				150.00					
Balance b/d		28.71									
Cash		121.29									

Main ledger

VAT account

	£		£
PCB	9.39		

Postage account

	£		£
PCB	24.06		

Travel expenses account

	£		£
PCB	42.69		

Sundry office expenses account

	£		£
PCB	25.15		

Cleaning expenses account

	£		£
PCB	20.00		

CHAPTER 14 Payroll accounting procedures

1   Income tax is paid by individuals on the income they earn. However it is paid at different rates depending upon the amount of income in a year. For example for 2007/2008 the first £2,230 of taxable income is taxed at 10%, the next band up to £34,600 is at 22% and any income over this amount is taxed at 40%. This means that if the income were taxed as earned then potentially in the first months the person would pay no income tax and further into the tax year more income tax would be paid.

This is further exaggerated by the fact that each employee will have a personal allowance which is the amount of income that can be earned before any income tax is paid.

The purpose of the PAYE system is to spread the payment of income tax by an individual over the whole tax year. Therefore by means of the tax tables issued to employers, the personal allowance and the lower tax rates can be evened out over the entire year meaning that the employee pays a similar amount of income tax each month or week, rather than none at the start of the tax year and a larger amount later in the tax year.

The PAYE system also means that the employer is responsible for calculating and paying the income tax for the employees, as each month the income tax deducted under the PAYE system is paid over to the HMRC, leaving the employee with no responsibilities in this area.

2   ■   PAYE to HMRC
     ■   employee's NIC deducted from gross pay to HMRC
     ■   employer's NIC to HMRC
     ■   any amount deducted for GAYE, SAYE, pensions, subscriptions to the appropriate source

3   a)   non-statutory
     b)   statutory
     c)   statutory
     d)   non-statutory

4

a)

	£
Gross pay £27,000/12	2,250.00
PAYE income tax	(418.16)
NIC	(189.00)
Net pay	1,642.84

b)

Gross wages control account

	£		£
CPB – net pay	1,642.84	Wages expense	2,250.00
PAYE/NIC creditor		Employer's NIC	274.50
(418.16 + 189.00)	607.16		
Employer's NIC	274.50		

Wages expense account

	£		£
Gross wages control	2,250.00		
PAYE/NIC creditor	274.50		

PAYE/NIC creditor account

	£		£
		Gross wages control	607.16
		Wages expense	274.50

CHAPTER 15 Bank reconciliation statement

1   Cash Receipts Book

Date	Details	Ref	Total £	VAT £	Cash sales £	Sales ledger £	Discounts allowed £
30/11	Burser Ltd	SL14	147.89			147.89	6.49
30/11	Crawley Partners	SL23	448.36			448.36	18.79
30/11	Breon & Co	SL15	273.37			273.37	
30/11	Kogart Supplies	SL06	552.68			552.68	42.67
30/11	Alex & Bros	SL09	273.46			273.46	
30/11	Minicar Ltd	SL22	194.68			194.68	

Cash Payments Book

Date	Details	Ref	Total £	VAT £	Cash purchases £	Purchases ledger £	Sundry £	Discounts received £
27/11	SO Loan Fin Rep	ML23	250.00				250.00	
30/11	Waterloo Part 001367	PL21	336.47			336.47		12.47
30/11	Central Supp 001368	PL16	169.36			169.36		
30/11	Gen Lon Tr 001369	PL23	268.38			268.38		10.58
30/11	Eye of the Tig 001370	PL19	84.50			84.50		
30/11	Chare & Cope 001371	PL27	447.39			447.39		19.86

2   Cash Receipts Book

Date	Details	Ref	Total £	VAT £	Cash sales £	Sales ledger £	Discounts allowed £
30/11	Burser Ltd	SL14	147.89 ✓			147.89	6.49
30/11	Crawley Partners	SL23	448.36 ✓			448.36	18.79
30/11	Breon & Co	SL15	273.37			273.37	
30/11	Kogart Supplies	SL06	552.68 ✓			552.68	42.67
30/11	Alex & Bros	SL09	273.46			273.46	
30/11	Minicar Ltd	SL22	194.68			194.68	

Cash Payments Book

Date	Details	Ref	Total £	VAT £	Cash purchases £	Purchases ledger £	Sundry £	Discounts received £
27/11	SO Loan Fin Rep	ML23	250.00 ✓				250.00	
30/11	Waterloo Part 001367	PL21	336.47 ✓			336.47		12.47
30/11	Central Supp 001368	PL16	169.36			169.36		
30/11	Gen Lon Tr 001369	PL23	268.38			268.38		10.58
30/11	Eye of the Tig 001370	PL19	84.50			84.50		
30/11	Chare & Cope 001371	PL27	447.39			447.39		19.86

STATEMENT

NATIONAL DIRECT

THAMES TRADERS

CHEQUE ACCOUNT

Account number: 15-20-40 10267432

Date	Sheet 136	Paid out	Paid in	Balance
23.11.06	Balance b/f			1,489.65 CR
26.11.06	Bank Giro Credit - Burser Ltd		52.00	1,541.65 CR
27.11.06	SO-Loan Finance Repayment	250.00 ✓		1,291.65 CR
28.11.06	Cheque No 001367	336.47 ✓		
	Credit		147.89 ✓	1,103.07 CR
29.11.06	Cheque No 001368	196.36		
	Credit		448.36 ✓	1,355.07 CR
30.11.06	Credit		552.68 ✓	
	Bank charges	34.53		1,873.22 CR

Unticked items in the cash book

- the entries in the cash receipts book are cheques that have presumably been paid into the bank but have not yet cleared – they will be agreed to subsequent bank statements

- Cheque no. 001368 – this cheque appeared as £169.36 in the cash payments book but £196.36 in the bank statement – this should be checked to the original cheque counterfoil and documentation and if the bank is correct the cash payments book must be adjusted

- the remaining cheques in the cash payments book have not yet cleared the banking system and they will be checked to subsequent bank statements.

Unticked items in the bank statement

- 26/11 bank giro credit from Burser Ltd – this has not been entered into the cash receipts book yet and the cash receipts book must therefore be adjusted to reflect this

- 29/11 – cheque no. 001368 – as has already been noted this has been incorrectly entered into the cash payments book and must be adjusted for

- 30/11 – bank charges – these have not been entered into the cash payments book and this must be adjusted for.

3 Cash Receipts Book

Date	Details	Ref	Total £	VAT £	Cash sales £	Sales ledger £	Discounts allowed £
30/11	Burser Ltd	SL14	147.89 ✓			147.89	6.49
30/11	Crawley Partners	SL23	448.36 ✓			448.36	18.79
30/11	Breon & Co	SL15	273.37			273.37	
30/11	Kogart Supplies	SL06	552.68 ✓			552.68	42.67
30/11	Alex & Bros	SL09	273.46			273.46	
30/11	Minicar Ltd	SL22	194.68			194.68	
30/11	Burser Ltd BGC	SL14	52.00 ✓			52.00	
			1,942.44			1,942.44	67.95

Cash Payments Book

Date	Details	Ref	Total £	VAT £	Cash purchases £	Purchases ledger £	Sundry £	Discounts received £
27/11	SO Loan Fin Rep	ML23	250.00 ✓				250.00	
30/11	Waterloo Part 001367	PL21	336.47 ✓			336.47		12.47
30/11	Central Supp 001368	PL16	169.36 ✓			169.36		
30/11	Gen Lon Tr 001369	PL23	268.38			268.38		10.58
30/11	Eye of the Tig 001370	PL19	84.50			84.50		
30/11	Chare & Cope 001371	PL27	447.39			447.39		19.86
30/11	Adjustment to 001368	PL16	27.00 ✓			27.00		
30/11	Bank charges	ML	34.53 ✓				34.53	
			1,617.63			1,333.10	284.53	42.91

Note that the amount 169.36 (cheque no 1368) is now ticked because the adjustment of £27 means that they can both be ticked against the amount (£196.36) on the bank statement.

4

	£
Opening balance	1,489.65
Add: receipts for the period	1,942.44
Less: payments for the period	(1,617.63)
Bank account trial balance figure	1,814.46

5   Bank reconciliation statement as at 30 November 2006

	£	£
Balance per bank statement		1,873.22
Outstanding lodgements		
Breon & Co	273.37	
Alex & Bros	273.46	
Minicar Ltd	194.68	
		741.51
		2,614.73
Unpresented cheques		
001369	268.38	
001370	84.50	
001371	447.39	
		(800.27)
Amended cash book balance		1,814.46

6 a) Main ledger accounts:

		£	£
Debit	Sales ledger control account	9.00	
Credit	Bank account		9.00

    b) Main ledger accounts:

		£	£
Debit	Bank charges account	15.80	
Credit	Bank account		15.80

    c) Bank reconciliation:

       Unpresented cheque

    d) Main ledger accounts:

		£	£
Debit	Gas expense account	300.00	
Credit	Bank account		300.00

(Note that if an analysed cash book is used and the postings are made to the main ledger from the totals of the analysis columns at the period end, the above amounts would be included in the totals and posted via the totals.)

7   ■   compare the receipts and payments in the cash book, bank statement and opening bank reconciliation statement and tick each item that agrees:

Cash Receipts Book

Date	Details	£	
4 March	J Killick	365.37	✓
	D Francis	105.48	✓
5 March	I Oliver	216.57	✓
6 March	L Canter	104.78	
7 March	R Trent	268.59	
8 March	P Otter	441.78	
		1,502.57	

Cash Payments Book

Date	Details	Cheque number	£	
4 March	L L Partners	002536	186.90	✓
	P J Parler	002537	210.55	✓
5 March	J K Properties	002538	500.00	✓
	Harmer & Co	002539	104.78	✓
	Plenith Ltd	002540	60.80	
7 March	Wessex & Co	002541	389.40	
8 March	Filmer Partners	002542	104.67	
			1,557.10	

Bank reconciliation statement at 1 March 2006

	£		£	
Balance per bank statement			835.68	
Less: unpresented cheques				
002530	110.46	✓		
002534	230.56	✓		
002535	88.90	✓		
			(429.92)	
			405.76	
Add: outstanding lodgement			102.45	✓
Amended cash book balance			508.21	

STATEMENT

first national
30 High Street
Benham
DR4 8TT

SOUTHFIELD ELECTRICAL LTD   **Account number:** 20-26-33 3126897

CHEQUE ACCOUNT

Date	Sheet 023	Paid out	Paid in	Balance
1 Mar	Balance b/f			835.68
4 Mar	Cheque No 002534	230.56 ✓		
	Credit		102.45 ✓	707.56
5 Mar	DD - National Telephones	145.00		
	Bank charges	7.80		554.77
6 Mar	Cheque No 002530	110.46 ✓		
	BACS J T Turner		486.20	930.51
7 Mar	Credit		470.85 ✓	
	Cheque No 002537	210.55 ✓		
	Cheque No 002536	186.90 ✓		
	Cheque No 002538	500.00 ✓		503.91
8 Mar	Cheque No 002535	88.90 ✓		
	Credit		216.57 ✓	
	Cheque No 002539	104.78 ✓		526.80
8 Mar	Balance c/f			526.80

■ amend the cash book for the un-ticked items on the bank statement

Bank account

	£		£
Balance b/d	508.21	Payments	1,557.10
Receipts	1,502.57	Direct debit	145.00
BACS	486.20	Bank charges	7.80
		Balance c/d	787.08
	2,496.98		2,496.98
Balance b/d	787.08		

- use the un-ticked figures in the cash book to prepare the bank reconciliation statement

Bank reconciliation statement at 8 March 2006

	£	£
Bank statement balance		526.80
Less: unpresented cheques		
002540	60.80	
002541	389.40	
002542	104.67	
		554.87
		(28.07)
Add: outstanding lodgements		
L Canter	104.78	
R Trent	268.59	
P Otter	441.78	
		815.15
		787.08

CHAPTER 16 Control account reconciliations

1 Main ledger

Sales ledger control account

	£		£
Opening balance	1,216.26	CRB	1,078.97
SDB	1,602.32	CRB – discounts	8.73
		Balance c/d	1,730.88
	2,818.58		2,818.58
Balance b/d	1,730.88		

Subsidiary ledger

Virgo Partners

	£		£
Opening balance	227.58	CRB	117.38
SDB	94.70		
SDB	210.00	Balance c/d	414.90
	532.28		532.28
Balance b/d	414.90		

McGowan & Sons

	£		£
Opening balance	552.73	CRB	552.73
SDB	582.69	Balance c/d	582.69
	1,135.42		1,135.42
Balance b/d	582.69		

J J Westrope

	£		£
Opening balance	317.59	CRB	308.86
SDB	163.90	CRB – discount	8.73
SDB	271.57	Balance c/d	435.47
	753.06		753.06
Balance b/d	435.47		

Jacks Ltd

	£		£
Opening balance	118.36	CRB	100.00
SDB	105.47		
SDB	173.99	Balance c/d	297.82
	397.82		397.82
Balance b/d	297.82		

Reconciliation

	£
Virgo Partners	414.90
McGowan & Sons	582.69
J J Westrope	435.47
Jacks Ltd	297.82
Sales ledger control account balance	1,730.88

2   **Main ledger**

Purchases ledger control account

	£		£
CPB	959.39	Opening balance	839.46
CPB – discounts	30.07	PDB	1,573.72
Balance c/d	1,423.72		
	2,413.18		2,413.18
		Balance b/d	1,423.72

Subsidiary ledger

Jenkins Suppliers

	£		£
CPB	423.89	Opening balance	441.56
CPB – discounts	17.67	PDB	215.47
Balance c/d	657.37	PDB	441.90
	1,098.93		1,098.93
		Balance b/d	657.37

Kilnfarm Paper

	£		£
CPB	150.00	Opening balance	150.00
CPB	150.00	PDB	150.00
Balance c/d	150.00	PDB	150.00
	450.00		450.00
		Balance b/d	150.00

Barnfield Ltd

	£		£
CPB	235.50	Opening balance	247.90
CPB – discounts	12.40	PDB	310.58
Balance c/d	616.35	PDB	305.77
	864.25		864.25
		Balance b/d	616.35

Reconciliation

	£
Jenkins Suppliers	657.37
Kilnfarm Paper	150.00
Barnfield Ltd	616.35
Purchases ledger control account balance	1,423.72

3

Sales ledger control account

	£		£
Opening balance	16,339	Sales returns	3,446
Credit sales	50,926	Cash received	47,612
Returned cheque	366	Settlement discounts	1,658
		Bad debt written off	500
		Balance c/d	14,415
	67,631		67,631

4

Purchases ledger control account

	£		£
Purchases returns	2,568	Opening balance	12,587
Cheques paid	38,227	Credit purchases	40,827
Settlement discounts	998		
Balance c/d	11,621		
	53,414		53,414

5

Sales ledger control account

	£		£
Original balance	41,774	Sales returns	450
SDB undercast	100	Bad debt written off	210
		Balance c/d	41,214
	41,874		41,874
Balance b/d	41,214		

	£
Original total of list of balances	41,586
Less: invoice misposted (769 – 679)	(90)
Less: discount (2 x 16)	(32)
Less: credit balance included as a debit balance (2 x 125)	(250)
Amended control account balance	41,214

6

Purchases ledger control account

	£		£
Settlement discounts	267	Original balance	38,694
		Purchases returns – overcast	300
Balance c/d	38,997	CPB error (3,415 – 3,145)	270
	39,264		39,264
		Balance b/d	38,997

	£
Original total of list of balances	39,741
Less: settlement discount omitted	(267)
Less: credit note adjustment (210 – 120)	(90)
Less: debit balance omitted	(187)
Less: credit balance misstated	(200)
Amended control account balance	38,997

7 Total cash

	£
£10 note	10.00
£5 note	10.00
£2 coin	2.00
£1 coin	5.00
50p coin	1.50
20p coin	3.00
10p coin	0.80
5p coin	0.55
2p coin	0.28
1p coin	0.06
	33.19

Total vouchers

1256	14.67
1257	6.30
1258	10.00
1259	4.47
1260	13.80
1261	15.90
1263	8.95
1264	7.45
	81.54

Reconciliation of cash and vouchers

Petty cash total	33.19
Vouchers total	81.54
	114.73

This is less than the imprest amount which means that some cash is missing, £5.27 (120.00 – 114.73). You may notice that petty cash voucher 1262 is missing and this may be the reason for the difference. The petty cash voucher should be found to ensure that this is the reason for the £5.27 difference.

The cash in hand that should appear in the trial balance is £33.19.

CHAPTER 17 Preparing an initial trial balance

1

VAT account

	£		£
Input VAT	3,778	Opening balance	2,116
Cash paid	2,116	Output VAT	6,145
Balance c/d	2,367		
	8,261		8,261
		Balance b/d	2,367

Sales account

	£		£
		Opening balance	57,226
Balance c/d	80,738	Debtors control	23,512
	80,738		80,738
		Balance b/d	80,738

Sales ledger control account

	£		£
Opening balance	4,689	Cash received	20,963
Sales	23,512	Discounts allowed	2,019
		Bad debt written off	542
		Balance c/d	4,677
	28,201		28,201
Balance b/d	4,677		

Purchases ledger control account

	£		£
Purchases returns	1,334	Opening balance	2,864
Cash paid	13,446	Purchases	14,552
Discounts received	662		
Balance c/d	1,974		
	17,416		17,416
		Balance b/d	1,974

2

	£		
Discounts allowed	1,335	–	debit balance
Discounts received	1,013	–	credit balance
Purchases returns	4,175	–	credit balance
Sales returns	6,078	–	debit balance
Carriage inwards	2,114	–	debit balance
Carriage outwards	1,478	–	debit balance
Bank interest received	328	–	credit balance
Bank charges	163	–	debit balance

3

	Debits £	Credits £
Motor vehicles	64,000	
Office equipment	21,200	
Sales		238,000
Purchases	164,000	
Bank overdraft		1,680
Petty cash	30	
Capital		75,000
Sales returns	4,700	
Purchases returns		3,600
Sales ledger control	35,800	
Purchases ledger control		30,100
VAT (credit balance)		12,950
Stock	19,200	
Telephone	1,600	
Electricity	2,800	
Wages	62,100	
Loan		30,000
Discounts allowed	6,400	
Discounts received		3,900
Rent	12,000	
Bad debts written off	1,400	
	395,230	395,230

CHAPTER 18 Errors and the trial balance

1 ■ the discounts received have been entered on the wrong side of the account
  ■ the closing balance has been incorrectly calculated – it should be £16,890

2 Transposition error

3 This is not correct.
  Error of reversal – the debit and credit entries have been reversed

4 Error of commission

5 The difference between the two figures (£270) is exactly divisible by 9. Therefore the error may be a transposition error in one of the balances in the trial balance.

6 Credit balance of £2,121

7

			£	£
a)	Debit	Suspense account	900	
	Credit	Sales ledger control account		900
b)	Debit	Suspense account	1,000	
	Credit	Discount allowed		1,000
c)	Debit	Purchases ledger control account	900	
	Credit	Discount received account		900
d)	Debit	Suspense account	1,088	
	Credit	Purchases returns account		1,088

Suspense account

	£		£
Sales ledger control	900	Balance b/d	2,988
Discount allowed	1,000		
Purchases returns	1,088		
	2,988		2,988

CHAPTER 19 Business transactions and the law

1 Agreement, value or consideration and an intention to create legal relations.

2 i) Yes. An offer and acceptance can be made verbally.

   ii) No. The purchase order is just part of the documentation that often accompanies contracts but the contract was made verbally and the purchase order itself adds no more to the contract.

3 No. The price attached to the item is an invitation to treat. The offer is made by the purchaser at the till and the acceptance is then made by the cashier. Therefore the customer is making an offer to buy the item at £15.99 and this can be rejected by the retailer.

4 21 November, the date on which the acceptance, the purchase order, is posted.

5 Yes. A valid contract was in existence even though this was with a friend. There was an agreement, consideration (the promise to pay £100) and an intention to create legal relations.

6 No. The consideration was past ie, it was offered after the performance of the act.

7 The clock/radio is clearly not of merchantable quality as part of it does not work therefore the retailer is required to give a refund.

8 The coat does not conform to its description, ie leather, and therefore an implied term has been breached and you are entitled to a refund.

9 The eight principles of good information handling state that personal data must be:

- fairly and lawfully processed

- processed for limited purposes

- adequate, relevant and not excessive

- accurate

- not held for longer than is necessary

- processed in line with the data subject's rights

- kept securely

- not transferred to countries outside the European Union unless there is adequate protection in those countries.

CHAPTER 20 Introduction to management information

1
- the cost of making each unit of the product
- the selling price of each unit
- the number of labour hours required to make the product
- any alternative use for these employees
- the potential future market for the product
- any alternative products that could replace this one
- the effect that discontinuing this product may have on other product sales.

2
- the revenues from the shop
- the costs of the shop
- the number of employees
- the effect of closure on these employees – would they be used elsewhere in the organisation or would redundancy payments have to be made
- the effect of closure of this shop on the profits of any other shops of the organisation
- the effect on competitors of closing this shop.

3 Sales budget – the expected unit sales of each product and unit selling price for the next year.

Production budget – the number of each product that must be produced to provide the amount planned to be sold in the sales budget.

Materials cost budget – the cost of the raw materials that need to be purchased in order to meet the production budget.

Labour hours budget – the number of labour hours required in order to make the units planned for in the production budget.

4   A variance is the amount by which the actual costs or revenues for a period differ from the budgeted costs or revenues.

Variances are an important tool to management in their control of the organisation. If there are significant variances then management may change plans or make decisions on the basis of these variances.

5   ■   throwing (making the pot) – production cost centre
     ■   baking – production cost centre
     ■   painting – production cost centre
     ■   packaging – production cost centre
     ■   stores – service cost centre
     ■   maintenance – service cost centre
     ■   selling and distribution – service cost centre
     ■   canteen – service cost centre
     ■   administration – service cost centre

6   ■   van deliveries cost centre
     ■   motorbike deliveries cost centre
     ■   maintenance cost centre
     ■   marketing cost centre
     ■   booking cost centre
     ■   administration cost centre

CHAPTER 21 Elements of cost

1   50kg Throwing clay   –   throwing cost centre
     10 litres paint   –   painting cost centre
     100kg frozen chips   –   canteen cost centre
     48 chicken pies   –   canteen cost centre

2
		£
Basic pay 41 hours @ £9.60		393.60
Overtime premium 3 hours @ 9.60		28.80
Total gross pay		422.40
Throwing cost centre – labour	26 hours @ £9.60	249.60
Baking cost centre – labour	15 hours @ £9.60	144.00
Throwing cost centre – expense		28.80

3

	£
Throwing cost centre – expense – rent £15,000 x 15%	2,250
Throwing cost centre – expense – cleaning	200
	2,450
Baking cost centre – expense – rent £15,000 x 40%	6,000
Baking cost centre – expense – servicing	600
	6,600
Painting cost centre – expense – rent £15,000 x 15%	2,250
Packaging cost centre – expense – rent £5,000 x 20%	1,000
Stores cost centre – expense – rent £5,000 x 80%	4,000
Maintenance cost centre – expense – rent £15,000 x 10%	1,500
Selling and distribution cost centre – expense – rent £3,000 x 0.5	1,500
Selling and distribution cost centre – expense – advertising	400
	1,900
Canteen cost centre – expense – rent £15,000 x 20%	3,000
Administration cost centre – expense – rent £3,000 x 0.5	1,500

4

	£
Audit cost centre – consumables 489.00 x 30%	146.70
Tax cost centre – consumables 489.00 x 40%	195.60
Consultancy cost centre – consumables 489.00 x 20%	97.80
Administration cost centre – consumables 489.00 x 10%	48.90

CHAPTER 22 Coding

1

INVOICE

Purbeck Clay
Granite Yard
Compston BH3 4TL
Tel 01929 464810
VAT Reg 1164 2810 67

To: Pole Potteries

Invoice number: 36411

Date/tax point: 16 Nov 2006

Order number: 11663

Account number: SL 42

Quantity	Description	Stock code	Unit amount £	Total £
50 kg	Throwing clay	TC412	6.80	111 340.00
10 litres	Paint - Fuchsia	PF67	2.80	131 28.00

Net total	368.00
VAT	64.40
Invoice total	432.40

Terms
Net 30 days
E & OE

```
                            INVOICE        IndCan Suppliers
                                                High Street
                                            Hamware BH3 7SP
                                            Tel 01929 432432
                                          VAT Reg 2214 6182 93


         ┌─                        ─┐
To:       Pole Potteries            │    Invoice number: 61212
                                         Date/tax point: 17 Nov 2006
                                         Order number: 11668
         └─                        ─┘    Account number: PP 02
```

Quantity	Description	Stock code	Unit amount £	Total £
100kg	Frozen chips	46112	1.20	181 120.00
48	Chicken pies	61297	0.90	181 43.20
			Net total	163.20
			VAT	28.56
			Invoice total	191.76

Terms
Net 30 days
E & OE

2	Throwing cost centre – labour 26 hours @ £9.60	249.60	112
	Baking cost centre – labour 15 hours @ £9.60	144.00	122
	Throwing cost centre – expense – overtime premium	28.80	113
	Throwing cost centre – expense – employer's NIC	26.42	113
	Baking cost centre – expense – employer's NIC	15.25	123
3	Throwing cost centre – expense – rent £15,000 x 15%	2,250	
	Throwing cost centre – expense – cleaning	200	
		2,450	113

Baking cost centre – expense – rent £15,000 x 40%   6,000
Baking cost centre – expense – servicing   600

                                                           6,600   123

Painting cost centre – expense – rent £15,000 x 15%   2,250   133

Packaging cost centre – expense – rent £5,000 x 20%   1,000   143

Stores cost centre – expense – rent £5,000 x 80%   4,000   153

Maintenance cost centre – expense – rent £15,000 x 10%   1,500   163

Selling and distribution cost centre – expense – rent
   £3,000 x 0.5   1,500
Selling and distribution cost centre – expense – advertising 400

                                                           1,900   173

Canteen cost centre – expense – rent £15,000 x 20%   3,000   183

Administration cost centre – expense – rent £3,000 x 0.5   1,500   193

CHAPTER 23 Comparison of costs and income

1   Comparison of cost centre costs – November 2006 to October 2006

	November 2006 £	October 2006 £
Throwing		
Materials	12,145.76	11,374.83
Labour	7,442.46	6,526.46
Expenses	6,335.49	6,103.78
	25,923.71	24,005.07
Baking		
Materials	1,336.48	1,263.78
Labour	2,447.28	1,984.05
Expenses	10,492.43	10,145.83
	14,276.19	13,393.66
Painting		
Materials	4,263.98	3,982.56
Labour	13,572.41	11,457.20
Expenses	2,684.50	2,155.83
	20,520.89	17,595.59

2 i) If a business is seasonal then its sales and production are likely to vary from month to month. Therefore comparison of one month's figures to those of the previous month may not be particularly meaningful. More useful information may be gathered by comparing the current month's figures to those of the same month in the previous year.

ii) **Comparison of cost centre costs – November 2006 to November 2005**

	November 2006 £	November 2005 £
Throwing		
Materials	12,145.76	12,672.84
Labour	7,442.46	6,627.31
Expenses	6,335.49	6,301.83
	25,923.71	25,601.98
Baking		
Materials	1,336.48	1,382.14
Labour	2,447.28	1,646.23
Expenses	10,492.43	10,646.29
	14,276.19	13,674.66
Painting		
Materials	4,263.98	3,896.22
Labour	13,572.41	12,118.29
Expenses	2,684.50	2,375.08
	20,520.89	18,389.59

3 Comparison of November 2006 cost centre costs to budget

	Actual £	Budget £	Variance £
Throwing			
Materials	12,145.76	11,202.67	943.09 adv
Labour	7,442.46	6,158.20	1,284.26 adv
Expenses	6,335.49	7,135.52	800.03 fav
Baking			
Materials	1,336.48	1,505.60	169.12 fav
Labour	2,447.28	2,490.82	43.54 fav
Expenses	10,492.43	11,356.50	864.07 fav
Painting			
Materials	4,263.98	3,660.30	603.68 adv
Labour	13,572.41	11,240.25	2,332.16 adv
Expenses	2,684.50	2,800.00	115.50 fav

Variance as percentage of budget

Throwing – materials   943.09/11,202.67   ×   100   =   8.4%
        labour   1,284.26/6,158.20   ×   100   =   20.8%
        expenses   800.03/7,135.52   ×   100   =   11.2%

Baking –   materials   169.12/1,505.60   ×   100   =   11.2%
        labour   43.54/2,490.82   ×   100   =   1.7%
        expenses   864.07/11,356.50   ×   100   =   7.6%

Painting – materials   603.68/3,660.30   ×   100   =   16.5%
        labour   2,332.16/11,240.25   ×   100   =   20.7%
        expenses   115.50/2,800.00   ×   100   =   4.1%

The variances to be reported are:

throwing – labour and expenses

baking – materials

painting – materials and labour

INDEX